The Daily Telegraph

BOOK OF

FORMULA ONE

The Daily Telegraph

BOOK OF

FORMULA ONE

edited by MARTIN SMITH

First published in Great Britain
2009 by Aurum Press Ltd
7 Greenland Street
London NW1 0ND
www.aurumpress.co.uk

Photographs: p xxii–1, the British Grand Prix, Silverstone, 17 July 1954,
courtesy of Getty Images; p 32–33, Stirling Moss, trapped in his car after a
crash at Goodwood, 23 April 1962, courtesy of Getty Images; p 60–61,
Niki Lauda (*left*) and James Hunt, courtesy of Getty Images; p 90–91,
Nigel Mansell in his Williams during the British Grand Prix,
Brands Hatch, 13 July 1986, courtesy of Getty Images; p 116–117, Ayrton Senna
ahead of the San Marino Grand Prix, Imola, 30 April 1994, courtesy of
AFP/Getty Images; p 248–249, Michael Schumacher at Interlagos,
São Paulo, 20 October 2006, courtesy of Getty Images.

A catalogue record for this book is available from the British Library.

ISBN 978 1 84513 495 2

1 3 5 7 9 10 8 6 4 2
2009 2011 2013 2012 2010

Typeset in Spectrum and Gill by Saxon Graphics, Derby
Printed and bound in Great Britain by the MPG Books Group

For my elder son Alexander,
who could say 'Schumacher' almost before he could say 'Daddy'

CONTENTS

INTRODUCTION

When Sebastian Vettel shot past Lewis Hamilton's McLaren on the ante-penultimate lap of the Brazilian Grand Prix in 2008, the collective air expelled from the lungs of a thwarted nation could have powered a fair-sized wind farm for a month. For a population of sports-loving couch potatoes, this was another example of the snatching-defeat-from-the-jaws-of-victory we had seen all too often before from the likes of Tim Henman, Frank Bruno and England's penalty-shy footballers; another example of being so near, yet so far. Hamilton had just put his kick in the sudden-death shootout wide of the target: the world drivers' title was heading elsewhere. It was *déjà vu* all over again.

Indeed, we had been in this position before with the prodigious young man from the council house in Stevenage. Twelve months earlier, in his rookie season, Hamilton had taken a lead of four points (over Fernando Alonso) and seven points (over Kimi Räikkönen) into the final race of the season, again at the Interlagos circuit in the south of São Paulo. On that occasion, he suffered a poor start, followed quickly by gearbox problems, and was running 18th at one point in a race in which he needed to finish no lower than second (if Alonso won) or fifth (if Räikkönen won). Though he charged through the field in the later stages to finish seventh, the die had already been cast, and the championship went to Räikkönen.

Now, on a particularly dark, dank, late-autumn teatime in Great Britain, we had again been enticed back to our sitting-room sofas to see if the latest *wunderkind* of Formula One could go one better than his runners-up spot of 2007 and become the ninth British driver to be crowned world champion. It shouldn't be too difficult this time, should it? He had a seven-point cushion over Felipe Massa, and only really had to coast round and finish no worse than fifth, assuming a Brazilian home win, and the title was his. He looked comfortable enough in the rain as he started the 69th of the 71 laps in that 'winning' fifth place. It was then that Vettel, the young German in a Toro Rosso, pounced – in a move that looked as if it would enthrone Massa as Brazil's fourth world champion, the heir to Emerson Fittipaldi, Nelson Piquet and Ayrton Senna. Everyone slumped exhausted, disappointed, deeper into their sofas.

But wait. There's a calm voice coming out of the television set: Martin Brundle, ITV's expert commentator and a former F1 driver, has spotted a metaphorical change in the wind's direction. Nigel Mansell once said the fans at Silverstone had helped blow him to victory, providing him with another 300 revs, and now it seemed that the intake of breath that followed the sharp exhalation moments earlier had zipped across the Atlantic Ocean like a zephyr and come to Hamilton's aid. Keeping a cool head while those around him were losing theirs, Brundle pointed out in a matter-of-fact way that up ahead, Timo Glock's decision to stay out on dry-weather tyres on a wet track was starting to unravel: his Toyota was losing speed and control at a rate that meant Hamilton would overtake him well before the line.

Hurrah! A nation perked up again.

To make the *dénouement* even sweeter, as Massa took the chequered flag the television screen flicked across to the Ferrari garage, where Massa's father and entourage were toasting the 2008 world championship. Bolstered now by Brundle's knowledge, and watching the wheels metaphorically fall off Glock's car, we allowed ourselves a degree of smugness as the Brazilian jubilation turned to shock, and the wild celebrations switched to the McLaren garage. In that instant, it was as if Tim Henman had just produced a backhand winner down the line to beat Pete Sampras at Wimbledon; Frank Bruno had knocked out Mike Tyson to become world heavyweight champion; and Chris Waddle's penalty had flown *under* the crossbar and England were through to the World Cup final. We were no longer a nation of losers: we could snatch victory from the jaws of defeat, after all.

As the cameras panned back to a McLaren garage in tumult, they sought out Hamilton's father, Anthony, for an immediate reaction; for once, the man who had been the sporting parent *in extremis*, who had taken on three jobs at one time to finance the son's ambitions, and for whom this was the ultimate justification, was absolutely speechless. Even he could not have thought the six-year-old boy for whom he bought a go-kart as a Christmas present would become world champion by the age of 23, the youngest in the history of F1, and the first black winner.

Lewis Hamilton first appeared in the pages of *The Daily Telegraph* as far back as 1995 when, aged ten, he won the British Cadet Karting Championships and received acclaim at the prestigious *Autosport* Awards. It was there that Hamilton famously introduced himself to Ron Dennis, the team boss at McLaren, and told him he wanted to be an F1 driver when he grew up. Dennis advised him to come back in nine years, but recruited the young driver to McLaren's scholarship scheme well before then. Timothy Collings, the *Telegraph*'s motorsport correspondent at the time, wrote for the paper's 'Focus on Schools Sport' column a piece (reproduced here) about Hamilton, and his relationship with the young driver and his family stood him in good stead when it came to choosing a co-author for Hamilton's autobiography in 2007. Hamilton has rarely been off the *Telegraph*'s radar for the last decade and a half.

The first grand prix was held a little more than 102 years before Lewis Hamilton slipped past Timo Glock's ailing Toyota at Interlagos. There had been motor races before the Automobile Club de France organised the inaugural grand prix. Indeed, the innovative French had been running races as early as 1895, less than a decade after Karl Benz had started selling the first production cars. In 1900 the Paris-based American newspaper owner James Gordon Bennett Jr initiated the annual Gordon Bennett Cup in an attempt to encourage other countries to challenge France's early domination of the sport. His races, a national team competition, ran for six editions and were the catalyst for the grands prix.

Early motor races were held over city-to-city courses, and consequently were much longer than the present-day 300-mile, two-hour, comparative sprints. In fact, the *Telegraph* reported that the third Gordon Bennett Cup, in 1902, which ran from Paris to Innsbruck and was won by Englishman Selwyn Edge, was raced over 870 miles as part of a larger race to Vienna. 'The events on the road between Bregenz and Innsbruck, and Innsbruck and Salzburg, were exciting,' said the *Telegraph* correspondent. 'The Chevalier de Knyff was first in at Bregenz on Friday. On Saturday morning he was the first to start, followed by Henry and Maurice Farnan. Then came Selwyn

Edge, who was destined to win the Gordon Bennett Cup, although there is some talk of disqualification in his case as he employed peasants to help him out of trouble on the road.' In those days, if cars suffered mechanical problems or punctures, only the driver or his travelling mechanic could fix it with tools and spares carried on the car. It was not until racing was confined to specially built, self-contained circuits several decades later that teams could station mechanics around the track to carry out repairs, and later set up their own garages and pits. 'The run to Innsbruck,' continued the *Telegraph*'s man, 'was of importance owing to the prize which it was confidently asserted would fall to M de Knyff. That motorist met with a mishap about 30 kilometres from Innsbruck. Edge, therefore, had the race to himself, and got on his Napier car after the Farnans and others who were not registered for the run for the cup to Innsbruck. Thus, an Englishman obtained the international prize, which has hitherto been in French hands.'

Unhappily, there were fatalities in the Automobile Club de France's Paris to Madrid race that same year – at least eight people died, mainly spectators, but including the driver Marcel Renault, a founder of the French motor company – and that ended city-to-city events for nearly a quarter of a century. The final three Gordon Bennett races were held on circuit courses, which set the template for the grand prix series.

The Daily Telegraph sent one of its band of 'Our Own Correspondents' to report Ferenc Szisz's victory in the first grand prix, held in 1906 on the Sarthe circuit, outside Le Mans. It was not, though, a race that Hamilton or other modern drivers, or indeed spectators, would recognise a century on. For a start the cars departed at 90-second intervals, and it was not all over in two hours with the winner spraying Champagne from the top of a podium. 'The automobiles were removed from the resting places, each drawn by one horse,' the man on the spot informed his readers. 'Each was handed over to the particular driver, who had then to take in his supply of petrol and to make whatever repairs were requisite. Some lost about half an hour while so engaged.' The race was a 'terrible ordeal', the heat of the late June day was 'overpowering'. The circuit was in a 'shocking state', 'rugged stones in many places meant serious danger to tyres, with consequent pauses for repairs'. Szisz's combined winning time in his Renault was 12 hours 1 minute 7 seconds, and the Hungarian's average speed was 63¼mph.

The *Telegraph* was also there at the significant races over the next 40 years or so before the introduction of the world championship as we know it. For instance, its representative was in Lyon for the French Grand Prix in 1914, six days after the assassination of Archduke Franz Ferdinand. A thrilling race was won by Christian Lautenschlager, his sixth title, and second in a Mercedes, but the *Telegraph* noted that the French crowd refused to applaud the German success; within a month the two countries would be at war. When peace was restored, the *Telegraph*'s motoring correspondent was at Brooklands, 'the Ascot of motor racing', for the first British Grand Prix in 1926. He was struck, and disappointed, by the size of the crowd. 'Last Saturday proved that the English public will not take that keen interest in motorcar racing our friends do across the Channel,' he wrote. 'Only between 10,000 and 12,000 spectators paid to see the first international motor event run in this country at Brooklands, compared with the hundreds of thousands who flock to the grands prix motor races held on the Continent'. He was particularly disappointed as the Royal Automobile Club had provided vantage points around the circuit for spectators to see every section of the race. Robert Sénéchal and Louis Wagner, sharing a Delage, gave France her first grand prix victory, covering the 110-lap, 287-mile course in just under four hours at an average speed of 72mph. They were followed home – albeit nearly ten miles behind – by two Britons, Captain Malcolm Campbell and Major Henry Segrave, who would find greater fame during the Twenties and Thirties by alternating the world land and water speed records between themselves. Segrave, who three years earlier had been the first Briton to win a grand prix, took the Stanley Cup at Brooklands for the fastest lap, and the *Telegraph*'s man was keen to point out that the successful French cars used Dunlop tyres, which was 'a tribute to England', he said. The tyres 'well withstood the gruelling treatment of constant and severe braking to negotiate the 880 hairpin bends'.

The unnamed motoring correspondent was at Donington less than a year before the outbreak of the Second World War, and would have been as impressed by the size of the crowd for the grand prix as he was by Tazio Nuvolari's storming victory. The crowd was officially reported as 61,000 and the spectators saw 'a race packed with incident'. Nuvolari, despite gaining the lead at the first corner, had fallen behind by the time the cars came in for fuel and tyre changes. Not for long. 'Driving like a demon, the little man was gaining on his rivals by two seconds a lap. [Otto] Müller dropped back, [Manfred] von Brauchitsch was suffering from blistered hands, [Richard] Seaman was a lap behind, [Hermann] Lang drove his hardest but he could not stave off Nuvolari, and 13 laps from the end the Auto-Union shot past the Mercedes on the straight down to Melbourne corner, not to be caught again'. Though the report gave no mention of the type of dubious sportsmanship towards the German cars which had marked the 1914 French Grand Prix, the 1938 race was run against the background of the Munich Conference and the onset of war, and the defeat of the Mercedes would surely not have been unwelcome.

Unfortunately, Nuvolari was 46 when he won that Donington Grand Prix, and 54 when the war ended and he was finally able to climb back into a racing cockpit. He won the Milan Grand Prix in 1946, using one hand to steer, the other holding a bloodstained handkerchief over his mouth, but that was the swansong for the man who had dominated pre-war motor racing. The Formula One world drivers' championship, which began in 1950, came too late for him, and it was left to marginally younger rivals like Alberto Ascari, Giuseppe Farina and Juan Manuel Fangio to dominate the fledgling series.

Formula One was first defined in 1946 when the FIA, the Federation Internationale de l'Automobile, carried out a re-classification of the motor racing categories under their control. Under the regulations for the premier single-seat racing category, non-supercharged 4.5-litre pre-war grand prix cars could race against the pre-war 1.5-litre supercharged cars. In 1950 the first world championship was held (a year, incidentally, after motorcycling introduced its own championship) – and that is the starting point for this book. The first race counting towards the championship was the British Grand Prix, held at Silverstone, won by Farina, and reported by *The Daily Telegraph*. The *Telegraph* has faithfully chronicled every engine cough and splutter ever since.

———————

… through the tight chicane, and it's a sharp, uphill right-hander into the long straight, fifth gear all the way, up and down Vale, until you reach Stowe corner. Hang a left, second gear. It twists and turns from here through Copse, but no more than a flick between fourth and fifth gears, down towards Farm, back into fifth past Club, down into second at the chicane as you approach Bridge. Then it's a 90-degree turn with the chequered flag in sight, and then into *parc fermé* …

All right, it's not a high-speed guide to Silverstone through the eyes of a Formula One driver. It's a section of the 30-mile journey from *chez* Smith to one of the car parks at the circuit. It's the second half of the journey, starting in the quiet county town of Buckingham, whizzing through the back roads to Clackmore, Stowe House, through Dadford and past (Silverstone Golf) Club. On the Sunday morning of a British Grand Prix, providing you leave before seven o'clock, it can take a smidgen over half an hour. With the sun establishing itself in the sky it can be one of the most pleasant jaunts imaginable through the green, leafy countryside, the complete antithesis of what lies ahead: fuel-guzzling cars streaking round the track at speeds in excess of 200mph. With that in prospect, it is tempting to bury the right foot into the floorboards and hope to avoid the flashing blue lights of the Buckinghamshire-Northamptonshire border constabulary, who are just dying to ask speeding motorists: 'Who do you think you are, Stirling Moss/Michael Schumacher/Lewis Hamilton?' (As an aside, Stirling Moss was actually pulled over by police in America, who stopped just short of asking him who he thought he was. The *Telegraph* report of the incident is included within these pages.) Later, by mid-morning, you will be lucky to get out of second gear within fifty miles of Silverstone, unless you're fortunate enough to arrive by one of the fleet of omnipresent helicopters flying into the former airfield. But what do you expect when there are 100,000 spectators heading for a sporting event? It takes 90 minutes or more to get away from Old Trafford after a Manchester United home game. The traffic jams in the vicinity of Silverstone have eased slightly since the A43 by-pass was upgraded, better sign-posting put up, and more accessible car parks made available. Anyway, why leave straight after the grand prix? My *modus operandi* has always been to stay and watch the historic car races (septuagenarian Stirling Moss and all), preferably from one of the grandstands vacated by the hospitality crowd, have an ice cream or carton of chips from one of the franchises opposite the pits and catch up with colleagues who have just filed their copy for the following day's newspapers, while letting the hordes drift away. It is a day out, after all.

That, broadly, is a personal declaration of interest in keeping the British Grand Prix at Silverstone. Now, though, the chase through the villages of Buckinghamshire for the GB GP looks as if it might become a thing of the past, and more's the pity – and not just from a selfish point of view. Sadly, the politics of Formula One are becoming more unfathomable and less in tune with the paying punters. It is bad enough that the cheapest ticket to the 2009 race was £49, and that was for track admission to Friday pre-qualifying. But then to threaten to up sticks for 2010 and move to the circuit at

Donington that has held one grand prix in the last 70 years — albeit a memorable one as underlined by the reports of the 1993 European Grand Prix that follow — defies understanding. The owners of Silverstone and the Government have gone through hoops to upgrade the infrastructure in and around the circuit, using tax-payers' money to do so, to meet the demands of Bernie Ecclestone and his F1 management company. But the continual dispute with the British Racing Drivers' Club, the guardians of Silverstone, has the appearance of an unpleasant little feud that is harming the sport in this country, and affecting the credibility of both sides. The *Telegraph*'s Paul Hayward was particularly forceful on the subject when Silverstone was again under threat a few years earlier, and his words then have resonance now.

Silverstone, as we have seen, hosted the first grand prix of the world championship era in 1950, and has been the permanent home of the British leg of the series since 1987. You play with history at your peril. F1 is a success because it is established, and has a tradition and a format that people recognise and understand. Holding a British Grand Prix at an historic track like Silverstone, and continuing to use Monaco, Imola, Monza, Spa-Francorchamps and Nürburgring, offers a feeling of permanency and grounding. By all means introduce others — like Bahrain, Shanghai, Istanbul and Abu Dhabi — to freshen up the series and attract new audiences, but do so sparingly, intelligently and with sensitivity to the newcomer's place in the overall scheme of things. The validity of F1 is through its history that goes back to Farina, Ascari, Fangio, Moss and company.

Similarly, Ferrari's threat, at several points during the 2009 season, to withdraw from F1 and set up a rival competition smacked of a team who feel they have become bigger than the sport. They need reminding that the F in F1 doesn't stand for Ferrari! Formula One has coped with the disappearance over the years of such iconic marques as Lotus, Vanwall, Maserati, Cooper, Alfa-Romeo, Brabham and Matra. Ferrari need the publicity and prestige generated by competing in front of a global audience of 850 million once a fortnight for nine months. Let's not forget, either, that like Manchester United and the absence of the First Division trophy between 1967 and 1993, Ferrari went more than 20 years without winning the drivers' world title, and 16 without the constructors'. Besides, where would they go? Ferrari and their cronies can talk all they like about setting up a rival series, but who would watch something that lacked the authority that tradition and history bestow on F1?

It has almost become a cliché to call Formula One a soap opera. Yet some of the storylines that underpin it are as ridiculous and outlandish as any dreamt up by the script writers of *EastEnders*, *Coronation Street*, *Howard's Way* or even *Dallas*, which was also fuelled by oil. This, after all, is a sport which changes the rules for no apparent reason almost every year. (The regulations governing qualifying have changed eight times in the last six years. Leave it alone, chaps! Now they are debating race wins to decide the championship rather than points. Illogical!) You don't have to delve too far back into history to come up with some of the cliff-hangers that would be laughable if those in and around Fɪ didn't take them so seriously: the baffling 'diffuser' affair; the Max Mosley sex scandal, and his eventual (unrelated) decision to stand down as FIA president; the budget-capping saga and the will-they-won't-they-break-away brinkmanship of the teams, led by Ferrari; Bernie Ecclestone's *faux pas* about Hitler; the McLaren 'spygate' story; the McLaren/Hamilton 'liargate' revelations; Ron Dennis standing down at McLaren (was he pushed or did he jump?); the half-cock introduction of KERS (Kinetic Energy Recovery System) technology; the arrival and instant domination of Brawn GP, and Jenson Button's long overdue successes; Michael Schumacher's aborted return; the manufactured feuds between drivers; even the manufactured results (if you believe Damon Hill in an interview with Giles Smith in 1998); and the annual round of driver transfer speculation. It's as bad as football! You presume the stories are planted to keep interest alive in a sport where nearly all the danger and excitement and overtaking manoeuvres have been squeezed out. Yes, it is easy to be cynical about it – and Martin Johnson takes that cynicism to extremes in his witty forays into the world of Fɪ, of which there are examples further on – but it is a sport that needs holding up to the light every so often; FISA, FIA and FOTA are acrimonious acronyms which are less transparent than alphabet soup.

It was so different when W.A. McKenzie was covering the embryonic world championship for *The Daily Telegraph* in the days of those magnificent men in their racing machines. You get a whiff of petrol fumes and burning tyres in the reports; the drivers in their goggles, looking like miners just up from the pit-face; the stories of car-swapping, acts of bravery, wives and girl-friends compiling lap charts in between making the sandwiches. McKenzie chronicled the first world champion, Giuseppe Farina – though in those days winning races was what mattered, the world title an afterthought; the rise of Juan Manuel Fangio; the first British winner of both a grand prix and the world title, Mike Hawthorn; and the striving in their wake of Stirling Moss, arguably the greatest driver never to have won the world title.

Sadly, like his successor Colin Dryden in the 1960s and 1970s, McKenzie also had to be a dab hand at writing an obituary at short notice. One day, for example, two-times world champion Alberto Ascari was driving his Lancia into the harbour at Monte Carlo, a few days later he was crashing fatally during testing at Monza; one week, Peter Collins was winning the British Grand Prix at Silverstone, the next he and his wife, the former Broadway actress Louise Cordier, were featured alongside the Mosses in the *Telegraph*'s women's pages – and the week after that he was killed in a crash at the Nürburgring. Furthermore, the ink was barely dry on McKenzie's retrospective review of the just-retired Hawthorn's career when he was rewriting it as an obituary. In no other sport has death stalked the playing arena with such determination.

Motor racing could also be a driver of newspaper sales. The *Telegraph* recognised very early on the enduring appeal for both sexes of fast cars and glamorous drivers; it became the foremost forum for informed and authoritative reporting of the sport that would become a multi-million pound industry. On occasions McKenzie's reports even came off an inside page and on to the front. It did in 1958, when Hawthorn clinched the world title in Morocco – though top billing was given to Moss winning the race. It was also McKenzie's by-line on the front-page lead in 1960, when British drivers Chris Bristow and Alan Stacey were killed at Spa-Francorchamps, and Moss broke both legs. And it was there again two years later when Moss crashed at Goodwood, leaving him in a coma and partially paralysed down the left side of his body (Moss got the message that time and, aged 32, retired from top-class competition). Much later, the death of Ayrton Senna would provide another unwelcome splash headline for the sport.

Dryden, with occasional help from other members of the *Telegraph*'s motoring staff (including the long-serving John Langley), reported the golden age of British F1 success. In the 15 seasons from 1962 British drivers shared nine world titles between them, starting with Graham Hill (twice a winner), Jim Clark (twice), John Surtees, Jackie Stewart (thrice) and finally, in 1976, James Hunt. However, during the same period there were still all-too-frequent fatalities – the list of those lost in action include Clark, Jochen Rindt (the only posthumous world champion), Piers Courage, Bruce McLaren, Jo Siffert and François Cevert – and so the all-too-frequent necessity to dash off a quick obit remained. If the articles in this book covering that period suggest carnage on the track, and raise the questions of why and how the sport could continue, then they nonetheless, however selectively, only reflect the tragedy and soul-searching of the time.

In fact, Enzo Ferrari, the founder of the eponymous manufacturer, went a long way towards trying to answer those questions in the early 1960s, when he became probably the first figure from within motorsport to write a first-person piece for a *Telegraph* title. It was the Daily's then baby sister, *The Sunday Telegraph*, who enticed the Godfather of motor racing to pen a wide-ranging article about his credo, crammed full of lively anecdotes and a fair smattering of self-justifications. It is reprinted in this book as a defence against the sport's critics; how successful it is depends on the reader.

Later, the *Telegraph* would widen its coverage of F1 to embrace regular columns from drivers past and present. Arguably the best of the lot was James Hunt, the playboy maverick who enlivened journalists' copy with tales of excess on and off the track during his racing career, and whose Tuesday-morning articles in the first part of the 1993 season were a must-read for anyone seeking a deeper understanding of the weekend's race. The size of this book makes it impossible to include them all, but the selection here shows what a delight they were. His analysis of Ayrton Senna's momentous drive through the torrential rain at Donington is a masterpiece. Poignantly, he did not live to see in print his very last column, written after the Canadian Grand Prix. The following day's paper carried front-page news of his death, at the age of 45, from a heart attack, and the first of many appreciations of a life lived to the full. As an aside, buried under piles of paper on *The Daily Telegraph* sports desk in Canary Wharf was a telephone so rarely used it was almost redundant. For some reason the only person to call on it was James, checking his copy had arrived and was all right, to the extent that it was usually answered: 'Hello, James ...' Spookily, the morning after he died it rang, to a stunned response from the staff on duty. From memory, when it was finally answered by the least timid sub, it turned out to be James's brother and agent, David, with details of the funeral arrangements. The phone never rang again after that, though, and was eventually disconnected.

Over the years Damon Hill, world champion 20 years after Hunt, has written a number of one-off articles, at times acerbic, at others revealing; David Coulthard was insightful, Eddie Irvine sometimes spiteful, but always readable. But some of the more recent columnists have not always lived up to the refreshing honesty and self-deprecation of their predecessors; it is perhaps indicative of an era when 'spygate', 'liargate' and PR have dogged F1.

Formula One benefited as much as any sport from the expansion of the *Telegraph*'s pagination and its championing of quality writing under the sports editorship of David Welch. Already in the late 1980s, Brian Allen, the then motorsport correspondent, would find himself accompanied by feature writer Michael Calvin at a growing number of races, particularly at the height of Mansell-mania. Allen's successor, Timothy Collings, was frequently joined in the paddock by F1 specialists like Sarah Edworthy and Andrew Baker, as well as occasional heavyweight appearances from chief sports writer Paul Hayward and the witty and irreverent Martin Johnson and Giles Smith. The arrival of the ground-breaking, stand-alone sports supplement in the early 1990s, initially only on Mondays, but eventually embracing the whole week, meant Collings was regularly filing 1,000-word race reports and sidebar analysis pieces compared to the truncated efforts of his forebears. The weekend's grand prix report would invariably end up on the front page of the broadsheet supplement, and sometimes across a page or two inside. One memorable cover was dominated by the fireball in the Benetton pit-lane when Jos Verstappen's car was engulfed in flames during refuelling at the German Grand Prix (it doesn't seem possible that it was as long ago as 1994); another was taken up with the shocking incidents over the weekend at Imola that claimed the life of Ayrton Senna, the causes and effects of which justifiably take up a considerable chunk of this book. On a more upbeat note, the front of the Monday sports pages also celebrated the return of the world title to Britain after 16 years, in 1992, when Nigel Mansell finally achieved his destiny, followed four years later by Damon Hill, the only son to emulate a father.

However, the *Telegraph*'s recognition of the importance of F1 was shown as early as 1955 when the newspaper sponsored the British Grand Prix at Aintree; they were rewarded with a crowd of 150,000 and a memorable home win by Stirling Moss, holding off the great Juan Manuel Fangio. Nearly half a century later, in 2004 (the year Kevin Garside succeeded Collings as motorsport correspondent), the *Telegraph* signed as title sponsors of ITV's television coverage. Viewers could not fail to be aware of the *Telegraph*'s association with the sport, as the newspaper was heralded noisily before and after each advertisement break. An F1 Fantasy Game, a brother for the well-established football and cricket leagues, was also introduced.

Garside's coverage received acclaim in the wider world of journalism when he won the specialist correspondent of the year award in 2008, and he went on to be appointed the *Telegraph*'s chief sports writer, passing the F1 baton to Tom Cary.

Anyway, you've seen the newspaper, now read the book.

As in any sport, the editor of a book like this requires a good team around him, not only to reach the chequered flag, but just to get to the starting grid. Consequently, thanks must go to Keith Perry, one of my former sports editors at the *Telegraph*, for coming up with the idea in the first place; to Caroline Buckland, Head of Books and Entertainment, for commissioning it; to the always helpful Gavin Fuller, Lorraine Goodspeed and the rest of the staff in the *Telegraph* library for facilitating the research; to Graham Coster, Sam Harrison, Dan Steward, John Wheelwright and Clive Ellis, my editors at Aurum, for keeping the show on track; to my trusted former colleague Andrew Baker for his excellent advice, as always; to the writers, the men and women who travelled to the glamorous corners of the world, breathed in the high-octane fumes and described what they saw so evocatively; and, not least, to the many members of the 'pit crew', who performed the original editing, and wrote the headlines, when the copy landed via copytaker or laptop in the bowels of Fleet Street, South Quay, Canary Wharf or Victoria. They have my admiration and appreciation.

Martin Smith
June 2009

CHAPTER ONE
THE 1950s

ALFA ROMEO PUT UP BEST TIMES

LAP RECORD BROKEN

Our Special Correspondent

Silverstone, Thursday

Dr Giuseppe Farina, driving an Alfa Romeo, set up the fastest lap here this afternoon in practice runs for the Grand Prix of Europe next Saturday. He went round in 1 minute 50.8 seconds – an average speed of 93.85mph. Two other Alfa Romeo drivers also beat the existing Silverstone lap record of 93.35mph. They were L. Fagioli, 53, the oldest entrant among the 21 drivers, and the Argentine, J.M. Fangio, the favourite for the race. Both returned 1 minute 51 seconds, equal to 93.69mph. Reginald Parnell, of Derby, who is also driving an Alfa Romeo, put in a time of 1 minute 52.2 seconds, equal to 92.68mph. He said that he and other Alfa Romeo drivers touched 152mph on sections of the course.

Fastest lap times qualify drivers for positions in the front rows of the starting line grid. It seems inevitable that Italian cars will have this advantage. The best British ERA time was 1 minute 57.4 seconds by Bob Gerard, of Leicester. The best French Talbot time was 1 minute 53.4 seconds.

BRITISH DRIVERS PROTEST

Our Special Correspondent

Silverstone, Friday

I understand that three British drivers taking part in the Grand Prix car race here tomorrow have refused an invitation from the RAC, the organisers of the meeting, to the race dinner and prize-giving in London on Monday. They complained that their wives and chief mechanics had not been included. They described the invitation as 'cold and ungenerous'.

Italian Alfa Romeo 1½-litre super-charged cars fill all four positions on the front row of the starting grid for the Grand Prix, over 70 laps of the 2.88-mile airfield circuit. Reginald Parnell, of Derby, will be one of them.

The King and Queen, who will be watching a motor race for the first time since they visited Brooklands as Duke and Duchess of York, will arrive by train at Brackley at 1.45 p.m. tomorrow.

16 MAY 1950

ITALIANS' EASY CAR VICTORY

120,000 SEE TEST RUNS BY BRM

Our Special Correspondent
Silverstone, Sunday

The 120,000 spectators who watched the Italian Alfa Romeo team win the first three places in the Grand Prix of Europe here yesterday, were thankful that earlier they had seen the nationally made British BRM [British Racing Motors] grand prix car show something of its paces. Raymond Mays, after driving the pale green BRM three laps at varying speeds, said: 'I am pleased with the car. I only accelerated spasmodically, but she topped 11,500rpm in low gear.' The British Motor Racing Research Trust announced over the loudspeakers that one or more BRM cars would compete in the International Trophy race here on 26 August against the best Italian opposition.

The Alfa Romeo chief tuner, Signor Satta, at his pit, said: 'The BRM car looks right. It has a fine engine note and it sits well.' The King and Queen, Princess Margaret and Earl and Countess Mountbatten examined the BRM after its demonstration laps.

From the start of the Grand Prix of Europe the four red Alfa Romeos were never headed until number one, driven by the favourite, J.M. Fangio, coasted in at the end of the 63rd lap. It had a broken oil pipe. Reginald Parnell, of Derby, drove his Alfa Romeo with tremendous verve and was only 52 seconds behind the winner, Farina, at the end of 70 laps. Farina had a brilliant opening lap in 1 minute 50.6 seconds, an average of 94.02mph. But when the race settled down the Italians realised that an average of 90 to 91mph was sufficient to win and maintained it to the end.

The private British entries in their out-of-date machines strove valiantly against the Italian factory team. T.C. Harrison, in his 1937 ERA, whipped around determinedly; P.D.C. Walker, nominated to drive the BRM in future races, had to stop his ERA for gearbox adjustment after the first lap. Reserve driver, A.P.R. Rolt, took over, but had to retire. Bob Gerard, of Leicester, got the best out of his 1937 ERA, but was checked by pit-stops.

FARINA WINS GRAND PRIX

WORLD RACING TITLE

Monza, Sunday

Italy's ace driver Giuseppe Farina, driving his Alfa Romeo, won the Italian Grand Prix at Monza today and at the same time gained the title of world motor racing champion of 1950. He led almost throughout the 315-mile race, conceding the first position during only two of the 80 laps, to Alberto Ascari (Italy).

In the classification for the world championship, the Grand Prix of Italy being the last event of the year, Farina obtained 30 points, according to an unofficial calculation, while Luigi Fagioli (Italy), who came third today, obtained 28. Farina's average speed today was 110mph.

25 SEPTEMBER 1950

SPECIAL DOCTOR

Dr Giuseppe Farina, world champion racing driver, has crashed at last, but not in a race. It was in a road accident on his way to a race meeting at Genoa. He is famous for his 'safety first' driving. While his brilliant colleague, Fangio, tears up the course in spectacular daring, Dr Farina – he holds his degree in engineering – drives in the approved Nuvolari style, safe but fast.

After he had won the Silverstone race last month he received a telegram from his wife. It read: 'Tell Giuseppe, after the race, to fly home at once. His mother is ill.' Farina flew back and nursed his mother in Turin while his rivals for the Italian Grand Prix practised. But he left the sick bed to get on the starting line and went on to win. This, with his other international victories this year, made him world champion.

10 OCTOBER 1950

FARINA WORLD CAR CHAMPION

Paris, Monday

The world racing drivers' championship in future will be based on results in the grand prix events organised by Britain, Belgium, France, Germany,

Italy, Switzerland and the United States. This was decided today by the International Automobile Federation.

Giuseppe Farina, the Italian ace who won the Grand Prix of Europe at Silverstone in May, was confirmed as world champion driver. The Alfa Romeo manufacturers won the year's constructors' award.

2 JULY 1951

ALFA ROMEO'S GRAND PRIX

110MPH AVERAGE OVER 373 MILES

W.A. McKenzie
Rheims, Sunday

Juan Manuel Fangio, of Argentina, team-mate and great rival of Giuseppe Farina, last year's champion driver of the world, won the fastest Grand Prix de Europe on record here today. Driving an Alfa Romeo, he covered the 373 miles of the famous triangular Rheims circuit in 3 hours 22 minutes 11 seconds, at an average speed of 110.97mph. Fangio beat Farina handsomely, squaring the score for the latter's victory in this race last year, when it was held at Silverstone.

But while Fangio's win upheld the all-enduring supremacy of Alfa Romeo, this race saw the nearest thing to victory by its national rival, the Italian Ferrari. Yet in the last judgment of this record race, Ferraris achieved glory in their failure, for they were second, third and fourth. The fourth place was taken by Reg Parnell, driving the privately owned Thinwall Special Ferrari. To the several hundred visitors from Britain the drive made by Parnell was a glorious failure. Handicapped by defective brakes and without the elaborate factory organisation behind him, he drove the Vandervell-owned Thinwall Special Ferrari on its limit and gradually, from an early position in eighth place, walked up into fifth. He just made the line, to uproarious cheers, coasting in neutral after his rear axle had sheared. Britain's only other driver, Peter Whitehead of Le Mans fame, broke down and retired on the first lap.

The Italian Sanesi, who finished tenth in a 'works' Alfa Romeo, earned not a little applause. He had driven magnificently among the fastest but, dogged by trouble, had been forced again and again to the pits. Towards the end the car broke down altogether. To be classed as a finisher the driver had to push the car to the line against a slight upgrade. Many times he had to rest. Farina established a new lap record (in a race) of 117.797mph.

29 OCTOBER 1951
ARGENTINE WINS GRAND PRIX
Our Own Correspondent
Madrid, Sunday

Juan Manuel Fangio, driving an Alfa Romeo, and Froilán González, driving a Ferrari, both of them Argentines, were first and second respectively in the Spanish Grand Prix at Barcelona today. Fangio's time for the course of nearly 275 miles was 2 hours 46 minutes 54 seconds. Gonzales completed the course in 2 hours 47 minutes 48.38 seconds. Third place was filled by Giuseppe Farina, of Italy, driving an Alfa Romeo, who returned a time of 2 hours 48 minutes 39.64 seconds. Alberto Ascari, of Italy, was fourth in a Ferrari after completing 68 of the 70 laps in 2 hours 47 minutes 6.16 seconds.

Fangio now becomes world champion driver with 31 points, followed by Ascari with 26, Gonzales with 24 and Farina with 19 points.

Our Motoring Correspondent writes: Fangio's victory was badly needed by the Alfa Romeos in this last grand prix of the season to restore some of the prestige lost this year to their national rivals, the Ferraris. The BRM was recently scratched from the race to continue its tests at Monza, Italy. But according to recent statements on the BRM's progress, both the Alfa Romeos and Ferraris will face a serious challenge from the British car next year.

18 AUGUST 1952
TWO BRITONS WERE RACE HEROES
HAWTHORN FOURTH IN DUTCH GRAND PRIX
W.A. McKenzie
Zandvoort, Holland, Sunday

Britain's two youngest motor racing stars, Stirling Moss and Mike Hawthorn, both aged 23, were the heroes of the 50,000 crowd at the Grand Prix of Holland here today. The race, for Formula Two cars up to 500cc supercharged or 2,000cc unsupercharged, went to the all-conquering Ferraris. But the home-tuned Bristol-Cooper, which Hawthorn drove, was the only car in the race that seriously challenged the Ferraris and finished fourth.

For the first four laps Hawthorn was in the middle of the Ferrari team, and was not passed by them all till after five of the fastest laps ever seen on this circuit. Even then he hung on their tail with determination that delighted the crowd. After a dozen laps rain made the course treacherous, and everyone except Hawthorn slowed. Unfortunately for him the rain stopped. But the Ferraris, the world's fastest Formula Two cars, costing £10,000 a piece, had to be kept flat out to keep the Bristol-Cooper, worth less than the price of many a saloon car in England, at bay.

Earlier, Moss won the international 500cc race, his first win abroad for several months.

19 AUGUST 1952

ASCARI WINS RACING TITLE
Our Motoring Correspondent

By his win in the Dutch Grand Prix on Sunday Alberto Ascari, of Italy, qualifies for the title 'world champion driver of 1952'. The championship will not be conferred until after the last official Grand Prix of the season at Barcelona, Spain, on 26 October. Ascari has already won four of the eight grand prix races which count for the championship. In each of them he made the fastest lap in the race. He receives eight points for each win and one for the fastest lap in each case, thus earning 36 points.

Theoretically, Piero Taruffi, of Italy, who is in second place, can tie. He has nine points for the Swiss Grand Prix, and if he is equally successful in the remaining three races, in Italy, Spain and Brazil, he also could amass 36 points. But Ascari would still be champion, for in the event of a tie other races are taken into consideration. Ascari's fifth victory in Holland, and its nine points keeps him in the lead. Taruffi only won six points in the British Grand Prix. The injured Juan Manuel Fangio, of Argentina, was last year's champion.

KILLED IN MOTOR RACE CRASH

Our Own Correspondent
Buenos Aires, Sunday

Seven people were killed during the Argentine Grand Prix in Buenos Aires this afternoon when a Ferrari driven by Giuseppe Farina ran into the crowd. Farina was uninjured. The race was won by Alberto Ascari, Italy, driving a Ferrari. Second was another Italian, Luigi Villoresi (Ferrari), third Froilán González, Argentina (Maserati) and fourth Michael Hawthorn, Britain (Ferrari).

BRITISH DRIVERS TRIUMPH IN TWO RHEIMS RACES

GRAND PRIX & 12-HOUR EVENTS WON BY HAWTHORN AND MOSS

W.A. McKenzie
Rheims, Sunday

British drivers had their finest hour in international motor racing today at Rheims. They won two of the chief events of the European calendar. In the 12-hour sports-car race Stirling Moss and Peter Whitehead won another brilliant Jaguar victory. They thus confirmed the Jaguar triumph in the 24-hour race at Le Mans three weeks ago, when these cars took first, second and fourth places.

Later, Mike Hawthorn, the 24-year-old British engineering student, who joined the Ferrari team six months ago, won the 310-mile Grand Prix of Rheims for his Italian firm in the closest-fought grand prix on record. His average speed was 113.6mph, one second better than Fangio in a Maserati.

The grand prix for stripped Formula Two racing cars was notable for the new Maseratis threatened the hitherto all-conquering Ferraris with defeat. But after the halfway mark, when Fangio took his Maserati into the lead, Hawthorn in his Ferrari was never more than two cars' lengths behind. He frequently passed the ex-world champion, only to be re-passed. None of the other Ferrari drivers, Ascari, Villoresi or Farina, could get near enough to fight it out with the Maserati. Right to the last half-mile the result was in doubt. Then, as the two leaders swept at 160mph to the finishing line, it was seen that Hawthorn, just behind when they last passed, was in front. González (Maserati) was third, and Ascari (Ferrari) took fourth place.

3 AUGUST 1953

DEFECT ROBBED BRITON OF RACE

W.A. McKenzie
Nürburgring, Sunday

But for a mechanical defect, Mike Hawthorn, the British driver, would have won his second grand prix of the season here today. It developed after he had taken the lead. He finished third in the Grand Prix of Germany, which was won by Dr Nino Farina in an Italian Ferrari. The race was packed with incident.

The winner covered 18 laps of the 14¼-mile Nürburgring road course in the Eifel mountains, west of the Rhine, in 3 hours 2 minutes 25 seconds. His average speed was 83.88mph. Juan Manuel Fangio, Argentine, and, like Farina a former world champion, in the new Italian Maserati, was second, 1 minute 20.4 seconds later. Third to these two was no mean feat for the 23-year-old Briton, driving for the Ferrari team.

After the first lap Hawthorn was lying third to Ascari's Ferrari and Fangio's Maserati. By the third lap he was catching Fangio, and by the fourth had passed him. Towards the end of the fifth lap, when Ascari was slightly in the lead, one of his front wheels leapt 60 feet in the air. It made an arch over Hawthorn and Fangio, and while Ascari coasted they passed him, Hawthorn now in the lead.

Ascari could not stop at his pit, but came to rest 100 yards past it with the brake drum on the ground. With the front jacked up it was reversed back, a new wheel was fitted, and he was sent off again, but now well back in the rear.

For the next two laps Hawthorn still led, at first extending his lead, but then, as some loss of power developed, only holding the lead by desperate driving that brought the German crowd to its toes. Fangio and Farina were on his tail, and on the eighth lap got past, the Argentine losing his place to Farina in the process.

Ascari broke the record with a lap of 85.44mph, trying to get back the time lost in the pits, but he was forced to retire on the tenth lap with brake trouble. Villoresi, last of the works Ferraris, was called in, and his car was given to Ascari. But this went up in a cloud of smoke on the 14th lap, and at 15 laps he retired again.

Meanwhile, the other British cars had been fighting a losing battle from the start. Stirling Moss, in a Cooper, built in 12 days for this, its first race, however, held his own against a host of French and German cars, but was defeated by the formidable cars from Italy. Despite two emergency stops for petrol, he finished sixth. Benetto and De Graffenried, in Maseratis, were fourth and fifth.

24 AUGUST 1953

ASCARI WINS SWISS PRIX

SECOND YEAR AS WORLD CHAMPION

W.A. McKenzie

Berne, Sunday

Alberto Ascari, in a Ferrari, today won the Swiss Grand Prix for Formula Two cars. He qualifies for the world championship for the second time in two years. It was a long, furiously fast race, chiefly between the Ferraris and Maseratis of Italy, fought on the Bremgarten circuit, outside the capital. The speed stripped tyres, caused minor crashes and brought the best cars to the pits for repairs.

The position of the leaders was changing all the time. But always in the picture was Mike Hawthorn, of Farnham, Surrey, driving a Ferrari. When at three-quarter distance Ascari lost the lead to change an oiled plug, Hawthorn came up from fourth to second. In front was Farina on a team car. Hawthorn got to within 300 yards of him when the race reached the stage where – under pre-arranged orders – the Ferraris were to remain in whatever position they found themselves, provided one was in the lead. Only Ascari was permitted to improve his position to secure his world championship. This he did ten laps before the end. The winner's speed was 97mph – one mile per hour less than that for the motorcycle grand prix, but roughly twice the distance.

12 APRIL 1954

BLAZING CAR LEAP BY MIKE HAWTHORN

Our Own Correspondent
Rome, Sunday

Mike Hawthorn, 25, the British racing driver, was badly burned today when his Ferrari car was involved in a crash during the Syracuse Grand Prix in Sicily. Doctors said he had suspected fractures and would be unable to drive for weeks. Hawthorn jumped from the car with his clothes alight. He flung himself in a cornfield beside the road and rolled about while track attendants ran to smother his overalls in overcoats and blankets.

The accident occurred on the fourth lap. His 2½-litre Ferrari crashed into a Maserati driven by Onofre Marimón, which skidded on the Florida Corner. Froilán González, his team-mate in the Ferrari works team, tried to help the British driver. But González's own car touched the blazing wreck and also caught fire. González was unhurt. Seconds later, Giuseppe Farina, of Italy, also in a Ferrari, came round the corner, saw the chaos in front, braked hard and spun round twice. He managed to regain control and carried on to win the race. Trintignant, of France, was second in another Ferrari.

Meanwhile, questions were asked in the House of Commons last month about Hawthorn's deferment from call-up for military service. He is at present under contract to Ferrari in Italy, and will be above the age limit if he stays abroad another year. His home is at Farnham, Surrey. Mr Watkinson, Parliamentary Secretary to the Ministry of Labour, said Hawthorn would get a 'very rapid' call-up for military service if he returned to Britain. Hawthorn plans to return to England soon, his Ferrari team colleagues said last night. They said he told them that as soon as he could leave hospital he would go to Rome and then to Britain.

2 AUGUST 1954

FANGIO WINS IN MERCEDES-BENZ AT 82.7MPH

GRAND PRIX SECOND FOR HAWTHORN

W.A. McKenzie
Nürburgring, Sunday

Mercedes-Benz gained world supremacy here today when Juan Manuel Fangio, the Argentine driver, won for them the Grand Prix of

Europe at 82.766mph, a notable speed for such a course. Mike Hawthorn, of Britain, took over from a tiring González, captain of the Ferrari team, towards the end. He drove so well to gain second place that the Germany crowd of about 500,000 gave him almost as great a reception as the winner.

The German win was not the proud win of the Mercedes-Benz racing cars' debut at Rheims. It barely made up for their subsequent defeat at Silverstone, due partly to unsuitable bodies for the circuit and to gearbox trouble. The effort was almost too much for them. A full team of four started, with new bodies giving the drivers a better view of the track and of their front wheels on the corner. Only two Mercedes cars finished. These were the winner, after a trouble-free run, and the car driven by Karl Kling, which fell back to fourth place by the end. It let Hawthorn's Ferrari into second place and the Ferrari driven by Trintignant, of France, into third place.

At the start it was a close fight between the Mercedes cars of Germany and the Ferraris and Maseratis of Italy. Fangio took the lead, with González hot on his tail, and Stirling Moss, of Britain, who had put up the fastest time in practice with his Maserati, in third place. Behind them sped 17 other cars, ten of them costly 'works' models in the hands of the world's greatest drivers. Only the official Maseratis were missing – withdrawn after Fangio's team *protégé* Marimón, 31, was killed when his car skidded over a precipice during practice yesterday.

The pace was devastating. Despite the 170 corners, steep gradients and blind horizons of this course among the Eifel hills, the leaders were lapping the 14¾-mile circuit in under ten minutes. It was anybody's race. Moss was one of the first casualties. He went out on the second lap with engine trouble. Hawthorn, sixth on the first lap but up in fourth place by the second lap, went out next, also with engine trouble.

After six laps Hans Hermann's Mercedes, lying sixth, limped into the pits and retired. By the 11th lap it was joined in the dead-car park by Lang's Mercedes, the third of the three leaders. The two remaining Mercedes kept their lead. González, who had been deeply affected by the death of Marimón, was well in the rear and appeared to be tiring, losing seconds on every lap.

It was decided to put Hawthorn in his place. The British driver had just walked a mile across country to get back to the pits. When he took over there was a gap of nearly five minutes between himself and his nearest rival, Kling, in a Mercedes. Then Kling, who had been running scarcely a car's length behind Fangio, was missed, pulled in for attention to the rear axle. Just before the trouble, he had put in a record lap at 86.27mph. He returned to the fray, but the Ferraris passed him, and gradually Hawthorn, in the first of them, began to overhaul the leaders. What had begun as a great battle between works car teams became a duel between Fangio and Hawthorn. Picking up seconds at every lap Hawthorn was still two miles behind Fangio at the end.

23 MAY 1955

CAR HURTLES INTO SEA

FERRARI WINS AT MONTE CARLO, ALL MERCEDES DROP OUT

W.A. McKenzie
Monte Carlo, Sunday

Maurice Trintignant, of France, won the Grand Prix of Europe at Monte Carlo today in a Ferrari. He averaged 65.8mph for three hours over the winding circuit through the streets of the city. He secured the lead after the Mercedes drivers, Fangio and Britain's Stirling Moss, had dropped out with mechanical trouble while leading, and Ascari, in a Lancia, plunged into the harbour as Moss retired.

It was one of the most sensational of all post-war grands prix. Trintignant owed his victory to the misfortunes of a dozen more likely winners. The only British car, the Vanwall, driven by Mike Hawthorn, retired before halfway. The race should have gone to world champion Juan Manuel Fangio and his Mercedes. But, after leading from the first quarter-lap, his car retired with back axle trouble on the 50th, at exactly half distance. Then it should have been his team-mate, Stirling Moss, always running in second place. But 30 laps after Fangio's retirement, Moss, too, was in trouble. He limped to the pits, smoke pouring from the bonnet. Hermann, in the third Mercedes, retired in the 27th lap.

Ascari, world champion in 1952 and 1953, was running a minute behind Moss on the Englishman's last lap. But he found the race ended dramatically, too. He brought his Lancia through a bend on to the Quai des Etats-Unis beside the harbour just as Moss pulled into the pits a mile ahead of him. At that moment the Lancia dived off the road, crashed through straw bales and a palisade, and leapt 50 yards through the air before plunging into the sea. Car and driver disappeared in a mountain of spray. Then Ascari was seen to be swimming. He made for a small yacht and was pulled out of the water uninjured.

The appearance in this race of at least four teams which, for the first time since the war, are all potential grand prix winners, augurs well for the sport. These teams are Mercedes-Benz, Ferrari, Lancia and Maserati.

27 MAY 1955

ASCARI DIES IN MONZA CRASH

FORMER CHAMPION'S CAR OVERTURNS

Our Own Correspondent
Rome, Thursday

Alberto Ascari, 36, Italy's most successful racing driver and world champion in 1952 and 1953, was killed today in a crash at Monza. A three-litre Ferrari he was trying out left the track and overturned. Last Sunday he escaped with minor injuries when his Lancia went off the road and leapt 50 yards into the sea during the Monte Carlo Grand Prix. He swam to a nearby yacht.

This morning he drove from his home to watch colleagues practising on the Monza track for the '1,000 kilometres' races next Sunday. He told the Ferrari driver Castellotti, who had just completed 20 laps without incident, that he would like to try out his car, although still in some pain from Sunday's accident. 'I'll make two or three laps,' he said. 'I'll drive slowly.' He completed two laps and started on a third. An eye-witness said: 'It seemed Ascari braked just as he had emerged from a bend and entered the straight opposite the stands. The car swerved to the right, with its left wheels slightly in the air. It overturned and reared up. Ascari was flung out. He landed ten yards away in the grass beyond the track.' Castellotti, Villoresi and other drivers ran over and found Ascari badly hurt. His mechanic immediately offered a blood transfusion, but the driver died within a few moments.

Among races Ascari had won were the British Silverstone Grand Prix, the German, Belgian, Swiss, Dutch and Argentine Grands Prix, the Grand Prix of Pau and the Italian Mille Miglia. His father was killed 30 years ago in an Alfa Romeo taking part in the French Grand Prix at Montlhéry. Ascari's body is lying in state tonight at Monza Hospital. It is draped with the Italian racing colours, and the hands are still covered with his driving gloves. He leaves a widow and two children.

Our Motoring Correspondent writes: Grand Prix racing has lost one of its greatest exponents in the death of Alberto Ascari. A stocky, powerfully built man, he was a gentle, courteous, diffident personality off the track. He possessed the charm and ready smile of the Italian, with none of the racial 'temperament'. His devotion to his children earned him the title of 'the racing father'. His death leaves Italy with very few drivers of grand prix calibre, apart from veterans like Villoresi and Farina. At one time the majority of the world's greatest drivers were Italians.

20 JUNE 1955

MOSS WINS BRITISH GRAND PRIX BY ONE-FIFTH SECOND

150,000 AT DAILY TELEGRAPH EVENT

W.A. McKenzie
Aintree, Liverpool, Sunday

Watched by the greatest crowd ever at a motoring contest in this country, Britain's young racing champion, Stirling Moss, achieved the ambition of his life here yesterday. He won the British Grand Prix by a fifth of a second over Juan Manuel Fangio, the world champion. The two silver-bullet Mercedes-Benz cars they drove were followed over the finish line by another pair from the same 'stable', the 'Mercs' of Karl Kling and Piero Taruffi. The German team won the first four places. They were never seriously challenged.

But for the rest of the field, the Maseratis and the Ferraris from Italy, the Gordinis from France, and the Vanwalls, Connaughts and Cooper of Britain, it was a grim enough struggle. Two drivers had to be replaced during the 270-mile contest, overcome by heat and strain. Only nine of the 24 starters finished, the remainder standing in the dead-car park, or on the circuit where they had 'died'.

The race, sponsored by *The Daily Telegraph*, began with Aintree's grandstands and enclosures being filled by crowds approaching 150,000. Even the Grand National had never seen this multitude. The county police force engaged for traffic control, had to be augmented by 250 extra men. It was reported two hours before the race began that traffic formed a solid queue from Chester to Liverpool. Vehicles were taking between one and one-and-a-half hours to traverse the two-and-a-half-mile Mersey Tunnel.

Over the crowd the sun blazed from a clear sky. Hundreds of high-masted flags of the nations, in honour of the foreign cars and drivers, completed the carnival scene, which had all the atmosphere of any grand prix meeting on the Continent.

At the 'off' the field screamed away, Fangio took the lead with Moss on his tail. Only the French ace, Jean Behra, in a Maserati, separated them from their team-mates, Kling and Taruffi. Two more Maseratis, the works cars of Roberto Mieres and Luigi Musso, followed Taruffi. The best of the Ferraris, Eugenio Castellotti's, lay eighth. Its team fellows, driven by Maurice Trintignant and Britain's Mike Hawthorn, lay ninth and tenth. The best Gordini, Robert Manzon's, was as far back as 12th. The best of the British cars, the Connaught of Tony Rolt, was 15th with Harry Schell's Vanwall behind.

From the first lap the cars were in trouble. Andre Simon's Maserati came to the pits with a broken gear selector, and stayed there. A lap later the superiority of Fangio and Moss was evident. Even Behra, in the Maserati, and Kling and Taruffi in 'Mercs', were left behind. On the third lap the crowd thrilled to see Moss, an imperturbable, white-helmeted figure, driving at arms' length and with a replica in style of the great Fangio, slipping past the world champion and then, yard by yard, widening the gap behind him.

By the fifth lap Behra, driving with every ounce of power extended, was 300 yards behind Fangio, with Moss 50 yards in the lead. Four laps later Behra's Maserati began to pour smoke from its bonnet. It passed the grandstand but we did not see it again. It was the second casualty. An oil pipe had burst. This put Kling in third place, three Mercedes-Benzes lying one, two, three. Only Mieres, in a Maserati, held Taruffi's Mercedes back from fourth place. Castellotti's Ferrari came to the pits on the 11th lap to change plugs. Rolt's Connaught pulled in with a jammed throttle. Hernando da Silva Ramos stopped his Gordini to investigate lack of oil pressure. His team-mate, Manzon, gave up at Bechers.

By now, with only 15 of the 90 laps covered, Moss and Fangio were handicapped by the necessity for overtaking the back markers, whose drivers, not expecting so soon to be 'lapped', pulled over late. By the 18th lap, Fangio passed Moss and took the lead again. The two were genuinely fighting, a luxury not always allowed to team-mates in the lead. Moss clung to Fangio's tail, and on the 25th lap, rounding Tatts corner, he tried to pass. A third car, a back-marker being lapped, complicated the manoeuvre, and Moss had to pull rein. But next lap he came round yards in the lead. From then, until the finish, he never lost the lead.

But, meanwhile, the struggle behind him waxed as hot as the weather. Horace Gould's Maserati went out with failing brakes. Peter Collins's Maserati retired with a defective clutch. Ken McAlpine's Connaught gave up with lack of oil pressure. Rolt's Connaught followed it into retirement with a broke throttle control. Jack Brabham's Cooper went out with a bent valve. Leslie Marr's Connaught was finished, damaging an oil pipe when it spun off the course. Mieres's Maserati was having piston trouble. Lance Macklin, driving for the first time since he was involved in the Le Mans accident, went off the road on Tatts corner. He walked back to the pits, returned leisurely with two mechanics, restarted, and joined in the fray again.

About 30 laps from the end, Mike Hawthorn, running well in sixth place, brought his Ferrari to the pits. He was suffering from sunstroke and felt that he might suddenly collapse. Castellotti, standing by after his retirement, jumped into the car and took off. A little earlier, Ken Wharton had pulled in with his Vanwall. He was feeling ill. Immediately, Harry Schell, whose Vanwall had retired, took over.

The result of the race seemed a certain win for Moss. But on the last lap Fangio pulled out a surprise spurt, caught Moss on Tatts corner, and tried to pass. But the corner gave him no room. He swung behind Moss, tried again on the outside. But Moss, warned by the first manoeuvre, pressed his throttle pedal to the floor. The two cars raced to the finish line, apparently dead abreast. Moss, a wheel ahead, won the race.

He said afterwards: 'Fangio is the greatest driver in the world. He could easily have come up and made it a different story. But being a sportsman, he allowed me to realise my greatest ambition.' Fangio, called to the public address microphone, said, in Spanish: 'Moss is a brilliant young driver. I have enjoyed very much following behind him.'

3 SEPTEMBER 1956

FANGIO LOSES TO MOSS BUT WINS TITLE

COLLINS GIVES UP CAR TO CHAMPION

W.A. McKenzie

Juan Manuel Fangio, of Argentina, won the world championship yesterday for the fourth time when he finished second to Stirling Moss, Britain, in the

European Grand Prix at Monza. Ron Flockhart, Scotland, was third. Fangio's nearest rival for the championship was Peter Collins, Britain, driving in Fangio's Ferrari team. In yesterday's race Collins handed over his car to the Argentine, who had gone into the pits with steering trouble after 218 miles. Had Collins finished and won he would have equalled Fangio's score.

Although Moss achieved only second place in the world championship, his driving yesterday in an Italian works Maserati at Monza brought him two records. He covered the 50-lap course of 310 miles at an average speed of 129.73mph. The previous record was 128.49mph, set last year by Fangio in a Mercedes. The lap record by Moss for the 6.2-mile circuit was 2 minutes 45.55 seconds, making an average of 135.40mph. Last year Moss set the previous lap record in a Mercedes at an average speed of 134.02mph.

Collins said in Monza last night: 'I gave up my car voluntarily to Fangio. I was not forced to do so, but I wanted to demonstrate that there was no truth in all the talk of rivalry between Fangio and myself. However, I am glad the winner was another Briton, Stirling Moss.' Fangio said: 'I do not know whether, in Collins's place, I would have done the same. It was something admirable, something which all papers should stress and praise as a rare gesture of high sportsmanship.'

5 AUGUST 1957

FANGIO WORLD CHAMPION AGAIN AFTER GERMAN WIN

BATTLE WITH TWO BRITONS

W.A. McKenzie
Nürburgring, West Germany, Sunday

Juan Manuel Fangio, the Argentine, consolidated beyond further challenge his title to the world championship for 1957 when he won the Grand Prix of Germany here today. He was driving a Maserati. Close to 47 now, world champion three times running before today, after holding the championship once previously, he put up on this 14-mile Eiffel mountain circuit today the finest demonstration of skill and courage of his career.

But he was good enough sportsman to say to me tonight: 'I was inspired, but the inspiration came from the dire necessity of catching two of the finest drivers I have ever raced against – your Englishmen, Mike Hawthorn and Peter Collins.' It was a deserved tribute. Hawthorn and Collins in the Ferrari team, and Fangio for Maserati, made the race the fastest on record here. All three were acclaimed by the crowd.

Fangio's winning speed of 88.79mph for the 310-mile event, despite a wheel change halfway through, is one mile an hour more than the previous absolute lap speed record. This he established himself last year at 87.73mph. The record he still holds. But now it stands at 91.84mph with an astonishing cut in the lap time of 24.4 seconds.

Hawthorn took the lead at the start, making a breathtaking first lap, including the stationary start, of 87.73mph. His time was 9 minutes 42.5 seconds, only 1.4 seconds above the flying lap absolute course record set up by Fangio in a time of 9 minutes 41.4 seconds. Close behind Hawthorn lay Collins, with Fangio on his tail. Next lap Hawthorn broke the record, with a lap time of 9 minutes 37.9 seconds. Fangio, determined to take the lead, countered with a lap in 9 minutes 34.6 seconds and on the next lap passed both Collins and Hawthorn, reducing the record lap to 9 minutes 33.4 seconds. Thereafter these three had the race to themselves, away out in front of the field.

Lap records went time and again. On the fifth lap it was Fangio again in 9 minutes 33.0 seconds, then again on the ninth lap in 9 minutes 30 seconds, and still again on the tenth lap in 9 minutes 29.5 seconds. The wonder of it was that the two British drivers were more or less holding him. By the 11th lap, half distance, Fangio had a lead of only 27 seconds over Hawthorn, and Collins was like Hawthorn's shadow. The lead was little. In fact, on the next lap the world champion stopped at the pits for a wheel change, and when he went off again, with Hawthorn and Collins in front, he was 40 seconds adrift of the new leader

It was after this that the real drama, and the skill of the three men, brought the crowd to its toes to stand poised for the whole of the second half of the race. Hawthorn and Collins were signalled to go flat out – to keep, at any cost, the Ferrari lead, even to race each other at the risk of both cars 'blowing up'. They did race. Collins on the 14th lap broke the new record. He returned a lap time of 9 minutes 29.3 seconds, equal to 89.47mph on a course any first-class amateur in a costly sports car would be proud to average 80. The new record gave Collins the lead. But a lap later Hawthorn regained it. Together, almost, they raced ahead. But Fangio pulled out all the stops of which the maestro is capable.

On the 17th lap there was a new Fangio record, 9 minutes 28.5 seconds. On the 18th another, 9 minutes 25.3 seconds. On the 19th still another, 9 minutes 25.4 seconds, a speed of 90.53mph. This was the first time the course has ever been lapped at over 90mph. And now Fangio was only 13 seconds behind the leaders. A lap later, with only two laps to go, the Argentine received wild applause as he passed the finish of the lap 150 yards behind Collins, who himself was on Hawthorn's tail. Half a mile further Fangio passed Collins, and halfway round the circuit squeezed past Hawthorn to finish the lap four seconds ahead. To do this he had put the record for the course to a still new speed of 9 minutes 17.4 seconds on the 20th lap, and almost equalled it on the next. He took the lead to win by 200 yards and to hold the record at 91.83mph.

7 JUNE 1958

HAWTHORN WINS FRENCH GRAND PRIX

MUSSO DIES AFTER 150MPH CRASH

FANGIO SAYS HE IS TO RETIRE

W.A. McKenzie

Rheims, Sunday

An Italian Ferrari driven by Mike Hawthorn (Britain) today won the 262-mile Grand Prix of France at a record average speed of 125.6mph. It was the first time this year that a non-British car had won a Formula One race in the world championship series. Hawthorn, who led throughout, finished 24.5 seconds ahead of Stirling Moss (Britain), who was second in a Vanwall. The German von Trips took third place in another Ferrari, 35.1 seconds behind Moss.

Luigi Musso, of Italy, in a Ferrari, crashed at about 150mph on the fast bend just after the grandstands. His car finished upside down in a cornfield and he was taken by helicopter to hospital, where he died.

Fangio, the world champion, finished fourth in a Maserati after Peter Collins's Ferrari stopped just short of the finish. Collins pushed the car home but Fangio passed him and Collins was placed fifth. Later Fangio said he was thinking of retiring. It was ten years since his first grand prix, which was on this course. 'I think it would be a good opportunity to make today's race my last,' he said. But Marcello Giambertone, Fangio's manager, later denied that the world champion had decided to leave racing. 'It is not true.

He has said no such thing,' Giambertone declared. 'Fangio has undertaken to race in England and Portugal and must fill these commitments. He also has an invitation to race in Morocco, and may accept.' Fangio is 48.

Two of the British BRMs retired. The third, driven by Harry Schell, spent much time in the pits and finished last. Tony Brooks was an early casualty in the Vanwall team. He was out on the 18th lap with mechanical trouble and took over Lewis-Evans's car on its 20th lap. But this Vanwall had no better luck than its mate, and was forced to retire at about three-quarters distance.

This was the fifth race of the season for the world championship. Two have been won by British Coopers and two by British Vanwalls. Hawthorn's win makes him equal with Stirling Moss for this year's world champion-ship. Previously Moss had 17 points, and he gets six today for second place, giving him a total of 23 points. Hawthorn previously had 14 points. He earns eight for today's victory and one point for putting up the fastest lap. Musso was lying third, and his death puts Harry Schell (United States) third with 11 points.

Hawthorn's speed today was remarkable. His average for the whole distance was within 1½mph of the previous absolute course record of 127.1mph established by Fangio in a Ferrari in 1956. Hawthorn today set up a new course record of 128.19mph, though in practice he did a lap at over 130mph.

21 JULY 1958

COLLINS WINS GRAND PRIX

Our Motoring Correspondent

Peter Collins, of Kidderminster, Worcestershire, gave the Italian Ferrari firm the victory in the British Grand Prix at Silverstone, Northamptonshire, on Saturday, winning the 218-mile race at an average speed of 102.05mph. His speed could have been considerably higher. He slowed in the later stages on pit instructions. He led from start to finish. Mike Hawthorn, of Farnham, Surrey, also in a Ferrari, was second, 24 seconds behind. At one time Hawthorn was 58 seconds behind, having had a short pit-stop.

The Ferrari win consolidated that firm's hopes of winning the manufac-turers' world championship and it put Hawthorn well in the lead for the drivers' world championship. Stirling Moss, in a Vanwall, second to Collins until the 26th lap of the 75-lap event, came into the pits then with smoke pouring from his engine, and retired. Hawthorn now has 30 points in the championship, Moss 23 and Collins 14.

25 JULY 1958

THERE'S TENSION BEHIND THE COOL, CALM FRONT

FOR DRIVERS' WIVES 'MOTOR RACING IS NO RELAXATION'

Winifred Carr

One wonders, sometimes, watching motor races how the nerves of any racing wife could stand the strain. Typical of what these wives witness was last Saturday when, for two hours, in the burning, broiling heat, 26-year-old Peter Collins drove the Italian Ferrari at an average speed of 102.05mph for 75 gruelling laps of the Silverstone circuit to win the British Grand Prix. That means he drove, in effect, from London to Liverpool – and drove immaculately, never making the slightest mistake.

But of course, this was a race, and to increase the wives' worries there was the added problem of team tactics. In this race Collins was to be the bait for Stirling Moss, driving a Vanwall. The Ferrari tactics were for Collins to get into the lead, somehow, from the very start and drive at such a pace that Moss's car would not stand the strain.

He did this so effectively that he covered the first lap at 94mph from a standing start. For 25 laps Collins led, with Moss second and Mike Hawthorn, in another Ferrari, lying third. If Collins's car cracked up, Hawthorn would step in. But it was Moss in the 26th lap whose engine could not stand the strain. He retired and Collins went on to win.

If ever there was a sport that faithfully reflects the restless, speed-crazy and uncertain times we live in, it is motor racing. It draws the world's prettiest girls and most dashing young men by the thousand to its hot and dusty tracks – Goodwood, Silverstone and Brands Hatch in England; Spa in Belgium; Zandvoort in Holland; Rheims and Le Mans in France; Monaco, Oporto, Rome, Palermo, Casablanca, Buenos Aires and Caracas.

They turn up on their scooters and motor bikes or in their sleek sports cars – the girls in bright summer colours and silk headscarves, the men in sports jackets and tweedy caps – to watch their idols – Juan Manuel Fangio, Stirling Moss, Peter Collins, Mike Hawthorn, Jean Behra and Roy Salvadori – streak by at 150 miles an hour.

And in between the races, when the tension has eased, the dust has settled and the acrid smell of hot tyres and high-powered fuel has faded, they sit on the grass around the track and picnic. The men they have come to see are deeply bronzed through following the sun around the world's racetracks throughout the year. Motor racing is a summer sport that is risky enough on a dry day, but positively dangerous when the track is rain-soaked.

It is the tensest of sports, too. Even the wives of the driving aces will admit this while loyally struggling to put up a cool, calm front so that no one can accuse them of trying to persuade their husbands to give up this dangerous game. 'Motor racing is no relaxation,' said Katie Moss rather sharply to me last week in the pits at Silverstone when we were talking about it. It was the only give-away remark in a carefully guarded conversation. All the time, she kept glancing over her shoulder to where Stirling, in his dark green Vanwall, was waiting for the starter's signal.

Katie never misses a race or practice that Stirling is in if she can possibly help it. Each time he streaks out of the pits it is a major parting. No wonder she smokes a lot and has a habit of pacing up and down all the time he is out on the track.

The Mosses' way of relaxing is to go to the pictures or just sit at home doing nothing. 'When you are on the move from country to country all the time, it's wonderful to get back home,' she said with all the wistfulness of a wife who has been married for less than a year and hasn't had a chance to live more than three weeks at a time in either of her two new homes.

This spring they moved into the house they have had built at Nassau, 52 feet above sea level and called Blue Cloud because it is on the highest point of the Bahamas. This is to be their winter base while Stirling is racing in South America. Last month they bought a tiny house in Mayfair's Shepherd's Market as their main base for the rest of the year while he races in England and on the Continent.

'I hope we can be back there for Christmas,' she said. 'There's not much hope of moving in before then, because we're off to France tomorrow night. Then we go on to Germany, Italy, Portugal, Morocco and the Bahamas.' Even at home in Nassau, there's no escape from speed. Stirling keeps a fast motorboat in the harbour.

Left to herself, Katie isn't a speed fan. She would rather potter along in her ten-horse-power car than drive their fast sports model. In this, she is unlike Peter Collins's wife, Louise, who was a sports car enthusiast long before she married. American-born Mrs Collins gave up acting on Broadway to marry Peter. Perhaps it is because of her stage training that she seems so relaxed while she sits out a race or a practice in the pits. Soon after her marriage early last year, she said: 'Peter laughs all the time and I laugh, too, but we both know how desperately dangerous his life must be. It's the price he pays for his fun and his livelihood.'

But although they can't enjoy the races like the thousands who come for the thrills and excitement, these two wives would rather be there than anywhere, and they would rather see their husbands zip by in the cars they are devoted to than stand by miserably while some other dedicated driver raced past.

4 AUGUST 1958

GRAND PRIX DEATH OF PETER COLLINS

CAR OFF TRACK IN SOMERSAULT

RACE WON BY BROOKS

Our Own Correspondent
Bonn, Sunday

Peter Collins, 27, the British racing driver, died tonight after his Ferrari crashed at high speed in the German Grand Prix. Tony Brooks, Britain, won the race in a Vanwall. Collins's Ferrari left the track in the 11th lap of the 15-lap race on the Nürburgring. It somersaulted several times. The driver was hurled out and fractured his skull. He was taken to St Joseph's Hospital at Adenau, not far from the track, and given a blood transfusion.

Soon afterwards a West German Army helicopter flew him to Bonn. He was taken on by ambulance to the neurosurgical clinic at Bonn University. He was still unconscious on arrival there and was immediately X-rayed. Despite attempts lasting an hour to revive him, Collins never regained consciousness. He was dead when his wife, the former Broadway actress Louise Cordier, whom he married last year, arrived at the hospital. Mrs Collins was driven from the track at high speed in an Italian sports car belonging to the Ferrari team. Mike Hawthorn, whose Ferrari lay behind that of Collins when the crash occurred, also went to the clinic. He was greatly upset and leaned against the wall at the entrance before going inside.

Collins's father-in-law, Dr Andrew Cordier, is executive assistant to the United Nations Secretary-General, Mr Hammarskjöld. He spoke by telephone from New York to his daughter in Bonn. Mrs Collins did not see her husband crash. She was in the pits.

At the time of the crash Collins, in second place, was battling for the lead with Brooks and Hawthorn. He was taking a right-hand curve on a section of the track known as the Botanical Garden. Hawthorn, white-faced and clutching Collins's cracked crash helmet, described after the race how he saw his team-mate hurtle off the track. He said: 'Collins topped the bank and went over the hedge. I saw him flung out. I think he hit a tree.' Spectators said that when the car shot into the air Collins was hurled into bushes. The front and rear of the car were badly buckled. The windscreen snapped off.

The winning 2½-litre Vanwall of Brooks set a record average speed of 90.87mph. Roy Salvadori, of Britain, came second with Maurice Trintignant, France, third. Both drove Coopers. Hawthorn and Stirling Moss, who drove a Vanwall, fell out with mechanical trouble.

5 AUGUST 1958

PETER COLLINS HIT BANK

MIKE HAWTHORN TELLS OF CRASH

Daily Telegraph Reporter

Mike Hawthorn, who arrived at London Airport from Cologne last night, described in detail the moments just before the crash in which his fellow racing driver Peter Collins was killed in the German Grand Prix on Sunday. Hawthorn accompanied Collins's widow back to London. They were the last passengers off the plane. Hawthorn supported Mrs Louise Collins down the aircraft steps and into the control buildings.

He gave an interview at the airport as a tribute to his friend. Hawthorn was very distressed and broke down several times. 'I am taking a few days off,' he said, 'and am taking Louise back to Peter's parents.' Referring to the crash, Hawthorn said: 'There was a little dip and Peter went into that; then a sharp right-hand bend. He took it a little too wide and hit the bank and turned over. I don't know what speed he was going at. As a driver he was definitely the best, and as a friend – he was my friend. Peter and I raced as a team [both drove Ferraris] and at that moment he was in front and I was behind. We were chasing Tony [Brooks was leading in a Vanwall].' It is expected that Collins's body will be flown to London this evening.

MOSS WINS BUT HAWTHORN CHAMPION BY ONE POINT

W.A. McKenzie
Casablanca, Sunday

Stirling Moss, of Tring, Hertfordshire, today won the Morocco Grand Prix in a British Vanwall at a record speed of 116.2mph. His close rival for many years, Mike Hawthorn, of Farnham, Surrey, finished second in a Ferrari, but won the 1958 world championship by one point. He is the first British driver to get the title since it was instituted in 1950. Fangio, previous champion, retired this year.

The manufacturers' world championship goes to Mr Tony Vandervell, maker of the Vanwall cars, which have won six grands prix this year. Stuart Lewis-Evans, of Welling, Kent, in a Vanwall, crashed and his car went up in flames. Lewis-Evans, who is 28, was taken to hospital by helicopter with serious burns.

Hawthorn could have lost the championship to Moss had he failed to finish within the first three places. He appeared to be making sure of the title, ignoring the temptation to fight out the race with the Vanwall. But he had to be careful not to fall too far behind and lose second or third place. He came 84 seconds behind Moss.

It was obvious from the start that the two were out to win the championship. But their tactics were very different. Moss was eight points down on Hawthorn before today's race, the last this season counting for the championship. To win the championship, Moss would have had to finish first, scoring eight points, record the fastest lap, worth one point, and Hawthorn would have had to be fourth or worse. Moss went flat out from the fall of the flag, taking the lead on the second lap. He had the race to lose if the car 'blew up'. But he had a chance of the world championship if he stayed in front. He not only led from the second lap to the finish, but topped the lap speed record, too. However, Hawthorn, taking things comparatively easily, did not go off the course, break up his engine or fail to finish. He cantered in a comfortable second, scoring six points. But owing to the system of counting each driver's six best races only, he got the championship by one point, 42 to Moss's 41 points.

The Ferrari team manager gave Hawthorn what help he could by sending out the American driver, Phil Hill, to harry Moss for all he was worth. Hill for several laps hung on to Moss, and time and again when Moss raised the lap speeds Hill went faster still. But Moss never made a mistake, nor did his Vanwall falter. Hawthorn kept the pair in sight, but was letting them get gradually farther and farther ahead. He himself was being pressed hard by Tony Brooks in another Vanwall, but he never allowed Brooks to stay in front for more than a lap or two. In the end, when Phil Hill had to slow down with his engine sounding rough, Hawthorn moved up into second place. He then contented himself with maintaining the gap and did not try to pass the leader. Hill finished third, less than a second behind Hawthorn. Brooks retired.

Hawthorn was to have driven with the Ferrari number two. But because Peter Collins and Luigi Musso, two famous drivers who were his friends, were killed this year running on that particular number, he asked if his number could be changed with that of his team-mate, the Belgian driver Olivier Gendebien. Gendebien crashed towards the end of the race, in an incident involving two other cars, the Cooper-Climax of François Picard of France and the Cooper of Tom Bridger, who comes from Royston, Cambridgeshire. Gendebien is reported to have a broken rib. Picard is said to be seriously hurt. Bridger escaped with minor injuries.

The race was run on a 4.7-mile circuit of tarmac roads, running practically over desert ground outside Casablanca. The crowd consisted of tens of thousands of Europeans and Arabs. It was run in hot sunshine. Because of the high speeds possible on the circuit, with the cars at times reaching 180mph, the race took a big toll of engines and of drivers.

After the race Mike Hawthorn said that he was very happy and proud to become the first Englishman to win the world championship. 'One day I should like to do it in a British car,' he added. Stirling Moss said: 'It has been my ambition all my life to win this championship. Perhaps next year I shall pull it off.'

23 JANUARY 1959

OBITUARY: MIKE HAWTHORN

CHAMPION DRIVER AT AGE OF 29

Mike Hawthorn, who was killed yesterday in a road accident, had many escapes on the racetrack during his spectacular progress to the forefront of British drivers. World champion at the age of 29, Hawthorn announced in

December his retirement from grand prix racing. In a Ferrari he won the title at Casablanca last year by a single point after coming second to his friend and rival, Stirling Moss, in the Morocco Grand Prix.

In eight years as a race driver Hawthorn won prize money estimated at £40,000. In the course of collecting it he suffered mishaps which included:

> The collapse of a rear spring at Goodwood, which threw him out of the car at more than 100mph;
>
> Failure of brakes at Aintree, which sent him careering into a ploughed field;
>
> The dislodging of a bonnet-top, which blew off and hit him in the face in practice at Silverstone;
>
> A skid at Oulton Park, which caused his car to do a triple somersault and throw him 40 feet;
>
> A collision with two other cars while racing in Sicily, as a result of which his car burst into flames. He was badly burned and spent several weeks in hospital.

In 1955 Hawthorn, driving a Jaguar, won the 24-hour Le Mans race in which 85 spectators were killed when a Mercedes driven by a Frenchman ran into the crowd at 150mph.

Hawthorn was deeply affected by the death of his friend and fellow driver, Peter Collins, in the German Grand Prix in August last year. Hawthorn, driving in the race, saw Collins hit a bank and turn over. Many thought that the loss of his friend was a factor in Hawthorn's decision to retire.

Tall, fair and genial, Hawthorn was immensely popular with his fellow drivers. His father, Mr Leslie Hawthorn, himself a racing driver, bought him a motorcycle while he was still at Ardingly College. By the age of 18 he had won a cup. By 1950 he owned his first sports car, a 1934 1100cc Riley 'Ulster Imp' and drove it successfully in speed trials. In 1952 he leapt into prominence by beating the great Argentine driver Juan Manuel Fangio at Goodwood. Hawthorn drove BRM cars for a time, but in 1956 signed for Ferrari, the Italian firm, and by victories in race after race in many parts of the world established himself as a fearless and first-class driver.

W. A. McKenzie writes: Mike Hawthorn was the most colourful and unpredictable personality in post-war motor racing. He was practically unheard of until the Easter Holiday meeting at Goodwood in 1952. In a Cooper Bristol, and in the company of many of the world's leading drivers, he won two races and in a third finished second to the Argentine, González.

His entry into grand prix racing was just as precipitate. He joined the Ferrari team and won the French Grand Prix at Rheims in 1953. For over 150 miles Hawthorn and Fangio were never more than a length apart. Hawthorn won. But the race was so close that Fangio and the equally famous Ascari and González all finished within less than three seconds of the winner. One knew then that the big flaxen-haired young Englishman had the courage and skill of a champion. He was 23 at the time.

Hawthorn was in the news again at Le Mans in 1955, when his car was involved in an accident with Levegh's Mercedes-Benz which disintegrated and killed 85 spectators. I think that is the only time I ever saw Hawthorn's nerve shaken. He leapt out of his car, jumped across the tarmac and started to run wildly away, saying that he would not drive again. He was almost dragged back, and with the Mercedes-Benz opposite the pits an inferno, he went on to win the race.

Last year he lost his closest friend, Peter Collins, who was killed on the Nürburgring. His team-mate Luigi Musso crashed fatally a few weeks earlier, and Archie Scott-Brown, another friend, lost his life during the season. Finally, Peter Whitehead died in a high-speed car trial.

1 JUNE 1959

BRM SCORE FIRST GRAND PRIX VICTORY

W.A. McKenzie
Zandvoort, Holland, Sunday

Britain's BRM achieved their first victory in an international '*grande épreuve*' here today by winning the 200-mile Dutch Grand Prix in one of the most dramatic races I have seen. The driver was Joakim Bonnier, Sweden. Bonnier, considered not quite a top-flight Formula One driver, won against many of the greatest in the game. Zandvoort is a difficult circuit of sweeping curves, hairpin bends and gradients, winding through the sand dunes of the Dutch coast.

Raymond Mays, 'father' of the original BRM project, and team manager, was warmly congratulated by drivers and entrants who descended on him from every pit. Mechanics danced with joy: the success ends ten years of heartbreak. The other BRM also had a good run. It was lying fourth when it broke down with ignition trouble. The success ensures that BRM's sponsor, the industrialist Mr A.G.B. Owen, will continue to back the car.

Stirling Moss had bad luck. He was leading the race, with not many miles to go, when the gearbox of his Cooper broke. Many laps early in the race were a duel between Bonnier and Jack Brabham (Cooper). In the 29th lap Brabham put Bonnier behind him, only to be overtaken again on the 33rd lap. Moss, after a bad start, began to pick up speed and by the 27th lap had passed into third place. By the 31st lap he was about a quarter of a minute behind Bonnier and Brabham. On the 49th lap he passed Brabham and began to chase Bonnier, only five seconds ahead. After ten exciting laps he went into the lead with beautifully judged racing. But in the 52nd lap his broken gearbox gave Bonnier an easy victory.

13 DECEMBER 1959

JACK BRABHAM IS CHAMPION

CAR PUSHED HOME OUT OF FUEL

Our Own Correspondent
New York, Sunday

Jack Brabham, the Australian, became 1959 world champion racing driver yesterday when he pushed his Cooper-Climax half a mile after it ran out of fuel to take fourth place in the American Grand Prix at Sebring, Florida. As he crossed the finishing line he collapsed from exhaustion, deaf to the cheers of a crowd of 15,000. The race was won by his team-mate, Bruce McLaren, of New Zealand, at an average speed of 98.87mph. Second was Maurice Trintignant, of France, also driving a Cooper. Tony Brooks, the British driver, was third in a Ferrari. Stirling Moss, in a Cooper, retired early in the race.

Although it was a surprised McLaren who won the first American Grand Prix to be held since the Vanderbilt Cup days, the attention of the crowds and those in the pits was on the duel between Brabham, Moss and Brooks for the world crown. Moss, in a Cooper-Climax entered by Rob Walker, and Brabham were together at the starting grid in the 18-car race. But Brabham did not have to compete with his English rival for long. In the fifth lap the gearbox on Moss's car broke down, and he had to walk two miles back to the pits, the world championship having eluded him for the fifth time. Up to this point Moss had been in the lead. Now Brabham shot to the fore and held the lead until he ran out of fuel on the last lap. As he pushed his car to the line, McLaren flashed past to win the race.

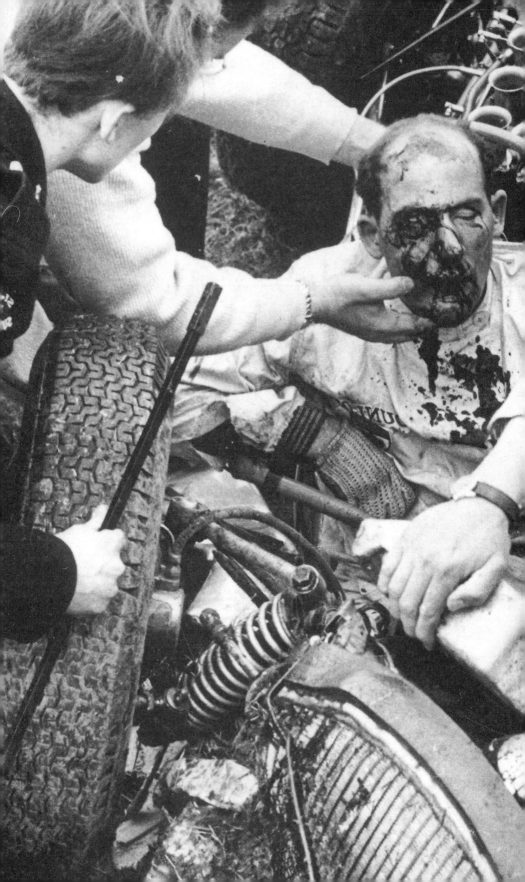

**CHAPTER TWO
THE 1960s**

20 JUNE 1960

TWO BRITONS KILLED IN GRAND PRIX

BRISTOW LOSES CONTROL: STACEY HIT BY BIRD
MOSS BREAKS LEGS: WIN BY BRABHAM

W.A. McKenzie

Spa, Belgium, Sunday

Two British drivers, Chris Bristow, 22, and Alan Stacey, 26, were killed in the Belgian Grand Prix motor race today. This followed serious accidents, in yesterday's practice, to Stirling Moss, 30, and Michael Taylor, 25. The race, won by the Australian Jack Brabham, reigning world champion, at an average of 133.631mph, was one of the fastest on any road circuit in the history of motor racing. Today's tragedies will arouse fresh controversy over the future of the sport.

Stacey's death seems almost certainly to have been due to a freak accident. M. Jean Bovy, a senior official of the circuit, confirmed that a bird hit Stacey's face, smashing his goggles. The body of a bird was found on the track. There were traces of blood and feathers on the goggles. It was at a spot called Fountain of the Bird that Stacey, driving his Lotus at nearly 140mph, crashed. The car left the path, hit a bank and burst into flames. He died in the ambulance.

Bristow was well up, lying seventh in his Cooper when, in the 19th lap, he took the long, fast bend known as Burneville, near Malmedy, at over 130mph, accelerated and overtook another car. Then he seemed to lose control. The car shot off the road and somersaulted three times. M. Bovy said Bristow was hurled through a row of bushes and small trees screening a wire fence. His neck hit a wire and was half severed.

Chris Bristow lived with his parents at Muller Road, Clapham, south-west London, and until recently helped his father in a garage business. He was a promising driver and had several successes. One of these was in a Cooper-Borgward, which he drove as a member of the British Racing Partnership, winning the important John Davy Trophy at the August Bank Holiday meeting at Brands Hatch, Kent, last year, when he beat such stars as Jack Brabham and Roy Salvadori. Today he was racing for the Yeoman Credit team, sponsored by the hire-purchase organisation of that name. The team lost a famous driver less than five weeks ago when the Franco-American Harry Schell was killed in practice at Silverstone.

Alan Stacey lived at Broomfield, Chelmsford, Essex, and had been driving particularly in important sports car events, including the Le Mans 24-hour race, with considerable success. He was single. He lost a leg in a motorcycle accident ten years ago. He never liked to talk about the accident and only a few of his friends knew. He had been riding a motorcycle only three weeks and was wearing L plates when a car ran into him. With the compensation he was able to start a garage business and then to enter motor racing.

The accident in which Bristow was killed happened on the bend at which Stirling Moss, in a Lotus, came to grief yesterday. Moss was swinging down the gradient at 140mph when a half-shaft to the left-side axle hub broke. The wheel collapsed, and the car went spinning round like a top, finally crashing into a bank. Moss was thrown violently on to the track. He fell on his face and knees and lay motionless for some minutes before a doctor could be brought to him. For some unexplained reason the ambulance that should have been stationed at Malmedy was not there and it was 20 minutes before one could be brought.

Moss was taken to the Malmedy Hospital where he was found to have both legs fractured just below the knee, three broken ribs, a badly cut and broken nose, two black eyes and several superficial cuts. I saw him in hospital just before the race. He was able to move his arms freely but lay otherwise inert. He smiled and seemed in good spirits. 'I shall be all right,' he said. 'It is a bit of a blow, though, to my hopes of getting the world championship this year. I am being flown back to England tomorrow but it is quite obvious that I shall have to miss quite a number of the grand prix races which count towards the championship.

'The funny thing is,' Moss said, 'in the accidents I have had in the past, none, of course, anything as bad as this, I have always seen it coming when it has finally been unavoidable and I have braced myself to stay in the car. This time I had no chance of staying in the car. One moment I was driving it and in a split second it was completely out of control. But if I had stayed in the car I think I would have been much worse.'

Moss's estranged wife Katie telephoned the hospital today and sent her love. Mr Rob Walker, the former racing driver, a close friend of Moss, said this evening the doctor had paid another visit and found Moss was progressing well. 'There would be no problem about his leaving tomorrow.' Moss would fly to London from Liège and would be taken to St Thomas's.

Michael Taylor, also injured yesterday, was driving a Lotus into a bend when the steering failed. The steering column had broken. The car plunged off the road into bushes and small trees. Taylor was thrown out.

After the failure to Moss's car the Lotus team manager withdrew the other Lotus cars from practice and had new axle-shafts flown over from the Lotus works at Cheshunt. These were fitted only a few hours before the race, but the cars were considered fit then to start.

Jack Brabham led from the start, his Cooper closely chased by the Cooper of Olivier Gendebien, the Ferrari of Phil Hill, the BRM of Graham Hill, and then Innes Ireland in a Lotus. Behind were Jo Bonnier, BRM, and the Cooper of Bruce McLaren. Brabham had earlier broken the lap record set up by Mike Hawthorn two years ago in a Ferrari in a time of 1 minute 58.3 seconds. The Australian world champion raised it by 6.4 seconds to 135.34mph. But later this record went too. Brabham, Innes Ireland and Phil Hill all did laps at a flat 116mph. Shortly afterwards Ireland was in and out of the pits. At 13 laps he retired. With only seven laps to go Phil Hill brought his Ferrari to the pits, leaving Brabham with no serious competition.

The championship position now, after four grand prix races – the USA, Monaco, Holland and Belgium – leaves McLaren with six points for today to add to his previous 14, a total of 20. Brabham, who had eight points, gets another eight today for a total of 16. Stirling Moss, who could not race today and was until now second in the table with 11 points, stands third, and Innes Ireland and Phil Hill are jointly fourth with seven.

Mr William Bristow, father of one of the dead drivers, heard the news of his son's death over the radio at his wife's hairdressing salon in Streatham. Mr Bristow, who runs a car-hire firm, said he had been trying to persuade his son to give up racing. 'I was worried about him with all those other drivers getting killed lately. When Harry Schell died, I thought things were getting too hot, and told Chris so. But being only 22, he had no fear of death and wanted to carry on. It has come as a terrible shock, but in that game it is always hanging over you. All I can say is that he was too young to die.'

15 AUGUST 1960
BRABHAM WINS PORTUGUESE GRAND PRIX
MOSS DISQUALIFIED
W. A. McKenzie
Oporto, Sunday

Jack Brabham, of Australia, the reigning world champion driver, won the Grand Prix of Portugal here today. It was his fifth grand prix victory in a row this season, and makes him certain of taking the championship title again for 1960. It was no easy victory. He won by only a little more than a minute over the New Zealander, Bruce McLaren, his chief rival for the championship. Both were driving 'works' Coopers. Jimmy Clark, Britain, in a Lotus, finished third with the German, Count von Trips, in a 'works' Ferrari only seconds behind in fourth place.

It was Stirling Moss's first grand prix since his serious accident in practice for the Belgian Grand Prix on 18 June. He drove his Lotus with his old dash and verve, but with his old ill-luck, too. He was dogged by mechanical trouble, and spun round off the road near the end, though he quickly went on again. He finished fifth, but when official results were issued tonight he was stated to have been disqualified for a breach of the regulations. The organisers of the race, the Oporto Automobile Club, said Moss had violated Article Six of the rules governing the event by pushing his car in the wrong direction on the track to take advantage of a downhill slope to get his engine started. He had stalled his engine when he skidded off the road.

Moss started well, ending the first lap in third place to the American Dan Gurney, in a BRM, who was in the lead with Jack Brabham a close second. A lap later, with Brabham suddenly dropping to eighth place, Moss was lying second and held on to Gurney until at the fifth lap John Surtees, the racing motorcyclist now driving for Lotus, overtook him. Surtees raised the lap record to 112.37mph. There were several incidents, but no one was hurt. The official announcer said that Surtees had 'turned over' while in the lead. But the Portuguese word used also means 'turned round'. Surtees apparently had spun off the course, damaging his car, though he was not hurt himself.

When the race started Brabham, who is 34, had 32 points towards the championship and McLaren 27 points. Brabham now has 40 and McLaren 33, so with the grand prix season approaching its end Brabham's lead is unassailable.

II SEPTEMBER 1961

13 DIE, 20 HURT AT GRAND PRIX

VON TRIPS KILLED: BRITON ESCAPES
SPECTATORS MOWN DOWN ALONG FENCE

W.A. McKenzie

Monza, Italy, Sunday

Thirteen spectators were killed and 20 injured when a Ferrari driven by Wolfgang von Trips hurtled into the crowd after a triple collision in the Italian Grand Prix here today. Von Trips, who was leading in the drivers' world championship, died almost instantly. The crash, one of the worst in motor racing since the war, occurred in the first lap. Von Trips's Ferrari was involved in a collision at a bend with Lotuses driven by Jim Clark and Gerald Ashmore of Britain.

Von Trips was flung out. His Ferrari and Clark's Lotus thrashed along the fences, leaving a trail of debris in their wake and ending upside down on opposite sides of the track. Ashmore was taken to hospital, but was not seriously hurt. Clark, who appeared none the worse when I saw him afterwards, told me he was running in Von Trips's slipstream when the Ferrari pulled across him. 'I pulled right over to avoid him,' said Clark. 'My front wheels touched his back wheels and we both went out of control. I hardly know what happened after that. I was quickly taken to the care of flag marshals who ran out on to the road to warn the cars behind. There was a lot of dust smoke and general melée. The details are a blank to me. I know I walked back.'

The spectators killed and injured were mown down as they pressed close to a wire fence at the roadside. The Ferrari crashed into the wire and ran along it for 50 yards before bouncing back into the road and overturning.

The race was won by Phil Hill, United States, von Trips's team-mate, in a Ferrari. Dan Gurney, United States, was second in a Porsche, and Bruce McLaren, New Zealand, third in a Cooper. Not until after the race had ended was Hill, runner-up to von Trips in drivers' championship points, and now 1961 champion, told of the crash and the tragedy officially reported.

Jack Fairman told me that he passed the spot a few seconds after the accident and had to weave constantly through a hundred yards of debris. There was a car bonnet, wheels and bits of chassis all over the road. Few of the crowd knew anything of the crash. No announcement was made, and as far as most of the spectators were concerned the race continued.

A similar accident occurred at the same spot a little later. John Surtees, the world motorcycling racing champion, turned car driver, appeared to be suddenly baulked by the Swede, Joakim Bonnier. Surtees could not stop or swerve his Yeoman Cooper, which struck Bonnier's Porsche, shot right over it and landed on its wheels to crash into a wall. 'I was lucky,' Surtees said. 'I must have jumped 20 feet in the air, but I wasn't even injured.' Bonnier also escaped injury.

24 APRIL 1962

MOSS INJURED IN 110MPH CRASH

TRAPPED FOR 30 MINS AT GOODWOOD

HOSPITAL TRANSFER AT 1.45A.M.

Stirling Moss, 32, champion British racing driver, was transferred from a Sussex hospital to one in London at 1.45 this morning after crashing at 110mph at Goodwood yesterday. He has 'moderately severe' head injuries and a broken leg. Moss, accompanied by his father, Mr Alfred Moss, was moved to the Atkinson Morley Hospital, Wimbledon, in an ambulance escorted by two police cars. He was apparently unconscious. His father stayed the night in the hospital.

Mr Jason Brice, a consultant neuro-surgeon, examined Moss and stated: 'It is unlikely we shall operate on him in the next few hours. We shall know better at 10a.m. He is here for observation.' Moss crashed as he was about to overtake another car. His Lotus Climax hit one bank and shot across the track, burying its nose in the opposite bank and trapping him in its crumpled bodywork. It took rescuers 30 minutes to free him.

'NOT TO WORRY' MESSAGE

W.A. McKenzie at Goodwood

Stirling Moss, four times runner-up to the world champion, crashed here at 110mph. He was taken to the Royal West Sussex Hospital, Chichester, with what the track medical officers describe as 'serious injuries', which included a broken rib, a fractured leg and head injuries. A late-night report to me from the hospital said he was unconscious and being moved to the Atkinson Morley Hospital, Wimbledon, because of head injuries.

His Lotus Climax car was so badly smashed in the crash that he was trapped in his seat, and it took the crew of the Goodwood emergency breakdown truck, eight marshals and two doctors half an hour to release his legs from the wreckage. He was unconscious when the first track marshal reached him, but he regained consciousness and remained in a dazed condition when they took him to hospital. While he was still trapped he dictated a message to be sent to his mother, Mrs Aileen Moss, at the White Cloud Farm, Tring, Hertfordshire. It said: 'I am fine, not to worry, will ring you when I get back.'

The accident happened in the chief race of the day, a 42-lap event for this season's 1½-litre Formula One Grand Prix cars. It turned out to be the fastest race ever held at Goodwood. Spurred on by the advent of some Formula One cars with new, eight-cylinder engines, with which Britain hopes to challenge last year's supremacy of the Italian Ferraris, the entrants of the older four-cylinder types had obviously got more power for their machines than ever before. But the eight-cylinder models, two BRMs driven by Graham Hill and Richie Ginther, a Lola Climax driven by John Surtees, and the Lotus Climax of Stirling Moss, were still their masters. Moss's car was entered by United Dominions Trust.

The race started off at a record pace, with Hill's BRM in the lead and Bruce McLaren, on a four-cylinder model, a fighting second. Surtees was third, with Moss, four times runner-up to the world champion, in fourth place. Very soon Hill broke the lap speed record for the course, previously held by Moss in a 2½-litre Cooper Climax at 102.13mph. Then Surtees broke the new record, bringing it to 105.37mph.

By that time Moss had been to the pits. His gear lever had stuck in fourth gear. When the car rejoined the race, Moss was more than two laps behind Hill. But only six of the 42 laps had gone, and he obviously thought it worth while to continue the struggle. He set off at a faster speed than he had done before, and overtook many cars. About the 36th lap he equalled the new circuit record, which he now shares with John Surtees. On the 39th he passed Innes Ireland's four-cylinder Lotus Climax, which was lying second. He then set out to catch Hill, but with only four laps to go it was a vain effort. He never quite caught the BRM. Just as he appeared to do so before St Mary's bend, he crashed. Shortly before he was released from his car Moss was visited by his father, 'Pop' Alfred Moss, who accompanied him to hospital.

The race was won by Graham Hill, who led from start to finish, at 102.65mph, a new record for any race at this circuit, and higher than the previous lap speed record.

Two years ago Moss broke both legs in a 130mph crash at Spa, when a Lotus he was driving in the Grand Prix of Belgium shed a wheel.

While Moss was lying ill in the West Sussex Hospital, it was announced in Nairobi that his sister, Pat Moss, and Ann Riley were placed third in the 3,000-mile East African Safari, which finished in Nairobi tonight.

9 OCTOBER 1962
STIRLING MOSS SUMMONED
STOPPED BY U.S. POLICE FOR SPEED
Our Own Correspondent
New York, Monday

Stirling Moss was summoned for speeding last night near West Windsor, New York State. He was stopped by a police patrol car as he drove his 1962 Austin Cooper back to New York from the United States Grand Prix at Watkins Glen. He served as an honorary steward there. Moss told the police he was leaving the country today, and asked to be allowed to plead by letter. He was given a 'mail waiver' which he must return to the court by next Wednesday. He was said to have driven at 65mph on Route 17. There is a 50mph limit.

The police said Moss joked with the two State policemen who stopped him. Trooper van Wagenen reported that Moss said the only thing that bothered him was that 'all those cars he had passed were now passing him'. Trooper van Wagenen said: 'There was no argument. He was driving a real tiny car and when we asked him why he was driving that kind of car, he said, "I like it".'

Moss gave his address as Park Avenue, New York. He caught a plane today from Idlewild Airport for Nassau, Bahamas. He said at the airport that he would plead guilty to the charge. He had asked a friend to pay any fine. 'It was my own damn fault. I was going at 65mph, but it was a dual carriageway and I wasn't endangering anyone. The cops were very good about it.'

He expected to leave for London next weekend. Asked about his future, he said: 'I will drive again if I am satisfied I can challenge Jim Clark, Graham Hill, Innes Ireland and that crowd. Otherwise I won't.' Moss was seriously injured racing at Goodwood on 23 April. After leaving hospital on 22 June, he said in July that he was driving a car again.

31 DECEMBER 1962
QUARTER-INCH WASHER COSTS
JIM CLARK WORLD TITLE
Leslie Beilby
East London, South Africa, Sunday

A missing washer about a quarter of an inch in diameter deprived the Scot, Jim Clark, 27, of the world motor driving championship in the South Africa Grand Prix yesterday. It cost the Lotus racing team, for whom he was driving, the car manufacturers' championship. The absence of the washer caused the loss of a plug and an oil leak which forced Clark to retire three-quarters of the way through the race. He was heading for a runaway victory and the championship.

After leading from the beginning, he was half a minute ahead of his rival for the title, Graham Hill, and so clear of the rest of the field that the race was turning into a procession. The crowd of 90,000 simply waited to cheer Clark home. Then suddenly a cloud of smoke emerged from Clark's engine. It was in the 61st lap of the 82-lap race that smoke started pouring from Clark's Lotus. He could have been called in to the pits, but continued for two more laps. The leak took some time to find. This in any case would probably have cost Clark the race.

Hill said afterwards that he would have preferred to beat Clark in a straight race. 'What happened to Jim today happened to me in the French and Monaco Grands Prix.' Congratulating Hill, Clark said: 'Hill had the measure of me. He gave me a hard time.'

Hill is the second British world champion since the championship was instituted in 1950. The first was Mike Hawthorn. He scored 42 points from his five best performances in this year's nine races, with four wins and one second. Clark, who had three wins, was runner-up for the world title with 30, and Bruce McLaren, of New Zealand, was third with 27.

Hill gave up a job to work on racing cars without pay. He became a first-class mechanic. He began this year well by winning the Dutch Grand Prix. Practising for the German Grand Prix, he was unhurt when his car hit a television camera at 140mph and ran into a ditch. Hill won the German

Grand Prix. He later won the Italian Grand Prix. His wife Bette sometimes acts as timekeeper at his races.

JIM CLARK WINS WORLD DRIVING CHAMPIONSHIP

QUESTIONED ON 1961 CRASH

John Langley
Monza, Sunday

Jim Clark, 27, became the youngest driver to win the world championship when he took the Italian Grand Prix in Monza today. Later he was interviewed by police about a crash in the 1961 race. He was involved in the crash in which the German driver von Trips and 13 spectators were killed. Clark said today that the police wanted him to sign a form. This is understood to mean he agreed to go to the police to make a further statement. He refused to sign this as he was 'not sure what it was all about'. It was thought that there might be some connection with legal action threatened by relatives of one of the dead spectators.

Clark said he was 'amazed that this trouble has come up again as I thought the matter was completely closed. During last year's race here the police called me away during practice and I had an interview lasting three hours. I thought I had been entirely exonerated. I cannot understand why they had to wait until just after the race to bring all this up again.'

Clark won the 307-mile grand prix today in 2 hours 24 minutes 19.6 seconds at an average speed of 127.74mph. Richie Ginther, of the United States, in a BRM, was second, and Bruce McLaren, of New Zealand, in a Cooper, third,

Clark, of Duns, Berwickshire, clinched the title by winning what is generally agreed tonight to have been the most hotly contested championship grand prix this year. The lead changed 23 times during the 86 laps. Clark, who had been forced to use a less powerful engine than usual in his Lotus after having practice troubles with his regular engine, clung on grimly. One by one his rivals disappeared or dropped back with mechanical troubles. The championship finally came within his grasp on lap 62, when Dan Gurney spun his Brabham Climax and was later forced to retire. By this time Clark had lapped every other driver.

Although there are three more championship events, Clark has made sure of the title by winning five of the seven so far held. The other two were won by Graham Hill, BRM, last year's champion, and John Surtees, Ferrari.

3 NOVEMBER 1963

TRAGEDY ON THE TRACK

DESPITE ACCIDENTS, MOTORSPORT BENEFITS
ORDINARY MOTORISTS TOO

Enzo Ferrari

Cynics have asked me whether, after a crash, I think first of the car or of the driver. Of course I think of the driver, and this would still be the case, even if I only cold-bloodedly considered my material interests. A car can be built in six months, but it takes up to ten years to make a driver.

Much of the responsibility for the results of accidents lies with present-day Formula One cars, which are so fragile that the slightest impact turns them into cages from which the driver can often be freed only with oxy-acetylene torches and hacksaws. But, in terms of causes, most accidents on the track are due, unhappily, to the human element. With few exceptions, these tragic crashes result from insufficient attention to physical fitness, slow reactions, misjudgments, over-confidence and other factors affecting a driver's physical condition or mental alertness. Race competitors should, of course, always behave sportingly and according to the rules. But it must be admitted that excitement, daring and the will to win, the applause, and all the things that stimulate a driver while he hurtles along the track, do not always make for fair play.

There are two sorts of drivers: the enthusiasts and those who are ambitious. The enthusiasts either kill themselves or go on racing till they have white hair. The ambitious give up at their first failure or after their first success. The racetrack is a maelstrom of conflicts, ambitions, determination and complexes.

An example of the enthusiast was Peter Collins, of whom I had the highest opinion, both as a driver and as a man. To give some idea of his generosity of character I cannot do better than revert to the year 1956. The world championship was developing in a way that made it look as though Collins might well carry off the honours. I therefore called him one day and said to him: 'Look here, Collins, I'm not asking you to step down for

Fangio; I wouldn't ask anybody that, because I've raced myself and I know what it means. All the same I would like to know what you think about the position, now that it's touch and go.'

Without hesitation, Collins replied: 'I never imagined that anyone who was only 25, like me, could get to be world champion. I've still plenty of time. Fangio must stay world champion this year, too, because he deserves it, and I'll let him have my car every time it might help him.' Unfortunately, Collins had not the time before him that he thought, for only two years later he was killed at Nürburgring whilst fighting it out with Brooks on that treacherous and very difficult course.

Peter was a fine-looking lad. His enthusiasm for racing was equal to his interest and skill in mechanics. He would get into a car and, after one round on the track, would be able to say exactly what number of revs gave the maximum torque, what was the highest advisable engine speed before changing gear, etc. He was a driver, in short, who assimilated his machine. Even Moss admired him and wanted him with him in one of the Targa Florio races in which the two of them put up a memorable performance.

Crashes often occur in the early stages of a long race, owing to over-eagerness on the part of drivers, who forget that the first lap or two will not decide the result. Often the real reason for a crash is never discovered, as in the case of Alberto Ascari, who was killed while practising at Monza in a three-litre sports car. He had slammed on his brakes inexplicably in the middle of a long, gentle curve, and the car had reared up on its front wheels. It was afterwards rumoured that a workman had walked on to the track, thinking it was not in use. The car afterwards proved to be 100 per cent serviceable, which at least set my mind at rest on that score.

Every time a serious accident occurs, voices are raised demanding that motor racing should be forbidden, and questioning whether it serves any useful purposes. There are four kinds of reason for racing, though not all of them are necessarily good ones. They are technical, sporting, political and moral.

It is generally recognised that races are useful because they stimulate technical progress. It is true that the president of Volkswagen has always declared that racing serves no useful purpose, but it is well known that Porsche and Volkswagen are basically the same firm, and Porsche gains much valuable experience by competing in sports car, Grand Tourism, prototype and Formula One categories. Speaking in Bristol in 1962, Rudolf Uhlenhaut, of Mercedes, explained: 'Manufacturers of sports cars can make more rapid technical progress than others, since their designers can risk using very advanced ideas, which they could not do if they were mass-producing cars for family use.'

While there is much that can still be done to improve motor cars, I do not see much scope for revolutionary invention – even rocket propulsion was tried in 1923, when an Opel rocket car exceeded 120mph. But it is experience with racing cars which yields improvements that can then be used in production models. For instance, the micro-tread tyre, a British patent, came out for racing cars about 1927. It consisted of small transverse cuts in the tread, to increase the adhesion of the tyre. (I won a race at Alessandria in 1928 with these tyres, but not having a micro-thread machine, I had to work on my tyres all night with a small hand-saw.) Today, if we can drive ordinary cars safely on wet roads, it is as a result of this historic racetrack experiment.

The petrol consumption of an ordinary family saloon has dropped considerably since 1930, as a result of reduced weight, abolition of super-chargers, and higher compression ratios. All this derived from racing experience.

The list of improvements in production cars which were first evolved on the racetrack is a long one. Disc brakes, streamlining, long-lasting lubricating oil, special lightweight metals, independent suspension, indiumised bearings, and even effective windscreen wipers – they all derive from racing experience. One technical advance is particularly striking. Engines of one-and-a-half litres are today beating all the records set up by cars with six-litre engines. In the near future we may expect to see cars with one-litre engines developing 90 horsepower, and one-and-a-half litre engines developing 140 to 150 horsepower.

Motor racing is, of course, a sport in its own right. It is useless to discuss why anyone should want to risk his life racing: why do people climb mountains, make parachute jumps, take part in bobsleigh runs and ride in steeplechases? Human beings obviously get a kick out of risking their necks to do something better than the next man.

Races are an entertainment, but this entertainment must preserve its technical content. It is unfortunate that racing is now organised too often simply with an eye to business, and something should certainly be done to reduce the excessive number of formulae and championships. A leading grand prix driver can make up to £10,000 a year, though very few reach this top bracket. Yet a driver with a good car, who can race for a whole season, can end up with a nice little nest-egg. Though earnings are good, they do not compare with the pay of stars in other sports. And, making allowance for changed purchasing power, the 10,000 lire which I won in the Targa Florio in 1920 was worth a good deal more than the 1,000,000 lire (about £600) now offered in a race counting towards the world championship. Juan Manuel Fangio undoubtedly made more out of racing than any other driver, not only through prize money, but also through his publicity value to business interests. Today he is a big car-dealer in the Argentine.

Manufacturers pay drivers a retaining fee which covers expenses for trials, travelling and so on. In addition, they are entitled to a 50 per cent share in starting money, in prize money for leading places, and in bonuses offered by car accessory makers. In the old days, contributions made to the costs of my *équipe* by manufacturers, who used our successes in their advertising, even gave us a small margin of profit. But today costs are so inflated and competition so severe that any firm that wants to keep a place in the car-racing world needs an annual budget of several hundred thousand pounds. At the Ferrari works, car-racing activities alone keep 94 people fully employed all the year round.

Racing is now being kept alive practically by the seven big oil groups. The oil companies are free to make use of racing successes in advertising their products. Tyres are the most important accessory, and it is very fortunate that Dunlop, at least, maintain their interest in motor racing. Dunlop, the ancestor of practically all European tyre companies, today provide tyres for 95 per cent of the world's racing cars.

We build Ferraris for road use, of course, as well as for the racing track. We have all sorts of customers, but I can divide most of them into three groups – the sportsmen, the 50-year-olds and the mere exhibitionists.

The sportsman usually likes a Grand Tourism coupé. He is often a gentleman of private means who drives pretty well, and may take part in road races. (Such owners like to change their cars every year, and even wealthy men with big names often seem to think they should get their cars for nothing!) A market survey has shown that 60 per cent of Ferrari owners are men over 50. These are men who have awarded themselves a sort of prize for their financial success in life and who want to recapture something of their youth by taking the wheel of one of my high-powered and expensive cars each weekend. Finally, we have customers who know nothing whatever about cars and simply buy a Ferrari because it is, so to speak, the mink or chinchilla of the automobile world. These customers, who are much fewer than you might imagine, usually turn up accompanied by high-powered blondes who distract the attention of all the mechanics. Such people spend hours debating the colour of the coachwork and the internal fittings.

An outstanding example of a 'gentleman sportsman' was the Marquis de Portago, who was ready to risk his neck on motor tracks, bob runs, in steeplechases, or anywhere where there was danger. Though tall and good-looking, he was often unshaven, shabby, and in need of a haircut; yet he had a great reputation as a Don Juan. He lost his life in the 1957 Mille Miglia disaster. [Besides the Marquis de Portago, 13 people, most of them spectators, were killed in this race. The previous year's race had caused the deaths of six people. There was an immediate outcry in the Italian Parliament and press: Manuel Fangio publicly attacked Ferrari. Typical newspaper headlines were 'These Massacres Must Cease' (*Unito*), 'The Last Time!' (*Giornale d'Italia*) and 'Finish This Insane Slaughter' (*Il Paese*). The Mille Miglia was abolished.]

After the disaster which marked the end of the Mille Miglia, my cars were officially sequestrated, and monstrous attacks on me appeared in the press. Finally, I was charged with manslaughter and with negligently causing grievous bodily harm. It was alleged that I had fitted unsuitable tyres to the Ferraris, made by the Belgian firm of Englebert, and that this had caused over-heating and the stripping of the tread on one of de Portago's tyres. [It was four and a half years later before Ferrari were acquitted. The court pointed out at the same time that the other Ferrari cars which took the first three places in the race had been fitted with the same tyres.]

What had actually happened was that the drift of de Portago's car on the Volta Mantovana bend had nipped the front tyre against one of the cat's eyes set in the middle of the road. Those cat's eyes have been removed from the bend – only to make their appearance in the curving tunnel of the new Bologna-Florence motorway!

Prince Bernhard of the Netherlands is a youthful 50-year-old sportsman who finds relaxation from the cares of the State in cars, aircraft and yachts. When he married he bought a supercharged, eight-cylinder Alfa Romeo, at that time the latest sensation. He has been a Ferrari customer for many years, and likes to join race mechanics in the pits. Whatever the result of a big race, Ferrari always gets a telegram from Prince Bernhard.

Ex-King Leopold of Belgium is perhaps our most remarkable royal client, and would have made a first-rate manager for a car works. In correspondence on highly mechanical matters he showed himself a first-class engineer. This impression was confirmed in later conversations over a good glass of red wine and dish of lasagne. He bitterly regretted that he had never been able to follow his technical bent, and I found him very determined at the wheel.

26 OCTOBER 1964

SURTEES WINS WORLD DRIVING CHAMPIONSHIP

Daily Telegraph Correspondent
Mexico City, Sunday

John Surtees, 30, of Britain, took the world championship title from Jim Clark, also of Britain, when he came second in the grand prix in Mexico City today. Clark, 27, was winning until the last lap of the 65-lap race. Halfway through this his Lotus sprang an oil leak. Dan Gurney, of California, won the race in a Brabham. Lorenzo Bandini, of Italy, in a Ferrari, was third.

The six points earned by Surtees gave him a total of 40. Graham Hill was struck in the tail by Bandini in the 31st lap and retired with a broken exhaust. Bandini, Surtees's team-mate, waved Surtees to pass him in the final lap to make up the points needed to win the championship.

Clark told correspondents after the race: 'It has been a season of it. It is all in the jam pot.' He was awarded fifth place for finishing 64 laps. This put him in front of Pedro Rodríguez, of Mexico, in a Ferrari, who finished fifth. Mike Spence, of Britain, was fourth in a Lotus.

27 OCTOBER 1964

MOTOR RACING LAURELS

Leading Article

It is a happy idea to give racing cars and drivers a prominent place in the forthcoming Lord Mayor's Show, for Britain excels in the production of both. Motor racing is a sport in which the merits of man and machine are hard to separate. In becoming world champion driver on Sunday, John Surtees won the manufacturers' championship for Ferrari; but it is no secret that the Italian car owes its outstanding performance this season in large measure to the engineering improvements suggested by the British driver. Graham Hill in a BRM was but a single point behind in the championship table; sheer ill-luck cheated Jim Clark, last year's champion, of victory with his Lotus in Sunday's thrilling race at Mexico City; and for good measure, it was in a British-designed Brabham that an American driver took first place there.

Surtees himself has now gained a unique 'double first' in such contests. Seven times he was world motorcycling champion before taking to four wheels, and it is an astonishing achievement to have won the new championship only four years after he started motor racing. He deserves Britain's congratulations and thanks.

12 JULY 1965

CLARK'S WIN FILLIP FOR RACING

W.A. McKenzie

Jim Clark's victory in Saturday's Grand Prix of Britain at Silverstone, and what was almost a defeat in a tight finish, has given Formula One racing a much-needed fillip. The last ten laps, in which Graham Hill narrowed the young Scot's lead of 30 seconds to three, provided a tense lap-by-lap struggle between a Lotus short of oil and at risk of seizure and a BRM whose brakes were going. For Clark, this was his fourth successive British Grand Prix, and his fourth grand prix win out of the five so far run this season. He took the lead at the start and kept it to the end.

Hill, who must have been astonished to find himself behind Richie Ginther's Japanese Honda, after the first lap, went into second place on the next lap, with John Surtees's Ferrari in third when, a lap later, the Honda fell back to fourth place. It was in this order that the first three finished, after 80 laps. Only trouble with Clark's engine, the still somewhat experimental four-valves-per-cylinder Coventry Climax unit, saved the contest from boredom.

Clark's victory by no means ensures him the world championship for this year. But it gives him a commanding lead of 36 points against the runner-up, Graham Hill, with 23 points, Jackie Stewart, 19 points, and John Surtees, 17 points.

2 AUGUST 1965

CLARK REGAINS WORLD DRIVERS' TITLE

W.A. McKenzie
Nürburgring, Sunday

Jim Clark won the Grand Prix of Germany at Nürburgring today in the fastest contest ever held on this 14-mile Eifel mountains circuit. It was his sixth grand prix victory this season, all those he has competed in, which is a record. He is also now assured of the drivers' world championship, which cannot be taken from him in the remaining races of the series. He took the world title from Graham Hill at the end of the 1963 season, then, a year later, lost it to John Surtees. His win today also consolidates the lead of the Lotus concern, whose cars he drives, for the manufacturers' world championship.

The speed of the race, coupled with the punishing nature of the course, brought early troubles for the cars. Of the 19 starters, only eight cars finished. Clark won at an average speed of 99.79mph, nearly one-and-a-half miles per hour above the previous lap speed record. He beat Graham Hill's BRM by 15.9 seconds, and the American Dan Gurney, in a Brabham, by 21.4 seconds. He also raised the lap speed record held by John Surtees, Ferrari, at 98.33mph to 101.2mph, the first time the 'Ring' has seen lap speeds in excess of 100mph.

Surtees, the reigning champion, who won this race last year and in 1963 for the Ferrari stable, was in at the pits with a jammed gear lever after the first lap, the fastest standing start lap ever made here. He lost 21 minutes, and although he subsequently made the second fastest lap of the race, the trouble recurred and the car – the new 'Flat 12' Ferrari – was withdrawn. Lorenzo Bandini, in the V8 Ferrari, finished sixth. Clark, his inevitable shadow, Hill, and Gurney ran in a procession from the second lap to the end of the 15th and last lap. The rest of the struggling field was so far behind they were in a separate race.

BRABHAM WINS CHAMPIONSHIP IN THE PITS

John Langley
Monza, Sunday

Jack Brabham, 40, of Australia, today became the first man to win the racing drivers' world championship in a car of his own construction. He was standing in the pits here at the time. Brabham's third world championship was clinched on the 32nd lap of the Italian Grand Prix. His car had been wheeled away with engine trouble when he was leading the race after only eight laps of the 68-lap event. It was on lap 32 that John Surtees, the only other driver who could beat him, pulled into the pit and retired his Cooper-Maserati with a severe petrol leak.

Italian Ferraris finished triumphantly first and second, driven by the young Italian Lodovico Scarfiotti, and the Englishman Michael Parkes. Scarfiotti, a comparatively new boy in the Ferrari grand prix team, won at an average of 135.9mph, and also set a lap record of 139.1mph. Brabham's team-mate, Denis Hulme from New Zealand, was third in the other Repco-Brabham after a dogfight with Parkes's Ferrari in the closing laps. The Austrian, Jochen Rindt, finished fourth, a lap behind, sliding his Cooper-Maserati over the finishing line with a punctured front tyre.

After four laps Brabham was leading and seemed to be settling down for another victory run. But at the end of the eighth lap, the Australian roared straight into the pits to retire, letting first Parkes and then Scarfiotti into the lead. The world champion, Jim Clark, after a hesitant start, worked his way up fast in the new Lotus, but three pit-stops to deal with wheel and electrical troubles put him out of the running.

CLARK WINS RACE: WORLD TITLE FOR HULME

Donald Saunders
Mexico City, Sunday

Denis Hulme, 31, became the first New Zealander to win the world drivers' championship here today by finishing third in the Mexican Grand Prix, after being lapped by the winner, Jim Clark of Scotland. Hulme began the race knowing that Jack Brabham, his Repco-Brabham team-mate and employer, must win to prevent his taking over as world champion. Brabham had to be content with second place.

Hulme, never further behind than seventh, moved into fourth place after 18 laps. He was happy to stay there until the opportunity to move up came when Chris Amon, another New Zealander, in a Ferrari, ran out of petrol when lying second. Meanwhile, Brabham could make no impression on Clark's Lotus-Ford, though he, too, benefited by one place from Amon's bad luck. John Surtees, in a Honda, was fourth. Clark, who started in the pole position, was overtaken by his team-mate, Graham Hill, and Amon on the opening lap, but moved in front on the third and stayed there throughout. When it was all over he described the race as 'an armchair ride'.

This is the third time the Scotsman has won this race and it brings his total of grand prix victories to 24, which equals the record held by Juan Manuel Fangio. Despite his triumph in this final Formula One grand prix of the season, Clark, with 41 points, had to be satisfied with third position in the drivers' table behind Hulme, who totalled 51, and Brabham (47).

8 APRIL 1968

JIM CLARK DIES IN 125MPH ROAD CRASH

CAR HURTLES INTO TREES AFTER SKID

Daily Telegraph Staff Correspondent
Bonn, Sunday

Jim Clark, 32, the British racing driver, was killed today when his Lotus-Cosworth skidded off the Hockenheim circuit near Heidelberg at 125mph, somersaulted and crashed into trees. Clark was competing in the first of two heats for the AVD-Deutschland trophy race for Formula Two cars. He is believed to have died almost instantly. Witnesses said that he went off the circuit in a long, right-hand bend while the track was still wet from rain. After the start of the next race an official told the 80,000 spectators of the crash over the loudspeaker.

He said: 'Probably because of a suspension fault, Clark went into a skid and 500 yards further on left the track. A technical investigation commission is working to find the cause of the accident.' None of the other 19 starters were near the crash. Late tonight it was stated that a legal inquiry into the crash will be conducted by a West German State prosecutor.

There was speculation that Clark – he was world champion in 1963 and 1965 – might not have been very familiar with the circuit as he had not had enough training on it. Witnesses also said that he was believed to have chosen inadequate tyres for the wet circuit. The race was the first of 11 in this season's unofficial European Formula Two championship.

8 APRIL 1968

OBITUARY: JIM CLARK

TWICE WORLD CHAMPION

Jim Clark, who has died, aged 32, after an accident in a car race at Hockenheim, Germany, was considered by many knowledgeable students of motor racing to be one of the greatest drivers of all time. Twice he won the world championship. In four attempts at the classic Indianapolis 500 Miles Race he finished twice in second place and once in the lead – the first non-American ever to be placed, let alone win, the event.

There have been world champions to whom the title fell more than twice. Fangio was the holder no fewer than five times, and Jack Brabham held the title on three occasions. But Jim Clark won his world championship crowns in the most decisive manner. On the first occasion, 1963, he won no fewer than seven of the events which counted towards the championship, and became the youngest driver ever to win the world title. In that same year he finished a brilliant second, beaten by the cruellest luck, at Indianapolis, driving the smallest-engined car in the race. On the second occasion, 1965, he won again with seven grand prix victories in a row – all those in which he was engaged, missing only the Grand Prix of Monaco because, at the time, he was in the United States winning the Indianapolis race.

His victories in top-class international events in both Formula and *grande tourisme* categories, were legion, but it was not only his total of wins that impressed: the manner in which they were won – the apparently utterly relaxed, and polished style of his driving – helped to create the reputation of being 'the greatest'.

His father farmed in Fife when Jim was born – the only son among five children – and moved to Berwickshire when the boy was six, to farm Edington Mains, where he first learnt to drive at 17 on the family Sunbeam. He had been at Loretto School from the age of ten, and between helping his father in caring for herds of sheep and cattle, he entered local car trials and rallies, and subsequently club races.

His first international race was a sports car event at Spa in 1958, finishing eighth with a fine drive in a D-type Jaguar. The next year he won over 20 national races. In 1960 he shared the Formula Junior championship with Trevor Taylor, signing up at the end of the season for Colin Chapman's Formula One Lotus team. But it was in 1962, when the long awaited V-8 Coventry Climax engine came into the sport, that Clark's great series of grand prix victories began. In 1964 he was leading for the championship halfway through the season, but in subsequent contests was defeated by mechanical trouble. In 1965 he had another decisive championship win, and came second at Indianapolis. Largely to mark his astonishing performance at 'Indy' he was appointed OBE in 1964.

Clark gave Britain's new Lotus-Ford racing car a brilliant victory in its first race, in June 1967, the Dutch Grand Prix. In January this year he won the South African Grand Prix, bringing his victories in grand prix races to a record 25, one more than Juan Manuel Fangio. The British Racing Drivers' Club awarded him a special Gold Star to mark the achievement. He won the Australian Grand Prix in February. Clark was a bachelor.

Our Motoring Correspondent writes: Clark was Britain's most successful racing driver and, so far as one can assess these things, possibly the greatest driver of all time. That at least was the opinion of such expert judges as the great Juan Manuel Fangio and Stirling Moss – both of whom have lived to enjoy their retirement.

5 NOVEMBER 1968

CHAMPION HILL DRIVING BETTER THAN EVER

Colin Dryden

Mexico City, Monday

So Graham Hill, often described as motor racing's best ambassador, has become world champion for the second time because of his superb winning race here in the Mexican Grand Prix yesterday, when he lapped most of the field. Nobody will begrudge him the title; Hill's winning speed of 103.802mph was faster than the late Jim Clark's lap record last year. But Jo Siffert (Lotus) set the lap record at a blistering 106.87mph.

Few of Hill's unique record of 103 grand prix drives can have given him more pleasure than this. For in 1964 he had only to finish third in Mexico to be the world champion, when the late Lorenzo Bandini's Ferrari collided with his car and put Hill out of the race. World champion in 1962, runner-up in 1963, 1964 and 1965, and now champion again in 1968, Hill will be 40 in February. He is driving better than ever, and is furious at any suggestion that he should give up now.

Before the race Denis Hulme (McLaren), last year's world champion, was six points behind Hill, while Jackie Stewart (Matra) was three behind Hill. But both had cruel luck on a day which was pure Olympic Gold for Graham Hill. Starting from the second row of the grid, Hill streaked into the lead, followed by Stewart, Gurney (McLaren), Hulme, Siffert and Brabham. But by lap five it was Stewart's blue Matra which was to lead for four laps.

On lap ten, Hill lost his second-closest rival for the championship when a rear suspension damper broke on Hulme's car. The McLaren struck a safety barrier and careered across the track, but the New Zealander managed to bring the car to rest safely after a quarter-of-a-mile skid from over 100mph. The car burst into flames as it came to rest, but Hulme jumped out unhurt.

Hill was soon back in the lead and held it until lap 21 when Jo Siffert, the Swiss who drives a Lotus privately entered by Rob Walker, was in front for three laps. But Siffert's throttle linkage broke. This let Hill back into the lead, which he held for the next 40 laps of the 65-lap race. Stewart was holding a seemingly secure second place. But then he started dropping back with fuel pump problems and finished seventh. He told me: 'I thought I had the measure of Graham until that happened.'

The pace, altitude and heat took a heavy toll of engines, with Gurney (McLaren), Surtees (Honda), Rindt and Brabham (Brabhams), Amon and Ickx (Ferrari) all retiring. Jack Brabham, driving the only car in the race with two aerofoils, looked certain for third place until five laps from the end when he lost all oil pressure. But it was a great day for Lotus and Ford, with Hill first, and his team-mate Jackie Oliver third.

8 SEPTEMBER 1969

STEWART TRIUMPHS IN WHEEL-TO-WHEEL DUEL BY INCHES FOR TITLE

Colin Dryden at Monza

Jackie Stewart, of Scotland, driving a Matra, clinched the world championship at Monza yesterday after a wheel-to-wheel fight to the finishing line with Jochen Rindt to win the Italian Grand Prix by inches. He now has an unassailable lead with 60 points. It was one of the closest grand prix races – only just over a second separating the first five cars after 60 of the 68 laps of the terrifyingly fast Monza circuit.

Stewart completed the distance in his dark blue car in 1 hour 39 minutes 11.26 seconds at a record average of 146.97mph. Rindt was timed at 1 hour 39 minutes 11.34 seconds. But the fastest lap, a record, was put in by Jean-Pierre Beltoise at 150.97mph. The French Matra driver finished third. Bruce McLaren (McLaren) was fourth, and Piers Courage in a privately entered Brabham was fifth. Pedro Rodríguez, of Mexico, brought the sole Ferrari into sixth place, two laps behind the leaders.

Stewart was in the lead for 59 laps, but the result was not certain until the chequered flag fell. Rindt, second for the first six laps, led on lap seven, followed by Stewart, Hulme (McLaren), Courage, Siffert (Lotus) and McLaren. Courage kept well up with the leaders in a brilliant drive throughout the race to finish fifth, but Hulme and Siffert were forced to drop back with mechanical troubles. At quarter distance Stewart led, followed by Courage, Siffert, Rindt, McLaren, Hulme, Beltoise and Graham Hill (Lotus). As the race went on, fiercely fought lap by lap, Hill wormed his way through the field to challenge Stewart and Rindt. He was fourth on lap 25 and third on lap 38. Ten laps later, he was second behind Stewart, and heading his Lotus team-mate Rindt. Courage was fourth, Beltoise fifth and McLaren sixth.

Hill, the reigning world champion, looked almost certain of second place until he slipped back to third five laps from the end and then disappeared from the race altogether, with a broken drive shaft. In the closing stages, Rindt was harrying Stewart every inch of the way with Beltoise close behind. The Scot and the Austrian took the finishing flag side-by-side, followed by Beltoise. Then came the orange McLaren car. Fifth man Courage was only 33 seconds behind Stewart after 68 laps of superb racing which thrilled the vast Italian crowd.

RINDT TRIUMPHS, HILL HURT, STEWART OUT

Henry Miller in New York

Jochen Rindt, the Austrian driver, scored a runaway United States Grand Prix victory in New York yesterday in a Lotus designed by Britain's Colin Chapman. Piers Courage, 27, of Britain, finished second in a Brabham, and another British driver, John Surtees, was third in a BRM. It was Rindt's first grand prix victory, and he set such an incredible pace throughout the 108-lap race that he was almost out of fuel at the end of the 248 miles. His winning time was 1 hour 57 minutes 56.84 seconds and his average speed 126.26mph – nearly 2mph faster than last year's winner, Jackie Stewart, Britain's world champion.

Graham Hill, the British driver who was No. 1 in the Lotus team, was feared to have broken his right leg in two places when his car overturned after blowing a tyre towards the end of the race. Another big disappointment for Britain was the failure of Stewart to finish the race. He retired on the 36th lap with engine failure following an oil leak when he was in a challenging position. The Matra international team that Stewart headed was eclipsed; none of the Matra cars finished the course. In fact, only seven of the original 17 starters were still running at the end.

Rindt's win was as much a triumph for Colin Chapman as anything else. The Lotus responded magnificently throughout and kept on breaking lap records as Rindt pushed it ahead of his rivals. Courage's performance was also impressive. Though he was a long way behind Rindt – a gap of more than 40 seconds – he held off Brabham's persistent challenges in a stylish way and earned a special £850 award as 'man of the race'.

CHAPTER THREE
THE 1970s

McLAREN KILLED AT 150MPH

Daily Telegraph Reporter

Bruce McLaren, 33, the racing driver and designer, was killed yesterday while testing a new 200mph racing car on the Goodwood circuit, near Chichester, Sussex. The engine exploded as McLaren roared along the Lavant Straight at more than 150mph, hurtling the car into a bank. McLaren was dragged clear of the wreckage, but was dead on arrival at Chichester Hospital three miles away.

Workers at the nearby airfield heard the car's engine explode and then saw 'flames and smoke pouring 40 feet into the air'. McLaren and members of his company, Bruce McLaren Motor Racing, were trying out the new 7½-litre M8D car they had specially designed for the Canadian-American Challenge Cup series of races this summer.

Goodwood was closed as a racing circuit for public meetings in 1966 because the track surface was too bumpy for complete safety. Since then it has been used extensively for testing new sports and racing cars at high speeds. McLaren, a New Zealander, was a frequent visitor.

OBITUARY: BRUCE McLAREN

Colin Dryden

Bruce McLaren, who was killed in a crash at Goodwood yesterday, was not only a first-rate grand prix driver but one of the leading racing car constructors. The orange Formula One cars were familiar sights in world championship events, but McLaren completely dominated the Canadian-American sports car series. Driven by McLaren himself and his fellow New Zealander Denny Hulme, world champion in 1967, the vastly powerful cars were reputed to have won £100,000 in prize money last season.

Because of the growing pressures of construction and design, McLaren had been talking of doing less racing. Although not as fast as Hulme, McLaren was always a force to be reckoned with. He finished second to Jackie Stewart's March in the Spanish Grand Prix at Jarama in April, and was lying fifth, equal with Graham Hill (Lotus), in this year's world championship.

Aged 33, McLaren came to Britain in 1958 under a scheme organised by the New Zealand Grand Prix Association to send the most promising local driver to Europe. He made his mark immediately in Formula Two racing and the following year was offered a drive in a Cooper Formula One car. He won the American Grand Prix and became the Cooper team leader when Jack Brabham left to start his own team.

McLaren soon followed Brabham into design and construction, and McLaren Motor Racing Ltd, at Colnbrook, Buckinghamshire, near London Airport, now employ a staff of nearly 50. As well as designing cars for others, McLaren scored many successes as a driver himself, winning the Belgian Grand Prix in 1968 and the Le Mans 24-hour race with Chris Amon in 1966.

The Royal Automobile Club were about to announce that he had been awarded the Seagrave Trophy for 'his outstanding performance in winning every race in the 1969 Can-Am Challenge Cup series with cars of his own design and construction'. Mr Wilfrid Andrews, chairman of the RAC, said yesterday: 'This is one of the most terrible blows suffered by motor racing. Bruce was not only a very good driver but also an outstanding manufacturer and designer. More than that, he was a gentleman and a good fellow.'

Quiet and unassuming, Bruce McLaren seemed unaffected by the immense pressures of being a top international racing driver and designer. As well as racing in Europe and America he also competed in races in Australia and New Zealand. When other drivers became temperamental, McLaren would just smile a little but less. He admitted: 'I guess I worry enormously, but I try not to. One oughtn't to worry, ought one?'

Graham Hill, world champion in 1962 and 1968, said: 'This is a tragic loss to racing. Bruce was the most likeable of people, friendly and easy-going, but in the top eight of grand prix drivers.' McLaren leaves a widow, Pat, and daughter, Amanda, aged four. He lived at Walton-on-Thames, Surrey.

22 JUNE 1970

PIERS COURAGE DIES IN DUTCH GRAND PRIX CRASH

Colin Dryden in Zandvoort, Holland

Piers Courage, 28, the racing driver, was burned to death when his car crashed and caught fire in the Dutch Grand Prix at Zandvoort yesterday.

His Italian Grand Prix de Tomaso car left the track on the 23rd lap, hit a bank and rolled over. Dutch firemen tried desperately to release him, but he was trapped in the blazing wreckage which burned for half an hour.

Mr Courage's wife, the former Lady Sarah Curzon, who was watching the race from the pits, was led away by Mr Louis Stanley, secretary of the Grand Prix Drivers' Association, and a woman friend. Lady Sarah, the daughter of the late Earl Howe, himself a former racing driver, married Mr Courage, son of Mr Richard Courage, head of the Courage brewery business, in 1966. They have two sons, Jason, three, and Amos, one.

As smoke billowed over the circuit, an official announcement said that the car had crashed but that the driver was all right. Organisers said later that the announcement was a mistake, due to the smoke and confusion. The heat from the blaze was so intense that surrounding woodland was set on fire. Mr Courage's charred body was found in the wreck of the car, which was completely destroyed.

Mr Courage, who always raced with the Old Etonian colours on his helmet, was tall and diffident in manner. He was a first-rate professional racing driver and he scored many successes in Formula Three events before becoming a works BRM driver in 1966. Although he never won a Formula One Grand Prix, he was always a force to be reckoned with. He was second to Graham Hill at Monaco in 1969, driving a Brabham. He was lying seventh yesterday in his new de Tomaso Ford, entered by Mr Frank Williams, when he crashed.

7 SEPTEMBER 1970
INQUIRY INTO RINDT CRASH
Colin Dryden in Monza

An inquiry will be held into death of Jochen Rindt, 28, the Austrian racing driver who was killed when his Lotus crashed at 150mph on the Monza circuit on Saturday. Rindt crashed into a barrier on the 'parabolic curve' while practising for the Italian Grand Prix. He was well ahead on points for this year's world championship.

Denny Hulme, the New Zealander who won the world championship in 1967, was following Rindt at the time in a McLaren. He estimated their speeds approaching the corner at 190mph. On braking, Rindt's car had slewed left, then right, and hit the barrier at about 150mph. The car was torn in half, but did not catch fire. Rindt was taken alive from the wreckage. He had severe chest and throat injuries, broken legs and a broken arm.

Instead of being taken to the grand prix medical unit, a mobile hospital equipped for major operations, Rindt was taken out of the circuit in an ambulance. The police escort turned left outside the circuit to head for Monza hospital, five minutes away, but the ambulance took the road to Milan – a 40-minute journey in heavy traffic. Hand-operated resuscitation equipment was used, although the medical unit had automatic resuscitators, and Rindt died in the ambulance.

Questions that need to be answered are: What caused Rindt's car to go out of control? Why were the facilities of the Grand Prix medical unit not used? Why was the 40-minute journey to Milan undertaken when there was a hospital much nearer in Monza? Why was there not a helicopter standing by?

Mr Louis Stanley, secretary of the Grand Prix Drivers' Association, said that Rindt might have died anyway, but the facilities of the medical unit should have been used. The association insist in future that the unit must be used.

A brilliant and forceful driver, Rindt had to wait five years in grand prix racing for his first victory – the American Grand Prix in 1969. This year he had won five races. His death leaves the world championship wide open. Jack Brabham with 25 points, Denny Hulme with 20, Jackie Stewart and Jacky Ickx both with 19 points, all now have a chance.

17 JULY 1971

STEWART EXTENDS CHAMPIONSHIP LEAD WITH SUPERB WIN

Colin Dryden

With his superb victory in the British Grand Prix at Silverstone on Saturday, Jackie Stewart tightened his grip on the world championship. In the Tyrrell he has won four out of six races this season. Stewart won as he liked after the challenge of the 12-cylinder Ferraris and BRMs had faded early. France's Matras were uncompetitive, although Jean-Pierre Beltoise finished seventh.

Stewart took command after the fourth lap and set race and lap records. So hot was the pace that the race was won in only 1 hour 31 minutes 31.5 seconds. His average speed was 130.48mph for the 199 miles. He broke his own outright Silverstone lap record which now stands at 1 minute 19.9 seconds, a speed of 131.88mph. Few people could have expected Stewart to have 42 points and the nearest Ferrari driver, Jacky Ickx of Belgium, a mere 19 halfway through the season with six grands prix to come.

Last year the Italian cars cleaned up four out of the last five races as well as 1971's opening events in South Africa. Since then they have lost their winning ways, and Saturday was no exception. Stewart's Tyrrell ran away from the field, and Ronnie Peterson, the dashing young Swede in his March, proved that his Monaco second place was no flash in the pan by finishing half a minute behind the Scotsman.

All the other places on the leader board were filled by Ford V8s: Emerson Fittipaldi of Brazil was third in a Lotus, Henri Pescarolo of France in Frank Williams's March was fourth, Rolf Stommelen's Surtees was fifth, while his boss, John Surtees, the 1964 world champion, was sixth.

All the excitement was in the early stages, such was Stewart's domination. The start was uncertain, and Jack Oliver, having his first Formula One drive this season in a McLaren, rammed the rear of Graham Hill's Brabham, putting both cars out. A complaint by Ron Tauranac, the Brabham team manager, was upheld by the stewards, and the luckless Oliver was fined £50 for 'careless driving'.

The sight of the blood-red Ferraris of Ickx and Clay Regazzoni thundering round in the lead at the end of the first lap recalled last season. Stewart was having none of it, though. Driving tigerishly he split them on the second lap, led the field from the fourth, and then pulled inexorably away. Jo Siffert (BRM) also had the bit between the teeth, and followed Stewart past the two Ferraris, breaking the existing lap record on lap seven at 131.55mph. Misfiring due to a loose coil slowed the BRM and led to a three-minute pit-stop, so that Siffert finished ninth. Both Ickx and Regazzoni ended their races in the pits.

16 AUGUST 1971

STEWART CHAMPION DESPITE LOSING WHEEL AND CRASHING

Colin Dryden in Zeltweg, Austria

It was a great day for Britain in the Austrian Grand Prix at Zeltweg yesterday. A Yardley BRM, driven by Jo Siffert, of Switzerland, won the race, and

Jackie Stewart won the world championship despite a 150mph crash in which he was unhurt. Although Stewart did not finish, his nearest rival for the world title, Jacky Ickx, of Belgium, was also unlucky with his Ferrari. Stewart cannot now be overtaken in the championship. His 51 points make him secure.

A drive shaft sheared on Stewart's Tyrrell, and a wheel flew off on a bend during lap 35 of the 54-lap race. The car left the track but Stewart walked away unhurt. The 1971 world title is Stewart's, but the race was Siffert's. He led from start to finish, crossing the line with a flat tyre. He last won a grand prix in 1968 driving a Lotus for the private entrant Rob Walker.

Although Siffert set a cracking pace, Stewart and his French team-mate François Cevert managed to stay with him until the 21st lap. The Tyrrells were obviously in difficulties, though. Stewart fell back and waved Cevert past him to do battle with the BRM. At this stage Siffert had a 10½-second lead. He pulled away from the Frenchman, while Stewart had to be content with third place. After Stewart had gone out, Cevert also retired on lap 41, letting Emerson Fittipaldi, of Brazil, leader of the Lotus team, into second place.

25 OCTOBER 1971

JO SIFFERT KILLED IN 140MPH CRASH

Colin Dryden

Jo Siffert, 35, the Swiss racing driver, was killed when his BRM swerved off the track at 140mph at Brands Hatch yesterday and burst into flames. The car collided with a bank at Hawthorn's bend. Firemen in aluminium suits tried to get Siffert out of the wreck but they were beaten back by fierce flames. The 40-lap race to celebrate Jackie Stewart's world championship victory was stopped because the track was blocked by a sea of flames.

Siffert had been working his way through the field after a poor start. He had just passed Tim Schenken's Brabham to take fourth place when the crash came on the 14th lap. No other car was involved. John Surtees, the 1964 world champion, who was following Siffert, said that the gearbox at the rear of his car appeared to break up. But last night Mr Louis Stanley, managing director of BRM, produced a statement from Mr F.C. Matthews, chief scrutineer of the Royal Automobile Club, which said the gearbox was intact and coupled to the lower part of the rear of the engine. 'Any suggestion that the gearbox fell out was pure suggestion and was not true.'

Siffert, known as 'Seppi', was one of the world's fastest drivers. He first made his name in hill climbs and as a motorcycle champion and joined the BRM team this year.

· I I SEPTEMBER 1972

FITTIPALDI STREAKS IN FOR MONZA GP AND WORLD TITLE

Colin Dryden at Monza

Motor racing has its youngest world champion with Emerson Fittipaldi's victory yesterday in the Italian Grand Prix. At 25, the Brazilian took the title in his John Player Lotus after only three years as a grand prix driver. His rise to the top has been one of the quickest in the history of motor racing, and at 25 he obviously has many more years as champion ahead of him. It is Lotus's fifth team title. He drives with a determination, flair and a calmness that recalls Jim Clark, probably the greatest grand prix driver of all time, and one of his predecessors with Lotus.

Jackie Stewart surrendered his title on the start line. He needed to win at Monza and in the United States and Canada with Fittipaldi not finishing in three races – a forlorn hope. The field stormed away – all but Stewart on the second row. Those behind streamed around him while the Tyrrell, which is having an ill-starred baptism in races, limped up the track and pulled off at the chicane, its race run.

Mike Hailwood, many times motorcycle world champion, scored his best grand prix result to come second in his Surtees. Denny Hulme (McLaren), runner-up in the championship table, was third, followed by his consistent American team-mate Peter Revson. Still probably the most popular grand prix driver, Graham Hill, was fifth but only just, because his Brabham's engine was very sick in the final lap.

15 OCTOBER 1973

STEWART KEPT SECRET HIS DECISION TO QUIT

Colin Dryden

Jackie Stewart, 34, three times world champion driver, said yesterday that he had decided last April to quit motor racing. 'But I could not let it be known until now,' he added. 'If I had said in April that I would still drive in five, then four, then three grands prix until the finish of the season, it would have been an unreasonable strain on my wife. But as from today I am no longer a racing driver. I have retired and I am very happy about it.

'Last week my son Paul said it was about time I should retire. I asked him what I should do instead and he replied, "Write some books and drive our school bus". But I will now be able to do things for motor racing which I have been unable to carry out before. I hope to be able to get involved in the organisation and safety aspects of motor racing.'

At no time had his wife Helen put any pressure on him to leave motor racing, and he had not told her of his decision until a week ago. Only Mr Ken Tyrrell, Stewart's team manager, had been told earlier, so that he could make plans for the future. In his announcement Stewart made no reference to his close friends who have been killed in races, but the deaths of Jim Clark, Piers Courage, Jochen Rindt, and his Tyrrell team-mate François Cevert a week last Saturday, must have weighed heavily on him.

Statistically Stewart will go down in the record books as the most successful grand prix driver since the world championship was instituted in 1950, with 360 points in nine seasons. Jim Clark scored 274 points and Juan Fangio 277 in the same number of seasons. Stewart drove in 99 grands prix and won 27 of them, while Clark won 25 out of 72, Fangio 24 out of 51 and Stirling Moss 16 out of 66. Apart from Fangio with five world titles, only Jack Brabham, now retired in Australia, has equalled Stewart's record of three championships.

A champion clay pigeon shot who just failed to get into the Olympic team, Stewart developed the competitive instinct early, but the first association with motor racing was in preparing cars for his brother Jimmy. After his brother had to give up following a bad accident, Stewart competed in local Scottish events under a pseudonym so that his mother would not know.

In 1964, his first year of international motor racing, Stewart made his name in the newly instituted Formula Two and Formula Three categories driving Cooper cars for Tyrrell. The following year he was driving a BRM in Formula One. From the moment he graduated to Formula One, his success was assured. Allied to superb natural skill, he brought an ice-cool detachment to his racing. He trained himself to be completely drained of any emotion at the start of a race and thereafter saw 190mph situations in 'slow motion'.

Stewart was the first driver to wear his hair long and adopt fashionable, trendy styles in clothes. He has seemed to enjoy a greater following in Europe than in Britain. This may be because he became one of the 'new Europeans' and went to live near Geneva and its international airport.

7 OCTOBER 1974
FITTIPALDI REGAINS WORLD TITLE
Special Correspondent in New York

Emerson Fittipaldi, of Brazil, in his McLaren, finished fourth in the United States Grand Prix at Watkins Glen, New York, yesterday. The placing was enough for him to regain the world drivers' championship. The race was won by Carlos Reutemann, of the Argentine, in a Brabham, with an average speed of 119.12mph for the 199-mile race over 59 laps.

Fittipaldi's only remaining challengers, Clay Regazzoni, of Switzerland, and Jody Scheckter, of South Africa, were out of luck. Regazzoni had tyre trouble when he was 11th and then ran into suspension problems. Scheckter pushed the issue before he had to pull out of the race at the start of the 45th lap because of overheating. From that point Fittipaldi's victory was not in doubt.

Reutemann, the fastest man in practice, took the lead from the start to capture his third grand prix victory this year. Fittipaldi, who first won the world championship in 1972, seemed almost content to see the rest tearing out themselves and their machines. Ahead of him Carlos Pace, Fittipaldi's countryman and Reutemann's team-mate, drove superbly to finish second, and Britain's James Hunt in his Hesketh Ford was little behind him, clearly justifying his position on the front row with Reutemann.

Fifth was John Watson, of Northern Ireland, in a Brabham, with Graham

Hill eighth in his Lola. Chris Amon, the New Zealander, was ninth in his BRM to give the race a somewhat unexpected British flavour.

19 MAY 1975

RACE CRASHES BLAMED ON DRIVER ERRORS
Colin Dryden

Mistakes by drivers caused nearly half the accidents in grand prix motor racing, says a report by the Jim Clark Foundation published today. Italian drivers were 'significantly more prone to accidents than the average', says the report, which covers 224 crashes between 1966 and 1972, including those in which Jochen Rindt and Piers Courage died.

The often expressed opinion that 'mechanical failure is a major cause of accidents' was not supported by computer analysis. Weather conditions were found to have no significant effect on the number of accidents or the severity of driver injury. In 85.8 per cent of accidents drivers were not injured, and a quarter of the crashes took place during the first two laps of the race. Of the accidents investigated, 122 occurred during races, 91 in practice and 11 during testing. After driver error, at 48.6 per cent, collision at 7.6 per cent was the next biggest cause. But various kinds of mechanical failure, including defects in suspension, wheels, wings, wheels and drive shafts, added up to a total of 24.7 per cent.

In Lorenzo Bandini's fatal accident at Monza in 1967, the report believes fatigue caused his driving to become erratic. He misjudged the chicane, hit the chicane barrier and crashed into straw bales. The car overturned and caught fire and Bandini was critically injured and later died. Jo Schlesser's fatal crash at Rouen-les-Essarts in 1968 is also attributed to driver error, although eyewitness reports suggested that the Honda's engine cut out before the car went out of control.

The cause of the crash that killed Courage at Zandvoort in 1970 is still unknown, the report says. He was in seventh place, running alone at the time with nearly a third of the race run at an average speed of 112.95mph. 'It would appear that something failed as Courage took the fast (150mph) corner, sending the De Tomaso car off to the left of the road.' The car knocked down three poles on the outside of the track, climbed the bank, rolled over and caught fire at once. Courage, trapped in the wreckage, was probably killed immediately.

The cause of Rindt's Monza crash the same year is also unknown. His Lotus 72 was geared for a top speed of 205mph. In dry weather and good visibility the car veered sharp left under braking for the Parabolica curve. Cars reach over 180mph along the preceding straight and take the corner between 120–130mph. The car crashed into a guard-rail but, instead of sliding along it and bouncing off, the Lotus stopped almost instantly, because the guard-rail broke and the car hit an upright post.

In 94 appearances, triple world champion Jackie Stewart, now retired, had ten accidents, with only one due to his own error. Figures for the other leading drivers:

	Races	Accidents	Driver Error
J Brabham	64	7	0
J Clark	22	3	2
E Fittipaldi	40	2	1
G Hill	95	10	5
J Surtees	76	4	0
C Regazzoni	31	8	4

The report concludes that despite welcome improvements in vehicle design and track safety – many made following the accidents – driver skill and concentration remained the most important factors in keeping death and injury off the circuits.

8 SEPTEMBER 1975

LAUDA CHAMPION IN DOUBLE FOR FERRARI

Colin Dryden at Monza

Ferrari supporters saw all their wishes fulfilled yesterday when Clay Regazzoni won the Italian Grand Prix while Niki Lauda, who was third, clinched this year's world championship. Monza erupted to acclaim its heroes, and spectators swarmed across the track as Lauda landed Ferrari's first drivers' championship for 11 years. Ferrari must also be sure of the manufacturers' world championship by half a point, even if Brabham win the last race of the season, the American Grand Prix.

It was Regazzoni's second Monza victory, and he led from start to finish, breaking the lap record on the 47th lap. Lauda was second for all but the last seven laps, when Emerson Fittipaldi overtook him. But Lauda was in no hurry. As long as anyone but Carlos Reutemann (Brabham) led the race, he was certain of being confirmed as world champion. With his team-mate Regazzoni leading, Lauda needed to take no risks. Reutemann finished fourth, while Britain's James Hunt, in the latest Hesketh, and Tom Pryce (Shadow) were fifth and sixth respectively.

Lauda's success this season made up for his bad luck last year, when many felt he deserved to be champion. Nine pole positions last year and eight this prove that the 26-year-old Austrian is consistently the fastest man in grand prix racing. Much effort and money has gone into ensuring Ferrari's success, and, unless the Ford-powered team can come up with some extra horsepower, it is difficult to see anything but an era of Ferrari domination stretching ahead.

The race was run on a dry track which had miraculously dried out after torrential rain and thunderstorms the previous night and morning. There was drama as the field negotiated the chicane on the main straight for the first time. The leaders were safely through but during the jostling for position Tony Brise (Embassy Hill), Jochen Mass (McLaren) and Mario Andretti (Parnelli) were all put out of the race.

Regazzoni was completely in command, and the main interest in what was not a classic Monza race was the progress of Fittipaldi, last year's world champion, who was not giving up his title without a fight. He passed Reutemann for third place on the 14th lap and then gradually reeled in Lauda to take a fine second position.

I DECEMBER 1975

OBITUARY: GRAHAM HILL

WINNER WHO HELPED LOSERS

Colin Dryden

Graham Hill, known to millions throughout the world as a world champion racing driver, used his fame to help the less fortunate. After giving up competitive driving he devoted much time and effort to causes like the Disabled Drivers' Association and the Springfield Boys' Club in the East End. His record on the circuits will probably never be surpassed: twice world champion, in 1962 with BRM and in 1969 with Lotus, winner of the Indianapolis 500 and Le Mans and participant in 176 grands prix, including five victories at Monaco.

To survive appalling race crashes and die in a routine flight returning from a testing session in the south of France with members of his Embassy Hill Formula One team is a tragic irony. The motor racing world had heaved a sigh of relief last July when Hill, married with three children, formally announced his retirement just before the British Grand Prix and decided to stick to team management. As Jackie Stewart said yesterday: 'He had retired from motor racing to be safe, grow old, and be with us for the rest of his life.' Hill's death away from the track which claimed so many of his fellows, parallels that other great English world champion, Mike Hawthorn, who retired only to die in a road accident on the Guildford by-pass in 1959.

Not a 'natural driver' like his friend Jim Clark, who was killed in a racing crash in 1968, Graham Hill epitomised grit and determination. This was never more evident than his fightback from a terrible crash in the 1969 American Grand Prix, when both his legs were shattered. Confined in a wheelchair for months – some thought for ever – Hill willed himself back to the cockpit. Asked about his greatest achievement Hill described it as 'coming sixth in the South African GP after my accident'. But even an iron will cannot completely heal severed nerves and sinews. Hill walked with a limp and was often in pain, but would never admit to it. His many friends urged him to retire after he had proved he could drive again.

The spectacle of a world champion no longer able to be ultra-competitive seemed inappropriate. But, although he was destined never to win another grand prix after his 1969 accident, Hill answered his critics by winning the 1971 International Trophy Formula One race at Silverstone and crowned a great career with victory in the 1972 Le Mans 24-hour endurance classic.

As he said in his autobiography, *Life at the Limit,* Hill did not know what he wanted to do with his life even at the age of 24, when he had just bought his first car, a 1934 Morris 8. As a young man rowing was his sport. He stroked the 1955 London Rowing Club eight in the Grand Challenge Cup at Henley and afterwards wore their blue and white colours on his racing helmets. Rowing gave him a physique which was to stand him in good stead for the rigours of motor racing. One pound's worth (four laps) of Brands Hatch in a 500cc Formula Three car in answer to an advertisement was enough to decide Hill. He was bitten by the motor racing bug there and then. Having given up his job at Smiths Industries, he was on the dole and later worked as a mechanic to get into motor racing.

He won his first world championship with BRM in 1962 and was runner-up in 1964 and 1965. Then he won Indianapolis in 1966 and bought a twin-engined aircraft with the winnings. The following year he joined Jim Clark in the Lotus team and in 1968 held the team together — severely shaken by Clark's death — and went on to win the world championship.

The fact that he had been able to fight his way out of a wheelchair left him with very real compassion for those condemned to immobility for life. He became an ardent campaigner for better transport for the disabled, describing the official issue invalid tricycle as 'the worst thing I have ever driven'. At a test session in 1973 for *The Daily Telegraph Magazine,* he likened the tricycle to a 'motorised bathtub'. He took part in deputations to Downing Street, calling attention to the invalid tricycle's defects and also attracting the help and support of the Earl of Snowdon. As well as giving his time Hill paid some of the bills for the Disabled Drivers' Action Group and gave £500 to launch the Invalid Tricycle Action Group.

Whatever cause Graham Hill took up received his full attention and energies. President of the Springfield Boys' Club in Upper Clapton, he was no figurehead. Despite a hectically busy life, Hill still found time to attend management committee meetings at the club. Since running the Embassy racing team left him with even less spare time, Graham and Bette Hill had boys from the club to camp at their country house in Hertfordshire.

With the deaths of Hill's brilliant new young driver Tony Brise, tipped as a future world champion, designer Andy Smallman, team manager Ray Brimble and two mechanics, the Embassy Hill Formula One team has been wiped out.

30 MARCH 1976

ANGRY HUNT FORCED OFF TRACK

Ian Brodie at Long Beach, California

James Hunt, of Britain, had a blistering exchange after the United States Grand Prix West, at Long Beach, California, with Patrick Depailler, of France — the man accused of ramming him into a wall on the fourth lap. At one point Hunt shouted angrily: 'The first thing you must do is learn to drive.' The unusual, public row started when Depailler denied to reporters that he bumped Hunt's McLaren off the track.

Hunt, still furious from the incident, was standing nearby and strode over to ask Depailler: 'If you didn't hit me where do you think I got all those tyre marks on my car?' Depailler, startled, said: 'James, I'm so sorry. I didn't see you.' Hunt retorted: 'You did see me. You looked in your mirror.' The incident, shortly before a left-handed turn, shunted Hunt into a wall, damaging his nose cone and putting him out of the race when he was lying second. Depailler (Tyrrell) went on to finish third, keeping his second position in the world drivers' championship. Hunt, who had been second equal with Depailler, is now fifth.

Depailler said he had brake trouble at the time of the collision. Hunt replied: 'I don't argue that you were having braking trouble but we weren't in a braking area. You made a complete cock-up of that corner before, and the first thing you should do when you make a cock-up is to look where all the others are.' Before turning on his heel, Hunt said Depailler had acted 'stupidly' and could have overturned both cars, causing a major accident. The McLaren team decided not to lodge an official protest. The stewards' report on the incident said Depailler 'shut the door' on Hunt, but apportioned no blame.

Later, a calmer Hunt said Depailler was known on the Formula One circuit for his aggressive driving. He said the points loss for the world championship had been 'a hell of a setback'. But then, with a boyish grin, he added: 'I'll beat Depailler yet – there are plenty of races left.'

2 AUGUST 1976

NIKI LAUDA CRITICAL

Colin Dryden, Motoring Staff

Niki Lauda, the Austrian world champion driver, was critically ill last night after being trapped when his Ferrari crashed and caught fire during the German Grand Prix at Nürburgring. As flames leapt round him three drivers, Guy Edwards, Brett Lunger and Arturo Merzario, fought desperately to free him.

Edwards, whose hands were burned in the rescue, said that it took them over a minute because his belts were jammed. 'We were trying like hell to get Niki out, but we couldn't get the seat belts undone and the fire was getting hotter and hotter.'

One of the drivers dashed for a fire extinguisher and played it on the flames, and Lauda was finally freed and dragged to safety. Edwards said: 'Niki was conscious after about ten seconds and he was screaming, "Get me out". The skin was coming away from his face and his hands. He was sitting in a sea of flames.'

After treatment at a burns unit Lauda was transferred to an intensive care ward of the Mannheim University clinic where he again recovered consciousness. But doctors were still battling to save his life, mainly because of the effects of inhaled fumes and flames.

2 AUGUST 1976

THIRD WIN IN A ROW EDGES HUNT NEARER THE WORLD TITLE

Colin Dryden in Nürburgring

By winning the West German Grand Prix at Nürburgring yesterday – his third consecutive victory – Britain's James Hunt edged nearer to the world championship that only a few weeks ago seemed totally beyond his reach. With world champion Niki Lauda crashing and sustaining burns that are likely to put him out of action for the rest of the season, Hunt must now have a real chance of winning the title. Hunt has 44 points, subject to the Ferrari protest over his Brands Hatch victory, compared with Lauda's 58. With only 14 points separating the two leading drivers, and Hunt and his McLaren being on top form, the English driver should be able to overhaul Lauda.

Jody Scheckter (Tyrrell) was second in yesterday's race, which was stopped and re-run after Lauda's accident on the second lap, and Jochen Mass made it McLaren's day by finishing third. Carlos Pace (Brabham) was fourth, to equal his team's best result this year, while Gunnar Nilsson was fifth in the John Player Special. Rolf Stommelen was the second German driver to finish on the leader board in another Brabham.

Uncertain weather at the start probably caused Lauda's accident and put many of the other drivers in difficulties. Rain on part of the 14¼-mile circuit led to all drivers, apart from Jochen Mass, starting on wet-weather tyres. But the rain was slight, and half the field rushed into the pits at the end of the first lap to change on to dry tyres. Lauda changed two tyres on his Ferrari and, like other drivers, experienced handling problems on the damp patches under the many trees that line this most dangerous of circuits. The

Austrian spun out of control in the second lap and crashed into the rails protecting the spectators, his Ferrari bursting into flames.

When the race was stopped, Mass had a lead of 48 seconds over Hunt, who was the first driver to change his tyres. If there had been no accident, an interesting battle would have developed between the McLaren drivers. But Hunt led the re-run race from start to finish and never seemed in any difficulty over the world's most difficult circuit.

25 OCTOBER 1976
IT WASN'T WORTH DYING FOR, SAYS LAUDA
Colin Dryden in Fuji

James Hunt had just one ambition last night after his nail-biting finish in the Japanese Grand Prix made him world champion driver by a solitary point at the end of one of the most dramatic motor racing seasons in history. 'I am going to get bloody well drunk,' he said as he struggled through hundreds of cheering Japanese.

The dethroned champion Niki Lauda threw in the towel after completing only one lap in the blinding rain and spray on the track at the foot of Mount Fujiyama. The immobility of Lauda's scarred face masked his disappointment as he left quickly for Tokyo with his wife Marlene. But a friend claimed that the Austrian driver told him: 'I simply lacked courage to continue the race under the conditions as they were. The track was far too dangerous. And I was scared.' And a reporter said Lauda – who was making his fourth appearance since being almost burned to death at Nürburgring – explained: 'I saw next to nothing. I am not crazy to drive at 180 kilometres an hour into a nothing. There are more important things than winning a world championship – life.' Lauda, who is still undergoing plastic surgery for his burns, said he will be back at the wheel of a Ferrari next season. His wife added: 'I am happy he retired from the race.'

Hunt himself paid a generous tribute to his rival. 'I am only sorry that Niki was unable to make it a straight fight. It was very difficult to see, and I feel the race should have been cancelled. I think Niki made the right decision, and in such weather everyone would agree with him.'

The 73-lap race was postponed for 96 minutes because of torrential rain and mist over the circuit 65 miles west of Tokyo. Most of the drivers, including Hunt, did not want to race because of the conditions. Hunt's tremendously fast practice time on Saturday gave him the great advantage of starting the race from the front row alongside the eventual winner Mario Andretti, of America. This meant that until slower cars were overtaken, he was not blinded by the great plumes of spray being thrown up. The Old Wellingtonian, driving superbly in the deluge, led for 61 laps.

But then a weak sun appeared over the snowy shoulder of Fujiyama, and as the track began to dry out the paper-thin wet-weather tyres on Hunt's Marlboro-McLaren started to wear badly, slowing him appreciably. On the 62nd lap both Patrick Depailler, in a Tyrrell, and Andretti, in his Lotus, slipped past Hunt. The 29-year-old Englishman, who began the race with 65 world championship points to Lauda's 68, needed to finish no lower than third (four points) to win the title outright. Fourth place (three points) would also be enough, because Hunt had won more races this season – six, to Lauda's five.

After 67 laps, however, Hunt, who complained about a breakdown in signals from his pit, was forced to come in to have new tyres fitted. He surged back into the race in fifth place. But, surefooted now on the driving track, he overtook both Alan Jones (Surtees) and Clay Regazzoni's Ferrari two laps from the end to finish third.

Hunt becomes the first English champion since Graham Hill won the title in Mexico in the last race of 1968. He is also the sixth Briton to hold the title. The others were Mike Hawthorn (1958), Hill (62, 68), Jimmy Clark (63, 65), John Surtees (64) and Jackie Stewart (69, 71, 73).

30 OCTOBER 1977
HUNT WINS: LOSES TITLE TO LAUDA
Special Correspondent in New York

James Hunt, driving a McLaren, won the £170,000 United States Grand Prix at Watkins Glen, New York, yesterday, but finally relinquished the world title to Austria's Niki Lauda, who finished fourth. Lauda, needing to be only sixth or better to make sure of regaining the championship which he lost to Hunt last year, gained three points to clinch overall victory with 72 points.

For Hunt it was his second US Grand Prix victory in succession, a feat achieved only once previously – by the late Jim Clark, also of Britain, in 1966–67. Hunt averaged 100.98mph despite an intermittent drizzle, but the nine points he gained by yesterday's victory leave him in fifth position in the world standings.

HUNT SAVES PETERSON FROM FLAMES

Colin Dryden in Monza

James Hunt helped to save Swedish racing driver Ronnie Peterson from being burned to death after a spectacular Italian Grand Prix crash yesterday. Nine cars piled up as they surged into the first chicane a few minutes after the start at Monza. Peterson's Lotus was hurled into a guard-rail and caught fire. Hunt leapt from his stalled McLaren at the centre of the shunt. He and the Swiss driver Clay Regazzoni tore off Peterson's safety belt and eased him from under the twisted steering wheel as a track marshal played foam on the wreck.

Both Peterson's legs were broken, and he suffered burns and lung damage from inhaling fumes. The only other serious casualty of the crash was the Italian Vittorio Brambilla, who fractured his skull. It was a day of triumph and disaster for Lotus. The team's No.1 driver, Mario Andretti, by finishing sixth in the re-run race – won by Niki Lauda – captured the 1978 world title. Peterson had been the only man with a chance of beating him.

LAUDA'S DOCTOR LOSES FIGHT TO SAVE PETERSON

Ronnie Peterson, the Swedish racing driver at first thought to be recovering from an emergency operation after crashing in the Italian Grand Prix at Monza on Sunday, died yesterday because of blood clots caused by his multiple fractures. 'Complications started almost immediately,' said Dr Eric Watkins, a London surgeon called in to help, along with Dr Rafael Roblais, the Brazilian who treated the world champion, Niki Lauda, after his near-fatal crash two years ago. Peterson, 34, fell into a deep coma early yesterday and died four hours later, before his wife Barbra could arrive from Monte Carlo.

'We worked on him for six hours on his thighs and foot,' said Dr Watkins. 'We had been optimistic after the operation because the circulation to his lower limbs improved.' But clots then began to block the blood and oxygen supply to the brain, kidneys and lungs, he said.

According to eye witnesses of the multiple crash at the start of the race, James Hunt's McLaren was rammed from behind into the back of Peterson's Lotus, causing it to slew across the track into the path of Vittorio Brambilla's Surtees. Brambilla, whose car hit Peterson's broadside, was the only other driver seriously hurt in the nine-car pile-up. He was said to be improving in Niguarda hospital yesterday with skull fractures.

Hunt escaped injury and leapt from his car to drag Peterson from the flames of his wreck. Being the start of the race, the 55-gallon tank was full, and fumes were thick. Peterson's team-mate Mario Andretti, who automatically became world champion because only Peterson could have caught him in this year's title race, said yesterday: 'It could have been the happiest day of my life; instead it has turned out to be the saddest. That's how racing is.'

Emerson Fittipaldi, who visited the hospital just before Peterson died, left white-faced, saying only that the Monza track was 'too old, too fast and too dangerous'. After a meeting of the Monza Sporting Committee last night, Bernie Ecclestone of the Brabham team and a committee member, said that the crash was caused by driver error and was not the fault of the track. The track has claimed many famous names in racing, the most recent being Jochen Rindt, of Austria, whose Lotus lost a wheel during practice in 1970. Alberto Ascari, the Italian world champion, was killed there in 1955 testing a Ferrari.

The Swedish press, who have devoted pages to the tragedy, have called it 'a natural death in a sick sport'. The state-owned television has a policy of not showing blood sports, which apparently include motor racing. But public pressure resulted in the Monza race being shown because of Peterson's chance to win the world title. Racing officials and the Milan prosecutor have opened separate inquiries.

5 MARCH 1979

TRIUMPHANT NEW FERRARI LEAVES RIVALS STANDING

Ray Kennedy in Johannesburg

Ferrari's decision to race their new 'ground effect' 312 T4 cars in the South African Grand Prix, third event of the world championship, was fully justified at Kyalami, outside Johannesburg, on Saturday, when Gilles Villeneuve and Jody Scheckter brought them home first and second, streets ahead of their rivals. The Ferraris had a distinct edge on the Lotus of Colin Chapman which last year proved almost unbeatable after he had refined the 'ground effect' or 'wing car' principle which greatly improves adhesion and cornering speeds.

It would appear that the reigning world champion, Mario Andretti, though he finished a good fourth, is soon going to need the new Lotus to catch the flying Ferraris. It seemed clear that the Lotus lacks something of the sheer speed that enabled Villeneuve to clip three seconds off the lap record and go round the 4.7-kilometre circuit in 1 minute 14.4 seconds.

The race was dominated by the weather and tyres. It was stopped after two laps, when a cloudburst flooded the track, and restarted an hour later. Scheckter, a South African, gambled on his knowledge of local weather conditions and went out for the restart with smooth racing 'slicks' on the Michelin-shod Ferrari, relying on the weather to clear up and the track to dry out rapidly, which it did. Villeneuve chose to start on wet-weather tyres, as did most other drivers, and, though he had to make a pit-stop to change them, it was the right decision.

Scheckter was leading the race and heading for his second popular home win at Kyalami when the front Michelins began to blister, and he headed in to change them on the 54th of the 78 laps. Third was Jean-Pierre Jarier, in a Tyrrell, followed by Andretti, his Lotus team-mate Carlos Reutemann, and Niki Lauda in the Brabham.

29 APRIL 1979

WHERE IS HUNT GOING NOW?

MOTOR RACING HAS BROUGHT HIM WEALTH, FAME ...
AND DISILLUSIONMENT?

Roger Heywood
Telegraph Sunday Magazine Feature

Whoever wins the Spanish Grand Prix on the Jarama circuit near Madrid this afternoon will not necessarily be the best racing driver in the world — or, for that matter, a man with the flair, skill and experience to be ranked among the top four or five. But, barring unforeseen accidents, it is safe to wager he will be driving the fastest car. This is why James Hunt, Britain's former world champion, is quitting motor racing at the end of this season. He is completely disenchanted with the sport which gave him so much pleasure as a young man, and made him a millionaire – and, therefore, a tax exile in Spain – before his thirtieth birthday.

'What is called the world drivers' championship is, in fact, a car manufacturers' championship,' he says rather bitterly. 'It's still a challenge to the skill of the designer, but drivers are becoming irrelevant.'

No other Formula One driver has been so publicly critical of modern grand prix racing, although no doubt several of the biggest names in the sport share his views. But Hunt has always been outspoken; and some who know him well might add the words arrogant, brash, uncompromising and bloody-minded.

Many others prefer to see him as intelligent, articulate, provocative, controversial and almost frighteningly honest. He is a character who could so easily have come from the pen of the young John Osborne, for he literally bombards you with a constant stream of angry yet rational arguments which leave you numb with word-shock. It is a relief to escape to the nearest bar and try to paraphrase the verbal avalanche into a pithy snowball or two to throw back at him.

'There used to be a time,' he said, almost accusingly, 'when all grand prix cars, give or take the odd technicality, had more or less the same potential performance. So the outcome of every race depended entirely on the skill and experience of the drivers. But those days are gone – probably for ever. There's no fun, no joy in the game any more. It's boring. Look back last year, for example. The Lotus was so far ahead of all the other cars, it ran away with nearly every race. The rest of us didn't have a chance. But I suppose that was an exceptional year.'

The fierceness of his argument sometimes makes you feel personally responsible for the whole shabby mess of the world at large. But then the obvious begins to sink in. You are talking to someone who is a naturally aggressive competitor. It was probably this innate killer spirit, as much as his driving ability, which made Hunt into a world champion.

Only an hour earlier, he had been playing squash, his favourite exertion (it would be ridiculous to apply the word relaxation to any sport he takes seriously), with a professional at the Los Monteros Hotel, a few miles from his Marbella home in southern Spain. The exercise revealed more about the real essence of the man many people in motor racing love to hate than all the thousands of words he can pour forth when trying to explain his attitude in life. Within a few minutes of being on court, he suddenly shouted: 'I may as well be playing by myself. Make me work. Stop making it easy.' The professional shrugged his shoulders, smiled up at the gallery and proceeded to treat James Hunt, the racing driver, as though he were Geoff Hunt, the Australian squash rackets champion of the world. James Hunt came off court sweating but happy. He had been forced to play to his limits. He had *competed* with a better player as hard as he knew how. And he had obviously enjoyed himself.

It is a pity that such a natural competitor does not get similar pleasure these days out of Formula One racing. Is it because he is unhappy about the new Wolf car he is driving? Or is he just sickened by the number of deaths and serious accidents he has seen on the tracks over the last few years?

'No, it's not the car,' he says emphatically, again fixing me with his cold, blue eyes, 'although obviously it has not been as fast as some of the others in the early races. But I knew exactly what I was doing when I switched from Marlboro McLaren to Wolf at the end of last season. Of course I enjoyed myself with McLaren – I won the world championship three years ago in a McLaren – but I wanted a change. And I have faith in the Wolf, and the entire Wolf team. They are all marvellous blokes. Maybe we'll get the car right sometime during the season. I hope so. It won't be for want of trying if we don't.

'As for the danger, the accidents ... well, I'd be a half-wit if I ever thought deaths couldn't happen in motor racing. Of course deaths upset me. Ronnie Peterson's death last year upset me greatly – and so did the terrible accident to Niki Lauda in the year I won the championship. Niki is my greatest friend in racing. We are very different men, but we think alike – and we respect each other. That's what really matters.

'But I suppose if I'm honest with myself, the thing that worries me is not being killed but being seriously injured. I'd hate to be crippled – or to badly injure an ankle, knee or hip. Then I wouldn't be able to play squash or golf. I'd be lost.

'Strange though it may seem, you don't think about such things when you first start driving fast cars. You are too busy learning and trying to prove yourself – hoping to be recognised. Very few youngsters make it from Formula Three to Formula One. I was one of the lucky ones.'

He was. At the end of his first season as a full-time professional, in 1969, he received the second prize of £300 when the Grovewood Motor Racing Awards were handed out. The other promising newcomers of that year were Mike Walker, who took the £500 first prize, and Tony Trimmer, who came third. Neither was destined to become internationally famous – or rich – like Hunt.

Within another four years, by then driving a Formula One Hesketh, he had taken fourth place in the British Grand Prix, third in the Dutch and second in the United States, and motor racing writers were talking about his 'spirited driving' and tipping him as a possible world champion.

Fittingly, he won his first Formula One race in Britain – the International Trophy at Silverstone – in April 1974; and then, in June the following year, his first grand prix, the Dutch at Zandvoort, driving the all-British Hesketh. He had arrived.

When the enormous financial demands of Formula One racing became too heavy for the young and enthusiastic Lord Hesketh, who had already ploughed a fortune into his racing team, Hunt joined McLaren and began to enjoy the benefits of the huge promotion from Marlboro. He was then not only financially secure but on the road to vast wealth.

He had married Suzy Miller, a 25-year-old model, but this ended in divorce and Suzy is now married to Richard Burton; and he moved to southern Spain to avoid paying back most of the enormous earnings he made from motor racing and the lucrative spin-offs from promotion and advertising. It was a wise decision, because although he will not discuss the exact amount he made from becoming the world champion in 1976, he admits that he is a millionaire. But he pays the price: he can spend only three months in Britain in any year.

Although he enjoys the lifestyle of a wealthy and famous celebrity in Marbella, which has attracted so many film stars and successful international businessmen trying to escape paying penal taxes in their own countries, Hunt still gives the impression that he misses Britain. Now 31, and on the brink of retirement, Hunt, one suspects, still hankers after the much-abused middle-class values of Britain in 1979. He is not, whatever the gossip writers have suggested over the last ten years, one of those natural 'beautiful people' who are supposed to make up the Jet Set.

Of course, he drives up to Malaga Airport in his dark-blue Mercedes and flies off to all points of the compass nearly every fortnight throughout the year. But it is all strictly business. He is committed to compete in every grand prix this year.

Of course, he owns a beautiful and extremely expensive house – by modern Spain's inflationary standards – in the foothills behind Marbella and he can easily afford to employ a middle-aged English couple – George and Joan – to look after it and his beloved pets, three dogs and two cats.

Of course, he hobnobs with the Sean Connerys of this world, because he also lives in Marbella and is among his friends. But Hunt still remains an ordinary middle-class boy who was educated at Wellington and who had a natural aptitude for driving fast cars daringly and brilliantly. Perhaps the British class and educational system has always created men like Hunt, with an overwhelming desire to compete. It could be argued that there would not have been an Empire without them. The outspoken, arrogant, and sometimes abrasive Hunt also has another side to his character. 'I realise,' he told me, 'that I need responsibility. That is why my girlfriend, Jane, is trying to have our baby. Then I would have a real meaning to my life. Someone to take care of.'

Jane is a 26-year-old photographers' agent who also has to spend her time travelling. She is a beautiful, long-legged girl who, as the gossip writers would say, would look just right with Hunt at a film premiere.

In what kind of a family would their baby grow up? He or she would soon know that father had been a famous world racing driver – hence the wealth – but father would also always be his own man, voicing his own views.

The child would inevitably hear this kind of basic philosophy: 'I don't get involved in the local social life of Marbella because they are all a bit weird. The trouble is, I suppose, that the place lives on tourists who are here for a couple of weeks a year. When they're here, they freak out, which is okay, but many people *living* here join in. They're not just freaking out for two weeks of the year, like the tourists, it's for 52 weeks of the year. In the end, they just rot.'

Hunt has no intention of rotting. He has a major share in a nightclub in Marbella, although he says he hates such places, and is involved with a Munich squash club. So his business interests, which are bound to increase as he approaches his retirement towards the end of the year, will keep him active and alert.

And maybe he will return to live in Britain eventually – to play squash at least up to county standard and to bring down his golf handicap so he can compete against the better amateurs. So even when he leaves the glamorous motor racing world we shall hear much more of James Hunt.

But it would be unwise to write off his chances of confounding the experts in his last season in racing. There are still 12 main grand prix this season, and Hunt is entered for them all. He obviously has faith in the

Wolf, the whole team behind the car and himself, despite the early-season failures.

He will always have the urge to succeed at anything he does and he is determined to win another race as early as possible – and prove the foolishness of calling him a has-been.

10 SEPTEMBER 1979

SCHECKTER VICTORY GIVES HIM TITLE

Colin Dryden in Monza

Helmeted police had to fight their way through ecstatic crowds and escort Jody Scheckter to the rostrum to be acclaimed the world motor racing champion after his victory in the Italian Grand Prix at Monza yesterday. Despite the new points system, the South African, with three victories and three second places, cannot be overtaken with two races yet to come.

Scheckter, 28, realised the main ambition of his career in his 97th grand prix – and it was his tenth victory in a Formula One career which started with McLaren in 1972. Since then, he has driven for Tyrrell, Wolf and now Ferrari, and has matured into a worthy world champion. To the delight of the chanting flag-waving crowd at Monza, the race was a clean sweep for their beloved Ferraris, with Scheckter's team-mate Gilles Villeneuve taking second place.

Clay Regazzoni, the veteran Swiss, celebrated his 40th birthday last week by being third in a Williams, and Niki Lauda, the former double world champion, in his Brabham, was fourth. Mario Andretti (Lotus), who lost his title to Scheckter, beat Jean-Pierre Jarier (Tyrrell) for fifth place.

Although Alan Jones's winning streak ended at Monza, he put in an heroic drive to finish ninth after being left on the line and having to make a pit-stop. The Australian fought his way up from last place, and two laps down, by setting one record lap after another. Then Regazzoni, battling to catch the Ferraris, went even faster – lapping in 1 minute 35.60 seconds, a speed of 135.71mph.

VILLENEUVE TAKES THE FINAL FLAG

Bob Lloyd in New York

Canadian Gilles Villeneuve, in a Ferrari, almost lapped the field in driving to an outstanding win in the United States Grand Prix at Watkins Glen, New York, yesterday. The win was Villeneuve's third and Ferrari's sixth of the now-concluded 15-race 1979 grand prix season, in which South Africa's Jody Scheckter had already clinched the world title for Ferrari.

Only seven cars were officially classified as finishers. Alan Jones, of Australia, in the Williams favoured by many to win the race, took the lead from Villeneuve after 31 of the scheduled 59 laps. Villeneuve was first into the pits to change from rain to dry tyres on lap 34 and fell 20 seconds behind Jones, who was still on rain tyres. Jones stopped to change tyres on lap 35 and after a 35-second pit-stop, in which he left the pits before one wheel had been properly secured. Jones lost the wheel during the next lap and was forced to retire. Scheckter also retired when he lost a rear tyre after 48 laps while running in second place.

CHAPTER FOUR
THE 1980s

JONES WINS BY SEAT OF HIS PANTS
Colin Dryden in Montreal

After celebrating the world championship, a relaxed Alan Jones said in Montreal yesterday that he would rather drive for Frank Williams's team than any other. 'I have had a couple of offers that I have to think about but I really want to stay with Frank and make it two in a row with Williams,' said Jones. He added that he would be signing his new contract after the final race of the season at Watkins Glen next Sunday.

Drinking black coffee and Vichy water the morning after winning the Canadian Grand Prix and clinching the championship, Jones said he knew he would win because his lucky underpants had arrived on Saturday night. They were sent out especially by his wife Beverley and he had worn them at all the races he had won last year. Very superstitious, Jones admitted that he had only really started to relax since Nelson Piquet overtook him by one point at the Italian Grand Prix.

'I have always lost championships in the past when I have been leading right up to the last round. I was twitchy in Zandvoort and Imola, but I have been relaxed here and I knew everything would work out when the underpants arrived in time,' he added.

Jones said he was disappointed that his rival Nelson Piquet had not congratulated him after the race. 'I would have said something to him if he'd won, even if I didn't mean it,' said Jones. He was delighted, however, to hear that the last Australian to win the world championship, Sir Jack Brabham, had remarked in Australia: 'Jones will probably drink more Fosters lager than I ever would.'

A measure of the man is that before leaving Montreal as the new champion, he was visiting Jean-Pierre Jabouille, who is in hospital here with a badly broken leg after crashing in his Renault Elf turbo-charged car during the race on Sunday.

The final race of the 1980 season takes place at Watkins Glen, New York State, on Sunday, but Jones is secure as champion because, even if Piquet wins, the Brazilian has to discard points under the complicated scoring system. The grand prix season is divided in half, and drivers' points count for only five races in each half. Piquet has scored in the second half in Britain, Germany, Austria, Holland and Italy. He, therefore, has to discard his lowest score – two points won in Austria. Even if Piquet won nine points in Watkins Glen, his total of 65 would have to be reduced to 61 – one point less than Jones's total after the Canadian Grand Prix.

19 OCTOBER 1981

FIFTH PLACE MAKES PIQUET CHAMPION

Ian Brodie in Las Vegas

Nelson Piquet, of Brazil, was in such pain that he was on the verge of quitting just over halfway through Saturday's Grand Prix at Caesar's Palace in Las Vegas, but he hung on to fifth place, which was enough to make him the world champion by one point. While Alan Jones, the retiring champion from Australia, was popping Champagne in the winner's circle, Piquet was slumped in his Brabham, having finally blacked out from exhaustion and pain racking his neck, back and shoulders. At 29, Piquet has triumphed in only his third full Formula One season. He came second last year – an incredibly rapid ascent.

He took up motor racing in defiance of his father, a doctor in Rio, who wanted him to be a lawn tennis star. Piquet adopted his mother's maiden name to hide his motor racing successes from his family. Presumably they know by now. 'It's difficult to believe I'm the champion,' he said after Saturday's race. 'I didn't know if I could finish, my neck was so sore and my head was going out of the car on all the bends.' Piquet had been troubled by back and neck pains all week, exacerbated by the tight 2.26-mile course with its 14 turns. He had needed a 90-minute massage before he could get into his car for the race.

The race was a disaster for Carlos Reutemann, of Argentina, who started it with a one-point lead over Piquet for the championship, having made all the fastest running in practice. At the start of the race, his Williams car apparently lost its fourth gear, forcing Reutemann to nurse it through the 169.5 miles. He finished eighth, out of the points.

26 APRIL 1982

DEFIANT PIRONI IS FERRARI WINNER

Didier Pironi, of France, defying team orders, won a tough battle with Ferrari team-mate Gilles Villeneuve, of Canada, in the strife-torn San Marino Grand Prix at Imola, Italy, yesterday. The Ferrari drivers, who had overcome the challenge of René Arnoux, in a similarly turbo-charged Renault, had a fierce 'private' race in the last 16 laps. Pironi passed Villeneuve on the final lap and held a narrow margin to the finish for a one-two triumph before a partisan 80,000 crowd.

Third place went to Tyrrell driver Michele Alboreto of Italy. His British-based but Italian-sponsored team decided to break ranks in the Formula One Constructors' Association (FOCA) boycott which left the race with 14 cars – 12 cars short of the normal complement.

The first Ferrari victory for almost a year failed to ease tension, and Pironi and Villeneuve did not shake hands after the race. Ferrari officials emphasised that they displayed a 'slow down, keep positions' signal ten laps from the end, when Villeneuve was leading. However, the aggressive Canadian had attacked Pironi repeatedly and triggered off a determined reaction. Piero Lardi Ferrari, son of team boss Enzo, said diplomatically that 'the victory of Ferrari here was the major achievement and we did it'. However, he could not hide the fact that relations between the team drivers were tense.

10 MAY 1982
VILLENEUVE KILLED IN 170MPH RACE CRASH
Colin Dryden

Gilles Villeneuve, 30, the French-Canadian driver, died in hospital a few hours after his turbo-charged Ferrari touched the rear of a slower car during practice for the Belgian Grand Prix at Zolder, Belgium, on Saturday, and was launched into the air. The Ferrari cartwheeled end over end, with Villeneuve being catapulted out of it into safety fencing. Taken to hospital with neck and brain injuries, he never regained consciousness.

The accident happened in the last few minutes of practice for yesterday's grand prix with Villeneuve, who had a reputation as the hardest driver in Formula One, trying desperately for a fast lap. A special meeting is to be held to consider grand prix safety measures following Villeneuve's death. One of the factors the safety committee of the sport's governing body, FISA, will probably consider is the danger involved where cars are travelling at very different speeds. The March being driven by Jochen Mass was slowing down and moved over when Villeneuve came up to it at about 150mph.

Racing drivers are by nature highly aggressive but can be divided into those who drive with their heads and those who drive with their hearts. Villeneuve was one of the latter. He never failed to give of his utmost whether his Ferrari was going well or not. This enabled him to win races against all the odds on circuits unsuitable for his car, as in Spain and Morocco last year. Sadly, the Ferrari's unreliability, in 1980 particularly, meant that his tally of grand prix victories was only six out of 67 starts. With his undoubted talent and ability it should have been much higher. His unfailing verve and zest for driving made him the idol of spectators throughout the world.

The pale, slight French-Canadian was cast in the heroic role of grand prix drivers whom crowds take to their hearts, like the late Jochen Rindt and Ronnie Peterson. His legendary car control enabled him to brake later and take corners off the right line that other drivers would not attempt. But even Villeneuve could do nothing after his car touched the rear of Mass's March.

Villeneuve is the first Formula One driver to be killed since Lorenzo Bandini at Monaco in 1967. Seemingly nerveless, he had survived some appalling accidents since he started in grand prix racing in 1977. His Ferrari left the track during the Japanese Grand Prix at Fuji in 1978, killing two people standing in a prohibited area, but Villeneuve was unhurt. A native of Montreal, he lived in Monte Carlo with his wife and two young children.

27 SEPTEMBER 1982

ROSBERG HOLDS ON FOR WORLD TITLE

Ian Brodie in Las Vegas

Keke Rosberg, of Finland, was confirmed as the world champion driver at Las Vegas after the final race of the Formula One season had been won by Michele Alboreto for an ecstatic Ken Tyrrell team on Saturday. John Watson, the British challenger, starting from eighth on the grid in sauna-bath heat, brilliantly took his McLaren past Rosberg's Williams and other cars to finish second.

Watson, 36, from Ulster, had to win to become the first British world champion since James Hunt, with Rosberg finishing seventh or worse and out of the points. But Rosberg drove a conservative race to make sure he came fifth. For the last third of the race around the bumpy Caesar's Palace Hotel car park, Watson had such vibration that he could not close the 12-second gap to the Italian Alboreto.

Alboreto, 25, rated as one of the best newcomers by Jackie Stewart, had set himself up for his first grand prix victory with fast practice times that put him third at the start behind the Renaults of Frenchmen Alain Prost and René Arnoux.

Rosberg, 33, is a trained computer software analyst, who worked his way up from kart racing. Short and broad-shouldered, he is engaged to be married and has homes in Monaco, Spain and Cookham Dean, near Marlow, Buckinghamshire. He is the first Formula One driver to capture the title after not scoring a single championship point in the previous year, and the first to win it with only one victory to his credit, this year's Swiss Grand Prix.

There have been 11 different winners in this season's 16 races, five of them first-timers. Rosberg's 44 points is the lowest total to win the championship since 1964, when John Surtees scored 40 from ten races. The turbo-engined Ferraris won the constructors' championship.

17 DECEMBER 1982

COLIN CHAPMAN, THE DYNAMO WHO MADE LOTUS THE WORLD'S BEST

Daily Telegraph Reporters

The immediate fall in the shares of Lotus Cars following yesterday's sudden death of Colin Chapman is a reflection of the domination which this tough, single-minded man exercised on the company he launched nearly 30 years ago in a London lock-up garage. His management style was tough and authoritarian, and none of his employees belonged to a trade union. But he attracted a dedicated workforce. The news of his death was broken to the 400 employees when they arrived yesterday at the Lotus factory at Hethel, a former airfield near Norwich.

Don Peake, the company pilot who flew Chapman home from a motor racing meeting in Paris late on Wednesday, a few hours before the heart attack which killed him, said: 'If you did your job properly, he would bend over backwards for you. He was the type of person who wanted you to work and prove you could do it. But if you could, there was nothing he wouldn't do in return.'

Fifty-four-year-old Mr Chapman — 'he was fine on the journey,' said Mr Peake — had arrived home at East Carlton Manor, three miles from his factory, at 12.30a.m., and gone to bed. About three hours later he woke his wife Hazel, who telephoned for a doctor. But Mr Chapman was dead before help arrived.

His death leaves an irreparable gap not only at Lotus, but in British motor racing. Mr Walter Hayes, vice-president (public affairs) of Ford US, said: 'He was a commanding figure in that long line of British motor car geniuses which stretched onwards from Henry Royce. He was a thinker, a man of extraordinary vision and ideas who played a larger creative role in the development of the grand prix car than any other person. He had all the virtues except patience — which was, perhaps, why he was occasionally in trouble with the motorsport authorities, who could neither think as fast as he could, nor see so far ahead.'

Anthony Colin Bruce Chapman — the ACBC monogram is incorporated in the Lotus badge — was born on 19 May, 1928. He studied aeronautical engineering at University College, London, and became an RAF pilot. He built his first competitions car in a lock-up garage in Muswell Hill, in 1948. It was based on a dilapidated Austin 7, and became the first of a long line of Lotus sports cars. With the aid of a £25 loan from Hazel, then his fiancée, he set up in business, concentrating on kit cars for home assembly by impecunious enthusiasts. By assembling the cars themselves, they were able to avoid the punitive purchase tax.

Chapman raced his car at weekends to publicise the Lotus name, and because he enjoyed it. He was a talented driver, fully able to compete with his customers in those early days. He was still working full-time for British Aluminium, but three years later he moved full-time into car production, and the path which would make him a millionaire. From his sports cars it was only a short step to racing cars, and in 1958 he had produced a front-engined Formula One car. A year later he constructed the first revolutionary Lotus, in such a way that it could compete in three different racing categories merely by changing the engine.

By 1960 a Lotus with a Coventry Climax engine driven by Stirling Moss achieved the first of 72 Lotus grand prix victories by winning at Monaco. But it was with the legendary Scottish driver, Jim Clark, that Chapman and Lotus enjoyed their greatest success. Clark's 1963 record of seven victories in a season has never been surpassed. When Clark's Lotus hurtled off the road at Hockenheim during the relatively unimportant Formula Two race in

April 1968, killing him instantly, Chapman was so upset that there was talk of his quitting motor racing. But Graham Hill took over and went on to become the 1968 world champion. Jochen Rindt, of Austria – who died in a crash at Monza – Emerson Fittipaldi of Brazil, and Mario Andretti, of America, also became world champions in Chapman-designed cars.

When other cars seemed to have reached a plateau of performance and could go no faster, Chapman's Lotuses employed the ground-effect principle, using the underside of the car as an aerofoil in reverse to suck the car down on to the track and increase cornering speeds. Before the opposition caught up, Andretti and Ronnie Peterson won eight races between them in 1978 to give Andretti the drivers' title and Lotus the seventh of their manufacturers' championships, a feat equalled only by Ferrari.

But the lean years now began, with few opportunities for Chapman to indulge his victory salute of throwing his little beach cap in the air. His attempt to baffle the opposition again failed in 1981, when the revolutionary Lotus 88B with two chassis was ruled illegal. After four years with only one victory (in Austria this year), Lotus seemed poised for success in 1983 after persuading Renault to provide some of its immensely powerful turbo engines to marry to Chapman's brilliant chassis designs.

Chapman, appointed CBE in 1970, was a private, almost lonely figure, with few close friends apart from his wife, son, two daughters and his immediate circle. He had a reputation for being 'difficult' and fiercely independent and had several brushes with the law. The most celebrated incident was during the Dutch Grand Prix at Zandvoort in 1965, when he was remanded in custody, accused of assaulting a policeman. He was eventually fined £25.

Frank Williams, head of the TAG Williams team who provided the car for the current world champion, Keke Rosberg, said yesterday: 'Britain has lost one of her greatest and most outstanding innovative engineers.'

17 OCTOBER 1983
PIQUET REIGNS BUT RENAULT TO BATTLE ON
Colin Dryden in Kyalami

Before the cars were packed away after the finish of the South African Grand Prix at Kyalami on Saturday, the Brabham of Nelson Piquet was carrying the world champion's coveted No. 1. The transfer had been unpeeled from the Williams of Keke Rosberg, the previous champion, and handed over in a little private ceremony.

For the last four seasons the world championship has been held alternately by drivers from the British Williams and Brabham teams – Alan Jones, Piquet, Rosberg and now Piquet again. To the chagrin of the French Renault team, the challenge of Alain Prost, who had led Piquet by two points before the start of the final race, had ended in the pits before the halfway mark. Despite having started the turbo-charged revolution at Silverstone in 1977 and the expenditure of many millions of francs, Renault have not produced the first French world champion. Undaunted, Jean Sage, the Renault team spokesman, said: 'Naturally we are very disappointed, but there is no question of our withdrawing from grand prix racing – we want that championship.' With the fine form of Piquet, who will have a new Brabham within days for testing, plus the promise of the Williams and the McLaren teams, Renault's task now seems even harder.

Piquet's race for the championship was planned meticulously by the Brabham team and went like clockwork. The 1981 world champion leapt to the front from the start followed by the eventual winner, his team-mate Riccardo Patrese. The two blue and white Brabhams were obviously the fastest cars on the hot, dusty circuit near Johannesburg, and pulled steadily away from Prost's Renault and the Ferraris of Patrick Tambay and René Arnoux.

22 OCTOBER 1984

LAUDA'S WORLD CHAMPIONSHIP BY HALF A POINT

Special Correspondent in Estoril

Niki Lauda, of Austria, won the world drivers' championship by half a point when he finished second to Alain Prost, of France, his McLaren team-mate, in the Portuguese Grand Prix at Estoril yesterday. 'I want to win the championship for a fourth time,' said Lauda, after describing the race as the hardest he had driven. 'The back-markers were more difficult than I can ever remember.' Lauda was champion in 1975 and 1977 and was badly burned at the old Nürburgring in 1976, being given the last rites. He retired in 1979 but returned to grand prix racing in 1982.

Prost started on the front row of the grid yesterday, with Nelson Piquet's Brabham in pole position, and Lauda had to work his way up from 11th, needing second place to win the title if the Frenchman won the race. For the second successive year Prost's championship hopes evaporated in the final grand prix of the season. Last year he was pipped by Piquet in the South African Grand Prix, when his Renault failed. Yesterday he scored his seventh grand prix victory of the season – equalling the record of the late Jim Clark of Scotland – at 112.185mph. Lauda's half-point margin was the smallest in the drivers' world championship since the series began 34 years ago, and a Frenchman has still to win it.

22 OCTOBER 1984

THE HERO WHO ROSE AGAIN

Colin Dryden

When Niki Lauda made his comeback in 1982 and took only three races to return to winning form, a third world championship was obviously on the cards. It seemed he might have clinched it three weeks ago at Nürburgring, where he had so nearly died in a fiery crash eight years previously. But a brilliant win by Alain Prost, his McLaren team-mate, meant that the fight had to go the full distance to Portugal.

Already the slightly built, scarred Austrian had scored more championship points than any other grand prix driver, but mere figures mean nothing to him. The man is a paradox ... uninterested in statistics, yet desperately wanting to become world champion for the third time and join Sir Jack Brabham and Jackie Stewart as the sport's only triple title-holders. Highly competitive and determined to win every race he enters, if humanly possible ... yet he gives his trophies away afterwards to his local garage. 'I'm not here to get the most points or wins – I am in the sport for as long as I am able to do it and enjoy it,' he says.

In 1976 the sport he loves nearly took his life, and he was given the last rites. Unbelievably he was back in the cockpit within six weeks, finishing fourth in the Italian GP at Monza in September. But even Lauda's stoicism deserted him in the rain-soaked Japan GP in October. After the opening lap he pulled into the pits complaining that he could not see and adding that the race was 'not worth dying for'. Almost unnoticed, Mario Andretti won the race, but James Hunt finished fourth to take the title by one point, 69–68. Enzo Ferrari can not have been best pleased, but Lauda made it up to him the following year by taking the drivers' world championship a second time to add to the team's constructors' championships for 1976 and 1977.

After success with Ferrari he switched to Brabham, and, without even waiting for the end of his second indifferent season with the team, he quit. During practice for the Canadian GP in Montreal he announced he was tired of 'going round and round in circles' and abruptly left without stopping for the race. His interest in aviation went beyond the usual GP driver's private aircraft. Lauda started his own airline, Lauda Air.

In 1982 he was back in grand prix racing, reputedly the highest-paid driver, such was the magic of the Lauda name. Within three races he was on the winner's podium, as if he had never been away, as chief executive of Lauda Air. 'The principle of grand prix racing for me has not changed at all – it is always difficult but competitive,' he said. 'Even the people are almost the same, except that we all seem to have more wrinkles.'

7 OCTOBER 1985
MANSELL AND PROST SHARE BRANDS GLORY
Brian Allen

The victory of Nigel Mansell, a British driver, in the Williams, a British car, in yesterday's Grand Prix of Europe at Brands Hatch overshadowed Alain Prost's winning of the world drivers' championship. An estimated 90,000 spectators saw Mansell, 31, though suffering the effects of incidents in the two previous grands prix, forget the aching ribs as he forged into the lead on lap nine of the 75-lap race and coolly hold his advantage to the finish. He comfortably beat off a challenge from Marc Surer, of Switzerland, which ended when, 13 laps from the finish, the Brabham expired in flames.

Prost, by finishing fourth, became the first Frenchman to win the championship. With only two races left he cannot be caught. Michele Alboreto, of Italy, his only challenger, saw his hopes disappear in huge clouds of smoke as his Ferrari engine blew. But Prost had his worries on the way. He was clearly ill at ease in the opening stages, and opted to come in for fresh tyres, which cost him valuable time but transformed his McLaren's handling. From eighth place he made a strong charge to take three points and put himself out of Alboreto's reach.

Ayrton Senna, of Brazil, mercurial in qualifying, had to be satisfied with second place in his Lotus, 21.4 seconds behind Mansell, who averaged 126.527mph. Third was Keke Rosberg, of Finland, who had been confident of winning in his Williams, but lost out when he spun – 'my own fault' – trying to take the lead from Senna. The Finn collided with Nelson Piquet's Brabham, bringing about the Brazilian's immediate retirement, but Rosberg limped back to the pits, had a damaged rear tyre replaced, and went off in pursuit. 'I have never driven so hard before,' he said.

The spectators were in raptures as they scented the first grand prix win by a British driver since John Watson's victory at Long Beach two years ago. In a flurry of Union Flags, embraced by his wife, Rosanne, and presented with the chequered flag which signalled his victory, Mansell thanked the fans for their faith in him. 'I've been trying so hard for so long to do this for England,' he told the crowd. 'And I've done it for you.' It was victory for Mansell at his 73rd attempt, but he is convinced that beating the barrier will lead to further successes.

14 APRIL 1986

SENNA PIPS MANSELL ON THE LINE

Brian Allen in Jerez, Spain

The closest finish for years saw Ayrton Senna just beat Nigel Mansell across the line in yesterday's exciting Spanish Grand Prix. What at one time seemed to be a processional race, with hardly any change of positions, flared suddenly to life as Mansell, in his Williams, began to close on Senna's Lotus. On lap 40, with just over half the race run, Mansell took over the lead from the rival with whom he clashed on the first lap of the recent championship round in Brazil. This was the signal for a classic duel between two supreme drivers, with Mansell trying all he knew to keep Senna at bay while preserving his tyres and keeping a tight watch on his fuel consumption.

Senna finally threw caution to the winds, badgering Mansell at almost every corner and once taking desperately to the grass. Mansell refused to give way, but, with nine laps to go, much against his will, he was pulled in by his team to change tyres. When he came out of the pits he was more than 20 seconds behind Senna, with Alain Prost's McLaren sandwiched between. But with fresh tyres, Mansell's car was rejuvenated and, as soon as they warmed up to working temperature, he began to cut the gap.

His attack on Prost probably cost him the race for it took him some two-thirds of a lap to get by on the twisty Jerez circuit. Then it was Senna in his sights. The Brazilian, teetering on the edge of disaster on badly worn tyres, went into the last corner sliding slightly as Mansell loomed large in his mirrors. As they both accelerated hard for the line, Mansell nearly had more traction, but his effort came just too late. Senna won his third grand prix by less than a car's length. It was good to see Senna and Mansell making congratulatory waves at each other on their cooling-down lap after what had been a memorable encounter.

12 JULY 1986

SECONDS OUT – THE WAY OF LIFE IN THE FAST PIT LANE

THE PIT CREW: MEN WHOSE PRAISES ARE UNSUNG

Brian Allen

When the grand prix car flicks into the pit-lane to collect fresh tyres, usually just before the halfway distance, it is time for the pit crew to take their brief place in the sun under the eyes of the packed grandstands and the TV cameras.

These are the glamorous moments that compensate for the endless hard graft that goes into making a winning racing team – the uncomplaining all-night sessions with a sick engine, the constant commuting to test tracks and Continental circuits, the snatched meals, the snatched sleep in the transporter, the sacrifices and selflessness demanded of the volunteers and true believers.

A dream tyre change like Mansell's in Belgium is the result of constant practice, and no team works harder than the Williams squad to achieve it. Frank Williams insists on it. After his fearful road accident in France in March, one of the first questions he asked when he eventually came on the phone to his headquarters in Didcot was: 'How much wheel-change practice have we done?'

The rehearsals go on throughout the year. Out of a sequence of 30 tyre changes, a large number are under six seconds, and the team's quickest ever was a staggering 4.3 seconds; though these times are achieved under non-race conditions.

'During a race the mechanics have to take just that little more care to ensure that the wheel gun has tightened the wheel nut right home,' says

Alan Challis, the chief mechanic. The effect of losing an inadequately secured wheel at speed is unthinkable.

Challis, a veteran who started an apprenticeship with BRM in 1958 before working on their race cars three years later, has attended umpteen grands prix in the last 25 years, and is now in his sixth year with Williams. 'Pit-stops are a critical time for the lads,' he says. 'The pressure is really on. They know only too well that a good tyre change can make all the difference between victory or defeat.'

The quickness of the mechanics practically defeats the eye. Have you seen a Williams tyre change on TV? Can you say how many were involved? You're in for a surprise. The answer is 15. There are three men at each corner of the car, one with the wheel gun, another to remove the wheel, and a third to put on the replacement. One mechanic operates the front jack, one the rear jack, and the last man holds the crash hoop behind the driver's head to steady the car while it is on the jacks. Curiously, it is not a situation the pit crew really relish. It is fraught with the possibilities of a slip-up; just one sticking wheel nut, one man unable to fling arms up in the all-clear signal, and the race can be lost.

Like all the top teams, Williams's approach to motor racing is akin to a military operation, with movement programmes carefully worked out well in advance. It is not often realised just how much effort and how many people are required to get Nigel Mansell and Nelson Piquet on to a grand prix grid.

Williams are a team who make a high proportion of their cars in-house, and getting those cars built, prepared and transported to a race calls on the services of more than a hundred devoted people at Didcot. And that does not include the Honda staff in Japan, whose numbers sometimes reach 30 during the season, occupying their own special section in the Didcot factory.

The movement sheet from a recent grand prix shows that the Williams team was represented by 33 people, 13 of them from Honda. To the list of mechanics have to be added transporter drivers, and one member whose sole job is to see that the stickers are in order on the cars, ensuring that the presentation of the cars is perfect and keeping them impeccably clean. Another's responsibility is the tidiness of the garage and operating the speed trap.

Logistics are something of a nightmare when there are grands prix on successive weekends. Last Sunday the Williams team were at the Paul Ricard circuit for the French Grand Prix. On race morning they were already packing up everything not essential for the event, so that as soon as it was over the cars could be loaded into the transporter ready to begin the 800-mile haul back from Marseille to Didcot. With two drivers taking turns at the wheel, the aim was to be back at base by Monday afternoon. Then it was a late night for the mechanics working on the cars, followed by two full days of preparation on Tuesday and Wednesday, so that the transporter could be on its way to Brands Hatch, probably around Thursday lunchtime. It is a turn-around that calls for tremendous efficiency and the maximum devotion of the mechanics, who have virtually no let-up.

A team spokesman told me: 'We get a lot of requests from our sponsors – and we have a lot of sponsors – asking if they can come down to Didcot to take some pictures of the cars. We always have to say no, regretfully, because our Formula One cars are never in one piece except when they are on the racetrack. The rest of the time they are in bits, usually a bare monocoque with nothing on it. Racing cars never spend any time assembled between races, so the only time we see them complete is at a race circuit. Our racing cars are constantly undressed. It's like a model with her make-up and all her nice clothes. She only wears them when she is actually on display.'

There are a few months between the end of one racing season and the start of the next, but the mechanics – if their contracts are renewed – are kept busy, helping to build up components for new cars and travelling to circuits for the most intensive testing programmes which take place in the off-season.

Before the current season the Williams team went testing in Rio, not only with the test car but also with a race car. Even more mechanics went to Rio than go to a race. And it is more arduous for them than racing, with the cars running from nine to five, followed by a late-night session rebuilding them.

How long does Alan Challis feel he can stand the pace? 'I'll only stop when I stop enjoying it,' he promises. 'I still get a lot of satisfaction out of this job. Williams are a great team to work for.' Two things give him satisfaction. One is how competitive Nigel Mansell is now. 'The other is when we get both cars running in a race without any major problems from our point of view. That means we've done our side of the job.'

MANSELL GOES INTO LEAD IN CHAMPIONSHIP

Brian Allen

The fairytale success of Nigel Mansell continued yesterday at Brands Hatch, when he fought off a stern challenge from his Williams team-mate Nelson Piquet to win the British Grand Prix. On this circuit only last October he won his first grand prix, and the pressure on him to continue his winning streak – three wins from four races – was dauntingly high. He rose to it magnificently despite a setback in the opening second, when his transmission exploded and left him to limp round with his Honda engine driving only one rear wheel.

Angry and disappointed, he was surprised to see black flags waved indicating that the race was stopped because of a multi-car pile-up, in which Jacques Laffite broke his legs and pelvis, behind him at Paddock Bend. But for that he would have been a non-finisher there and then. But the officials declared a new race, which began 90 minutes later, and Mansell was able to take over the spare Williams which had been set up by Piquet during the two previous practice days.

It is a tribute to the professionalism of the smoothly oiled Williams team that Mansell's new mount was so competitive. By lap three he had moved up to second behind Piquet and overtook him on lap 23. Then came the sequence of tyre-change pit-stops, Piquet first and Mansell two laps later. Both were achieved with typical Williams efficiency, but Mansell held on to his lead as he hurtled out of the pits, and it was a lead he held to the finish, despite unrelenting pressure from Piquet.

There were no team orders, no one to tell Mansell to win. It was, said Williams's design director Patrick Head, completely open house, and, urged on by a vociferous record crowd estimated at 100,000, Mansell hung on grimly in the closing laps and extended his lead to finish five-and-a-half seconds ahead for his sixth grand prix win.

'I could see the crowd waving me on, Union Jacks and all that,' he said. 'It really started with four laps to go. They were the longest four laps in my life.' He admitted two problems: 'One was I did not want to lose,' he joked. 'The other was that Piquet's spare car did not have a drink bottle so I finished absolutely dehydrated.' Indeed, he looked completely drained, both physically and emotionally, as thousands of fans cheered him on the rostrum. Mansell, who sports a Union Flag on his helmet, dedicated his victory 'to all my fans and England'. He now goes into the drivers' world championship lead with 47 points, four points ahead of Prost.

27 OCTOBER 1986

GENEROUS PROST PRAISES MANSELL

Michael Calvin in Adelaide

The praise for Alain Prost's victory in a momentous Australian Grand Prix failed to prevent the Frenchman reflecting that Nigel Mansell would be a more worthy 1986 world Formula One champion. Such an unsolicited admission barely emphasised that a global television audience of 800 million had witnessed an extraordinary spectacle which will be installed in sporting folklore.

Every aspect of human emotion was explored in the early hours of yesterday morning at Adelaide's street circuit, set against mist-covered woods. The 82-lap race, drawn out over almost two hours, featured Mansell's utter despair, the belligerence and eventual frustration of Nelson Piquet, and the professionalism of Prost. He was able even to retain his perspective despite the elation of becoming the first man to retain his title since Jack Brabham won his second successive championship in 1960.

'It is fantastic for me,' Prost conceded. 'But I feel so sorry for Nigel. I know how he must feel, losing the title on the last race. I did the same in 1982, '83 and '84. Nigel really deserved to win the title – I think he will do so next year.'

Those did not have the ring of empty words. But, though the event centred on the ambitions of three men, there were equally absorbing side issues which highlighted the political nature of the captivating grand prix scene. Goodyear officials, blessed with the perfect vision of hindsight as they sought to justify their product, suggested after the race that Mansell could have afforded to stop to change the tyre which disintegrated with such devastating effect on the 64th lap.

Keke Rosberg's similar misfortune, two laps earlier, robbed him of apparent victory yet absolved him from a decision of conscience in his final grand prix. Though the Finn had promised Prost, his McLaren team-mate, that he would allow him to pass if he was in a position to thwart his chances of gaining the victory Prost required, Rosberg had established a 36-second lead at the front by the 44th lap. He was prey to the understandable temptation to end his career on a winning note. But his retirement, with a shredded right rear tyre, whipped away the safety net which protected Mansell from the early stages, when the Briton found himself in fourth place despite a flying start.

Prost, handicapped by a poor 33rd-lap pit-stop to change a punctured tyre, claimed second position from Mansell almost immediately. The eclipse of his British rival only served to accelerate his assault on Piquet, the other Williams driver. The success of that challenge was guaranteed by the cautious decision to order Piquet in to change tyres. Prost established an 18-second cushion with ten laps to go.

18 MAY 1987

MANSELL FLARES AS PROST CHARGES TO RECORD 27TH WIN

Brian Allen

The McLaren pair steam-rolled the opposition in yesterday's Belgian Grand Prix with Alain Prost leading home his team-mate Stefan Johansson after a typically smooth performance by the Woking-based team. The race was marred by a second-lap accident which sidelined both Tyrrells, mercifully without injury to either Philippe Streiff or Jonathan Palmer. Streiff's car suddenly snapped sideways and bounced off the barriers, breaking up and spreading wreckage which Palmer hit. Streiff took over the team's spare car and finished ninth in the restarted race.

This incident led to a controversial collision on the first lap of the restarted race. Nigel Mansell, who had a clear advantage on the original first lap, was outgunned by Ayrton Senna's Lotus at the start but was hounding him halfway round the first lap. Whoever was at fault – each blamed the other – the Lotus and Williams collided and went off into a sand trap. Senna retired on the spot and Mansell limped away only to give up later with his undertray damaged in the accident. Then followed an unsavoury incident when Mansell, adrenalin pumping hard, attacked Senna in the pits, and had to be restrained by Lotus mechanics.

Nelson Piquet led the race initially but fell victim to an engine problem, which left the pursuing Prost in the lead he was never to lose as he equalled Jackie Stewart's record of 27 wins.

MANSELL HAULS IN PIQUET TO SNATCH DRAMATIC VICTORY

Brian Allen

Shortly before he stepped into the cockpit of his Williams on the grid before the British Grand Prix yesterday, Nigel Mansell declared: 'I expect a very interesting race.' Interesting it certainly was, but little did he know just how he would have to battle for his tenth GP victory.

On the first Silverstone circuit the two Williamses of Mansell and Nelson Piquet were quite uncatchable. It was a tense and exciting duel between two talented drivers striving to demonstrate who was No. 1. After his criticism of Mansell a few days earlier and his avowal that his motivation was still strong, Piquet was determined to prove the point. He led from the start and, though he did not make a significant break, he seemed able to control his advantage over Mansell.

Around half-distance Mansell began to make a charge, but on lap 35, with 30 to go, he stormed into the pits for a rapid tyre change. It cured a serious vibration caused through a lost balance-weight but, despite the slick work of his mechanics, it cost him nearly half a minute. After a few laps he began to cut into Piquet's considerable lead, and everyone wondered when Piquet would call in for tyres. But he sailed through, though in the closing laps his tyre performance deteriorated, and he lost grip. He drove with all the verve of a twice world champion, but Mansell remorselessly closed the gap. With eight laps to go the margin was under four seconds, and on lap 63, with two-and-a-half remaining, the crowd went wild when Mansell slipped through on the inside of Piquet at Stowe corner. There was nothing Piquet could do to reply, and he had to be content with second place, 1.9 seconds behind Mansell, who averaged 146.208mph. It was an epic battle, a fitting climax to the intense duel they fought during qualifying.

Both drivers regularly set lap records during the chase, the honours eventually going to Mansell on lap 58. Mansell admitted afterwards that he had been driving ten-tenths for the final 20 laps, 'something I don't like doing on such a fast circuit'. The recriminations of previous days apparently dissipated, Piquet was dignified in defeat. And Mansell was generous, too, suggesting that Piquet might have won if he had come in for fresh tyres. The support of the crowd Mansell described as 'unbelievable'. He said: 'For the last 15 laps they were waving me on at every corner. Really they won the race for me. I knew I had to do my best.'

7 JULY 1988

SENNA GIVES PROST THAT EXTRA PUSH
Michael Calvin

Before they were sent out to dominate grand prix racing this season, Alain Prost and Ayrton Senna were summoned to Tokyo and reminded that even millionaire sportsmen are servants. Seated together on one side of a long table, they found themselves being lectured by ten of Formula One's power brokers drawn from the Honda empire and their own McLaren team. 'I could see the drivers were uncomfortable because it was all so different for them,' recalled Ron Dennis, who, as managing director of McLaren International, will pay Prost and Senna around £5 million this year. 'They were told, "This is how it is going to work this season". It was all designed to implant the knowledge that they should never lose sight of the fact that they are our employees.'

Dennis, 41, smiled at the memory. For, in a Formula One team who operate on an estimated £14 million annual budget, the human factor is just another variable to be controlled. McLaren have succeeded spectacularly, having won every grand prix this season. On Sunday, at Silverstone, they will confront dispirited rivals with cars which have been improved aerodynamically.

Dennis, the former Brabham mechanic who holds the title of McLaren team manager, runs what may well be the most professional operation in modern sport. He is a natural businessman, fond of relating their success to what he terms 'the Billy Butlin concept'. He explains: 'It is no longer enough to buy a few huts at the seaside, paint them white, and expect to make a million. Things progress. What applied to yesterday does not apply to today.' Dennis plans up to five years ahead, putting theory into practice behind grey doors at McLaren's Woking base which proclaim 'restricted area'. With its filtered air, controlled temperature and humidity, and firm instructions that 'white impervious gloves must be worn when handling materials', it is no ordinary factory. The life of every part is logged on computer. Each car is stripped of paint after a race and even the dirt pattern in the cooling system is photographed and analysed.

The human chemistry between Prost and Senna was subject to similar scrutiny. It has proved to be the classic case of a champion, Prost, being simultaneously threatened and inspired by his most likely successor. 'Alain would not be as motivated, were it not for Ayrton,' said Dennis. 'That was my plan in bringing them together: to put the pressure on. They wouldn't drive as hard if the other wasn't in the team. It's very close between them. Despite appearances, they both struggle with themselves. Alain has mellowed, and Ayrton will change for the better if he wins the world championship. He's too intense at the moment. They have got to respect each other, but neither will admit the other is better. Each, though, has total knowledge of what is in the other's car.'

Such drivers are among the most charismatic figures in sport – fêted for their physical strength, mental dexterity and acceptance of risk. But Dennis insists: 'I don't support all that stuff about them sticking their necks out. We don't pay them for danger. It's supply and demand. If there were ten drivers around like Alain and Ayrton, their price would be less.' Equally, when he is prepared to spend £50,000 impressing a sponsor with a presentation in McLaren's private cinema, he will not tolerate unseemly public behaviour. Mechanics are not allowed to visit other teams in the pit-lane in case they are accused of arrogance.

McLaren market their own lawn tennis rackets, skis and tea sets. At Silverstone this weekend they will house 300 sponsors' guests in a private village designed on the lines of the Chelsea Flower Show. The team are used to projecting such varied products as cigarettes, high fashion and motor oil. But, perhaps, the key to their commercial success lies in their technical alliance with Honda. Results back up the general belief that their engines are matchless. Yet other European teams – Williams are a good example – have lost their expertise through a basic misunderstanding of the Japanese psyche. When Honda are prepared to commit £25 million to their Formula One programme, little things, such as Japanese-speakers being on McLaren's 150-strong staff, create an essential atmosphere of mutual respect. As Dennis said: 'For them it is about how they win, how they progress. When you win a race with them the one thing you must avoid is saying, "Thank you". You are partners so do not need to be surprised that you are successful.'

In that case no one will be startled to learn that McLaren are not satisfied even with what promises to be a season of historic achievement. As Dennis summed up: 'You cannot suddenly say what you have got is good enough.'

SENNA TAKES TITLE WITH A RECORD EIGHTH SUCCESS

Brian Allen in Suzuka

Ayrton Senna yesterday emerged as world champion after a memorable performance against the odds in the Japanese Grand Prix. The Brazilian's hopes of clinching the title with a victory looked slim as his McLaren stumbled off the Suzuka grid and was passed by 13 rivals. Yet by the end of the opening lap he was eighth and by lap four was fourth. With that typical blend of instinct, skill and panache, he seized every available opportunity to overtake. Before half-distance he was hounding team-mate Alain Prost, and on lap 28 of the 51-lap race he was in front.

He owed something to the elements. The race began on a dampish but drying track, was later struck by light rain and again affected by a shower towards the end – conditions in which he demonstrated his uncanny car control. Prost, who had seemed so secure on lap one, fought back after losing the lead, but Senna held him off and when the Frenchman found trouble selecting a gear every lap or so, he resigned himself to concentrating on giving the team their ninth one-two of the season.

The title decided – Prost cannot now snatch it even if he wins in Adelaide in a fortnight's time – both drivers relieved the tension with a frenetic display of Champagne-wasting on the podium. Prost said: 'I am quite happy for Ayrton. He deserved to be champion.' An unusually emotional Senna said he believed Prost was the world's best. Nevertheless, Senna's great drive brought him his eighth win this season, smashing the record previously held jointly by Prost and the late Jim Clark.

LITTLE LOVE LOST AS MISERABLE SENNA EMBEDS ALL HIS HOPES IN GRAVEL

Michael Calvin

Nigel Mansell put personal ambition into perspective and voiced the growing suspicion that Alain Prost is destined to offer McLaren his third world drivers' title as a farewell present. He knows his challenge will have greater credibility next season, when the reliability that helped his Ferrari finish second in yesterday's British Grand Prix should be the rule rather than the exception.

Mansell is also, in a sport in which straightforwardness is rare, and as welcome as silence, unafraid to offer unreserved respect to a principal rival. 'I'll tell you one thing,' he announced, tapping Prost on the knee as they sat together afterwards. 'This is the one person in the pit-lane I could learn from.' Prost smiled. He, like the rest of us, probably had fleeting thoughts of Ayrton Senna, who had left Silverstone long before the Frenchman crossed the finishing line with his red-gloved hand pumping the air in triumph.

The Brazilian made a less than dignified exit, scurrying along the pit-lane and refusing all comment apart from a mumbled explanation, in Portuguese, that he had experienced problems finding third gear. That was more revealing than his immediate reaction to adversity, when he sat impassively after embedding his car in the gravel designed to rescue those caught out by Becketts corner. Anyone who divorces his wife because she distracts him from his career – as Senna did before he had even entered Formula One – is not the type of man to tolerate a fourth successive failure.

One's mind drifted back to the reflections of Prost before the race, which leaves him with the type of lead in the championship that marks earlier assumptions of Senna's superiority. 'On one lap,' said Prost, 'Ayrton is the quickest driver I've ever seen. That's his big advantage, especially when there's no strong competition from outside. Ayrton is a fantastic driver, no question about it. But one of his weak points is that, because of his character, he doesn't drive consistently, all the time.'

Prost has never shied away from the truth and, though that admirable trait has soured his relationship with Senna, it is at the very heart of his appeal as a master sportsman. He has none of the self-importance that is an occupational hazard for Formula One drivers, who live with a Faustian pact that trades adulation for danger beyond the comprehension of the ordinary mortal. Television, remember, sanitises the sport, and strips it of all its shrieks and smells. Stand and watch Mansell accelerate at 170mph towards Stowe corner, with his car quivering on the edge of control, and his supposed annual salary of £6 million does not seem so ludicrous.

Riccardo Patrese's accident at Club corner yesterday, which did not quite match the awful balletic qualities of Mauricio Gugelmin's crash in France, was startling enough. His Williams, trailing tyre smoke, was momentarily airborne and wrecked by the inevitable collision with the bank. Add such perils to an emotional cocktail of personal antagonism and frantic ambition, and the well-publicised strains between Prost and Senna begin to have some real meaning.

Though Prost was relaxed on the grid before the start, climbing out to joke with his pit crew, Senna sat sternly in the cockpit, locked in meditative silence with his bare hands clasped as if in prayer. Each knew the 190-mile race could be decided in the quarter of a mile before the first corner, and Senna was in no mood to relent as they accelerated away. As Prost said: 'If I hadn't moved ten centimetres to one side, we would have crashed.' Little wonder he admitted he was 'happy' to see his team-mate slide out of contention.

Mansell, too, was hardly grief-stricken. 'I could see Alain grinning, so I gave him a wave,' he said, adding that the Frenchman must be a 'very strong' favourite for the title he has yet to claim. The Briton is a veteran of many political battles and hinted that Prost made an important break-through when he complained publicly that Honda had been offering Senna favourable treatment. The Frenchman smiled again and conceded: 'I have had no problems since then.' But of one thing he was undoubtedly sure. At that moment, in the crowded skies above Northamptonshire, Ayrton Senna was planning the next word in a long-running argument.

25 SEPTEMBER 1989

MANSELL ERROR BRINGS REVERSAL IN FORTUNES

Brian Allen in Estoril

Nigel Mansell was at the centre of a raging controversy at yesterday's Portu-guese Grand Prix which was won by his Ferrari team-mate Gerhard Berger. After breaking the rules by reversing his car in the pit-lane and later ignor-ing a black flag instructing him to stop, Mansell and the Ferrari team were fined $50,000 (£32,000) by the stewards of the meeting. They also asked FISA, the sport's ruling body, to consider the exclusion of Mansell from one of the remaining three races this year. Ferrari have protested at the decision and maintain that Mansell could not get into his proper pit place when he came in for a tyre change because mechanics were standing in his way.

After his three main rivals – Ayrton Senna, Alain Prost and Berger – had stopped for fresh tyres, Mansell, driving superbly, had a very comfortable 27-second lead. He had plenty of time to stop for tyres and retain that lead but, coming in very fast, he overshot his pit. The Ferrari mechanics were in confusion as to whether they should push him back. Then Mansell engaged reverse gear and went back under his own power. His actions cost him 20.1 seconds at a standstill, but ultimately far more. As he fought to snatch third place from Senna he received a black flag for that reversing manoeuvre. Either Mansell did not see the black flag, along with his race number displayed at the start line, or he chose to ignore it. A member of the Ferrari team said: 'We put out a signal for him to come in.'

Whatever the reason, Mansell was putting Senna under extreme pressure and, going into the first corner, just got his nose ahead of the McLaren. The two cars touched and both went off the circuit. Mansell later went to the control tower for a discussion with race officials, then left the track without making any comment. Through a spokesman, he said: 'I am prepared to swear on the Bible I did not see the black flag because I was so heavily involved trying to overtake Senna.' The Brazilian has probably lost the chance of retaining his title since Prost finished second. The discard system, under which the best 11 placings count towards final totals, meant that Prost added four points to his score instead of six. Referring to the incident between Mansell and Senna, McLaren's Ron Dennis said: 'I am at a loss for words. Mansell should not have been on the circuit at all. He ignored the black flag three times running.'

Berger won his fourth grand prix by over half a minute. He had shot into an impressive lead at the start, but was later hauled back by Mansell, who overtook him after 24 laps as they lapped a close bunch of five cars. After Mansell's calamitous pit-stop, the Austrian had a comfortable cruise home. With three rounds to go, Prost now has a 24-point lead over Senna. It is still possible for Senna to retain his title, but the possibility begins to look remote.

CHAPTER FIVE
THE 1990s

WARWICK CRASH OVERSHADOWS SENNA'S PEACE

Timothy Collings at Monza

Derek Warwick last night paid tribute to Formula One's safety pioneers and his Lotus team's designers and engineers after escaping unhurt from the wreckage of his horrific high-speed accident in yesterday's Italian Grand Prix. Ayrton Senna ended both his barren run in the Italian race at Monza and his feud with Frenchman Alain Prost, but it was Warwick's almost unbelievable escape which stayed most vividly in the memory.

Warwick said: 'It is thanks to people like Niki Lauda, Jackie Stewart, Alain Prost and Ayrton Senna, and FISA, for all the safety regulations that I survived – and it is a tribute to my team and their car that I was able to run away from that.' The 35-year-old British driver, who has been grand prix racing since 1983, lost control of his car as he steered it round the long Parabolica curve at more than 160mph on the opening lap of yesterday's restarted race.

Instead of taking the corner, Warwick found himself careering straight on into the barriers. His car crashed heavily and, with debris flying in all directions, slid upside down across the circuit. Almost miraculously, Warwick clambered out uninjured, and jogged back across the circuit to the Lotus pits where, after a medical check, he took the team's spare car for the restart of a memorable race won in style by Senna.

The Brazilian, starting from pole position, drove his McLaren to a faultless victory, setting a new lap record, to establish himself as clear favourite for the world drivers' championship. It was his sixth victory of the year, the 26th of his remarkable career and his first in an Italian Grand Prix. The massed *tifosi,* hoping for a home win, were silenced as he came home six seconds clear of defending champion Alain Prost's Ferrari. With four races to come, he now leads the Frenchman, with whom Senna made his peace with a public handshake after the race, by 16 points.

He initiated making his peace with Prost – and so ending a silent and bitter feud which has lasted nearly 18 months since they were team-mates at McLaren – when he said: 'We are true professionals. What matters is this year. Now. I don't want to think about what happened last year. Not that that was not important. But we race now and here, and if he is ready in his heart to prepare to accept these facts, I will accept his handshake. We have to race this championship. The battle is tough and we, I hope, can do better if we are on better terms.' Prost, who was disappointed at finishing second, accepted Senna's offer with grace. He said: 'Ayrton is right. It really doesn't matter what happened last year if we both accept it that way.'

While the two leading protagonists in this year's title race were ending their feud, Warwick – forced to retire with clutch problems in the spare car after 14 laps – described his accident. He said: 'I was right up on Gugelmin and I just got too close. I lost front downforce and couldn't lift from the throttle. The car started to understeer, and as soon as I touched the grass it went into the barriers. I was conscious all the time, and as soon as the car started sliding upside down I began to organise mentally because I was afraid of fire. As soon as the car stopped, I thought of the scratches on my helmet and then of getting out, but I was scared of undoing my helmet in case someone hit me as I got out. Once I was out my first reaction was "I'm okay," and my second was to find the spare car. I had no second thoughts about it.'

11 SEPTEMBER 1990

WARWICK SAVED BY A MILLIMETRE
Timothy Collings

Derek Warwick would have been engulfed in flames in his accident in the Italian Grand Prix but for the revised fuel-tank regulations brought in to Formula One racing this season, Chris Whiting, the sport's specialist scrutineer, revealed yesterday. Mr Whiting, who examined the wrecked Lotus, said a life-saving millimetre remained of the car's fuel cell skin after Warwick's 160mph crash at the Parabolica on the opening lap of Sunday's race.

'If the old regulations had still been in force – the ones which were used before [Gerhard] Berger's crash last year – the tank would have burst, and there would have been a fire,' he said. 'Under the new regulations the skins of the fuel tanks are four times as tough, and that's what saved him. He was a very lucky guy.'

Whiting's views of the biggest accident in grand prix racing since Berger's Ferrari burst into flames during the San Marino race at Imola, in April 1988, were echoed by Jackie Stewart, one of the pioneers of improved safety standards in motorsport. But Stewart, who campaigned for increased security on the circuits and in the design of cars, criticised the decision to allow Warwick to rejoin the race for the restart. He said: 'The violence of the accident was very severe, and it's a tribute to the design of the car that Warwick survived unhurt. But had it happened at Indianapolis, for example, there's no way he would have been let back into the race. He would have been put into an ambulance and taken off to the medical centre. I know he was seen by Professor Sid Watkins, for whom I have the greatest respect. But he could have had concussion, and that may have affected him in all sorts of ways. In my view, he should not have been allowed to carry on like that. He should have been thoroughly checked, even if it meant him missing the race. No race is that important. I know that if I had had that sort of accident when I was racing I would have been killed. It could take a death to make drivers realise this sport is still very dangerous.'

20 OCTOBER 1990

SENNA CLINCHES TITLE BUT PROST IS DISGUSTED

Timothy Collings in Suzuka

Ayrton Senna clinched the second drivers' world championship of his career in the most dramatic and controversial circumstances yesterday when he collided with Alain Prost on the first corner of the Japanese Grand Prix and, in the process, revived the most acrimonious feud in motorsport. Senna's McLaren and Prost's Ferrari disappeared in a cloud of dust, sand and debris only seconds after the start of a stirring race, won in commanding style by Nelson Piquet, who led his Benetton team-mate and fellow Brazilian, Roberto Moreno, home in front of a record crowd of 141,000 at Suzuka.

The incident revived memories of their infamous collision at the Suzuka chicane last year. On that occasion, Senna recovered his car and went on to finish first before being disqualified when Prost was crowned champion. This time, it was Prost who was to lose out as Senna's kami-kaze-style attack prompted their abrupt removal from the race and wrecked the Frenchman's last hopes of retaining the title. Senna's 'success' and the subsequent retirements of both Nigel Mansell, in the second Ferrari, and Gerhard Berger, in the McLaren, also assured McLaren of the constructors' title.

Prost, aware that he and Senna had shaken hands on a new *entente cordiale* only last month at Monza, could not suppress his sense of injustice afterwards and, as a tearful Moreno dedicated his six-point Benetton debut to the injured Alessandro Nannini, he gave full vent to his own very different feelings. 'He did it on purpose,' said Prost. 'He knew that if I made a good start, my car was better than his and he would have no chance to win the race. So he pushed me out. This makes him world champion – and that is good for him. But it was more than unsporting. It is disgusting. I have no problems with losing the world championship. I have lost many. But not this way. We have done everything this year and worked very hard – and the outcome is no good from the sporting point of view. I mean, can you imagine what the young drivers and the young people looking at Formula One, at the sport, will think? They see things like this and they think they can do everything they want in their lives.

'I hate this kind of situation. Senna has completely destroyed everything again and I hope everyone could see he was not honest. Now I am going to tell the truth about the last two years. I am going to ask the Honda people to tell the press what they told me after 1988. They did everything they could to let Senna win and they told me that. I have bitten my tongue for two years but not any more. I never expected this. I thought he was one of the human race. But he is not. I thought he was fair on the track. But he was not today, not like this. He did not brake. He drove into me. I don't expect anything now from this guy.' Senna, defending his driving, shifted blame for the incident to Prost. He said: 'I cannot be responsible for his outbursts.'

Sadly, neither the euphoria of Benetton's win nor the Champagne celebrations in the McLaren offices could erase a deep sense of disappointment at the way in which the championship was settled. Cesare Fiorio, the Ferrari team manager, said it was 'scandalous' that the race was allowed to go on, and Prost later threatened to retire if the regulations could not be tightened up to neutralise Senna.

The incident dragged grand prix racing into disrepute again on a day when Honda were celebrating a championship, but not a victory, on their home test circuit, as Ford, Lamborghini and Renault-powered cars dominated the top six.

3 JUNE 1991

FINAL-LAP GEARBOX PROBLEM DEPRIVES MANSELL OF VICTORY

Timothy Collings in Montreal

Nigel Mansell's catalogue of misfortunes continued in the most amazing fashion at the Circuit Gilles Villeneuve yesterday when Nelson Piquet profited from the Englishman's last-lap retirement to end Ayrton Senna's run of wins and claim a sensational victory in the Canadian Grand Prix. Leading by more than 50 seconds on the closing laps, Mansell seemed certain to claim the 17th win of his career until he came to a halt on his final lap, leaving Piquet with a clear run to his 23rd victory and the first for the John Barnard-designed Benetton.

Piquet, like Mansell and almost everyone else at the trackside, could hardly believe what was happening. 'I was slowing down and then I heard it on the radio,' he said. 'They told me to push and push, "Nigel is stopping", and I was so excited I almost lost control of myself. It was such a long hard race and it was great to win.'

Mansell, having led from the first corner, was left stranded out on the circuit needing a lift home to the Williams garage, on the side of team-mate Riccardo Patrese's car. Patrese, who was equally disappointed though he finished third after an eventful race for which he had started in pole position, later said Mansell's retirement was due to a gearbox problem.

Mansell said: 'It feels very unfair. I can hardly believe it. It is more disappointing than losing the 1986 world championship in Adelaide. I just went into the hairpin for the last time the same way I had for the previous 68 laps and when I changed gear it went into neutral and the engine cut out as well. It was as if there was some kind of electrical or gearbox failure. I stopped and that was it. It was as simple as that. It was like someone switched something off.' Mansell was finally classified sixth and collected just one point.

MOSLEY MAKES QUIET ASSAULT ON BALESTRE'S POLE POSITION

Timothy Collings

Jean-Marie Balestre may not sleep well this week. The autocratic and often controversial Frenchman, who has been president of the International Motor Sports Federation (FISA) since 1978, could be removed from office on Wednesday. To make matters worse for the bombastic Mr Balestre, he is likely to be replaced by a softly spoken Englishman, Max Mosley, who is eminently qualified for the post and whose campaign and manifesto have carefully dissected his rival's 'achievements', leaving him floundering.

Mr Mosley, 51, is the son of Sir Oswald Mosley, the former British Fascist leader and an early advocate of a united Europe, and the author Diana Mitford. In many ways he is the antipathy of Mr Balestre, who declares himself a self-made man so frequently it raises eyebrows, particularly as his suggestion that Mr Mosley is supported by private, inherited wealth is inaccurate. In fact, as Mr Mosley, who has been president of the FISA manufacturers' commission since 1986, stressed last week, he had to scrimp and save to enter his own racing cars when he drove in Formula Two in the 1960s and he has earned all his income as a lawyer, in his private business interests and as a motorsports consultant in the years since.

This contrast in character between Mr Balestre as the streetwise, bullying, battle-hardened Frenchman of the campaign trail, and Mr Mosley as the quintessential Oxford-educated Englishman with a colourful family background, has resulted already in several personality attacks and one extraordinary piece of blatant electioneering. While Mr Balestre's monopoly of power, his age and his health (he is 70 and underwent heart surgery in 1986) have been questioned, for example, so too has Mr Mosley's stamina. Mr Balestre claimed: 'When Mr Mosley is just waking up, I have already done a day's work,' and accused the tall Londoner, who lives within a stone's throw of Harrods, of failing to fulfil his role as president of the manufacturers' commission.

In letters circulated to the national delegates who will be voting in the election at the International Motoring Federation (FIA) offices in Place de la Concorde, Paris, on Wednesday morning, both men have stated their case for holding down the top job in world motorsport and one of the biggest in international sports administration. Their manifestos have made extraordinary reading. For while Mr Mosley's, dated 18 September, consists of a carefully worded and well-reasoned explanation for change, for his own election and for his vision of the future for all motorsport from amateur club racing and rallying to sports cars and Formula One, Mr Balestre's, dated 25 September, consists of nothing more than point-by-point responses to his rival. In short, it is as if Mr Balestre had already put himself on trial before the electorate in his fight to keep his job.

It is a role which ranks alongside running the Olympic Games or football's World Cup in terms of worldwide interest, television figures and commercial activity, and much of its modern success – particularly the huge popularity of modern grand prix racing – is attributed to Mr Balestre and his liaison with Bernie Ecclestone, the president of the Formula One Constructors' Association. Indeed, the battle-hardened president takes no prisoners in claiming credit for the rapid growth and success of Formula One since the acrimonious days of the war between FISA and FOCA nearly a decade ago.

In some respects, after the rows and controversies of recent years, he has become just as synonymous with dissent in the pit-lane as the famous quarrels between Ayrton Senna and Alain Prost. Wherever there has been an accident, a row or a raging controversy, there has been Mr Balestre, gesticulating and shouting. It is this very central role that Mr Balestre has played in all these controversies, his high-profile style, his monopoly of power through holding the same position at FISA, FIA and his own French federation, which has become the target for Mr Mosley's sharpest attacks. Mr Mosley believes, as many who will support him do, that it is not possible for one man, however fit and able, to do all three jobs properly and simultaneously, and adds, with the sharp and accurate mind of the lawyer, that all three of Mr Balestre's posts conflict with one another.

For Mr Balestre, this suggestion has been tantamount to an attack on his very being, and during a bizarre press conference at the Spanish Grand Prix ten days ago he could not resist showing his machismo by comparing the workload of all three jobs to 'a game of croquet' as compared to his earlier workloads as the director of a French publishing company. This was typically flamboyant Balestre over-statement. As a former journalist, who joined the French army as a volunteer at 19, later entered the French Resistance and who was captured, arrested and sentenced to death by the Gestapo before being deported to a concentration camp, it has become almost obligatory for him to talk from the hip and behave in an unpredictable and sometimes ridiculous manner.

In 1986, after surviving a heart operation, he rushed back to the FISA offices in Paris and, in a wild show of authority, effectively challenged his delegated understudies to overrule any of his directives. Earlier this year, during a dinner with French journalists, he allegedly ripped his clothes to show the scars of his surgery on his bare chest as he sat in a crowded restaurant. These two incidents are only examples of dozens of stories of Mr Balestre's eccentricity and his insistence that, after a career launched by his days as clerk of the course at events in France and, later, as founder of the French Karting Association, he has warranted the power he wields now.

Compared to Mr Balestre, an adroit politician who rose to power through the French network of motorsport bodies and clung on with the great success of Formula One, Mr Mosley is a much less experienced candidate. But, as one who was educated in England, France and Germany, he does have several advantages, not least his fluency in foreign languages. Having driven in club racing and Formula Two (Mr Balestre's *curriculum vitae* does not include any racing) against the likes of Graham Hill, Jackie Stewart, Jochen Rindt and Jim Clark, he understands the driver's view. And as an Oxford graduate, a joint founder of March Engineering, a representative of the Formula One contractors and a major force in the negotiations which led to the Concorde Agreement, he has shown a real grasp of the technology, politics and business of this complex sport.

While Mr Balestre appears to be offering the same form of leadership as for the past 13 years, Mr Mosley offers something different, and with it a recognition that environmental, political and financial considerations will have a large bearing on the future of all forms of motor racing. In simple terms, Mr Mosley has a perfect CV for the job, a fashionable pan-global outlook and a desire to run FISA by consensus rather than conflict. Where Mr Balestre has issued his instructions, Mr Mosley favours a 'think tank' approach, making use of all the talent available within FISA. His quiet electioneering, much of it done by lobbying for support by telephone, has made him a popular candidate. He is the first man since the late Basil Tye, in 1981, to contest the presidency and has a fine chance of becoming the first Briton to hold the post since the inauguration of world motorsport's first recognised body, the Commission Sportive Internationale (CSI) in 1922. If Mr Mosley succeeds, when the 71 votes are cast, he can truly claim to have stormed the Bastille.

2 NOVEMBER 1991

LIFE'S THE PITS

WIVES AND GIRLFRIENDS IN THE HIGH-OCTANE WORLD OF FORMULA ONE

Sarah Edworthy

Telegraph Weekend Magazine Feature

'I give Riccardo a kiss before he starts every race,' says Susie Patrese, wife of the 37-year-old Italian Formula One driver. 'Then I stand for a minute by his car. It's not a ritual, more like a prayer.' And sure enough, with 15 minutes to go before this year's Spanish Grand Prix, Susie Patrese is there on the starting grid. In the whirl of over 300 mechanics, tyre engineers, fuel analysts and team officials attending to the 26 cars, she is the slim figure standing sentry by Patrese's yellow and blue Williams car.

It is not cold, but her arms are folded and she hovers from foot to foot, her diamond hooped earrings glinting through thick, blonde hair. Then, with a smile to Riccardo, she is off, weaving through the sponsors' co-ordinated umbrellas and brightly costumed girls, back to the paddock to watch the race on a television monitor.

Further down the grid, behind the Ferraris of Alain Prost and Jean Alesi, Stella Gugelmin waits by her husband's Leyton House car, his helmet clasped to her chest. With the reverence of someone serving at an altar, she hands Mauricio the helmet, and some towels to wipe the bottom of his shoes. Then she just stands there, fingering her necklace – a replica of his helmet wrought in three colours of gold.

In 16th position, Angela, the wild-blonde girlfriend of Andrea de Cesaris (once known as de Crasheris) is clearly fed up. De Cesaris is so tense that he looks as if he is simultaneously having trouble with a contact lens, shaking water out of his ears and shrugging off a fly. Angela wants to squeeze his hand reassuringly, but he won't acknowledge her. Hence her mood. 'He never looks at me or talks to me out there,' she says, 'but he says he needs me to stay with him.'

So she stays, like the other loyal wives and girlfriends who watch and wait as their men strap themselves into the uncomfortable cockpits of their low, squat, sharp-nosed cars. Like mini-Concordes with wheels instead of wings, the noise of their mass revving alone is said to break all accepted sound barriers, being 40 times above the recommended level of 'safe' noise. When they surge over the starting line, they are like a plague of locusts, charging with an exhilaration that threatens as much as it excites. As they race off, jockeying for position, you see man and machine as one.

Protected by ear plugs, Balaclavas and fire-proof overalls, the drivers accelerate to over 200mph, their bodies just six centimetres from the track. They negotiate corners where the G-force brings them close to blackout, and emerge bumped and bruised, their hands raw with blisters from over 5,000 gear changes, their bodyweight reduced by between 14 and 16lb after a single race. The risks are fearsome. Consider just the British drivers on the grid: Nigel Mansell has had a broken neck; Johnny Herbert has smashed his legs to pieces; Martin Brundle trapped a nerve and lost the feeling in his feet.

It was Niki Lauda, survivor of the most famous near-fatal crash, who summed up the Formula One driver's attitude most memorably. 'Living with death is my profession.' But he also encapsulated the sorry lot of the driver's wife. 'If a racing driver's wife says, "It's fantastic what my guy is doing", she must be mad, because it is bloody dangerous.'

It many ways, the women *are* a sorry lot. Mere waifs among men monitoring tyre insulators and aerodynamic fittings, they emphasise by their very presence the difficulties of being committed to a man whose job is to put his life at risk. The official view is that a wife cannot come unless she accepts the danger; the unspoken line is that they cannot afford to stay away – how would they feel if there were an accident and they were not there? The most they will say, as Kate Palmer did of her boyfriend, the Jordan driver Bertrand Gachot, who was recently released from jail for attacking a cabbie, is that 'your heart misses a beat if the car doesn't come round'. They come to watch their men at work, without getting silly about it. They have been told that emotions are what get you killed.

'The only real comparison of the lot of an F1 wife is with that of an astronaut's,' says Eric Silbermann of Honda. 'They have nothing to do except sit back and let their husbands experiment with all this speed and technology.'

It is one of the ironies of the role of a racing driver's partner that when they are not worried out of their minds, they are bored out of their heads. A Grand Prix does not just consist of the stomach-churning excitement of a race that lasts, at most, two hours. There are two, sometimes three, preliminary days of testing and qualifying, with intensive mechanical fine-tuning. The garage is a laboratory of micro-precision and computer read-outs, the drivers translate the 'feel' of the car's performance to the engineers, who set it up for the particular requirements of the circuit. The watching wives are reduced to the role of spare parts.

In the paddock – the village of motorhomes where only friends and guests are allowed – you can spot the wives a mile off: they are the only stationary people. Beautiful and surprisingly tall for wives of jockey-sized men, they wear an unofficial but immediately recognisable uniform: jeans, hooped earrings and watches with complex second-hand mechanisms.

Catherine Valentin is the undisputed leader of the paddock pack. She holds this position by virtue of being Nelson Piquet's 'number one' girl-friend – no mean feat, since Piquet's womanising is legendary, even in a world where that is all part of the image. For a time, the Brazilian housed two of his girlfriends, both mothers of his sons of about the same age, in flats above each other in a Monaco condominium.

Valentin and Piquet, who have a three-year-old son, Laszlo, met when she was working for the clothing magnate Hugo Boss (big in F1 sponsor-ship). Piquet enticed her away from arch-rival Ayrton Senna. Stories about Formula One PR girls and Nelson Piquet are always on an absurd scale, and the one about Valentin is that she tried out 19 drivers before settling for Piquet. The reality of race days is rather more mundane, as Valentin makes clear sitting in the Benetton motorhome, waiting by a monitor for the race to begin. Bouncing Laszlo on her knee, she shakes her waist-length blonde hair. 'This is the worst moment for us, all this confusion and boredom. Thank God Laszlo will be too tall to race.'

Marlene Pirro, an ex-lawyer from Belgium and the wife of Emanuele Pirro, is sitting outside the Scuderia Italia motorhome doing giant cross-words. A few yards along, under the Footwork Porsche awnings, the mothers' meeting of Italian wives is in full swing. Known as the stitch'n'bitch club, the collected wives of Tarquini, Martini, Morbidelli, Alboreto, Caffi, Patrese and Larini sound like a shopping list for a delicatessen, which is just the sort of thing they discuss, as Susie Patrese explains: 'We talk about every-thing girls talk about. You know, friends, family, clothes, shopping, where to eat, what to cook ...'

Elizabeth Brundle walks from motorhome to pit-lane, and back again, and back to the pits again, making sure Martin has everything he needs. Lisa Dennis, the beautiful American wife of Ron, the director of the McLaren team, sums up the role of F1 wife: 'It is knowing when not to be conspicu-ous, and when to comfort or cheer up. I won't even say hello to Ayrton

[Senna] on race day. He doesn't want his concentration disturbed. It's the delicate art of being there.'

James Hunt, the twice-married former world champion who now commentates for the BBC, takes a rather more dyspeptic line. An F1 wife, he says, must be 'completely thick-skinned, with as little brain as possible. If they had anything more than that,' he goes on, 'they wouldn't be here – unless they like being totally ignored.'

Yet this is another irony. A fair smattering of the wives and girlfriends hanging around F1 are highly educated and gave up significant careers of their own. There are lawyers, business graduates, public relations officers and – fair enough – the odd princess (such as the wife of Stefano Modena) among their number. Yet they choose to sit around all day, looking the part, being perfect, selfless wives. As the eight-month season progresses from South to North America, to Europe, Japan and Australia, they see more laps of the airport luggage carousel than of cars in races.

And even when they are not racing, many drivers pursue solitary, escapist hobbies. Prost and Mansell, for example, are as obsessive about golf as they are about driving. James Hunt, a breeder of budgerigars, used to spend seven hours a day between races in his Wimbledon aviary. Defending world champion Ayrton Senna lists model aeroplanes as his favourite pastime. Nora Tyrrell, who has missed only two races in the 24 years her husband, Ken, has been running his team, says: 'The girls are fantastic. You've got to be very special to be a top F1 driver's wife. Drivers are selfish sort of people really. Very self-absorbed.'

It was not always like this. In the 1960s and 1970s, wives and girlfriends were right in the thick of things. They used to sit along the pit-lane wall with stop-watches, recording each lap time down to the last hundredth of a second. 'It was all very informal and matey,' recalls Nora Tyrrell, who would do the lap charts and make the sandwiches for the mechanics. Jane Birbeck would be hovering among James Hunt's spare engines; Patricia Boutsen would be managing Thierry's business interests. Bob Constanduros, who commentates at all the races, recalls how the girlfriend of the Austrian Jo Gartner almost became an engineer: 'Gartner spoke very little English, and Doris started working very closely with the mechanics, translating demands for an adjustment here, a tweak there. Soon she was doing the work herself.'

In those days, women earned respect for their roles. But then Big Business woke up to motor racing, and it became a sponsored and politicised world of Learjets, grand hotels and briefcases. In marched an army of managers, caterers, press officers, fitness consultants, physios, psychiatrists and travel executives – making a business of what the wives used to do as a matter of course. Now money washes around the circuit. A team like McLaren invests between £10 million and £15 million a year. Top drivers are multi-millionaire tax exiles: Ayrton Senna will earn £12 million next year. The owner of the Leyton House team, Akira Agaki, has been convicted in Japan of nothing less than a multi-billion-pound fraud. The pit-lane garages look like space stations, and if someone offers you a lift at a circuit, it means a seat in a helicopter.

Nora Tyrrell describes the change. 'It's far more relaxing for me now – to the point of being bored. Before Longines [the computerised timing system] I used to take the times with a stop-watch, which was hectic – you had to recognise the helmets. But I am afraid I play truant more than I used to. I read books or take the first day off for sight-seeing. It's not that I don't enjoy it any more – it's as exciting now as it was then – it's just that I don't have much to do.'

Marlene Pirro has become a crossword addict. 'We arrive at the circuit at seven or eight in the morning and stay here often till ten at night,' she says. 'Most of this time Emanuele is busy, so there are many hours for me to kill. He spends a lot of time talking to engineers. Hours, they spend, *hours*, briefing, debriefing, briefing again. That's why all the girlfriends are friends.'

So much for the glamour of Formula One. Marlene met Pirro in Monte Carlo when she had a holiday job as a Champion sparkplug girl. The story goes that Pirro, having fallen for a Champion girl, decided to track her down. When he rang the office, the girl he wanted was out and Marlene found herself arranging to meet him. They have been together ever since. 'I gave up university to be with him. The first year was exciting, but then the stress gets too much. There is too much money involved. If you make a mistake and break a car it cannot be because you have been out until 4 a.m. Before a race we go to bed, to sleep, at 9.30 p.m. And at the circuit I have to behave perfectly: a sponsor does not want to see his driver arguing with his wife. He has to be 100 per cent dedicated.' Is she not tempted to go back to her law studies and lead a more independent life? 'No way. We would never meet. All the races are at weekends, so Emanuele would be working when I was off work and the other way round. It's not a big sacrifice to be at Emanuele's disposal all the time. I want to do anything if it helps him.'

Her thoughts are echoed by Nadine van de Poele, another Belgian lawyer who practised for five years before retiring to travel with Eric. 'I spend all day waiting; it's terrible, but I do it for Eric. It's so hard to arrive in Formula One that I have a lot of admiration for him. I try to stay near him all day; if he needs something I go for him.'

The heroic feats of the drivers make romantic figures of their women: they are Penelopes, models of domestic virtue, waiting for their Ulysses to come home. And yet Ayrton Senna has been described as 'having the spontaneity of a mainframe computer'; eating a biscuit is said to be more interesting than talking to Thierry Boutsen. What is it about such narrowly motivated, self-contained men that makes them so attractive? What is the fuel that feeds the flame? A unanimous, and ironic, answer: 'It's the overalls,' said Elizabeth Brundle shyly, vociferously backed up by Stella Gugelmin, Patricia Boutsen, Brunella Comas and Nadine van de Poele. '*La tua*,' Susie Patrese cried, and then more calmly, 'Well, it must be, because when you look at the drivers, none of them are *that* attractive.' Eric Silbermann says: 'If you could bottle Nomex [the flame-retardant with which the overalls are treated], you would have the first proven aphrodisiac.' Angela de Cesaris is more specific. 'They are very special men to spend time with. There are only 31 of them in the world. And they are big sports personalities. They do very dangerous things and never seem fussed. They are all extremely fit young men.'

The cult of the driver as demigod is a spectacle. Every time he drives into the pit-lane, he stays in the cockpit, his car jacked up while dozens of headphoned mechanics dance attendance around every inch of car. It is a little like a Roman senator being borne aloft in a litter. 'Most drivers have this thing called an ego,' said a man, who obviously wished he was a driver. 'It means they love attention, fans, the lifestyle: that's why their motivation lasts.'

The whole Formula One circus works as an ego-support system. The transporters, garage trucks, motorhomes, paddock village, loudspeaker systems blaring Madonna and track commentary in turn, the 2,300 tyres that Goodyear alone bring to one race, the army of journalists – all are there for only 31 men. Women are thus reduced either to the legion of worshippers or to the primal role of sex object in a macho world. There is no real place now for the women in the pits, except to lurk in the corners where the pit popsies of old used to seduce the cameras. Canny men have manipulated this masculine atmosphere: Cesare Fiorio, a former Ferrari team manager, is said to have set about spying on rivals by sending his daughter with a camera down to the McLaren garage in a revealing mini-skirt. The distracted mechanics did not realise until too late that she was taking zoom shots of their new aerodynamic fittings.

By the McLaren motorhome, an auburn-haired Frenchwoman hovers in an absurdly short skirt for a glimpse of Ayrton Senna. She has sneaked in, as she has to most European grands prix, but she is adamant that she is not a fan. She is more than that. Ayrton Senna is far more to her than the racing driver everyone else knew; they have a special relationship. No, she has never spoken to him. When Senna emerges, he gives her a tiny nod, as he apparently always does.

Catherine Valentin, who lives with Piquet on a 35-metre boat which moves around the Mediterranean, shrugs: 'When I chose Nelson I knew it would always be like this. Whenever we stay in a hotel, photographs of nude women are slipped under the door with names and telephone numbers. He also has this woman called Susanna, who sends flowers to every race. She once sent a friend to our boat who arrived saying she had come to spend the weekend with Nelson and Susanna – but he has never met her.'

In front of the Coloni motorhome, the girlfriend of the man who only that morning had bought the team, stands all day in one of the shortest, tightest dresses ever seen, 'advertising her tree trunks,' as one journalist put it. A newcomer to motor racing, she obviously feels this is the pose expected of her.

10 JULY 1992

F1 WUNDERKIND WHO HAS STIRRED UP A WHIRLWIND

Timothy Collings

Michael Schumacher might dismiss the idea as ludicrous, but he arrived at Silverstone yesterday established as a future world champion and arguably the hottest property in Formula One. Yet, less than 12 months into his F1 career, and after only 14 grands prix, in which he has accumulated 30 points, he has persuaded many seasoned observers that he is the best newcomer to the sport since Ayrton Senna burst through in 1984.

The Brazilian, three times a world champion, certainly appears to think so, judging from his reaction to his two brushes with the *wunderkind* in Brazil and France this year. After the first, when Schumacher accused him of poor driving, Senna kept a polite silence, but last weekend, in Magny-Cours, when a Schumacher error led to a collision which forced him out of the race, Senna was vehement in his protests and remonstrated with the young German on the reformed grid. The effects of Senna's outburst, only moments before Schumacher restarted the race and crashed again, are unconfirmed, but it is worth recording that Schumacher leads him in the championship by 26 points to 18.

His first win surely cannot be far away. Naturally quick, technically capable and as good outside the car — among the engineers, mechanics, media and sponsors — as he is in the cockpit, the 23-year-old German has also won the respect of his Benetton team-mate Martin Brundle. The Englishman, a former world sports car champion who has 91 grands prix under his belt, freely admits he found Schumacher's sheer speed difficult to cope with at first and confirms the view that he is a young driver with rare talents. Brundle said: 'Michael is fast, very fast. It has been hard for me to accept this and take it when he has gone quicker than me. He also has an old head on young shoulders, and he is definitely someone special for the future.'

It is likely that his natural speed and courage, allied to the excellence of his constantly improving Benetton, will make him hugely popular with the fans. His father started him karting at four, and he was German junior karting champion at 15, German and European senior champion at 18. He then graduated from the German academy of motorsport at Mercedes-Benz and is a more experienced driver than many of his rivals of the same age. He is certainly more forthright. He talks in a direct way, often mixed with warm humour, and does not suffer fools gladly. This was clear earlier this year when he spoke out strongly after his first clash with Senna, in São Paulo.

'When things are not going right, I have to say so,' he said. 'Even if it is someone like Senna or Mansell, it doesn't matter. If somebody is making a mistake, in my eyes, I have to tell it the way I see it. I still have the same opinion: if someone is wrong I say so. I tell it. I don't just shut up because I think I should. They all know what I think about them, and that is the important thing for me. They cannot just do what they want with me.'

To some, Schumacher's supreme self-confidence can smack of arrogance, but at close quarters he is anything but conceited. He is warm and humorous and seems surprised at his success since being drafted into the

Jordan team at Spa last August. His immediate success in qualifying seventh marked him out as special, and at the next race he was the subject of a huge controversy as Benetton pulled off a coup by 'transferring' him to their team on the eve of the Italian Grand Prix at Monza. Under great pressure he reacted coolly and finished fifth, sparking off a run of form which has gained him more and more attention. Nigel Mansell recognised this yesterday when he suggested it was Schumacher who had given him and his Williams the hardest race this year, in the rain at Barcelona. That recognition could be followed by Schumacher's succession to the championship, which Mansell himself hopes to claim for the first time this year.

13 JULY 1992

MARVELLOUS MANSELL IS MOBBED

CRUSHING SILVERSTONE VICTORY SETS RECORD
OF 28 WINS

Timothy Collings

Nigel Mansell sent Silverstone into a frightening frenzy yesterday with his seventh triumph this year in a stirring and memorable British Grand Prix. The Englishman crushed all opposition with a performance which included fastest laps, and established a record of 28 grand prix wins, eclipsing Jackie Stewart's 19-year-old landmark.

Then, as the 38-year-old Williams driver rounded Woodcote for the last time, his car was engulfed by thousands of supporters who invaded the circuit. Loudspeaker warnings not to go on the track were ignored as Mansell, arms aloft amid a sea of flags, completed his 59-lap victory in 1 hour 25 minutes 42.991 seconds, nearly two minutes inside his winning time last year, at an average speed of 134.109mph. One supporter was run over at slow speed by Mansell, but was unhurt, and no injuries were reported on a day of unashamed British celebration.

For many, knowing the superiority of Mansell and his Williams team this year, it was an early party to mark the long-awaited first championship Mansell looks certain to claim. Mansell now has 76 points, 36 ahead of his team-mate Riccardo Patrese, who followed him home to complete the sixth one-two in nine races this year for the Didcot-based team. Assuming Mansell can win the next three races, in Germany, Hungary and Belgium, he will be champion before the late August Bank Holiday.

However, the Englishman was reluctant to contemplate the prospect yesterday, after dedicating his victory to a crowd estimated at 150,000. 'I have never experienced a crowd like this anywhere in the world,' he said. 'They are just incredible. Fantastic. I had to leave the car at Club ... I ran one person over. He was a big man and I was going only a few miles per hour and I hope he got up okay. It was a great race ... but I'm not thinking about the championship being secured yet. I've been in the game too long for that. I remember how close I was in Australia in 1986, and I shan't count anything until it's in the bag.' Mansell said the crowd's support was so intense that he felt them blowing him down the straight, supplying an 'extra 300 revs', and blowing against the other cars. And he confessed that he had added his final fastest lap, two laps from the end, purely to entertain the fans.

17 AUGUST 1992

MANSELL REALISES DREAM

SENNA'S TRIUMPH IN HUNGARY FAILS TO PREVENT TITLE GOING TO BRITON

Timothy Collings in Budapest

Nigel Mansell realised his greatest dream amid emotional scenes here at the Hungaroring yesterday when he finished second behind Ayrton Senna's McLaren in an eventful Hungarian Grand Prix to confirm himself as Britain's first world drivers' champion since James Hunt in 1976. Overcoming a poor start, the many problems posed by a dusty, twisting circuit, the difficulty in overtaking and, finally, a late enforced pit-stop when his left rear tyre began deflating, the 39-year-old Englishman came home 40.139 seconds behind the Brazilian from whom he now inherits the title.

For Mansell, whose win sparked a Union-Flag-waving show of affection from many hundreds of Britons at the track, it was a precious moment and one which he dedicated afterwards to his fans all around the world, the Williams team, their sponsors and to England. He should, however, have spared a grateful thought for his staunch, but luckless Williams team-mate Riccardo Patrese, whose fateful mistake after leading for 39 laps effectively handed Mansell the championship. Had Patrese stayed on the track, instead of losing control and spinning off on to a kerb, from which he was helped back into the fray, the title race would almost certainly have continued for at least another two weeks.

As it is, Mansell, his family and the Williams team can now relax and celebrate a triumph which has installed the driver as Britain's seventh title winner since the championship began in 1950 and a worthy modern successor to Nelson Piquet, Alain Prost and Senna. Mansell, who was close to tears and whose arms were hoisted aloft on the podium by Senna and Berger, said he felt as if he had been 'carrying a hundred-ton weight around with me' recently and warmly thanked Patrick Head, Williams's technical director, for the volume of his voice with which he informed him of his slow puncture.

17 AUGUST 1992

ULTIMATE SUCCESS FOR AN 'ORDINARY MAN' WHO STARTED ON BOTTOM RUNG

Timothy Collings

Determination and tenacity finally paid off for Nigel Mansell yesterday when he clinched his first world drivers' championship and proved that, judged on talent and courage alone, he deserves his place among the elite. After three previous close challenges for the championship had ended in disappointment, the golf-playing Englishman had every reason after the Hungarian Grand Prix to celebrate a triumph which made him Britain's first champion since James Hunt in 1976. Not only had Mansell, 39, banished the old memories of failure and criticism, he had also made all the sacrifices and outbursts of a long, eventful and chequered grand prix career worthwhile. His title proved to him, and all his supporters, that guts and bravery can carry an ordinary man to the top.

For Mansell, the championship was not just a triumph. It was the realisation of a dream which has filled him with ambition throughout his 12 seasons in Formula One and since he first sat in a kart as a boy. Born in Upton-on-Severn, in central England, on 8 August 1953, Mansell followed the trail of nearly all the motor racing greats by starting in karting in the 1960s, progressing to Formula Ford by the 1970s. He also trained and worked as an aerospace engineer, a job which gave him insight into the Formula One world he was to join in the future. By 1977 he was showing some sensational form, winning 32 out of 34 races he entered, but he also broke his neck in an accident from which he made an extraordinary recovery to return to racing within a matter of months.

The following year, showing the single-minded determination which has characterised his career, he sold his home to finance the purchase of a Formula Three March drive. At this time, as she has throughout his rise to the top, his wife Rosanne gave him her unwavering support. Her reward has come in recent years with luxury homes in the Isle of Man, Portugal and Florida. The March season of 1978 yielded little success for Mansell, and in 1979 he suffered a further setback when he crashed badly and further damaged his spine. As previously, he showed his extraordinary powers of recovery and physical determination to return to racing in such fashion that he caught the eye of then Lotus supremo Colin Chapman.

Within weeks of his accident, he was offered a test drive for Lotus at Le Castellet in France. A heavy dose of pain-killers helped him blank out the pain as he drove a Formula One car in earnest for the first time and, four weeks later, he was offered a test contract. This in turn led, in 1980, to his grand prix debut in the Austrian Grand Prix. Even that was a typical Mansell affair as, after qualifying, he was badly burned around his buttocks when fuel was spilt as the mechanics topped up his car on the grid. In the race, an engine failure brought him a merciful release from the pain. He did enough, however, to earn a chance at Lotus, and in 1981 he signed up as the team's second driver and went on to win his first points by finishing third in Belgium.

The death of Mr Chapman the following year was a blow not only to Lotus, but everyone connected with the team, and Mansell in particular. For the English driver, it was the loss of his mentor, and it took him some time to recover his self-belief and direction. He had to wait until 1984 to claim his first pole position at the US Grand Prix in Dallas and a further year for his first win in the European Grand Prix at Brands Hatch. By then, reacting to problems with the new management at Lotus, he had moved to Williams, where he has since enjoyed great success.

From then on, it was as if Mansell had discovered a new person within himself, and he overcame all the previous obstacles which seemed to have held him back. He won again, in the South African Grand Prix, and went on to finish sixth in the championship, then carried his momentum into 1986 when he gained five more victories. Only a spectacular tyre blow-out in Adelaide robbed him of the title which was taken by Alain Prost. In 1987, by now recognised as a challenger for the title, he made another attempt on the championship but, despite eight pole positions and six wins, was pipped again, this time by his Williams team-mate Nelson Piquet when

Mansell crashed in qualifying for the Japanese Grand Prix, damaging his back again.

For the first time, Mansell truly realised that it was not to his own advantage to share equal top status in a team with another leading driver. A less successful season followed in 1988, when the Williams team lost their Honda engine supply, and Mansell moved on to Ferrari for 1989 and 1990. In Italy, he enjoyed spectacular success with the *tifosi* after winning his first race for the team in Brazil. He also won memorably that year in Hungary, coming through from 12th on the grid. The following season, he was partnered at Ferrari by Prost and, after a friendly start, their relationship deteriorated until Mansell wanted only to leave the team. One win and three pole positions were scant compensation for him, and it was during his deepest low of the year that he announced his intention to retire. This was quickly rescinded when he was offered a return to Williams as the British team's undisputed No. 1 driver for 1991 in a new car with the back-up and commitment to truly challenge for success.

After a slow start with the new Williams car — the now all-conquering FW14 — Mansell began to reel off the victories, scoring a mid-season hat-trick and challenging for the 1991 title before sealing the 1992 season and breaking most of the records this year. Five successive season-opening wins and a new British record number of victories ensured his entry among the greats long before this season ended in Japan.

31 AUGUST 1992

TEARFUL SCHUMACHER NOTCHES MAIDEN WIN AT RAIN-HIT SPA CIRCUIT

Timothy Collings at Spa-Francorchamps

Michael Schumacher, celebrating the first anniversary of his debut, became the third-youngest victor in Formula One yesterday when he won a rain-affected and tactical Belgian Grand Prix. Schumacher, 23, whose home in Kerpen, Germany, is only 100 miles from the Belgian track, took full advantage of changeable weather, unpredictable track conditions and a broken exhaust system which affected Nigel Mansell's late surge. The Benetton driver's victory was the first by a German since Jochen Mass won the crash-marred Spanish Grand Prix in 1975.

Timing his tyre changes from slicks to wets and then back to slicks with the judgment of a veteran, he took command of the final 11 of 44 laps. He finished in tears of joy, 36.595 seconds clear of Mansell, the new world champion. Yesterday also saw a magnificent achievement by the Williams team. They secured their fifth constructors' title when Mansell, making a British record 177th grand prix start, and team-mate Riccardo Patrese took second and third respectively. It was Renault's 200th grand prix and first title.

Schumacher said: 'I had good feelings about this weekend. I don't know why, but when I was in the motorhome today, thoughts went through my mind about a possible victory. But then I found I was running only third and fourth, which I would have been happy with, before it all changed. Suddenly, my luck was in. I came in for dry tyres at the perfect moment, the opportunity was there to win the race and I went for it.'

Schumacher, for whose services McLaren are said to be prepared to pay a king's ransom in 1993, admitted he made one mistake when he ran off the track at Stavelot on lap 30, just as the circuit was drying out. 'I ran wide and missed the apex,' he explained. 'I turned in too late and I was lucky not to hit the barrier. Martin [Brundle] passed me and I could see his tyres were blistered, so I decided to go in immediately for new tyres. It was the perfect decision. There will be a big party tonight.' Mansell warmly praised Schumacher. He said: 'I have to congratulate Michael and the Benetton team. I think this win is fantastic for Formula One.'

5 OCTOBER 1992

EX-WORLD CHAMPION DIES AT THE WHEEL
Timothy Collings

Denny Hulme, the first New Zealander to win the Formula One world drivers' championship, in 1967, died while competing in the Tooheys 1000 endurance race at Bathurst, Australia, yesterday. He was 56. According to reports, Hulme suffered a suspected heart attack at the wheel of his BMW on lap 33 of the 161-lap production car race. His car left the road and crashed into a wall, and, although rescue crews reached him within two minutes, they were unable to save his life. A spokesman for BMW said the team had continued in the race in Hulme's honour.

An unlikely world champion in the era of Jim Clark and Graham Hill, Hulme was held in affection and high regard and remained a popular, if infrequent, visitor to the Formula One paddocks. Indeed he attracted a large crowd of well-wishers to his table at Monte Carlo this year. By his own admission Hulme was a lazy man who always took the simplest and most direct routes and decisions. He was also a keen supporter of Jackie Stewart's quest to improve safety in grand prix racing. Behind his sometimes gruff exterior lay a sensitive and intelligent interior.

Hulme won universal acclaim when he edged out team-mate Jack Brabham to win the 1967 world drivers' championship by five points. He joined McLaren the following year, completing his career in 1974 with eight wins from 112 GP starts.

9 NOVEMBER 1992

SHUNT SOURS F1 FINALE

CHAMPION MANSELL LEFT FUMING AS SENNA ERROR WRECKS VICTORY PARADE

Timothy Collings in Adelaide

Nigel Mansell's triumphant championship year came to a frustrating end yesterday when his hopes of another record-breaking victory were wrecked by a collision with his old rival Ayrton Senna in a tumultuous Australian Grand Prix. Mansell, who was seeking a record tenth victory in a single season, had started the day full of confidence. The 100,000 crowd were backing him as he pulled away into the lead from a record 14th pole position this year in his Williams. But on lap 19, as he fought to keep ahead of Senna's McLaren, the Brazilian, driving on the limit, lost control under braking and swerved into the back of Mansell's car as the pair approached the Foster's hairpin.

'All I know is that I felt an impact and someone hit me at about 40 or 50mph, just as I was turning into the corner,' said Mansell. 'I hurt my back due to the impact in the side. I went to see the stewards, who said it was a sporting accident, but I don't see it that way. I'm very, very disappointed. I had everything under control. I'm disgusted and really I don't know what to say. I ran across the track because I wanted to avoid a big fight and that just isn't the way to end your Formula One career. I was so disgusted. There should be one rule for everybody. I've been fined thousands of dollars for much less. There are appalling standards in Formula One. I should have had the support of my team, but I didn't. They're just gutless.' Senna said:

'Nigel and I had passed the car that had been holding us up, then he braked earlier than I expected. He knew I was very close. I was at the limit and I could not stop my car when he braked early. There was a clear track ahead …'

Mansell stormed red-faced back to the team garage and later protested in vain to the stewards, before departing by car with his family. On the track, Gerhard Berger, in the second McLaren, took control to land his second win of the season in the year's most exciting race.

16 DECEMBER 1992

'I HAVE NO FEARS FOR SON DAMON'

Sarah Edworthy

Bette Hill, widow of Graham Hill, always said that as soon as her son Damon got a regular Formula One drive she would treat herself to satellite television. Right now, though, she is more worried about her telephone. Ever since her son was confirmed as successor to Nigel Mansell and team-mate to Alain Prost in the 1993 Williams team, her London home has been bombarded with calls. And now the answering machine has packed up.

'We're all slightly numb at the moment,' she admitted as a television news bulletin flickered in the corner of her living room, interspersing old black-and-white clips of her twice-world-champion husband in winner's garlands with Damon speaking from the cockpit at the hi-tech Williams headquarters. 'We've had so much has-he, hasn't-he all along that everyone's very excited now Damon *has* definitely got it. When he told me he was going to have a discussion with Frank Williams, I said, "Don't tell me anything. I don't want to know. Not until it's all signed, sealed and delivered".'

Now that it is, her modest terraced house in Clapham is in danger of becoming an alternative British motor racing hall of fame. Well-wishers ring to say what a right and proper decision it is for the sport, how good it is for the British boys, how wonderful it must be for her. Family friends say they have already had enough of the Hills on the news and have switched over to *Coronation Street*. You do not need to be a soap opera fan to see why Mrs Hill is so ecstatic. Her husband and son, between them, bridge more than 30 years of motor racing. 'It just became my life,' she says in her no-nonsense way, and it still is.

While Graham Hill dominates the record books as the only driver to win the world championship, the Indianapolis 500 and the Le Mans 24-hour race, his son now has the dream position of being the British driver with the best chance of staging a championship challenge, something that six months ago not even he realistically could envisage.

She once said that 15-year-old Damon was the one she felt most sorry for after her husband's death in a plane crash near Elstree in 1975. 'He and Graham were like one.' She has stood beside them both in turn, a familiar trackside character, holding the blue and white Hill helmet or screaming, by her young daughter Samantha's admission, 'like a fishwife' as she cheered them on. For, in the tradition of the Brabhams and Tyrrells, Hill's career is a family concern. His helmet, like his late father's, bears the colours of the London Rowing Club (his parents met through rowing circles – she represented Britain at international level; he stroked the London Grand eight at Henley in 1954). Damon's older sister, Brigitte, works in sport promotion; his wife, Georgie, is an enthusiast.

But it was Mrs Hill who steered Damon towards cars, seven years after his father's death. 'He was very keen on bikes, and very good on them, but it scared me. They're so dangerous. So I thought, "Let's stick him in a car". I made a deal with a friend and sent him to the Winfield Elf racing school at Magny-Cours.'

That was ten years ago, and there followed the long apprenticeship through Formula Ford and Formula 3000 that she acknowledges is so depressing for British drivers. 'Formula One is all down to money and not being British,' she used to say. Happy now to be proved wrong, her worries of wrongly encouraging her son to emulate his father have been quashed.

But what may be a dream come true for her would surely be any other mother's nightmare, especially for one who saw Riccardo Patrese's Williams somersault at 150mph at Estoril last season. She said: 'I have no fears at all. I love motor racing. I can relate to it. I just want him to do well, because it's been tough, and he's had the most dreadful struggle. He's tremendously talented and has real stickability.'

A truer sense of her pride can perhaps be gauged from her first-floor study. Every inch of wall is covered with her husband's trophies, yellowing photographs and marvellously dated paintings; a hand-sewn chequered flag is mounted in a box, his helmet sits prominently on a high surface. And in there, too, are some recent pictures of Damon. 'It won't change him or Georgie. Obviously it's a change of circumstances, which might mean a move of house, but it won't be difficult for either of them. Their first baby, Oliver, who's nearly four, is a Down's child, so they're very strong and level-headed.'

The only thing she wrings her hands about is the fact that Damon's name is so often mispronounced. 'It's Day-mon,' she has a way of saying, though she is adamant she will not be hovering at his heels.

8 APRIL 1993

DONINGTON ALL GEARED UP FOR FORMULA ONE

Timothy Collings

This weekend's European Grand Prix at Donington Park will have an atmosphere all of its own. Not the Latin passion and poverty of São Paulo, nor the pomp and pageantry of Silverstone, but a local feeling of history, pride and mushy peas as Donington, the only privately owned circuit to feature on the Formula One calendar, celebrates a personal triumph. The race on Easter Sunday marks not only the first time the East Midlands track has hosted a round of the FI world championship, but also the 60th anniversary of the first car race to be held on a licensed racetrack in England. It also marks the end of Tom Wheatcroft's long battle for FI recognition and the realisation of a dream which began when he first came to the track in its halcyon days in the 1930s as a wide-eyed teenager.

The first race, held at Donington on 25 March 1933, was not billed as a grand prix, nor did it feature the sort of high-powered single-seat cars to be seen blasting round the tight modern track this weekend. Instead, it featured the kind of open-air, leather-hat-and-goggles races better loved from flickering black-and-white newsreels than the Technicolor technology of modern racing.

But it was still hugely enjoyed, and by nobody more so than 80-year-old Max Turner and his brother Rodney, now 84, who ended up finishing second to Eddie Hall's MG Midget in their Austin Ulster 850. Mr Turner returned to Donington recently to relive his memories of the days when the track included the famous arches through which the cars would tussle for space. As he steered an ancient replica Ulster round the smooth modern circuit, where Ayrton Senna drove an FI car for the first time in a test for Frank Williams, he said: 'We used to race abreast down the hill and the curves [now named after Fred Craner, the former secretary of Derby Motor Club, who designed the circuit in the grounds of Donington Hall] on the approach. It was just the quickest and bravest who won. The track has changed a lot since those days. Up the top, where Coppice corner is now, there used to be a farm, and it really meant it was a blind corner as we raced up there and round the farmyard without seeing the track ahead. It was great fun, I can tell you. Care for a pint?'

Mr Turner, along with the circuit's owner, Leicestershire businessman Tom Wheatcroft, has fond memories of the 'golden age' when the drivers made traditional Le Mans-style starts, and he still revels in the history of Donington Park, which he recalled as 'a very spectacular circuit' for its time. The 1930s were the boom years for Donington. After successfully handling club racing, it won the Tourist Trophy races and then hosted four pre-war, self-styled Donington Grands Prix in 1935, 1936, 1937 and 1938. These drew crowds of up to 60,000 and in the latter two years they saw great battles between the German marques, Auto Union and Mercedes-Benz.

Mr Craner's success in those early days and his ambitions for expansion were brought to a halt by the outbreak of war. The track was used as a military vehicle depot and then fell derelict before Mr Wheatcroft bought it as part of a 300-acre purchase of part of the Donington estate, in 1971. Mr Wheatcroft, a multi-millionaire builder and property developer, dreamed of reopening the track, but found it required six years of struggle with red tape before he was permitted to bring back racing in May 1977. It was just as well he was rich, because Mr Wheatcroft, 70, has often had to dip into his coffers, not only to fight costly planning appeals but also to invest in the circuit itself, gradually upgrading it over the years until it achieved its present status as an F1 Grand Prix venue and the home, for the last six years, of the British Motorcycle Grand Prix. Mr Wheatcroft estimates more than £4 million has been spent to stage this European Grand Prix, which is the first in this country since Nigel Mansell claimed his first Formula One victory at Brands Hatch back in 1983.

'It is a tremendous boost for this area and will bring in £5.2 million for the local economy,' he added. 'I would never have started if I didn't believe I had a chance of getting a grand prix. It has been an uphill fight all the way. Like a man with a wooden leg chasing a hare ... but I always thought there would be a way.'

12 APRIL 1993

SENNA SHOWS HIS GENIUS IN DOWNPOUR AT DONINGTON

Timothy Collings

Ayrton Senna can have won few greater victories in his extraordinary career than that in the cloud-bursts which turned the European Grand Prix at Donington Park yesterday into a lottery. Starting fourth on the grid in a near downpour, he combined inspired tactics with sheer good fortune to steer his McLaren to the 38th win of his career. It was a victory to savour not only for the 33-year-old Brazilian, still driving on a race-by-race agreement with the team, but also for the drenched 50,000 crowd – a disappointing attendance for Tom Wheatcroft's first grand prix at his Leicestershire track.

Where others slid and spun in ever-changing track conditions, Senna was steady all the way from green lights to chequered flag. Showing uncanny car control on slick tyres, he finished a lap ahead of all his rivals except Damon Hill, who brought his Williams home 1 minute 23.199 seconds behind the McLaren. Alain Prost, who had challenged strongly early in the race before suffering a catastrophic pit-stop, was third in the second Williams, one lap down, ahead of Johnny Herbert's Lotus. Italians Riccardo Patrese, in the new Benetton, and Fabrizio Barbazza, in a Minardi, were fifth and sixth respectively. It was Barbazza's first championship point.

Senna's victory lifted him 12 points clear of Prost in the early stages of the drivers' championship and left McLaren and Williams level on 26 points in the constructors' title race. 'It was fantastic,' said Senna, who had been hoping for a wet race to negate the power advantage of the Williams cars. 'The conditions were unpredictable and, of course, unknown, too. On a circuit like this you have to commit yourself to a corner before you have any feeling for it. If you try too hard, you are off, and if you try too easy, they come and get you. So it is tremendous, not just for me but for Formula One.'

Looking back on the race, Senna said: 'I didn't have a particularly good start, I think. Not a fantastic one. I think I even lost a place. But then I started to recover at the first corner, under braking, and through the next few corners. I knew I was going for it. I had to go for the maximum while the conditions were very much unknown. Technically, they [Williams] are superior. There is no doubt about that and only in conditions like these can you make something up before they settle down and know what pace they had to go. It worked perfectly.'

There was an early departure, again, for Michael Andretti in the second McLaren, following a first-lap collision with Karl Wendlinger's Sauber. But, as the conditions changed after the opening laps, a fascinating tactical contest unfolded with Prost and Senna each attempting to anticipate the conditions with their pit-stops for tyre changes from wets to slicks and back again. Two pit-stops appeared effectively to decide the outcome. The first, after 33 laps, saw Senna slowed severely by a problem when his right rear wheel cross-threaded as he changed from wets to slicks. Prost, for the first time since he had failed to make the most of the 23rd pole position of his career, was in command again. Another weather change, however, persuaded the Frenchman to return early for a premature change back to wet-weather tyres after 38 laps, and this proved costly. Senna regained the lead, and Prost had to pit again to return to slicks on lap 48, this time stalling his engine.

'I was disappointed,' said Prost. 'It was not the way I wanted the race to go at all. I lost around 30 or 40 seconds because of it. The clutch was becoming difficult and that is why I stalled, but I had a gearbox problem from the start. The car was not handling badly on wet tyres but on slicks I think the front pressure was too low, and the car was very difficult to drive. At least I got four points, and there is still a long way to go in the championship.'

In the end, Prost totalled seven visits to the pits, Hill six and Senna five, though one of the latter's was literally a flying visit as he came in and drove by without stopping. 'I called for wets,' said Senna, 'but they were not ready. We do not communicate too well on the radio at the moment.' This came at the end of lap 57 after which Senna elected to stay out and perform near miracles before eventually pitting for the desired wet-weather tyres ten laps later. 'I made sure they were ready that time and we did a good stop,' said Senna.

Senna's brilliance could not completely overshadow several other splendid drives including those of Hill, who followed up his first podium finish in Brazil with another demonstration of his rapidly maturing talent, Herbert and Brazil's latest prodigy, Rubens Barrichello, who was classified 11th after running third for most of the race in his Jordan. Hill said: 'The race was a nightmare. I have to say it was the worst race you would ever want to be in because you just didn't know what was going to happen. You could see the clouds on one part of the circuit and the umbrellas up, and on another part it was dry. I don't really know how I came second, because I didn't know where I was for a lot of the race.'

Herbert showed the sense of a veteran in judging his pit-stops to a minimum and staying out of trouble. He stopped just once, after 12 laps. 'Unless it was really wet, there wasn't much difference between slicks and wets,' he said. 'And the wets wouldn't have lasted long in the dry periods. I just kept going and it paid off.'

Barrichello, 20, in only his third Formula One race, started 12th on the grid, was fourth at the end of the first lap and third when he retired with a broken fuel pump four laps from the end. Like many of the leading drivers, he had benefited from traction control in the conditions which saw only 11 of the 25 starters classified as finishers. Unfortunately, the lost included both the British Ligier drivers, Martin Brundle and Mark Blundell, and Derek Warwick, who had looked certain of scoring points in the first outing of the new Mugen-Honda until a gearbox failure after 66 laps. He was in good company, however, as both Ferraris, both Saubers, and Michael Schumacher's Benetton also departed early on a day which belonged to Senna.

13 APRIL 1993

HOW SLICK SENNA PUT THE SKIDS UNDER ARCH-RIVAL

James Hunt

His command of the race was so absolute that the Grand Prix of Europe became the grand prix of Ayrton Senna. While the changing weather caught out many drivers, it provided Senna with the opportunity to use his superior skills to overcome the handicap of having the second-best car. Displaying pure genius in mastering the constantly changing track conditions, his brilliant driving in the rain was matched by his superb tactics.

The alternating wet and dry surface produced a race that must have set a record for pit-stops to change tyres. Senna timed his four changes to perfection, not only with careful regard to the track conditions, but also in such a way that he covered any move by the vainly pursuing Williamses of Damon Hill and Alain Prost. Senna's win was set up by the most sensational first lap I can remember in a GP. Realising that the Williams cars have at least as big an advantage in wet conditions as dry, Senna resolved to get in front of them before Hill and Prost could hit their stride. However, Senna fell back to fifth place going into the first corner.

Then – on a wet track and on two difficult corners – he swept majestically round the outside of the two cars separating him from the Williams team-mates. They, too, were duly picked off before the end of the lap, and, while his rivals either fell foul of the conditions or gingerly felt them out, Senna stormed away to establish a seven-second lead in just five laps. With this lead and his genius on slick tyres in damp conditions, Senna was able to control the race, using the mastery of tactics which he began to add to his repertoire in 1990 and has now perfected to such an extent one wonders how Prost was ever regarded as the master tactician.

But for two pieces of minor misfortune, Senna would have had the race won before half-distance. While the Williams drivers had taken the soft option and changed to the more sure-footed wet-weather tyres as rain began to fall again, Senna, correctly, decided to stay on slicks until such time as he began to lap more slowly than those on wets – which did not happen.

Luck intervened for Williams just as their hastiness in changing tyres was beginning to look embarrassing. The rain suddenly increased to the extent that Senna was forced to go in for a tyre change immediately. Equally suddenly the rain abated and with Senna's lead reduced, the race was alive again. Had Senna been able to delay his decision for two laps he would not have needed to make those two pit-stops, and when the Williams cars changed back to slicks he would have been nearly a lap ahead. In any case, the proceedings were further enlivened by Senna's second misfortune.

During his stop to change back to dry tyres the McLaren team had a problem with replacing a rear wheel, and the delay cost Senna the lead. However, justice was soon done, and, appropriately, the architect was the man whom Senna had run rings round all day. As the next shower began, Prost immediately surrendered the lead by diving into the pits again, without any regard for the fact that the track was still much more suited to slicks. Indeed, it stayed that way, because the shower soon stopped. But the Williams team, doubtless influenced by Prost's supposedly superior race-craft, called in Hill. By the time the Williams pair made yet another pit-stop to change back to dry tyres, Senna had lapped them both.

Prost's oft-stated distaste for wet weather has seemed in the past to be accompanied by an inability to think, or compete. This was never more obvious than at Donington, where he seemed to get more flustered and distracted as the race progressed. He visited the pits with such frequency it appeared he might prefer to say there. Every time he saw a spot of rain he came in; his seven pit-stops set the record for the day.

Senna saved the final, crushing humiliation for the post-race press conference. There, a rather sheepish Prost cited a variety of technical trivia (incorrect tyre pressures, faulty gearbox, difficult clutch) by way of excuse. Senna, again with incisive timing, suggested that perhaps Prost would like to swap cars.

Hill again drove a well-managed race. Because he does not have enough experience, the timing of his stops was stage-managed by the team, but Hill did all the rest. This was an impressively competent job in the treacherous conditions, and he thoroughly deserved his second place.

Johnny Herbert showed what could be done by simply staying out on the track and driving as quickly as possible according to the conditions. The timing of his one and only tyre stop, from wets to dries, was well judged. He came in earlier, rather than later, and fourth place was just reward for himself and Team Lotus. Young Rubens Barrichello was terribly unlucky to miss out on the points he deserved. In only his third GP, he was running third or fourth all day until his Jordan failed with a few laps left.

Michael Andretti's third accident in as many GPs does not augur well, unless he changes his ways. He sorely needed a finish in this race but threw it all away on the first lap, when he drove his McLaren into the back of Karl Wendlinger's Sauber, taking them both off. Andretti came to F1 with a reputation as a charger and a winner in Indy Cars. But my fear was always that charging in that series is very different from charging against fit and fast young F1 drivers who also want to win badly. So far, Andretti has not yet shown the speed of a top F1 driver, nor the ability to avoid others when racing. He is under pressure to deliver soon.

22 MAY 1993

HILL STEADIES HIMSELF TO FOLLOW THE FAMILY LINE

James Hunt

The prospect of racing through the unforgiving streets of Monaco presents Michael Andretti with a particular dilemma. This race could be pivotal to his Formula One future, and Andretti must decide whether to attack the tightest street circuit of them all or treat it with the circumspection normally expected from newcomers. But the latter course of action is not really open to Andretti, whose poor season to date – only one finish in five starts and a marked lack of speed when he did finish – leaves him with little choice other than to drive hard. Andretti's recognised prowess on the street circuits in the American IndyCar Series should stand him in good stead, but none is as narrow and treacherous as Monaco.

Working against him is the new rule limiting drivers to only 21 laps in practice and 12 laps of qualifying, today and on Saturday. This is plenty of time for any competent driver to learn an ordinary circuit, where one's limits can be found by exceeding them, then tailoring back as required. But there are no run-off areas at Monaco, and any mistakes usually end in sharp contact with the barriers lining the track, which can result in a damaged car. Unless it can be repaired, its driver will be sidelined because of another new rule this season, which forbids the use of spare cars during practice and qualifying. For a driver trying to learn the circuit this would be disastrous, and it is the fear of falling foul of this rule that put tremendous pressure on Andretti during qualifying.

Monaco has to be learned slowly by inching up to the limit. To come to grips with the sinuous nature of its 2.886-mile circuit, a driver must develop a rhythm. Andretti is further disadvantaged by the fact that all his rivals have raced here before, even the newcomers. The race part of the Monaco Grand Prix takes place in qualifying and at the start, on the run to the first corner, Ste Dévote. This is a very tight, second-gear, right-hander which filters the cars into single file. Thereafter, the race becomes a high-speed procession in which places are normally only gained by way of another's misfortune, rather than by overtaking, which is normally at the peril of the cars involved.

This event will be a big occasion for Damon Hill, who can benefit from the splendid example of his father Graham, who won in Monte Carlo five times. Graham Hill achieved this by employing a simple tactic to great effect: steadiness, rather than speed, in order to finish the race. Using similar strategy, and the benefit of his Williams superiority, Damon can get a very good result without making the mistake of trying to compete, in terms of speed, with the two drivers who have monopolised this event for the last nine years. Ayrton Senna is also a five-times winner at Monaco, while Alain Prost has four victories to his credit.

Last year Williams's mechanical superiority over McLaren was enormous, with Senna being completely outpaced by Nigel Mansell, yet still managing to win, albeit luckily, when Mansell made a pit-stop. This year, though the Williams chassis is still better, I think the McLaren is greatly improved, with a much more driveable chassis and engine. Monaco's slower speeds will reduce the impact of the horsepower advantage Prost's Renault enjoys over Senna's Ford engine, and Senna's driving brilliance could well fill the remaining performance gap between the two cars. Of those who harbour hopes of breaking the monopoly, Michael Schumacher, Jean Alesi, Hill and Gerhard Berger have the most realistic, but still slim, chances. Monaco is a particularly important race for Senna, who must hope to win or at least outpoint Prost on one of the few circuits where they are on a more equal footing. Should he fail to do so the world championship may be beyond Senna's reach.

In qualifying, Monaco produces grand prix racing at its best. For the world's top drivers, wrestling half a ton of 800-horsepower car at full speed round these twisty, hilly and narrow streets is a unique and important challenge. To behold at close quarters it is truly awe-inspiring. I intend making my annual pilgrimage to the corner in the tunnel for Saturday's final qualifying session, a view of Formula One cars I consider to be the most dramatic anywhere.

They enter the tunnel by way of Le Portier, a slow first-gear corner, followed by hard acceleration through the gears along the short stretch of sea wall before entering the black hole that announces it on a sunny day. Halfway through the tunnel there is a sharp bend which, taken flat out, is right on the limits of adhesion. It is on the outside of the exit, just a few feet from the barrier and peeping from behind a huge pillar, there to protect the spectators from flying debris, that I station myself. I hear the muted engine note of a car leaving Le Portier, rushing up through the gears from first to fifth before it explodes into sight at 150-plus mph, entering the corner with an all-enveloping cacophony of amplified sound.

By the apex of the corner the car is heading straight at me, straining for the grip to hold the line to the exit, and, as the mind struggles to keep up, it passes at 160mph, still accelerating hard and hugging the road as it crests the brow of the hill down to the chicane. The tunnel at Monaco is unique for me, being the only place that's more exciting outside than inside a Formula One car.

BRAZILIAN CROWNED PRINCE OF MONACO

James Hunt

There was never a dull moment in the streets of Monaco, where the non-stop drama — aggressive driving, high-speed traffic jams, spins, collisions and retirements — tended to draw attention away from the considerable achievement of the winner. Ayrton Senna's drive was well-judged and immaculate in concept and execution, as he used all his Monaco experience and tactical skill to maximum effect. Though it owed something to the problems which afflicted his two main rivals, Senna's record-breaking sixth victory in one of the most difficult of all grand prix races was entirely deserved.

It was apparent from the start that Senna, nursing a sore thumb from his practice crash, was driving according to a plan. He avoided trying to race the quicker cars of Alain Prost and Michael Schumacher, both of whom had outqualified him. Instead he played a waiting game. His first bonus was the ten-second penalty imposed on Prost for jumping the start. I thought this was harsh, and Prost felt it was one of the best starts of his career. If he was guilty, then Prost was unlucky to get caught, because jumped starts are not often penalised. He was creeping forward before the start as a result of his clutch dragging — but this is normally ignored by the stewards — and he didn't actually 'hit it' until the green light.

Prost had a bad day at Monaco to add to his list of woes this season. Following his flawed performances in the Brazilian and European GPs, he managed to throw away the good chance he had of winning this race. He stalled his engine twice when trying to set off after his penalty, by failing to apply throttle when releasing the clutch, a process learnt by drivers the world over long before they shed their L-plates. A senior member of the Williams team seemed incredulous after the race as he explained that the telemetry (which records the movements of all the controls) had shown no throttle-opening at the two stalled attempts. Getting a Formula One car moving from a stationary position is a lot more difficult than a road car and always requires concentration. But a GP driver is expected to have it mastered long before he races an F1 car.

When Prost finally got away again it was initially at such a reduced pace that I mistakenly thought he had a problem with the car. However, as others fell out and he got a whiff of some points, he speeded up again to finish fourth, one lap down to Senna. If Prost is to take the world championship as comfortably as he ought to he will need to stop throwing away points and regain the concentration that has made him the most successful driver of all time in terms of wins and points.

Schumacher suffered even worse luck when enjoying the lead he inherited from Prost. The active suspension failure which caused his retirement before half-distance was costly for the spectators, too, because Senna was starting to push Schumacher to try to force him into changing tyres. With Schumacher's departure Senna was able to stop for fresh tyres of his own, and there were no further challenges to his lead.

Damon Hill, in his first Monaco start, wisely chose not to race Senna, and his second place came despite an admitted hesitancy when lapping slower cars. Hill was not afraid to admit his wariness in traffic, and most welcome, too, was his generous and touching post-race tribute to Senna, who took away the record of five Monaco wins established by Damon's father, Graham.

Though his criticism of Gerhard Berger was restrained, Hill had every right to be angry about the unprovoked attack which could easily have put him out of the race, as it did Berger's Ferrari. It was really quite over the top for a man as experienced as Berger to attempt such a wild overtaking move. However, in comparison to their poor form, this was an excellent race for Ferrari, and Jean Alesi's third place was a result of competitiveness rather than simply reliability. This will be an important morale-booster for the team and we must hope that Ferrari continue to make progress.

Monaco was always going to be difficult for Michael Andretti, but he made it even harder when he ran into another car on the first lap and had to stop for repairs. Andretti's plan was to drive conservatively and stay out of trouble. He failed in the latter, again, and also failed to show the speed which would make his frequent misdemeanours more forgettable. Andretti was 1.4 seconds slower than team-mate Senna in qualifying, a large deficit which was reproduced exactly in their respective fastest race laps. This time difference represents a different level of driving and is a gap which Andretti must start to bridge very soon if he is to make his mark in F1. Despite Andretti's contribution of only two points, McLaren are still only 11 points behind the mechanically superior Williams team in the constructors' championship. In the drivers' championship, Senna has again overtaken Prost: a remarkable accomplishment and testimony to the ability of the best driver in the world.

15 JUNE 1993

SENNA'S DISPLAY OF GENIUS HAS SCHUMACHER IN SLIPSTREAM

James Hunt

Though it tended to be processional, I found the Canadian Grand Prix thoroughly entertaining. While the intensity of action in the early laps made them quite thrilling, the last half of the race was equally engrossing. For Alain Prost this race must have come as something of a relief. His confident control and consistent speed in the race in Montreal, where he enjoyed probably his smallest car advantage to date, showed us that the Prost of old is alive and well. His performance did a lot to allay the criticisms of his driving that have tended to overshadow his season so far.

Ayrton Senna's opening laps were, I thought, those of a genius, and at least equal to the way he simply threw himself past the opposition in the rain at Donington. Spine-tingling to see, Senna's charge from eighth on the grid to third by the second lap was nevertheless supremely controlled. At no time did he look as if he was going to go off himself or take anyone else off. Thereafter, his momentum hardly slackened, and he was eventually able to take command of second place despite having a car inferior to his closest challengers.

The latter stages of the race, following the pit-stops for fresh tyres, were best appreciated by focusing on the gaps between the leading cars. We had the spectacle of the eventual winner, Prost, having to work hard to regain control of the race after his stop. Meanwhile, Michael Schumacher was charging after Senna and, though the traffic they encountered changed the interval between them from time to time, their battle for second place was riveting. Here we had probably the greatest driver of all time being chased by the heir apparent. Not to be outdone by Senna, Schumacher's early laps were similarly spectacular, if less visible, because he was back in the pack, after his car's traction control played tricks on him at the start, and he lost several places. That these two drivers should find places to pass where others feared to tread in Montreal is no coincidence. Schumacher quickly regained most of his lost ground and by the time the tyre stops were complete he was right back in the race, ahead of Hill and only a few seconds behind Senna. What a pity that within three laps of Schumacher finally catching Senna, their conflict was resolved by the mechanical problems – an alternator failure – which put Senna out of the race.

Damon Hill deserved his third place after driving a good, solid race, but when he found himself right behind Senna and Schumacher after the tyre stops I would have liked to have seen him stay with them. Earlier, Prost was able to drive away from Hill unchallenged in an identical car, and this, together with Hill's inability to keep pace with Senna and Schumacher in inferior cars, raises questions about Hill's outright speed. Granted, the other three drivers are among the fastest in Formula One, but Hill, quite rightly, has high ambitions and will be looking to pick up his pace.

Less becoming to the sport is the awkward way the powers-that-be announced that 24 of the 25 cars on the grid in Canada were illegal – though, it was decreed, they would be allowed to race. Although the cars in question were undoubtedly contravening long-standing regulations concerning aerodynamic devices moveable when the car is in motion, and similarly control of the propulsion systems of the car, most had been doing so for some time. It is transparently obvious that this development is a political manoeuvre by FISA, the governing body, to counter the intransigent and isolated position the McLaren and Williams teams have taken over the proposed rule changes that will ban some of the technology next year. But the fact that FISA are being forced to handle it in this very public way on the doorstep of the IndyCar series, by which Formula One feels it is being bruised, is unfortunate.

Everybody accepts that rule changes are urgently needed, firstly to halt the two-tier structure that has developed between the haves and the have-nots. The success of the top teams brings them more sponsorship to further develop the technical advantages they have over the others. Meanwhile, the consequent lack of success of the less financially endowed teams leaves them struggling more to survive than to improve.

Secondly, for sporting reasons, the insidious advance of computer technology needs to be reversed in all areas in which it has taken over the driver's job. What worries me is that, instead of wasting enormous amounts of energy in fighting each other over procedures and detail, FISA and the McLaren-Williams alliance should be combining all their considerable knowledge and experience on the real issue. This is to create a climate in which 30 or more cars – of which at least half should be fully competitive, if driven well enough – can compete for 26 places on the starting grid at an affordable price.

At a recent meeting of the teams on this subject, I understand that McLaren stated that the 'name of the game' is to win races. Robin Herd, of the Larrousse team, pointed out that this was secondary to the necessity of 'staying in business'. Hear, hear! To satisfy both requirements the goal should be to create an environment similar to the halcyon days of the mid-1970s when the sport was at its most competitive and affordable.

16 JUNE 1993

JAMES HUNT FOUND DEAD AT HIS HOME
Jenny Rees

James Hunt, the 1976 Formula One motor racing champion and BBC commentator, was found dead at his home in Wimbledon, south-west London, yesterday. It is believed he had suffered a heart attack in his sleep. The news of his death, at the age of 45, shocked everyone involved in motor racing, many of whom were making their way home from the Canadian Grand Prix in Montreal.

Mr Hunt's body was found by an old school friend who had stayed overnight after playing snooker with him on Monday evening. The friend said: 'When he had not come down to breakfast I went up to wake him, but could not rouse him. I immediately feared the worst. I called an ambulance, but it was too late. He had a heart attack in his sleep. I am absolutely devastated. James was in top form and seemed in good health.'

Mr Hunt, who retired from Grand Prix racing in 1979, was seen by BBC viewers on Sunday, commentating on the Canadian Grand Prix. He also wrote in the sports pages of *The Daily Telegraph* – his last column appeared yesterday. Murray Walker, a fellow commentator for the past 13 years, said: 'I am completely overwhelmed. On Sunday James was his usual ebullient self, and his commentary was as good as ever. He was one of those rare things, a sportsman who had not only risen to the top, but was highly articulate and could talk about it.'

Lord Hesketh, Mr Hunt's former Grand Prix team boss, said: 'It is no exaggeration to say that I am absolutely shattered. I would look at myself and then at him, and he seemed so fit. He not only drove with me, but he was a great friend. I know his record in racing will stand. He was truly outstanding and he represented the archetypal British sportsman.'

Lord Hesketh and Mr Hunt became Britain's most famous racing partnership of the 1970s when the peer spent a large part of his personal fortune to set up and maintain his racing team. 'He was known as Hunt the Shunt. No one would hire him. I had a machine no one wanted to drive. A few months later we were in Formula Two, and three months after that in Formula One. Eighteen months later we were fourth in the world championship.'

Jackie Stewart, a world champion three times, said: 'One of the great things for me has been the way he lived life his way. He was very unconventional.' Friends said that Mr Hunt, once a heavy smoker, had given up cigarettes and was not drinking. He had financial problems. Although he was reported to have left racing with more than £1 million, he had recently applied for legal aid to sue solicitors acting for him during his divorce from his second wife, Sarah Lomax. They parted in 1988, having had two sons. His first marriage, to Suzy Miller, the former model, ended in 1980, and she later married Richard Burton. Mr Hunt was frequently seen in Wimbledon riding a bicycle, telling friends he could only afford to run an old Austin A35 van.

16 JUNE 1993

FREE SPIRIT WITH ABILITY TO DAZZLE AS A TOP DRIVER

TRIBUTE TO JAMES HUNT, F1 CHAMPION AND FORTHRIGHT COMMENTATOR

Timothy Collings

James Hunt was a warm, generous and independent man. He was a free spirit who enjoyed a full and colourful life, adding both a waspish humour and a serious understanding of the business to any sporting company. He was also a brilliant driver who won the world championship in 1976. Motor racing suffered a deep loss with his death yesterday, aged 45.

No grand prix paddock will seem quite the same again, and he will be missed sorely next month when the British Grand Prix takes place at Silverstone. Always a maverick, James enjoyed a reputation for his eventful lifestyle, his sometimes light-hearted approach to conventions and his outspoken views as a television commentator with the BBC, alongside Murray Walker – and, of course, in his columns this season in *The Daily Telegraph*.

During his racing years he had an image as a playboy, with his blond hair, his sense of fun, his enjoyment of Champagne and pretty girls. All this was true, as two broken marriages and several years of adventurous living, which led to financial difficulties, proved. But none of it reflected the more relaxed and assured man he became in recent years, or threw sufficient praise on the talent which enabled him to become the first Englishman to win the world title since Graham Hill triumphed in 1968.

For much of his career, it seemed that James treated motor racing as a great pleasure, a 'wheeze', something done for fun. 'The only reason I ever walked up and down the pit road when I was a driver was to look at the crumpet,' he admitted a year or two ago. But this was only a superficial view of an inconsistent, but sometimes dazzling driver who had an enormous impact on Formula One. James captured the imagination of a generation of racing fans with his stylish progress to the championship, won by just one point, from Niki Lauda (who retired because of the conditions on the second lap), when he finished third in the rain at Mount Fuji in Japan on 24 October 1976. He had been running fifth with only a handful of laps remaining, but with typical competitive spirit fought his way through to take the title in utterly atrocious conditions.

'He was a bloody good driver, a very intelligent racer and so competitive that he would fight for every last fraction of an inch of the road,' said John Watson yesterday. 'He was very strong physically, and very athletic, and he brought those qualities with him into his driving. It is ironic that, after driving those 92 grands prix in the 1970s, he should go now in his middle forties. It's so hard to equate.'

This same competitiveness remained with him in his attitudes to all forms of sport. He lived his life the way he wanted, with his right foot down on the pedal, but he was fit and well, having given up drinking and smoking, and cycling several miles each day, before the heart attack while he slept at home in Wimbledon.

Born on 29 August 1947, he was educated at Wellington. His competitive sporting prowess showed early in his life, and he competed in Junior Wimbledon tennis and was a squash player to county standard. But it was cars not rackets which captured him, and he chose to race first Minis and then, in 1968, Formula Ford, before going on to break into Formula Three the following year, when his outstanding performances earned him the Grovewood Award and his less-outstanding ones the soubriquet 'Hunt the Shunt'.

In earlier times – particularly when he was driving for Lord Alexander Hesketh's charismatic, if small, team – James had earned himself a reputation as a leader of riotous parties. He had grown up in the 1960s and not been short of disposable income. On one occasion, in Rio de Janeiro, it is said James relied upon his instant good humour and adroit sense of fun when he was caught riding up in a lift in the old-fashioned Copacabana Palace Hotel one night with a lady whose skin was many shades darker than his own light complexion. When faced by an angry desk clerk, who informed him that ladies were not allowed in the guests' bedrooms, the instant reply was: 'What do you mean? This is my sister.'

Such adventures are just part of the folklore which went with Hunt from the earliest days of his career, when it was once supposed he would become a doctor. Instead, he worked in a hospital as a porter and later became an ice cream salesman in order to help fund his motor racing instruction.

In recent times, however, James had devoted himself to his children whenever possible, and on one recent occasion when I called him he told me he would ring me back because 'I've got to nip out and buy the fish and chips for their supper'. Life was different, but he seemed to enjoy the role of the middle-aged and responsible parent.

James was the icon of his age in the 1970s, and he will never be forgotten by that generation, who enjoyed his presence in the gossip columns as much as his speed on the track, or by modern admirers for his forthright commentaries.

19 JUNE 1993

LETTERS TO THE SPORTS EDITOR

DEATH OF HUNT LEAVES SAD VOID

Sir,

On a sad day for British and international motor racing, what a pleasure it was to read James Hunt's final column in *The Daily Telegraph* following the Canadian Grand Prix last Sunday.

It was with great sadness that I heard of his untimely death because it is my opinion that he was not only one of the finest racing drivers this country has ever produced, but was also one of the sport's finest commentators. Not only did he provide the perfect foil for the effervescent Murray Walker on BBC Television, but after every grand prix I would wait eagerly to read his views on the race as published in your paper. His intriguing personal insight into the turbo-charged world of Formula One motor racing was quite superb, and, though he was a great ambassador for his sport on the world stage, he was also willing to make constructive criticisms of the sport's running – suggesting, in his last article, how to make an increasingly professional sport more exciting to the public.

I can only say, as a young and avid follower of all motorsport, that his departure will leave a large void and I shall miss his informed comments.

Peter Harding, 19
Tavistock, Devon

Sir,

I for one will greatly miss James Hunt, both for his TV comments and, more especially, his superb articles in your paper on the Tuesday after each race. He seemed to understand the true nature of great driving far better than most of the scribes of the specialist motoring magazines. Those of us who like to read the unbiased truth (or at least reasoned opinion) are the losers.

Robin Sturrock
Arbroath

16 AUGUST 1993

FORTUNE FAVOURS HILL FOR HIS FIRST GP WIN

Timothy Collings in Budapest

Lady Luck finally smiled on Damon Hill in the scorching sunshine of the Hungaroring yesterday when he claimed his first Formula One triumph with a controlled, but nerve-wracking victory in his Williams after a battle of attrition in the Hungarian Grand Prix. After his jinx-riddled month of July, when he was denied victory when leading in both the British and German grands prix, the son of double world champion Graham had a full measure of good fortune yesterday as he took advantage of the problems which hit all his rivals.

Hill, 32, finished a comfortable 1 minute 11 seconds clear of second-placed Riccardo Patrese, in a Benetton, while two further Englishmen, Derek Warwick, who finished fourth in a Mugen-Honda, and Martin Brundle, fifth in a Ligier, were also in the points as temperatures reached 100°F. It was Warwick's best finish since 1988.

Hill had every reason to enjoy the celebrations which followed his first win in his 13th grand prix race. 'It is an overwhelming feeling, and I am a little lost for the words I need to describe it,' said Hill, who bowed theatrically from the podium to the cheering crowds, before he dedicated his win to the Hill family 'past, present and future'.

'I would like to thank everyone who has helped me get to the position where I can compete in a Williams and to thank the team for the opportunity to drive for them and to win grands prix. This is a tough circuit, and it was a long race. I had a big lead, and my greatest difficulty was in maintaining my concentration. That was my only problem, as both my pit-stops were perfect and I had a lot more luck than in the last few races. With about 20 laps to go I was thinking of what to say at the end, and I kept telling myself, "It's not over until it's over", and I thought of my dad. I thought of him telling me to concentrate. He was a hard task-master, and that was enough to clear my mind and keep my concentration.'

Hill's victory completed the first father-and-son grand prix double in the Formula One world championship since it started in 1950 and brought the Hills their first win since Graham triumphed at Monaco in 1969. 'I am thrilled for him,' said team owner Frank Williams. 'It was obvious from the first few races that he could win and that he could cut the mustard.'

27 SEPTEMBER 1993

PROST BOWS OUT ON BITTER NOTE
AFTER CLINCHING HIS FOURTH TITLE

Timothy Collings in Estoril

Alain Prost finally ended the suspense and Damon Hill's outside hopes of glory by claiming his fourth world drivers' championship yesterday. But he did it without delivering the victory he wanted, as Michael Schumacher overcame a weekend riddled with problems to win an eventful Portuguese Grand Prix at the Autodromo do Estoril.

Schumacher, recovering from what had seemed to be chronic handling difficulties by switching to his spare Benetton, took command of a remarkable race by making an early pit-stop, which helped him take the lead after 30 of the 71 laps, and then choosing to go the distance without another change of rubber. As in Belgium last year, when he won his maiden victory, it was an inspired tactical decision by the 24-year-old German. Not even Prost, in his faster Williams, could overhaul him as the pair raced home separated by only nine-tenths of a second.

Hill, the only man with even a slender hope of preventing his Williams team-mate from taking the title, finished third, eight seconds further back, after a memorable drive from the back of the grid, enforced by another calamitous Williams start. The result took Prost to an unbeatable 87 points in the championship, with two races remaining. Hill is second on 62, and Senna third on 53, one more than Schumacher. To his credit, Hill showed no disappointment and warmly congratulated the Frenchman, who will head into retirement with the 1993 title added to those he won in 1985, 1986 and 1989.

'It was my challenge to win the fourth title at the start of the year, and I have done it,' said Prost, who barely raised a smile. 'I'm glad to be retiring. There is no temptation at all for me to come back again. I chose to stop on winning my fourth title because the game just is not worth the candle any more. The rules are not the same for everyone.'

Instead of joy, there was a trace of bitterness. Instead of satisfaction, there seemed to be frustration. Prost seemed happier to have completed his last grand prix on European soil than to have moved into the history books as the only man, other than five-times champion Juan Manuel Fangio, to have secured four titles.

Prost's drive was not the story of the race, however, on a day of almost endless incidents and accidents. He had looked worried at the start, but he need not have been. At the start of the final warm-up lap, Hill struggled and then stalled. It was a Prost-style misfortune, and it left him stranded, forced to start from the back. Team orders had been the worry beforehand for Hill, but this seemed to obliterate any prospects of their use.

30 SEPTEMBER 1993

FAREWELL TO A LONE HUNTER WHO LIVED IN THE FAST LANE

Paul Hayward at James Hunt's memorial service

The last time James Hunt was involved in a memorial service he arrived by push bike and changed in the street outside the church. Yesterday it was his turn to be remembered, and everyone turned up the conventional way, knowing just what sport had lost by his death. It was a genteel and sober remembrance of a life that was anything but placid and reflective. Mercifully, there was no attempt to conceal the excesses. Hunt the Formula One champion was celebrated alongside Hunt the insatiable hedonist, and it made his departure at the age of 45 all the harder to countenance.

Everybody possesses a James Hunt story. Murray Walker, his fellow BBC commentator, recalled Hunt arriving for work one day with 'no shoes, a T-shirt, a pair of shorts that had seen better days and a bottle of rosé'. Lord Hesketh, for whom Hunt drove before joining McLaren, called him 'a combination of the Corinthian Casual and the anarchist'. 'In that,' Hesketh said, 'he represented something very, very English.'

Many of the tales are unprintable, but all are told with admiration and relish. McLaren's team manager in the 1970s, Alistair Caldwell, remembered the night Hunt enjoyed a liaison with the hotel band's female singer every time she took her 30-minute coffee break. 'I tried to get him to bed at ten o'clock,' Caldwell said outside St James's Church, Piccadilly, where the service was held yesterday, 'but this band went on till three in the morning, and James was a bit the worse for wear. The next day he drove the race of his life.'

This was one of the paradoxes of Hunt's life. Behind the indulgent tendencies that led him at different times to tobacco, alcohol, cocaine and marijuana, Hunt was a high achiever who brought to his television and newspaper journalism the same standards he applied on the track. Caldwell recounted the McLaren team feeling they 'had got stuck' with Hunt when he joined the operation as No. 1 driver – but that unflattering early judgment soon gave way to an appreciation of his ability and courage.

He danced perilously close to three evils of boredom, vice and poverty, but the abiding image of his final moments is of him cycling from Wimbledon to the BBC's headquarters in Shepherd's Bush and doing a full day's work just 24 hours before his death from a heart attack.

Some people are grotesquely inflated and purified by retrospective verdicts. Hunt was merely illuminated by a clearer, stronger light. 'Most of us stand out like grey outside black,' Walker said in a gentle indictment of the kind of conformity Hunt found so alien. 'James was a likeable, warm, different kind of human being. He didn't think like other people.'

Yesterday's service was, in part, an exotic gathering of fellow daredevils, spurned girlfriends and blue-blooded mavericks. It is 17 years since Hunt won his only world championship, but the fascination with him is undimmed. As Walker said: 'James raced in an era when it was possible to succeed and have fun at the same time.' We look at a life like Hunt's now and see the absence of humility and humour in contemporary sport. Hunt was 'a total non-conformist', Stirling Moss said. 'On occasions it was difficult to admit I knew him, never mind that he was my friend.'

The first time Walker worked with Hunt was at a 'very boring' Formula 5000 race at Silverstone, and he recalls the former champion lying on the floor with his foot in plaster, watching the race on a monitor. 'When I handed him the microphone and asked him to sum up, James just said, "What a load of rubbish".'

Nigel Davison, master in charge of Wellington College during Hunt's schooldays, told us that British motor racing's lost hero was 'not much interested in team games'. It was, Davison said, individual pursuits like 'squash, tennis, rackets and cross-country running that enthralled Hunt as a boy', and his words made sense, given the many descriptions of him as a lone hunter who would push his technicians to despair with his escapades during testing.

There were few of Hunt's old colleagues at yesterday's memorial service, but all spoke kindly of him when his absence from Walker's commentary box was eerily confirmed on the circuit this summer. 'James was the most charismatic person ever in F1,' Niki Lauda has said. When he was with McLaren, Hunt complained of being a 'human honey pot' for the media, yet only now is the full richness of his short journey emerging. In the words of the old hymn, Hunt was 'oft in danger, oft in woe'. 'Personal and financial problems had made things very tough for him,' Walker said of Hunt's later years, before he met Helen Dyson. 'But you'd never have known it.'

25 OCTOBER 1993

ROOKIE IRVINE DUSTS HIMSELF DOWN AFTER BUST-UP WITH RAGING SENNA

Timothy Collings at Suzuka

Eddie Irvine, the confident Ulsterman who was flattened by an angry Ayrton Senna after a controversial first drive on the grand prix circuit at Suzuka yesterday, is undaunted and already looking forward to his second appearance in Formula One. Irvine, who described Senna as 'a nutter' after being punched by the Brazilian, became the first debutant to earn a point since 1989 when he finished an incident-packed race in sixth place. He will drive again for the Jordan team in the Australian Grand Prix, the last of the season.

An old friend of Dubliner Eddie Jordan, the team owner, Irvine is the fifth man to have driven in the Jordan second seat this season, and his performance was by far the best of the five. The team's No. 1, Rubens Barrichello, finished fifth, and the three points earned by the pair were the first for the team in this year's constructors' championship.

Irvine, from Newtownards, is based in Japan and used his knowledge of the Suzuka circuit – he has won there on the Japanese F3000 circuit this year – to great effect, though he was criticised for his aggressive style by Senna and Derek Warwick. He drove extraordinarily well to qualify eighth on the grid, and again yesterday. Warwick, driven off the track at the chicane with five laps remaining and thus out of a potential sixth-place finish for Footwork Mugen Honda, contented himself with some finger-wagging before departing for a flight home.

The Brazilian, three times a world champion, had been incensed by Irvine's driving in his battle with Damon Hill for fourth position. Senna, a clear leader, was attempting to lap both British drivers, and had a clear view of what he described as 'unprofessional' driving by Irvine that was 'unworthy of Formula One'. He said: 'They were hitting each other and spinning off. I had to go off the circuit to avoid them. Then I managed to squeeze past when they were banging wheels, but suddenly I was disturbed again when the guy behind me came like a lunatic. If he [Irvine] is a back marker, he should respect someone who is one lap in front. It was dangerous.'

Hill had no complaints against Irvine, who started in Formula Ford 1600 in Ireland in 1983, drove Formula Three in Britain, then International Formula 3000. He is in his third full season on the Japanese Formula 3000 circuit, and with two races left he has a chance of the title. Formula Three driver Marc Goossens said: 'As far as I know he has never been rated as a wild driver.'

Senna, having driven quite superbly to claim the 40th victory of his career, should have been celebrating an afternoon of triumph with his McLaren team after a memorable race. Instead, with a near-perfect left hook in front of several witnesses, he flattened Irvine before being hauled away by two McLaren team officials and Jordan's commercial manager. Irvine's reaction was a mixture of surprise and disappointment. After rubbing his right temple and considering his position, he confirmed he was thinking of taking legal action against Senna, who was reported to the stewards for 'serious physical assault of another driver'.

The confident Irvine caught the full force of Senna's storm, chiefly because he refused to bow to him both on and off the track. 'He was between me and Hill when we were vying for fourth place,' he said. 'What does he want me to do, move over and follow him? Hill is not complaining. For him and me there were no problems. I think the guy [Senna] is a nutter. He is out of control. Completely out of control. And as far as the thing with Warwick was concerned, he was in big problems anyway. He braked far too early for the corner and I had nowhere to go.'

Given that he has been punished for previous misdemeanours off the track, Senna can expect a severe reprimand, at the very least, for his assault. It was the worst incident in Formula One since Nigel Mansell held Senna 'warmly by the throat' at Spa-Francorchamps in 1987.

8 NOVEMBER 1993

UNSENTIMENTAL SENNA HAS LAST WORD AS PROST EXITS WITH GRACE

Timothy Collings in Adelaide

Ayrton Senna made history and ended an era yesterday when he drove to his second successive victory and fifth win of the year with a flawless, emotion-charged performance in front of more than 97,000 spectators at the Australian Grand Prix. The Brazilian's 41st triumph, in his 158th race, was the perfect ending to his six-year roller-coaster career with McLaren. It established the Woking-based team as the most successful in Formula One history, with 104 wins.

It also denied Senna's great rival Alain Prost the victory he so wanted in his 199th and final grand prix. Prost, who finished second in his Williams, now heads into retirement with his family in Switzerland. His British teammate Damon Hill was third, but never threatened in a race which delivered little of the drama and melodrama which both preceded and followed it.

The race concluded one of sport's most intense and acrimonious rivalries. Senna admitted afterwards: 'Awards don't count very much to us. We both love motor racing. We both are world champions and despite the difficult times we've had in the past, today is the end of an era – for him and for me.' The post-race words from the two drivers who have dominated Formula One for a decade hardly amounted to reconciliation, though their half-embraces in the pit-lane and on the podium at least indicated a deep mutual respect.

Senna's performance – he dominated both qualifying and the 79-lap race – in his final drive for McLaren before replacing Prost at Williams, was one of his best of the year. Prost, who made a dignified exit after claiming four world titles in 13 years at the top, admitted as much. He was never in the hunt and had to save his energy for later in a race which had been preceded by two false starts for resisting a powerful challenge from Hill. The Englishman, third throughout except for pit-stops, ran within a second of Prost for several laps before attacking at the end of the straight on lap 68.

Ron Dennis, McLaren's managing director, seemed to greet his team's win with mixed feelings. 'It's a great way to finish the season,' he said. 'I hope Ayrton will enjoy his holiday in Didcot, though I also hope it's not too much of a success.'

The 38-year-old Prost was more generous to his old rival than might have been expected. 'I think we had good times,' he said. 'Very good times. Especially in 1988. And because I am retiring, I think it would be good to remember only the good times we had and the sporting aspect of our season in 1988, when he won the championship, and I finished second.'

Asked about his own future, Prost said: 'I think it will change very much. I hope I don't get fat and lazy, that's for sure. I will feel a little more free, and my life should be a little bit better. It's not easy to say what is going to be my life in the future. But I'm quite happy to change, and maybe I will be much, much happier. Or maybe not. I really don't know. But for sure my life will be different.'

25 MARCH 1994

SENNA TRACKS FOURTH WORLD CHAMPIONSHIP

Timothy Collings

Ten years after he made his Formula One debut with Toleman, Ayrton Senna's image, reputation and record set him apart from every other driver as he prepares for Sunday's Brazilian Grand Prix, the opening round of the 1994 world championship. He is the only former champion in the field, the only truly experienced race-winner, the richest and most confident, and he is acknowledged as the fastest and the best. He has also, by popular acknowledgement, the fastest car and most powerful engine in his Williams FW16.

For most observers, it is not a question of if Senna can win, but how he wins. Not only will he start the 1994 season as the outstanding favourite to claim his fourth world drivers' title, thereby drawing level with the tally of his arch-rival Alain Prost, but he will also be expected to set a host of records. The most vulnerable statistics will be Nigel Mansell's record number of wins in a season (nine in 1992) and Prost's record total of 51 victories. Senna has 41 now, but would have had more had his machinery at McLaren last year been as competitive as he demanded.

Determined but temperamental, Senna left McLaren for Williams last December to rekindle the motivation which had manifestly waned during his final months with the Woking-based team. With the threat of a return by the retired Prost (who flirted with the new McLaren in Estoril recently) now removed, Senna appears to have few true rivals outside his own team, unless the package of controversial rule changes is as effective as its creators hopes.

The rules have been altered substantially to ban computerised high-technology driver aids, such as traction control, active suspension, four-wheel steering and anti-lock braking, in an effort to make the racing more competitive after years of processions led by the technically superior and, usually, richest teams. All this, however, is unlikely to affect Senna, who will set the pace in what will be another season dominated by the power of the Anglo-French Williams-Renault combination.

Senna, who was 34 on Monday, is likely to have a commanding advantage over all his rivals, except Williams team-mate Damon Hill, who last year, in his first full season of Formula One, showed he was both a fast learner and a determined competitor by winning three races. Williams are seeking a third successive constructors' championship, and their supremacy has been such that in the 32 races since the start of 1992, when Nigel Mansell claimed the drivers' title, they have won 20 times. With Senna involved, there seems little likelihood of any dilution to their dominance.

The ever-improving Michael Schumacher, in the ever-improving Benetton, may run the Williams pair close on certain circuits, where handling counts for more than sheer power, and he may mount a challenge for the title himself, but he is unlikely to be able to sustain it unless Senna, or Hill, is handicapped by some unforeseen catastrophe. Thankfully, in an age of much greater safety this is unlikely, even with the return, after a decade, of refuelling during a race.

30 APRIL 1994

BARRICHELLO LUCKY TO SURVIVE SPECTACULAR 160MPH CRASH

Timothy Collings in Imola

Rubens Barrichello left the Autodromo Enzo e Dino Ferrari with a joke and a painful smile yesterday afternoon after escaping with his life from a spectacular 160mph crash during opening qualifying for tomorrow's San Marino Grand Prix. 'I'm off to play with the nurses now, but I'll be back tomorrow,' said the Jordan driver, through his lacerated and swollen lips, before being taken by ambulance to hospital in Bologna. 'I feel okay; it's just a bit difficult to breathe.' It was a brave display from a fortunate man. In reality, which will arrive for him this morning, he will know his part in this weekend's grand prix is over.

His accident overshadowed an outstanding performance from fellow Brazilian Ayrton Senna, who smashed the qualifying lap record to secure provisional pole position, and Barrichello's escape left even the most seasoned observers of Formula One's brushes with death amazed. The 21-year-old's accident, during which his airborne car flew over the tyre barrier, rebounded off the safety catch fence and, after pitching nose first into the ground, completed one-and-a-half barrel-rolls, came only 16 minutes into the opening qualifying session. For several minutes it appeared he must have suffered grievous injury, as Formula One's chief medical officer, Sid Watkins, attended to him with great care before he was transferred from cockpit to ambulance by stretcher.

His car, missing both right wheels, was hoisted away for examinations and repairs. At the same time, Barrichello — second behind Michael Schumacher in the drivers' championship after the opening two races this year — was undergoing X-rays and scans at the circuit medical centre. The examinations revealed no injuries other than those to his face — he broke his nose and bit through his lip. 'He's very lucky to get away with that,' said the head of his team, Eddie Jordan.

Senna, like Barrichello a man of São Paulo, admitted he was unable to concentrate on his work after the crash. 'I didn't feel I ever drove the car properly,' he said. 'It was all a bit chaotic. I was out there when he had the accident and after that I didn't drive well. I wasn't myself.'

Senna's supreme use of the powerful Renault V10 engine was enough, however, to lift him 0.4 seconds clear of Schumacher, who was disappointed with the handling of his Benetton on a hot afternoon which made the track more slippery.

I MAY 1994

FI WORLD LEFT SHAKEN BY RATZENBERGER'S DEATH

Timothy Collings in Imola

Roland Ratzenberger, one of the most popular drivers in Formula One, died at Imola after crashing during an attempt to qualify for only his second grand prix with the new Simtek team. The 31-year-old Austrian was a close friend of many of his fellow competitors. Nothing would have pleased him, his family or friends more than to have qualified for this afternoon's San Marino Grand Prix. And nothing could be a more sickening blow to them or his team. He rose to the top the hard way, and his death, in the anaesthesia and resuscitation unit at Bologna's Maggiore Hospital 38 minutes after his crash on the Autodromo Enzo e Dino Ferrari, came as a savage shock to a sport in which death, contrary to popular opinion, is a rare visitor, though it is accepted as the ultimate risk.

Ratzenberger, tall and humorous, had only arrived in Formula One this season after a journeyman career through the lower formulae, including years of competition with Britain's Damon Hill and five years in Japan, where Eddie Irvine established his reputation. Along with every other person in the paddock, they were both deeply shocked. Indeed, tears ran freely as the second serious accident in 24 hours on one of Europe's fastest circuits, claimed a life at a grand prix race meeting for the first time in 12 years. Not since the 1982 Canadian Grand Prix, when Riccardo Paletti was killed at the start when his Osella rammed headlong into Didier Pironi's stalled Ferrari, has a Formula One race meeting seen a fatality. Elio de Angelis, who died at the Paul Ricard circuit in France in 1986, was testing with Brabham when his car hurtled out of control.

This fatal accident, however, will doubtless revive claims that motor racing is a hugely dangerous sport, amid speculation that the revised technical regulations introduced in 1994 have deprived the cars of the levels of stability they had last year. But this terrible accident was not due to errors or oversights in safety measures, nor was it the result of the removal of traction control or active suspension from the cars. It was, simply, an accident which appeared to be caused by the loss of all, or part, of the front wing of Ratzenberger's car as he accelerated at almost 185mph from Tamburello towards the Tosa hairpin.

Jean Alesi, the Frenchman who is recovering from damaged vertebrae, was a spectator at Tosa and is understood to have told journalists that he saw the front wing fly off. If so, it accounts for what followed. Ratzenberger's car, out of control without the down-force provided by the wing, should have veered left around Villeneuve curve. Instead, it ploughed head on, sliding slightly to the right, into the wall. It then careered for fully 200 metres before finally coming to a halt, the left side ripped away from the monocoque. A gaping hole in the monocoque confirmed how serious this accident had been.

The medical and rescue crews arrived as soon as the car stopped. Ratzenberger, who was lifted on to a stretcher, received immediate heart massage and was taken to the circuit medical centre and then by helicopter to hospital, arriving at 2.07p.m. local time. His death was confirmed eight minutes later.

The qualifying session was red-flagged and did not restart for 48 minutes. When it did, the Williams, Benetton and Sauber teams pulled out. 'Our action is out of respect for life,' said the Benetton managing director, Flavio Briatore. 'I don't care if I have one place less on the grid. Life is more important.'

Ratzenberger was a close friend of Benetton drivers Michael Schumacher, the championship leader, and J.J. Lehto, the Finn for whom today's race is his debut with the team after recovering from two damaged vertebrae in a testing crash at Silverstone. Neither wished to drive again, and nor did Ayrton Senna, who will start from the record 65th pole position of his career with Schumacher alongside. The Brazilian, at his own wish, was taken in the course car to the scene of the crash before withdrawing.

Of the major teams, only Ferrari and McLaren continued. 'It was the first time that I have found myself shaking after an accident,' admitted Berger. 'I was sitting in the car. I watched it on the monitor and when they started to get him out of the car I could see it was going to be very bad. I went out from the car. I felt sick. Then the difficult situation was coming to say if I was going to drive or not. But I said to myself, "Do you want to race tomorrow, or are you not going to race?" I said I was going to race … But it was very hard.'

2 MAY 1994

SENNA DIES AFTER 165MPH CRASH

Tim King and Timothy Collings

Ayrton Senna, three times world champion of Formula One motor racing, died yesterday after crashing at 165mph during the San Marino Grand Prix at Imola, in Italy. The 34-year-old Brazilian was leading on the seventh lap when the car careered into a concrete crash barrier. He was dragged unconscious from the wreckage of his Williams car, and at one point the medical team had to restart his heart. Senna was taken by helicopter to a hospital in Bologna with severe head injuries. He never regained consciousness and was pronounced brain dead four hours after he was admitted. His heart stopped beating an hour later.

Dr Maria Teresa Fiandri, head of intensive care at the Maggiore Hospital, said: 'With the first aid at the track, during transport here and in the hospital, we did all we could.' Last night, it was announced that there would be three days of national mourning in Brazil.

The German Michael Schumacher, who was following Senna when the accident happened, said: 'Ayrton looked nervous from the very first lap. The lap before I saw he was a little unstable and skittish in that corner. The next time he went sideways and then lost it.' Senna had written in a German newspaper, published yesterday, that he was having handling problems with his Williams on the Imola track. 'My car reacts a bit nervously on this kind of race surface,' he said.

Senna was the second Formula One driver to be killed in little more than 24 hours. The Austrian Roland Ratzenberger died after crashing during a qualifying round on Saturday. On Friday Rubens Barrichello crashed his Jordan but escaped with a broken nose and concussion. The deaths were the first in Formula One racing since Italy's Ricardo Paletti died in the Canadian Grand Prix of 1982.

At the start of this season, rule changes were introduced to Formula One which were intended to restrict the use of computer technology and to put a premium on driving skill. Senna was widely regarded as one of the most skilful drivers in the sport's history. Former racing driver and BBC commentator, Jonathan Palmer, was confident Senna's accident would not be put down to driver error, since both car and driver would have been well within their limits taking what he described as 'merely a curve in the straight' at 165mph. 'We have to look at other causes, possibly mechanical failure,' he said. 'The Williams team are obviously devastated. They will be going through the car with a fine-tooth comb.'

The veteran British racer Stirling Moss described Senna as the benchmark for driving skill. 'He was the greatest driver ever seen,' he said. 'The only person to compare with him was Fangio.' Mr Moss said he had spoken to Senna a month ago. 'He was so looking forward to the new season. Because of the changes in the regulations, he felt this would truly be a season for drivers.' He added that it was too soon to speculate on causes but, while mechanical failure was most likely, there was also a chance that Senna passed out in the cockpit. 'He appeared to make absolutely no attempt to corner and that isn't Senna at all.' Mr Moss said that the way in which both Ratzenberger's and Senna's cars withstood the impact testified to the strength of their construction, but added: 'If you have cars going at 190 or 200mph, you can't have them going into a brick wall and expect to get away with it.'

Mr Martin Whitaker, spokesman for Grand Prix motor racing's ruling body, the Federation Internationale de l'Automobile, said there would be a detailed inquiry into both accidents. He explained that grand prix cars carried data recorders, like the 'black boxes' in aircraft, which recorded in minute detail what was happening to them. This equipment had been recovered from both cars. Mr Whitaker said he did not think regulations banning computer control systems had added to the danger of serious accidents. 'The experts we speak to, the engineers, say it is completely the reverse. They believe cars are safer without this equipment because there is less to go wrong,' he said.

Imola, one of the fastest tracks in the world, has a history of accidents. Senna's crash yesterday was one of three. As the race started, Pedro Lamy drove his Lotus into the back of J.J. Lehto's Benetton. Both drivers were unhurt, but seven spectators and a policeman were injured by a tyre that flew into the grandstand. Late in the race, three Ferrari mechanics and a Lotus team member were injured in an accident as Michele Alboreto's car was leaving the pit.

2 MAY 1994

THREE-TIMES CHAMPION KILLED ON BLACKEST OF GP WEEKENDS

SENNA TRAGEDY SPARKS SAFETY INITIATIVE
BY SCHUMACHER

F1 COMMUNITY GRIEF-STRICKEN AS BRAZILIAN'S FATAL
CRASH FOLLOWS DEATH OF RATZENBERGER

Timothy Collings at Imola

Michael Schumacher last night promised to lead a campaign for improved safety in Formula One following the deaths of Ayrton Senna and Roland Ratzenberger in motor racing's blackest weekend at the San Marino Grand Prix at Imola. Schumacher, who had emerged this year as the heir apparent to Senna as the finest driver of his generation, pleaded for the launch of a drivers' crusade for greater safety. 'What we have to do is make sure that we all learn from this,' he said, after winning for his Benetton team a race that had become almost irrelevant. 'There are things that can be improved, and we should have made the changes before. We were even discussing these further safety issues today with Ayrton, Gerhard [Berger] and Michele [Alboreto], and we intended to organise a meeting in Monaco. Now I would like to push to get as much done as possible.'

Senna, called upon by Niki Lauda on Saturday evening to act as leader of a new move for safety, had heeded his words only hours before his death, but lost his life 11 days before the drivers' planned first meeting in Monaco. Schumacher confirmed that a safety summit would still take place before the next grand prix when he said: 'I took the opportunity to talk to Roland Bruynseraede of the FIA [the official safety officer] about all the circuits where I personally thought safety could be improved. Although Roland is pushing very hard for something to be done, it cannot be accomplished in one day. Maybe there will be other drivers with different solutions, and they must be discussed. We agreed to try to have a talk at Monaco on the free day, Friday, and we want to get all the drivers together if possible.'

Lauda and Jackie Stewart, both three-time world champions, said a new drivers' association should be formed to deal with safety matters. Lauda, now a consultant with Ferrari, said: 'I have spoken to Gerhard [Berger] about it, and he agrees, but he has not said he will do anything because they [the drivers] are all the same now – lazy. Too lazy.' Stewart said: 'They will then be able to represent themselves against the sport's authorities and, united, they could refuse to drive on a bad circuit. What happened at Imola showed the circuit was dangerous.'

It was hard to find an explanation for Senna's accident or the series of tragedies which scarred the weekend. Debris on the circuit, a bump or a problem with the car seemed possible. Others suggested that the new technology-free technical regulations could have played a part, but this seems unlikely. Senna had written on Saturday in a German newspaper that he had encountered problems with his Williams on the uneven stretches with long bends at Imola. 'It's one thing that's giving me a headache because it exposes the technical weak points of my Williams. My car reacts a bit nervously on this kind of race surface. This stems from its special aerodynamics but it's also got to do with a difficulty in the suspension.' Another clue came from Senna's Williams team-mate, Damon Hill, when he said: 'There seemed to be cars going off everywhere. It did occur to me that there are more accidents than last year, but it would be impossible to put your finger on anything. I believe the cornering speeds are in excess of what the circuits are now capable of taking.'

The double tragedy at the Autodromo Enzo e Dino Ferrari was the worst incidence of driver deaths at a Grand Prix meeting since the 1960 Belgian Grand Prix at Spa-Francorchamps, when Chris Bristow and Alan Stacey were killed. No words could sum up the mood of the paddock last evening, when tears replaced the more familiar sight of Champagne after the race. Most of the drivers escaped quickly, without a word, amid mounting calls for more action on safety. Hill, deeply upset after the broken race was finally finished, could barely speak after finishing sixth, but agreed with suggestions that debris from a crash on the starting grid may not have been entirely cleared. He said it had been difficult to know what had happened, and he had raced on thanks to the 'safety sheen' in which drivers are able to focus on the race. But he added: 'It takes a weekend like this to scrape away that very thin veneer of apparent safety.'

The scenes were as harrowing as those on Saturday when Ratzenberger was killed in qualifying. The right side of Senna's car was destroyed when he slid off the track in a cloud of dust and hit the wall near the point where Nelson Piquet and Gerhard Berger crashed in 1987 and 1989 respectively. Both wheels were torn away as the car spun to a halt.

Senna's fatal crash followed serious accidents on Friday and Saturday. Rubens Barrichello escaped almost unscathed on Friday during qualifying, when his airborne Jordan barrel-rolled after hurtling out of control at the

Variante Bassa. He suffered a broken nose and bruised ribs in an incident forewarning of worse to come the following day. Ratzenberger, seeking to qualify for only his second grand prix, was killed when his Simtek ploughed straight on after losing at least part of its front wing at 195mph at Villeneuve curve. The death of the Austrian had deeply affected everyone, not least Senna, who went to the scene of Ratzenberger's accident to see it for himself before withdrawing from the final qualifying session, in which he secured pole position.

The sadness of Ratzenberger's death had barely dissipated before the cars lined up yesterday, with one place on the grid left vacant as a mark of respect, and further drama unfolded at the start. J.J. Lehto, the Finn who was making his debut for Benetton after recovering from two damaged vertebrae following a testing crash at Silverstone in January, stalled and his car was hit from behind by Pedro Lamy's Lotus. Cars were weaving in all directions to avoid Lehto as Lamy came forward unsighted, his car ripping into the left side of the Benetton and sending debris flying. Ten spectators were treated for cuts and bruises as the race was slowed by the introduction of a safety car. At this point, Senna was leading, and when the race resumed after five laps he rejoined his battle to stay ahead of the chasing Schumacher. But two laps later the tragic crash at Tamburello claimed his life.

As the scale of the tragedy unfolded, the race became irrelevant, though it continued to throw up drama. Gerhard Berger, the Ferrari driver who was a close friend of Senna after three years together at McLaren, retired from the race, leaving the pursuit of Schumacher to his team-mate, Nicola Larini, who, by finishing second, scored his first championship points in 44 starts.

There was almost a tragedy, too, for Ferrari when their former driver, veteran Michele Alboreto, lost a wheel from his Minardi after a pit-stop. The errant wheel flew into the Ferrari pits, injuring three mechanics, one suffering a badly fractured left leg and shattered kneecap. A Lotus mechanic was also slightly injured and was confined to hospital in Imola overnight. Eddie Jordan, owner of the Jordan team, said: 'This has been the most awful weekend our sport has known for a very long time.'

2 MAY 1994
OBITUARY: AYRTON SENNA
ONE OF THE GREATEST DRIVERS IN GP HISTORY
Timothy Collings

Ayrton Senna, who died yesterday after suffering head injuries in an accident during the San Marino Grand Prix, was widely regarded as the finest motor racing driver of his generation and one of the greatest of all time. He was 34.

Born in São Paulo, Brazil, on 21 March 1960, he started in 161 grands prix, winning 41 and claiming a record total of 65 pole positions. His final pole position was the one he took on Saturday afternoon during a final qualifying session at the tragedy-shrouded Autodromo Enzo e Dino Ferrari, when fellow competitor Austrian Roland Ratzenberger lost his life.

Senna's reputation as both a great driver and a man of deep feelings was demonstrated that afternoon as he decided to travel by circuit car to see the scene of Ratzenberger's death for himself. Afterwards, he was unable to take any further part in the session, a decision which reflected the depth of his feelings about the tragedy which enveloped the San Marino Grand Prix this weekend.

Senna will be remembered for his brilliant talent as a racer, but also for his unprecedentedly high level of commitment to winning grand prix races. It was this which cost him his life yesterday. He had dedicated his adult life to succeeding in the business of grand prix racing after travelling from Brazil to enter the British Formula Ford 1600 Championship in 1981. Prior to this he had enjoyed a hugely successful karting career, which had begun at the age of four, when he first climbed aboard a motorised vehicle.

By the time he was 13 he was racing in go-karts. He went on to win the 1977 Pan American Championship and finished as runner-up in the karting world championships of 1979 and 1980. He climbed the classic motor racing career ladder by driving in the British Formula Ford series, winning the British and European Formula Ford 2000 Championship in 1982. The following year he won the British Formula Three Championship with West Surrey Racing, before entering Formula One for the first time in 1984 with the Toleman team.

He made his debut in the 1984 Brazilian Grand Prix and that season collected 13 points to finish ninth in the championship, his startlingly brilliant and aggressive driving earning him admiration from many, but also incurring the wrath of several of his senior fellow competitors. 'Winning is like a drug,' he once said. 'I cannot justify in any circumstances coming second or third.' Senna had the rare ability, and the courage, to go through gaps which others either could not see or felt they could not get through themselves.

The following season he transferred from Toleman to Lotus in a disputed move which led to accusations that he had broken his contract. However, for Senna the only goal was success, and in that season he claimed his first grand prix win in emphatic style in the rain at Estoril, Portugal. He finished fourth in the championship that year with 36 points. That victory was the beginning of a dazzling collection as his career progressed from Lotus to the McLaren team, which he joined in 1988.

In his first season with McLaren he collected 94 points and won the world championship, despite a season-long duel with his team-mate and arch-rival, Frenchman Alain Prost. Senna remained with McLaren for six years, winning the world title three times for the British team before departing at the end of 1993. They were six glorious years for all those associated with the Woking-based outfit as Senna established himself as the master of motor racing and arguably the greatest of his generation, with the possible exception of Prost.

He made the decision to leave McLaren at the end of 1993 because he wished to continue his single-minded pursuit of Formula One success with the team he felt best equipped to deliver it this season – Williams. However, Senna was tragically unable to record a single race victory with the Williams team, whose owner Frank Williams had given him his first test in a Formula One car a decade earlier, before he joined Toleman.

Senna was an intelligent man, from a well-off family, and he accumulated great wealth of his own, commanding vast salaries for his work. Nothing, however, rewarded him so much as triumph on the track, something for which he will be remembered by everyone in Formula One.

He was married early in his racing career to his childhood sweetheart, but his young Brazilian wife found it impossible to cope in Europe, and they later divorced. He had established a durable relationship with his girlfriend Adriane during the last 12 months. He loved most sports, particularly water skiing and jet skiing and was synonymous with everything Brazilian, taking every opportunity to promote his country, its culture, language, food and character. An intensely religious man, Senna said: 'To survive in grand prix racing you need to be afraid. Fear is a very important feeling to have. It helps you stay together. It helps you race longer and live longer.'

Not only Brazil, but the world of international sport lost a great champion at Imola yesterday.

2 MAY 1994

AYRTON'S KINDNESS WAS AN EXAMPLE TO US ALL

Martin Donnelly reflects on the deaths at Imola

I feel very numb about Ayrton Senna's accident. Everyone in the sport knows his concern was always for the welfare of injured drivers. When I had my accident [Donnelly's Lotus disintegrated during qualifying for the 1990 Spanish Grand Prix] he came into the medical centre, and apparently I spoke to him. There were eight minutes of that qualifying session left, and he got back into his car, went out and took pole position. It takes a very special sort of driver to see someone in a bad state and get back into his car and put it on pole position.

Again last year, at Spa, Eric Comas had a big shunt, and Ayrton was the first on the scene to check that he was all right. This weekend he went to see Rubens Barrichello in the medical centre, got back in his car and went out and put it on pole position. And he went out to see Roland Ratzenberger. Unfortunately this time round circumstances have fallen on Ayrton. This will inevitably affect the team.

I don't think there is any particular reason why there have been so many accidents this weekend. Barrichello's was a freak accident. He obviously lost it at a very fast part of the circuit and was fortunate to get away with a broken nose. With Ratzenberger, something obviously went seriously wrong mechanically with the car, which meant he couldn't even contemplate turning into the corner. No one could survive the impact with which he hit the wall, no matter what they were in, even though the monocoque stayed intact, whereas in my accident it completely disintegrated.

Ayrton Senna seems to have picked up a slow puncture from debris from the starting accident with J.J. Lehto, and the tyre let go suddenly — because, again, his car made no effort to negotiate the corner. So he went straight off at high speed into a concrete wall. In the Simtek accident something broke on Roland's car. I presume the team know what it was but I am surprised that they actually took part in the race after losing one of their drivers.

Team managers will most definitely study what went wrong. They will re-run videos from different angles. Williams will want to interview Michael Schumacher, who was directly behind Senna, to see if the car exploded or something broke on the back suspension. Obviously they will want answers to accept what went wrong.

A lot of drivers believe it will never happen to them, and they are paid, they are professional drivers. If they are out there thinking, 'When is my wing going to fall off' or 'When is the wheel going to fall off', they will not be driving at 100 per cent. They will not be doing the job they are employed to do, which is to drive with total commitment and get every second out of the car. Ayrton Senna was racing his car.

There was a fatality on Saturday, the crowds were there and the race took place. The show must go on. Now it has happened to one of the top teams, the top driver, maybe the FIA will sit down and start thinking. Maybe they will make a couple of chicanes in that long straight. They keep trying to reduce the speeds. This year they took away driver aids and made qualifying tyres smaller. And yet Ayrton on Friday went out at Imola and did the fastest time ever. He was half a second quicker than Prost last year without the advantage of semi-automatic gearboxes or anything. The emphasis has come back on drivers, but that isn't why these accidents have happened.

Watching Imola this weekend on television makes me appreciate more what I have got in life. I still feel upset that I was cheated of Formula One through no fault of my own, and I tried desperately to get back to it in 1991. I love it, but my wife Diane would be very much of a different opinion.

13 MAY 1994

WENDLINGER FIGHTS FOR LIFE AFTER CRASH ON FIRST DAY OF PRACTICE FOR MONACO
Timothy Collings in Monte Carlo

Less than two weeks after the black weekend of the San Marino Grand Prix, Formula One was last night plunged into deep shock again, as Karl Wendlinger fought for his life in the intensive care unit of the Hospital Saint-Roch in Nice. The Austrian, attempting to qualify for Sunday's Monaco Grand Prix, lost control of his Sauber at the chicane in the closing minutes of yesterday's free practice session and sustained a serious head injury. Initially, he was taken to the Princess Grace Hospital in Monaco before being transferred to Nice, where he was put into the care of Professor Dominique Grimaud. After a lengthy period of wild rumours concerning his condition, Mr Grimaud said last night that Wendlinger had suffered 'a very serious head injury and is in a critical condition'. A later statement said his condition was 'stable'.

No further official details were forthcoming from the hospital where Wendlinger's parents were at his bedside, but unconfirmed reports said the driver was on a ventilator and in a deep coma, suffering from severe brain contusions and swelling. He did not damage his spine. These descriptions suggested that Wendlinger's injuries were similar to those of the British boxer Bradley Stone, who died two weeks ago after suffering fatal head injuries.

Wendlinger, 25, lost control of his car after coming out of the tunnel at about 180mph. According to his team, he braked 15 metres later than he had on his previous, fastest, lap as he slowed to about 65mph on approach to the chicane. His car spun and crashed into the central barriers separating the chicane from an escape road. It is believed he may have struck his head as the car collided with the heavy plastic impact-absorbent boxes, which contain water and which stood in front of the barrier. Wendlinger has not recovered consciousness since the accident.

16 MAY 1994

SCHUMACHER STAYS IN CONTROL ON DAY OF HIGH EMOTION

Timothy Collings in Monte Carlo

Michael Schumacher yesterday altered the name on the scroll of honour at the Monaco Grand Prix for the first time in five years when he succeeded Ayrton Senna as the master of the world's most famous street circuit. It was his fourth successive victory for the Benetton team this season and without doubt the most emotionally charged of the six wins of his career.

As one of four newly elected leaders of the reformed Grand Prix Drivers' Association and a prime mover in Formula One's crusade for improved safety, he had been at the focal point of media, public and political pressure throughout a weekend dominated by the aftermath of Imola, where Ayrton

Senna and Roland Ratzenberger lost their lives, and by the severe injuries suffered by Karl Wendlinger when he crashed last Thursday. Wendlinger last night remained in a stable condition in a deep medically controlled coma.

Schumacher let none of the pressures show as he produced a record fastest race-lap for the unforgiving street circuit, to add to the record qualifying lap which had earned him his maiden pole position on Saturday. It was an overwhelming demonstration of his, and the Benetton team's, superiority. The 25-year-old German leapt with glee after the race into the arms of Flavio Briatore, the Benetton team's managing director who has threatened to withdraw his cars from the next race if the latest safety measures are not enforced immediately. He finished more than 37 seconds clear of his nearest rival, Martin Brundle, who scored his first thoroughly deserved points for McLaren by finishing second. 'I had a lot of very strong feelings before the start, but they were private,' said Schumacher afterwards, when he recalled the minute before the race as the drivers stood together in silent homage to Senna and Ratzenberger. 'It was not easy for me, but I was able to put those feelings out of my mind for the race – as I think you could see.'

Whatever the state of his mind before he started the 52nd Monaco Grand Prix, Schumacher showed no ill-effects as he drove a faultless race. His victory in 1 hour 49 minutes 55.372 seconds was masterful, establishing him not only as a clear favourite for the drivers' title this year, but also as the heir apparent to the brilliant Brazilian, six times the winner of this race in the previous seven years.

Like Schumacher, Martin Brundle revealed many of the inner conflicts which had filled him with concern in the days after Imola. 'I had to show a lot of self-confidence over the winter to get the drive and then personally through the last fortnight, when it has been very difficult for us all, very difficult to keep your head together,' he said.

'So to come through all this and then to be on the podium at Monaco has to be one of the best things I have ever done. The soul-searching was very difficult – especially when my five-year-old daughter came in and asked if it was true Senna was dead and that sort of thing ... It was tough. But we all had to face the same thing. Did we want to do this any more? Is it crazy? It was a very emotional and very difficult time. I have to say I am very proud of the drivers now. We had a fantastic meeting on Friday, very productive. I think we can make some sensible steps in the next few months to try and make sure it does not happen again.'

No one will forget the sight of the drivers' final homage, when the two remaining Brazilians, Christian Fittipaldi and Rubens Barrichello, held a Brazilian flag carrying the message 'Adeus Ayrton' as they stood on the empty front row of the grid. Niki Lauda stood bare-headed in public for the first time since his own, near-fatal, accident in 1976. Senna played a prominent part in Brundle's career, and the Briton admitted: 'I had a tear in my eye. It was a very emotional moment for us all. But we wanted to do it.'

I AUGUST 1994

HOCKENHEIM FLASH FIRE RAISES NEW SAFETY DOUBTS

Timothy Collings at Hockenheim

Formula One was engulfed in a fresh safety controversy last night after a flash fire in the pit-lane during an incident-filled German Grand Prix at Hockenheim. Benetton driver Jos Verstappen and five of the team's crew suffering burns in the blaze, which broke out when the Dutchman pulled up to refuel. Verstappen and four of the mechanics were released from hospital after treatment for minor facial burns, but one mechanic was detained overnight for observation.

Ross Brawn, the beleaguered Benetton team's technical director, promised a full investigation into the cause of the fire, which was the first of its type since refuelling was controversially reintroduced to grand prix racing this season after a ten-year absence. Brawn, who on Friday convincingly denied allegations that the championship-leading team may have used an illegal 'launch control' device at this year's San Marino Grand Prix, refused to comment further on yesterday's fire until the internal investigation had been carried out.

Verstappen, who was sitting in his car when it was sprayed by leaking fuel for a second, was trapped in the blaze as the shocked refuelling crew, in their full fire-proof overalls, fell back with flames erupting all around the car. 'I thought it was water,' said the 22-year-old driver. 'But then there was a fireball and it all went mad.'

It appeared that after the fuel valve was knocked into position it sprang away just as the first of the pressurised petrol was pouring through the pipe. This suggests that the valve had not locked fully before the fuel began to flow. The fuel sprayed all over the car before igniting in a 20-foot ball of flames which threatened to burn many of the spectators immediately above the pits in the Formula One Paddock Club — a scenario which was uppermost in many observers' fears about refuelling last winter.

Verstappen was saved from serious burns by the prompt fire-fighting action of those in the garage, and particularly Greg Field, the team's operations manager, who brandished a large powder-filled extinguisher. It is believed Field then helped Verstappen escape from his car.

Gerhard Berger, who won the race in front of a 150,000 crowd, said he saw the smoke and flames as he raced to Ferrari's first victory since Alain Prost won the Spanish Grand Prix in September 1990. 'I think we all have to look very carefully at this before saying anything,' he said. 'It should be safe. If aircraft can be refuelled at 30,000 feet, we should be able to do it.'

29 AUGUST 1994

SCHUMACHER IS STRIPPED OF BELGIAN GP VICTORY

Timothy Collings in Spa-Francorchamps

Michael Schumacher was left stunned again last night when he was disqualified from the Belgian Grand Prix five hours after he had won the race. A stewards' inquiry found that his car contravened the technical regulations by running with an undersized skid block. For Schumacher, who is due to appear in Paris tomorrow to appeal against the two-race ban imposed on him for ignoring a black flag at Silverstone during the British Grand Prix, this latest and unexpected blow could prove devastating.

It has not only resulted in Damon Hill being handed an unexpected victory on a plank, if not on a plate, but also in Schumacher's seemingly impregnable lead of 35 points in the title race being reduced to 21. If Schumacher's appeal is unsuccessful tomorrow, it will give Hill the opportunity to reduce the gap to single figures, or even one point, while the 25-year-old German is absent from the Italian and Portuguese Grands Prix. Both Schumacher and Hill, who was travelling home after finishing second, left the circuit yesterday afternoon unaware of the drama which followed their 44-lap race. The Benetton team, who made no official comment last night, appealed against the decision. This will mean they become embroiled in yet another dispute with the sport's governing body, the FIA, as they attempt to land their first championship.

On top of the fiasco at Silverstone, where Schumacher says he did not see the black flag when it was shown, the team are due to appear in Paris in September to answer charges that they deliberately and illegally removed a filter from their refuelling rig before the German Grand Prix at Hockenheim, where Schumacher's team-mate, Jos Verstappen, was engulfed in flames. Benetton have vehemently denied that the removal of the filter caused that fire and also claim that they had permission to remove it from Charlie Whiting, the Formula One technical delegate, whose report yesterday triggered the events after the race which led to Schumacher's disqualification.

Whiting's report, produced after he had examined Schumacher's car in post-race scrutineering, found the skid block, a plank of wood attached to the underside of the car to reduce its aerodynamic efficiency and therefore make it slower, was undersized. A more detailed explanation revealed that the plank was thinner at one end than the other. Schumacher and the team, represented by Benetton's technical director Ross Brawn and team manager Joan Villadelprat, said that this inconsistency in the thickness of the skid block, throughout its length, may have been caused when Schumacher spun on the 19th lap of a race he dominated almost from start to finish.

The team also said that Schumacher's car had developed some technical problems after the first pit-stop and these may have caused the spin. The stewards responded by saying the thickness of the skid block was not attributable to the spin over the kerb 'because the accidental damage was clearly marked as located in the drawing submitted by the technical delegate'. This drawing showed the accident damage and the illegally thin areas to be at opposite ends of the plank. The stewards went on to conclude that 'not one of the defences offered is acceptable and therefore that car No. 5 does not comply as regards the skid block'.

For Schumacher, the announcement will have wrecked a weekend which had seemed to be a perfect example of his ability on the circuit where he made his debut, with Jordan, in 1991, and won his first race in 1992. The win he had taken from him last evening would have been the tenth of his career in his 49th race.

GERMAN TAKES TITLE BY A KNOCKOUT

Timothy Collings in Adelaide

No scriptwriter could have improved on the *dénouement* to the 1994 Formula One world championship. A season which has encompassed tragedy, controversy and intense rivalry ended in character as the two key players collided in a dramatic deciding race in Adelaide yesterday. What was expected to be a close race to the flag between the fastest men of the new era, Michael Schumacher and Damon Hill, ended for them before the halfway point. Their departure handed Nigel Mansell, the oldest man in the field, his 31st Formula One victory. Gerhard Berger was second for Ferrari, and Martin Brundle third in his McLaren.

Schumacher, at 25, became not only the first German champion, but the youngest since the championship began in 1950. But he did so, somewhat fittingly after all the political upheavals this year, in such questionable style that even he was not convinced he had succeeded until he was engulfed in his team's wild celebrations after the long walk back from his abandoned Benetton car. His collision with Hill's Williams was the result of instinctive and aggressive tactics in defence of his position. Hill admitted he took a risk in trying to pass through a gap which Schumacher closed in the most uncompromising fashion.

The outcome was a puncture and damaged suspension linkage on the Englishman's car and an abrupt end to his hopes of overhauling Schumacher's one-point lead in the championship. Schumacher's car flew into a wall of tyres, leaving him to climb free and watch in suspense as Hill limped to the pits before retiring. 'I got caught out on a bump when the car stepped out,' said Schumacher. 'It went sideways but I caught it. Then I had to go on the white line and I had to use the run-off area, went over the grass and touched the wall, but continued. I just wanted to turn in into the corner and suddenly I saw Damon next to me and we just hit each other. I went up in the air. I thought I was going to roll over but the car came back. The worst moment was being in the tyre wall and not being able to continue and yet seeing Damon still driving. I thought it was over. But then I heard on the loudspeakers that he had a problem – I wasn't sure what kind of problem. And then I saw Mansell going by two or three times without Hill coming through and I thought, "That's it!"'

Schumacher, with 92 points to Hill's 91, had achieved his ambition, and, after an apology for his verbal attack on Hill last month, he dedicated his title triumph to the late Ayrton Senna, whose fatal accident he had witnessed at close quarters in the San Marino Grand Prix. 'It was difficult at the time to show my feelings,' said Schumacher. 'I am not someone who likes to show his feelings on the outside, but I always thought about it, and it is the right time now to give something which I have achieved, something which he should have achieved, to him.'

Hill, to his enormous credit, did not grumble once in public about his fate, however much he was pushed to do so by observers convinced that Schumacher's manoeuvre contained more than a trace of calculation. 'I'm not making any comment about that,' said Hill. 'Motor racing often has incidents like that, and I did what I felt I had to do. If we had finished on the road in the positions we were in at the time, then that would not have been good enough for me. I saw an opening and I went for it. Race fans all over the world will debate what happened at that point.' Hill's dignity and his driving were of the highest order, the order of a champion.

18 JANUARY 1995

END OF AN ERA AS ONCE-PROUD LOTUS LOSE FIGHT FOR SURVIVAL
Timothy Collings

Team Lotus, the most famous marque in British motor racing, yesterday gave up their fight for survival in the cut-throat jungle of modern Formula One. Chronic financial difficulties, which had bedevilled them for years, finally overwhelmed the Norfolk team, leaving owner David Hunt with little option but to make the staff of 60 redundant.

Like Brabham, who perished two years ago, Lotus have lived too long on borrowed time, the laurels of a bygone age and the goodwill of old friends after falling into a downward spiral following the death of their founder Colin Chapman in December 1982. 'He gave the team direction and "oomph", and without him it was never the same,' said Derek Warwick, to whom Lotus remain the epitome of British racing despite his harrowing season with them in 1990 – their last season sponsored by Camel.

Hunt, who had announced in December that he was laying off all staff until the end of last year while he searched for new sponsors and backers, extended that stay of execution until 16 January. But when the deadline came nothing had materialised, and the team he had saved from extinction, when he bought them from court-appointed administrators last October, were left without the resources to race on.

Sadly, the heritage of Chapman's creations and the driving achievements of Jim Clark, Graham Hill, Jochen Rindt, Emerson Fittipaldi and Mario Andretti in a scroll of honour which boasts six drivers' championships and seven constructors' titles, is all that the team have left to trade. Ever since Chapman founded the first Lotus Engineering Company in Hornsey, London, in 1952, Lotus have been synonymous with innovative engineering. Moves to Cheshunt in Hertfordshire in 1959 and to Norfolk in 1965, saw that reputation enhanced with the pioneering of such features as monocoque chassis, four-wheel drive, gas turbine engines, ground-effect technology and active suspension.

The racing team, who made their debut at Monaco in 1958, won their first grand prix there two years later. Yesterday, after a total of 490 grands prix, 107 pole positions and 79 wins, the last supplied by the late Ayrton Senna at Detroit in 1987, that famous innovation was unable to keep them on the track.

11 MARCH 1995

COMING TO TERMS WITH TRIUMPH AND TRAGEDY

Timothy Collings interviews Michael Schumacher

Naturally gifted, yet accused of a sometimes haughty manner, Michael Schumacher, the Formula One world drivers' champion, has changed as much as his sport in the last 12 months. Part of the problem might have been that his achievement, after *that* collision with Damon Hill in Adelaide last November, when he became a champion after only ten victories and 52 grands prix since August 1991, turned Germany's 44-year dream into reality. For the country which is home to Mercedes, Porsche, BMW, Audi and Volkswagen, his win was unprecedented, and, while Britain protested the legality of the shunt which ended Hill's hopes at Flinders Street, the celebrations in Germany were unstoppable.

It might all have gone to Schumacher's head. However, the most remarkable change in Schumacher, 26, since last season is quite the opposite, for he now appears at ease with himself. 'I personally feel more relaxed because of having done it,' he said while taking a break from testing – and setting the fastest time – at Estoril this week. 'There are drivers who have not won races and not won the championship. I think there is more pressure on them now to win than on me. I am looking forward to the first race.' He did not mention Hill by name, but the inference was clear.

Of the widespread allegations that he collided deliberately with Hill to take the title, he admitted he has rerun the incident over and over again in his mind, and on video, but without changing his view that it was a normal racing accident. 'Yes, I have thought quite often about it. But I know I am champion. I feel quite satisfied and there is nothing else to say now. At the time, there was a lot of heat in the situation, but then it went. I feel that a lot of the people who said I did it on purpose will be changing their minds.'

Having swept that question aside, Schumacher added that winning the championship, after such a harrowing and pressurised season, did not leave him completely fulfilled. Although he acknowledged a feeling of immense personal pride, he explained: 'I still feel unsatisfied. I still expect a lot more. I don't feel over the moon, because I haven't achieved enough yet. It has always been the same for me. When I won my first race, at Spa, it was a great feeling, but then I came back to normal very quickly and started from there again. I just do not have this sort of up-and-down feeling. But to be Germany's first champion is special.'

In talking of last year, it was impossible not to mention Ayrton Senna. The Brazilian had been expected to dominate in 1994, but was left trailing his younger rival after the opening two races. There was obvious tension between them (they almost came to blows in Germany during testing in 1992), but Schumacher admitted he learnt from Senna and, with hindsight, understood him and the pressures he faced. He said: 'At the time I did not understand certain reactions from him, things he did. But I do now, because I am much more involved in the whole business. I can see things now I didn't before, and this is a strange situation to be in.' His car was only a fraction of a second behind when Senna's veered off at Tamburello and plunged into the perimeter concrete wall, ending one of motor racing's most dramatic and brilliant careers. That black weekend remains a scar on Schumacher's mind. He simply goes silent when prompted for further reflections.

Like all drivers he prefers to focus on the future, the new safety-conscious regulations and the closer racing promised this year when he defends his crown in his Benetton car, emblazoned No. 1. 'I feel, firstly, that the car should be capable of winning races. I have no doubt in my mind,' he said. 'It might take us a little while to achieve the maximum from the car, and I expect it to be very close. Certainly, it is going to be very interesting between Williams and us. I admit we are not as well prepared as we were last season, but, as we saw then, so many things can happen.'

Last year, Schumacher's Benetton was powered by a Ford V8 engine. This year, it will carry the same Renault V10 as Hill's Williams, putting the two favourites and rivals on equal terms. This parity should produce even more thrills than the showdown in Suzuka and Adelaide, where Hill's performances gained the respect of the German. Their relationship, however, remains a fragile thing. 'The only thing that I can really say is that I see him as a good competitor for the season,' said Schumacher. 'We have the same engine and, having spoken out about each other in the newspapers, we know what to expect from each other. We respect each other, which as it should be.'

Alongside Hill, Schumacher recognised the threat of David Coulthard and, potentially, Nigel Mansell, if the 41-year-old can overcome his and the McLaren team's initial problems. 'I think Nigel will drive all 16 races this year, but I don't believe he will finish them all,' he joked. 'It will not be because of him. He will try.' It has been widely predicted that Schumacher will be Mansell's replacement in Mercedes colours in 1996 (for him a return home, as it was with Mercedes that he raced in sports cars in 1990 and 1991), but he dismissed this assumption. 'I am free at the end of the season to do whatever I like, and it could well be that I will stay with the Benetton team. If I am satisfied there is no reason to change.'

Schumacher's long-term plans may remain open, but his short-term aims are keenly focused on the season's opening race in São Paulo and what he expects to be an emotionally charged first race. It will be his first return to the city since last year's race, weeks before Senna's death, but he will travel with a heavy heart. He did not attend Senna's funeral last May, and recognises that Interlagos will present him with greater psychological difficulties than the return later to Imola. 'To go to Brazil and race in Brazil without Ayrton is going to be hard,' he said, clearly upset. 'It is not going to be the same as it used to be.' No, nothing will. So much has changed.

24 MAY 1995

MANSELL WALKS AWAY FROM LOVELESS AFFAIR

Timothy Collings

It was at the Hilton Hotel in Park Lane in February that Nigel Mansell uttered the words that will haunt him. 'It's not a question of will we win this year,' he said, 'but when. With the might of Mercedes, the organisational prowess of McLaren, I'm feeling extremely confident.' Yesterday afternoon, exactly 110 days later, the man with the mighty moustache and the organisation with the mighty engines parted company like a loveless couple, victims of an unhappy arranged marriage that simply did not work and has barely been consummated. Of four grands prix this year, Mansell has taken part in only two, finishing only once and covering all of 250 miles.

Accountants will calculate that at an estimated cost of £4,000 per mile to McLaren, but the biggest blow is to their pride and Mansell's. The marvellous team of Ms — McLaren, Mercedes, Marlboro and Mansell — have collected only six points this year, and one of those was contributed by Mark Blundell, who will replace the 1992 world champion in both Sunday's Monaco Grand Prix and the Canadian Grand Prix next month. 'It's fantastic news for me and a great opportunity to show what I can do,' said Blundell, 29, an unfulfilled talent with 48 races behind him. 'I've been told I'll be doing the next two races, and then I'll sit down with Ron Dennis and see what the future holds.'

The statement yesterday from McLaren's Woking headquarters did not confirm the end of Mansell's career, but after 41 summers, and without a vacancy in sight, he has almost no option. All the top seats are taken, and a queue of younger men is pressing already for promotion. The news itself was almost greeted with a sense of relief, mere confirmation of what has been widely expected throughout the ten days since Mansell decided to pull up and retire, amid complaints that his car was 'virtually undriveable', after only 18 laps of the Spanish Grand Prix.

'I'm obviously disappointed that the relationship with McLaren and Mercedes, which could have achieved so much, has been concluded early,' said Mansell. 'At this stage of my career I had expected, on joining McLaren, that the total package would have given me the possibility to be competitive with the other top teams. I've certainly enjoyed many aspects of my relationship with the team and working with them has been a unique experience. I have no immediate plans in Formula One, but welcome the opportunity to keep in touch with the team, with whom I have parted on the best possible terms.'

Ron Dennis, the managing director of McLaren, who was once quoted as saying he did not understand Mansell and that he would never hire a driver he could not understand, was precise in his remarks. 'Nigel has not felt confident within the car and this has affected his ability to commit fully for the programme,' he said. 'In these circumstances, I believe that we have determined the most appropriate course of action.'

After 187 grands prix and a chequered career studded with spectacular accidents, premature retirements, two memorable championship seasons and some of the most courageous racing by any Englishman, it seems events here finally caught up with the self-proclaimed people's champion. He has 31 wins, 32 pole positions and 39 fastest laps to his name, mere statistics that do nothing to convey the essence of a man driven by a competitive thirst which has not been, and may never be, quenched. According to a recent survey, Mansell is the 367th richest man in Britain with £33 million; that league table will be another challenge to come if he concentrates, as expected, on his many business enterprises.

18 JULY 1995

CHAMPAGNE FINALE SOOTHES FRUSTRATION OF TRAFFIC JAMS

David Coulthard gives an insight into his British Grand Prix weekend

Friday

7.40: Arrived by car at circuit. Stepped out and mobbed by British fans. Sign autographs for 20 minutes. Over to motorhome where Francis, the team cook, gives me porridge and banana for breakfast, sloshed down with mug of tea. Change into overalls and rush through paddock, over bridge to BBC studio.

7.55: Live BBC *Breakfast Time* interview with Jonathan Maitland. Questioned about speculation that Damon is talking to other teams. I joke that it would be great if he goes to Ferrari. Not sure that anyone gets it.

8.50: Scooter over to other side of circuit to open new Autosport Tower. Back to motorhome for interview with Renault TV, an internal company station.

9.20:	Over to pits. Say hello to mechanics, talk to my race engineer Jock Clear (otherwise known as 'Nookie Bear', because he looks like a ventriloquist's puppet). Look at weather (cloudy and blustery) and revise set-up. Ritual check of helmet and ear plugs.
9.30– 11.15:	Free practice. Weather conditions affect me. Disappointed with fourth-fastest time after balance felt so good last week. But we have decent time to work from.
11.20:	Debrief with Jock, Damon and his race engineer, David Brown. They feel same problem but to a lesser extent. Small adjustments for afternoon qualifying.
12.00:	Bowl of soup. Start of building up fluid intake. Physio Pierre Baladier gives me energy-boosting mineral drink.
12.30:	Pierre takes me through stretching exercises for shoulder and neck, and tried to sharpen my mind (hits me over head with a bat). We do these alone in debrief room. Damon did not want to pay a contribution towards sharing. Retreat to truck, otherwise someone will grab me. Safest thing is not to come out.
1–2.00:	First qualifying session. Get into car (always from left-hand side). Sit and wait for another car to go out and clean circuit. Wind still gusting, but brighter. Disappointed with third-fastest time of 1 minute 28.947 seconds. The car felt bizarre, could be same problem as at Magny-Cours. Set-up not quite right. Hope weather fine tomorrow. I would love to be on front row with Damon.
2–3.00:	Debrief with Jock.
3.00:	Talk to jostling mob of journalists. Line of questioning is 'David in danger because of lack of performance'. Cannot believe things a tabloid reporter has read into questions I answered honestly. It is not the case that I feel threatened. Amused by simplistic interpretations of my seven-race season's record. How often do I have to repeat basic fact that I need to be fit and have reliable car to win races?
3.15:	Lunch at last. Salmon penne, fruit salad, cup of tea.
4.30:	Scooter over to Paddock Club for driver presentation to Rothmans and Renault guests. Talk through lap of circuit; answered questions.
5.00:	Back to motorhome for interview with *Dundee Courier*.
5.15:	Back to truck for more debrief. Engineers have produced information from telemetry print-outs. Relief to discover problem has been

isolated to downchange on gearbox. Group discussion degenerates into boys' talk.

7.30: Leave circuit. Fans bang car windows: 'Beat the German', 'Win for us'. Sign autographs in traffic jam.

8.00: Back at hotel. Massage with Pierre. My girlfriend Andrea orders from room service. My manager, Tim Wright, joins us to review the day.

10.00: Bath, watch Eurosport, flick through *Autosport*. Room above noisy bar. Don't sleep until well after last orders.

Saturday

7.00: Alarm call. Pull back curtains and despair over clouds. Fight over mirror with Andrea.

7.40: Set off for circuit.

8.00: Porridge and banana in motorhome. Signed autographs for 20 minutes.

8.30: Interview with Silverstone TV. Quick look at newspapers. Everyone else caught on to the 'Coulthard Knows He Must Perform' line. I maintain I have been misinterpreted.

9.30– Free practice. Track is patchily damp. Set third-fastest time only
11.15: managing one flying lap because of lengthy change of set-up with wet weather wings.

11.20: Debrief. Nothing clear-cut because not enough time to assess whether changes were improvement.

12.00: Soup and chicken pasta at motorhome. Physio.

1–2.00: Second qualifying session. Didn't push too much because rain meant yesterday's grid positions would remain. Happy to be quickest in wet session.

2–4.00: More debrief.

5.00: Live interview with Steve Rider on BBC *Grandstand*.

5.15: Scooter back to paddock.

5.30: Interview behind truck with BBC Radio Scotland.

5.40: Debrief. Discuss race strategy (one or two pit-stops), fuel and balance.

7.00: Dinner with Renault. Pasta and barbecued chicken.

8.30: Visit to fan club gathering at Towcester Cycling Club. Claire, secretary, has organised an amazing show. I am overwhelmed. Pictures on wall, books for sale (the one I did not officially endorse). Met

Cherry, who sent me a cake at Christmas. Signed everything. Several women wanted T-shirt signed across the chest.

10.00:   Back to hotel. Massage from Pierre, bath, chat through day with Andrea.

Sunday

7.45:   Leave hotel. Stuck in horrendous traffic.

8.50:   Leave car to walk to circuit. Man on motorbike gives me a lift. Arrive at circuit, no time for breakfast.

9.30–   Practice important because I need to try both race and spare cars.

10.00:   Warm-up. Race car bit lazy with full tanks. Too much understeer at high speed.

10.15:   Debrief. Final decision will be made 45 minutes before race. Not great difference between a one- and two-stop strategy. Will go for two as car will feel lighter and racier on new tyres.

10.30:   Pasta, chicken, banana and mineral drinks.

11.00:   Drivers' briefing. Clerk of course goes through race regulations and safety issues.

11.30:   Over to Renault Paddock Club for driver presentations.

12.30:   Talk to Jock, confirm race strategy.

1.00:   Massage from Pierre in de-brief room. Pit-lane opens. Quick talk to Jock. Final pee. Johnny Herbert comes over to say good luck and be careful. Last person I talk to before helmet goes on is always Andrea.

2.00:   Parade lap. Green lights. Ferrari makes a storming start. Frustrated at losing a place. Stuck behind Schumacher, who is stuck behind Alesi. Due to make first stop on lap 20 but team call me in on 15.

Reasonable stop but electrics fail, affecting pit-lane speed limiter and up and down changes on gears. Wait for gearbox failure, but car keeps running. Lap 43, second pit-stop. No speed limiter. Probably speeded. Saw Damon and Michael off on giant TV screen and P2 on my pit board. Catch Johnny Herbert easily and overtake in the lead. But see Coulthard ten-second penalty flash up on TV. In for penalty, back out, surprised to be third. Very torrid race.

Podium – great feeling. Couple of slugs of Champagne. No point wasting it. Genuinely happy for Johnny. Interviews.

Over to motorhome. Greet Georgie and Bette Hill. Damon and I discuss 'incidents'.

7.00:   Supper (salmon and potatoes) with a couple of beers. Join Eddie
            Jordan's band, The Pit-Stop Boogie Boys, on stage for post-race gig,
            along with Damon, Eddie Irvine and Mika Häkkinen. Biggest cheer
            for 'Go Johnny Go'.

18 JULY 1995

FATHER FIGURE WHO WAS THE FINEST CHAMPION OF ALL

Timothy Collings

Motor racing is mourning its greatest champion, Juan Manuel Fangio, who
died in a Buenos Aires hospital yesterday morning. 'The Maestro' was 84.
Fangio was no ordinary man, no ordinary sportsman. He was loved the
world over, respected and revered by his team-mates and competitors alike
and universally accepted as the greatest motor racing driver of all time. As
Stirling Moss put it, after hearing the sad news of his greatest friend and
fellow driver, he was 'a gentleman, not of birth, but of being'.

Fangio, who did not race in his first grand prix until he was 38, won five
world championships. 'I feel a great loss because he was such a wonderful
person in everything he did,' said Moss, who raced with and against Fangio
through his greatest years in the 1950s before he retired in 1958, aged 47. 'He
was not just a friend, I idolised him. He was always so helpful to me, a
marvellous person in everything he did. Not just in sport, but with everyone. We all adored and respected him. He was a father figure to me.'

Fangio was the son of a stonemason from a family of Italian immigrants
who built a monumental achievement in sporting history. His first race was
in a converted taxi in 1936, his first victory in a long-distance endurance
event in 1940 and his first grand prix, in Europe, in 1950 at Rheims. At an age
when most men are ready to retire from racing, Fangio's career began and
took off, carrying him to such heights that his achievements remain
untouched today. Every driver to have won a race since 1950 has been in awe
of him and his feats with Alfa Romeo, Maserati, Mercedes Benz and Ferrari.
Jackie Stewart once said: 'When Fangio comes in to a room the conversation stops. You hear us all just whispering about him. Everything else is
forgotten.'

Fangio survived in an era when death was a constant unwanted companion. He said in 1990: 'In my ten years of driving in Europe, I saw 30 of my

friends and rivals killed.' Fangio had two dreadful accidents. The first was in 1948 in Peru, late at night during a road race, when he missed a corner and went off the road, rolling his car. His co-driver was killed. Four years later, at Monza, he broke his neck after crashing on the second lap following an overnight drive from Paris and a race in Ireland the previous day. 'It was a short story,' he said. 'I arrived at two. I raced at 2.30 and I was in hospital with a broken neck by three.'

Fangio said once: 'Fear is not a stupid thing. Winning is not a question of courage, but of faith in oneself and in the car. A car is like a creature that lives, with its own emotions and its own heart. You have to understand it and to live it accordingly. I knew many drivers more courageous than me. They are dead now.'

He was famed for more than his racing. Stories of his love affairs were frequent, including one with the actress Gina Lollobrigida, but it was for his racing that he is remembered. His greatest win was in the German Grand Prix at the Nürburgring in 1957, when he was driving for Maserati. He had gambled victory on a pit-stop for fuel and tyres, but rejoined 48 seconds behind. 'It was a marvellous, great moment,' said Moss, who was watching. 'He caught the two Ferraris and then he passed Mike [Hawthorn] on one side and Peter [Collins] on the other, behind the pits. It was a masterly move.' Fangio, who broke the lap record ten times to win by 3.6 seconds, said: 'I was inspired that day. I never quite drove like that before and never drove like it again.'

On that day, there was no accident. On another, when Moss won the 1955 British Grand Prix at Aintree, there was no explanation. Moss still does not know if Fangio had allowed him through to win or not. 'He always told me, "Ah, that was your day" ... Now with his death, we have the end of an era. His is the passing of a very great man.'

18 JULY 1995
OBITUARY: JUAN MANUEL FANGIO

Juan Manuel Fangio, the Argentine racing driver who died aged 84, was to his sport what Pelé was to football and Bradman to cricket. Though Fangio did not compete in the world championship until he was almost 39 – at which age grand prix drivers are now regarded as over the hill – he won five championships between 1951 and 1957, and from only 51 starts wrested a remarkable 24 grand prix victories, 25 fastest laps and 22 second places.

Cool and seemingly fearless, Fangio had superb control over his car, and never drove faster than was necessary, though he could keep his foot slammed down longer than any of his opponents dared. His remarkable stamina had been built up in the marathon road races of South America in the late 1930s and 1940s, when he crossed and recrossed 6,000 miles of bad roads in unsuitable motor-cars, acting as his own mechanic. 'The man who wants to be world champion must cover himself in grease from head to foot,' said Fangio. 'He must work on his car with his hand and his heart. Before becoming a driver he must become a mechanic – almost a manufacturer ...'

He drove for all the top teams of the day: Alfa-Romeo, Ferrari, Mercedes and Maserati. Fangio's brilliance was encapsulated by his mastery of the old Nürburgring track. Racing on this, he said, was like 'getting to know a woman. ... You can't memorise 176 curves over more than 14 miles,' he observed, 'just as you can't memorise 176 feminine wiles after a short acquaintance.'

At Nürburgring in 1957 he notched up his last – and greatest – victory. After a lengthy pit-stop he had to make up almost a minute on the leading Ferraris of Mike Hawthorn and Peter Collins. Breaking the lap record ten times in his Maserati, he screamed past both his rivals. They applauded his victory as ecstatically as the crowd.

An immigrant Italian stonemason's son, Juan Manuel Fangio was born at Balcarce, 200 miles from Buenos Aires, on 24 June 1911. As a boy he was apprenticed to a blacksmith but soon found a job in a garage. Mechanics and football quickly became his passions, and it was his task to drive the team to away matches over the muddy tracks that passed for roads. Before long he set up his own garage, and entered his first races to win publicity for the business. In 1940 he became national road-racing champion.

In 1942 all motor racing ceased, and when it resumed, in 1947, European-style racing on purpose-built tracks was introduced to Argentina. For the first time Argentine drivers competed against Europeans. In 1949 Fangio enjoyed his first full European season, and caused a sensation by winning nine races. He returned to Argentina to find that the *Tango Fangio* had been composed in his honour. Such was his enduring popularity in South America and Europe that years later a dock strike was lifted at Genoa to allow Fangio's car to be loaded.

Some 30 drivers were killed during his seasons in Europe, and Fangio was vociferous in his complaints about the lack of safety precautions on the track. However, such was his skill – and luck – that his only serious accident, which cost him much of the 1952 season, was a result of exhaustion.

His good nature was exemplified by a bizarre incident in Havana in 1958, when he was kidnapped before a race by anti-Batista insurgents. Fangio later said that he had endured awful problems during practice with the car he was due to drive in the minor event, and was sure the kidnappers had done him a good turn. He said he had been well treated and even interceded on behalf of a kidnapper who was captured. On his retirement Fangio became an ambassador for motorsport as well as president of Mercedes-Benz (Argentina). His appearance was guaranteed to create a stir at any motoring event: even in old age he was a charismatic and dignified figure with piercing grey eyes.

For all his wide gifts – his friends said that if he had gone into the Church he would have become a cardinal – Fangio never mastered English. He made George VI laugh when he was presented at Silverstone in 1950. 'No spik English – spik Italian, spik Spanish,' stammered Fangio to the King, who looked a little embarrassed. Fangio turned to the interpreter by his side. 'Please tell His Majesty,' he said, 'that I don't have to speak English to be able to drive.'

Fangio had a long and mysterious relationship with a woman who was always with him at circuits and was mistakenly thought to be his wife, but he never married.

31 JULY 1995

LETTER TO THE SPORTS EDITOR

MAESTRO FANGIO

Sir,

Timothy Collings's article on Juan Manuel Fangio rightly stressed that he was the maestro of all motor racing champions, universally respected and revered on and off the track. He also had an almost mystical rapport with his cars. I saw him, in his sixties, during Birmingham's street 'race' of grand prix cars. Another driver finished a lap in a huge pulsating monster from the Thirties which was misfiring and belching noisily. Fangio stepped aboard, immediately the maniacal machine moved smoothly into gear and purred proudly away.

John Hollinshead
Leek, Staffordshire

25 SEPTEMBER 1995

FULFILMENT OF A DREAM I HAD FROM THE AGE OF 12

David Coulthard

Maybe it was an illusion and I had another lap to do. The sight of the chequered flag waving me across the line was fantastic – until I thought maybe I hadn't seen it at all. After controlling the race here in Portugal from pole position I was suddenly afflicted with nerves. I guess when it is your first win you want to make sure you have absolutely snatched it. I've experienced a few near-misses lately. I didn't talk to the team on the radio until I came out of the last corner and knew I could coast across the line. After retiring from the lead two races in a row on unlucky lap 13, I didn't want to tempt fate at all.

I knew I could start celebrating when Karl Heinz, the Rothmans chef, appeared on the track behind the pits on the slowing-down lap like he did last year when Damon and I finished one-two. He had a bottle of Champagne in his hand and sprayed it all over the car. Unfortunately he didn't manage to get any in my helmet – at that stage I could have done with a drink. Michael and Damon made up for that on the podium by drenching me right through to my underpants (not my lucky pair, as I couldn't find them in the race truck, but maybe these are my new lucky underpants).

My first victory feels special because it was a straight win against the main championship contenders, Damon and Michael. To take pole position again, post the fastest lap and then win a close, tactical race was the best way to prove to people who doubted that I was capable of stringing it together after the tonsillitis that affected my early season.

To win it in my 21st race is fitting, I guess, in that it's like a coming of age. It has come a bit late, to be honest, but better late than never. When I was 12 and had started to race in England, the dream while watching the grands prix on television was one day to be sitting on the grid and one day to be standing on top of the podium. Today I was able to realise that dream, and it's a day I won't forget. Despite wild celebrations, I feel quite reserved about it. The big picture has always been the world championship, and that requires a number of wins. I'm not the sort of person who shows emotional highs and lows – but that may change tonight. The race team and I will be partying through the early hours. It's their win as much as mine.

2 OCTOBER 1995

SCHUMACHER ON TITLE BRINK AS HILL REACHES END OF ROAD

Timothy Collings at the Nürburgring

The leap on top of the victors' podium signalled it all for Michael Schumacher: triumph, joy, relief, the fitness and vitality of a honed athlete, and a thrilling communion with the hordes of supporters, whose fanaticism inspired his electrifying surge to the greatest win of his career. All were there in the moment which followed his magnificent victory in yesterday's memorable European Grand Prix. It was a champion performance, more than worthy of clinching the title itself.

Thanks, in part at least, to the misfortunes which dogged Damon Hill, the defending title-holder now has only the formalities to complete before he is declared the 1995 Formula One world drivers' champion. Three more points, the equivalent of fourth place at Aida in the Pacific Grand Prix, will complete the academic issue, but ask anyone who was here in the mist which shrouded this circuit in the Eifel mountains where the title was truly settled, and they will say the Nürburgring.

Hill, disappointed but not distressed, was as gallant in his hour of defeat as he had been dogged and courageous in his fight for glory an hour earlier, before sliding and spinning into a tyre barrier with nine laps remaining. 'He drove a great race to win again in his home country,' he said in praise of Schumacher, the rival whose superiority was manifested in thrilling fashion. 'Hats off to the guy. He's a bloody good racing driver. ... I'm not going to be world champion this year, but I'll be back. I'm very disappointed, obviously, but I think I did everything I could, and I don't feel I disgraced myself. I don't have any regrets, nor am I too downhearted. Fortunately, I'm in full working order after hitting the barrier, so that's good news.'

Sorrow, then, for Hill, who stood to offer a thumbs-up sign to Schumacher and then to applaud him from the sidelines on his slowing-down lap at the end of the race. Euphoria for Schumacher. And a bank of fabulous memories for the spectators, all 100,000 or more who camped in the hills and forests, a canvas city of sore heads and damp bodies, to witness one of Germany's most exhilarating races in modern times. It was overwhelmingly Schumacher's day. In damp, drying conditions, on a track where the dry line was painfully slow in encouraging the use of slick tyres, he performed with a rare verve, unmatched speed, a competitive daring that he could hardly believe himself and with the backing of a strategy – three pit-stops, where his rivals chose two or one – which was calculated to secure a nail-biting triumph.

'When I made my second pit-stop, I did not think it was possible for me to win,' he said. 'And after my last pit-stop, I had to ask myself if it was best for me to take second for the championship or to push for victory. My fans made me push. So, I took the risk, I pushed, and it worked.' Emerging from the Benetton pits 22 seconds behind Alesi, with 14 laps remaining, Schumacher cut through the field in a manner reminiscent of the legends created on the original Nürburgring circuit nearby. He may have finished only 2.684 seconds ahead of Alesi, but such was his mastery of the treacherous conditions, it might have been a minute or an hour. Throwing aside any notion of cruising home second for the sake of six easy championship points, Schumacher scored the 17th win of his career in his 66th race. It was his seventh win of his final season with the Benetton team and, beyond much doubt, his greatest.

Hill, beaten when he ran into Alesi's Ferrari and snapped the front wing off his Williams after 39 of the 67 laps, left the final image behind with his lonely silhouette, clapping by the side of the track as Schumacher drove by. 'That showed his character; it made me feel very happy,' admitted the champion. 'We may not be friends, but we respect each other, and there is no war between us.' He did not say it, but the feud was over.

23 OCTOBER 1995

SCHUMACHER SETS NEW STANDARD

GERMAN RETAINS WORLD TITLE IN MASTERFUL STYLE

Timothy Collings in Aida, Japan

Michael Schumacher cancelled his waiting helicopter, revised his itinerary in Tokyo and organised a party. Unlike at Adelaide in 1994, this time he felt ready to let his hair down after clinching his second world drivers' championship with yesterday's masterful triumph of strategy and speed in the Pacific Grand Prix at the Aida circuit in Japan. All around him in the cramped confines of the Benetton team's temporary office, the celebrations ran amok. With a bottle of beer in his hand, Schumacher was in no mood to hold back after becoming the youngest driver to retain the world title. 'We have to change everything,' said his team's managing director Flavio Briatore. 'We go to Tokyo tomorrow. Tonight we party.'

When he awakes this morning, Schumacher may well have a race hangover. But, after watching the way in which he demolished all opposition again yesterday, it will be his rivals who have the biggest headaches of all. On form, Schumacher looks untouchable and after eight victories he can now aim with confidence to overhaul Nigel Mansell's 1992 record of nine in a season, after joining the ranks of such illustrious double champions as Alberto Ascari, Graham Hill, Jim Clark and Emerson Fittipaldi.

Ahead lie the targets set by five-times champion Juan Manuel Fangio, four-times champion Alain Prost, and the three-times winners Jack Brabham, Jackie Stewart, Niki Lauda, Nelson Piquet and Ayrton Senna. Schumacher will be in good company in the record books from now on after proving that he and Benetton have shrugged off the rumour and innuendo of 1994 and are worthy champions. At the end of yesterday's demonstration of his and Benetton's supremacy, he was 14.9 seconds ahead of David Coulthard, in second place, 48 clear of Damon Hill and had lapped the rest of the field. Gerhard Berger and Jean Alesi, in the two Ferraris, were fourth and fifth, and Johnny Herbert was sixth. It was a one-man show of massive superiority.

If his victory at the Nürburgring was a festival of daring and skill in atrocious conditions, this was a result of calculation, tactical acumen, stealth and the reliable fingers and instincts of his faithful pit crew. Indeed Schumacher himself paid his team a rich tribute when he chose to spend last night with them in Aida rather than fly on out towards the greater luxuries of the Japanese capital. 'To win my second championship like this, it is a beautiful feeling,' he said. 'At the beginning of the race it was hard for me to believe I had any chance of winning. I was fifth after the start, but as the race developed – and thanks to the guys who did a first-class job in the pits – I was able to pull out in front of Damon and Jean after the first pit-stops. That meant I was able to catch David and our strategy worked from there on.'

1 2 NOVEMBER 1995

THE MOMENT I REALISED SCHUMACHER WOULD FINISH MY TITLE ASPIRATIONS

Damon Hill

Looking back now, it looks as if I made a mistake by working through from last year's Formula One season without taking a break: testing in the winter; the promotion of my book; awards, like the BBC Sports Personality, which meant a lot, and media appearances; training; a round-the-world promotional tour with Rothmans in January; and then all the preparations for the new season.

After Adelaide it was non-stop all the way. I didn't have a holiday. I spent more time away from home. We moved house to Ireland, but I was never there. I was hardly at home at all, and the pressure was enormous. It stayed that way. I felt it, but I did not really feel affected by it, I don't think, until Silverstone, when on top of everything I was being called a 'prat', and it was across all the national papers. I had driven my heart out to win the British Grand Prix and taken a chance which didn't pay off. At Silverstone I felt I had done my best, given my damnedest, to win that race. I had taken pole position and I could have won it. For me, it was a new twist to everything to be completely slaughtered in the papers. In the space of six months I'd gone from being a brilliant loser to that.

The thing was, too, that I felt I was driving much better generally. I really did. I had been on a high since Suzuka the previous year, and then, in all honesty, I just made one or two fundamental errors, and it heaped more and more pressure on me. Without going into those things specifically, looking back now, I would say I was ill-prepared for the pressures which built up. The pressure you feel when you are trying to win a championship is something no one can understand unless they have done it. I talked to Alain Prost about it and he recognised it. He knew what I was talking about. He said he doesn't think anyone can keep up that level of performance, as required, over an entire season. There are always going to be ups and downs. Things change and things happen.

Last year it got to the point where I lost out by one point, but the way I felt at the time was that, in all honesty, if I had won the title, I would have been a very jammy bastard. Michael Schumacher had been thrown out of races and had races taken away from him, so I just wouldn't have considered it to be a worthy championship in the end. But, having said that, I felt I did a very good job. I had not let myself down. I had raised my game to a new level and I set myself up really for the coming season, this one, and that is why I started this one feeling so confident.

I thought my car was going to be good and, knowing that Benetton would be having a Renault engine, a new engine to them, I felt optimistic. I felt I might have an advantage and a great chance. In testing, our car was very good. I had finished third in the championship in my first year, second in my second, and I was just hoping 'a dream could come true', and I could finish first in the third.

In the winter the car was very good, and I had no doubts about it. I felt we certainly had the best car. We knew where we stood. Benetton did not get their act together at all in the pre-season, so I was full of confidence when we flew out to Brazil. I got pole, led the race, but went out with a suspension failure. I thought, 'Tough ... put it behind you, concentrate on the next races'. And I did that. I went out and won them both and found myself leading the championship.

And then, we went to Barcelona, and it all changed. It was the first time all season that Benetton had been fully competitive. From now on they were sharp and competitive all the time. I knew, in that race in Barcelona, that I could not win. It also started a run of things going wrong. We had a fuel pump problem, and from there on we seemed to be uncompetitive. Things began to fall away. The gap just got bigger and bigger. It was mystifying because we had been so competitive before. Two things seemed to be happening – we were losing reliability and we had lost some form. We tested like mad. I did more miles by half-season in 1995 than I had done in all the previous year.

Schumacher? He is a good driver and I won't take anything away from him. He is a brilliant driver. But Benetton have taken a completely different approach to the job. Their approach is that the tactics are crucial and that the best way to get the results is to concentrate on one guy, one driver. But that is not the way it is done at Williams. Nor will it be next year. I know that. I know I have to work within that structure and I cannot change it. I cannot say I have lacked support from the team. Frank has been very good. He has always helped and encouraged me when he can see the pressure. There have been times this year when it's been difficult to feel we are a perfect team. For example, it was not made obvious that the actual reason for my going off in Hockenheim was not my mistake, but a mechanical problem.

It has hurt me a lot that I have had so much criticism this year, and that people have said I make excuses. It hurts because I know a lot more than I have divulged and I don't want to get into that kind of scenario… I am not making any excuses for not winning the championship. I made my own mistakes because I was under pressure, because of a lot of things. But I cannot blame anyone but myself.

People cannot appreciate truly what it is like trying to win the world championship. I certainly didn't until I got caught up in it. I remember seeing a clip from Suzuka, after Ayrton had won one of his championships there, and he talked about being emotional, the strain and the stress, and I used to think, 'Give over! What are you making such a big deal about?' Now, he was the best ever, and if you could talk to him or Alain Prost or Jackie Stewart, then you know they understand what it can take out of you. It is one thing to drive a car for 70 laps without making a mistake, and it's another thing to try and do that when your confidence is being attacked on all fronts and you are losing points through mechanical problems.

It has been a difficult year. I know I have often been told I restrain myself too much, hold back my deepest feelings, but if I said what I really felt, I'd be scared of the consequences. I have always believed that you should think first, take a deep breath before you speak. But, maybe that is not immediate enough for this business.

And as to the future, I will only say that there are more disciplines in this sport which I need to address if I am going to improve my chances of success. But I think that also goes for my team. I hope 1996 will see Hill and Williams being the major force in Formula One.

20 DECEMBER 1995

FAMILY AFFAIR HAS HAMILTON ON RIGHT ROAD FOR SUCCESS

Timothy Collings
Focus on Schools Sport

At the age of ten, Lewis Hamilton is a star. He is the first black boy to emerge as a junior champion in British motorsport and the youngest winner of his age group in the national karting championship. As winner of the Vauxhall Autosport Cadet Karting trophy, awarded at a black-tie dinner at the Grosvenor House Hotel in London, he has already experienced the media spotlight, speaking before a vast audience, being interviewed on television and radio and seeing his photograph in magazines and newspapers. Yet, he remains not only disarmingly modest and polite, but also unspoilt. Indeed, his first ambition, after strolling off stage following the *Autosport* Awards ceremony, was to seek out David Coulthard and Damon Hill for autographs.

To all those who met him, Lewis was manifestly a credit to his parents and his school, Peartree Spring Junior in Stevenage, Hertfordshire. His headmaster, John Seal, admitted he had nothing but praise for the achievements of his pupil, who had transformed himself from aimlessly average into one of Britain's best prospects of sporting success in the next millennium.

'We always make room for those who achieve and encourage them to bring their trophies in to school assembly,' he said, brushing aside questions about the Government's policy of supporting team sports in schools. 'It makes no difference if they are for team sports or individual sports. We have one young lady who is fourth in archery in Hertfordshire, but we also have a good soccer team. The main thing, I think, is that there is room for both individual and team sports together. In Lewis's case, he had to prioritise to succeed, and he chose to give up football to concentrate on his karting. His success has helped him a great deal in many things, and he has proved he is a bright lad with lots of smiles.'

Lewis's father, Anthony, is proud of his son and keen to point out also that his karting success has paid off in the classroom. 'Before he started, he was average at school, but with the ability to do a lot better. Now, he is much more focused, and I think that is down to the deal I made with him.' This 'deal' came about after Lewis, around his eighth birthday, in January 1993, was taken to the Rye House kart track in Hoddesden in Hertfordshire. 'He saw it and wanted to have a go,' said Anthony. 'I said immediately that if he wanted to do it I would support him, but only if he improved at school. It was an attractive offer.'

Since then, Anthony Hamilton has spent at estimated £35,000 on his son's career ('a drop in the ocean,' he said, compared to others, some of whom have invested up to £300,000). Lewis, in return, has become the dominant force in his age group (eight to twelve-year-olds) and established himself as the British No. 1 while at the same time impressing his teachers with his academic performance. 'We have done it all as a family,' said his father. 'It is hard work and it costs a lot of money, but I feel the results have fully justified the expenditure. To be No. 1 at the age of ten when the majority are 11 or 12 is something exceptional.'

In his father's words, the competition is equivalent to Formula One on a miniature scale. It is taken very seriously by all involved and administered by the RAC/MSA, who maintain the rules and regulations, ensure the drivers race in the correct equipment – they all run in 60cc karts – and wear the correct helmets and race suits. Lewis, who talks about racing with all the aplomb of a grand prix veteran, has two Zip karts. One is for testing and the other for racing. He also has sponsorship, which helps pay for his engines and tyres. His family, including his younger brother Nicholas and his mother Linda, camp down at each event in a motorhome for their trips, which can take them as far away as Scotland.

To keep fit, Lewis has taken up karate – he is already an intermediate black belt – and adheres to a controlled diet. He goes to bed at 8.30p.m. and regards it as all part of his programme aimed at this ultimate goal of racing in Formula One. Next year his horizons will be broadened further when he travels to Italy to take part in the world championships. 'He has his own bank account for the prize money,' said his father. 'And as far as I know, he has not spent a penny of it yet. It is very satisfying because he has turned out to be just the sort of nice, disciplined young lad I hoped he would be.'

And it all started so innocently and so simply. 'I just wanted to do it,' he said. 'I asked for a kart for Christmas and I got it. When I first got into it, it was really fun. I didn't feel any fear at all. It was just great. I loved going fast, I always have.'

At his first race, however, Anthony thought it was all over when he saw Lewis crash. He crawled from the wreckage of his kart with blood streaming from his nose. 'I thought that would be the end of it, there and then,' he said. 'But astonishingly he just asked me if the kart could be fixed for the race the following day. … It could. We did it. And he won. And he has been winning ever since.'

16 JULY 1996
SURVIVING THE SILVERSTONE SYNDROME
Sarah Edworthy

Early in the morning of the British Grand Prix, Damon Hill expressed amazement at the number of supporters who had been queuing at the autograph hatch near the Williams motorhome since 5a.m. A guest of another British driver, taken aback by the alert faces pressed up against the paddock's perimeter chicken-wire fencing, felt embarrassed that he, a fan for the day, could stroll freely where *aficionados* who had paid £95 a ticket could but gawp through security controls.

Fiat's supremo, Gianni Agnelli, one of the most powerful men in the world, spent 15 minutes getting his pass accepted by the swipe machine. The three-year-old grandson of Yamaha's president was charged the full £650 Paddock Club price for a Saturday–Sunday ticket, despite the fact he was unlikely to be partaking in much of the complimentary Champagne. Jean Alesi preferred a bunk in the Benetton truck to the inevitable hassle of leaving the circuit.

For 72 hours of the year, Silverstone is twinned with Bangkok in terms of standstill, bumper-to-bumper frustration. Physiotherapists, faced with the annual increase in Achilles tendon injuries in mid-July (damage wrought to your brake and accelerator foot in marathon stop-start conditions) will soon have enough cases to alert the *Lancet* to The Silverstone Syndrome.

While workers from catering staff to journalists exhausted by global deadlines dossed down in the back seats of their cars to prevent road rage on race-day morning, and the police advised ticket-holders to come into the circuit throughout the night to ease congestion, the question had to be asked: why bother? Why not stay at home and watch it on television? What do you really get at the circuit that outweighs the hassle and herding?

Noise, buzz and the ritual of an annual pilgrimage were the unanimous answers. Vox pop surveys among punters yielded a unanimous 'brilliant, hope it goes well for Damon', changing only to 'brilliant, pity about Damon'. 'What do you mean *why* come?' some replied with genuine incredulity. Tickets for Sunday had been sold out well in advance.

What is it about Silverstone that works? The secret is to treat it as an adventure. Those who camp know this can be an escapade in itself, full of fireworks, partying through the night and banter over the barbecue. Those who make a weekend of it, having bought tickers and booked hotels in advance, make a holiday of a logistical nightmare. Ditto, the awayday package, with its dawn start and late-night crawl-away.

At the more privileged end of the scale, the Paddock Club provides activities for those who may not particularly like motor racing but have been invited as a guest by one of the team's sponsors. Poor things. Coming in by helicopter, tucking in to *cordon bleu* lunch, meeting drivers – who was it? Johnny Herbert? – and getting personalised pit-lane tours. If the race is just a nasty noise, Paddock Club guests need not waste the time. Within its tented enclaves (after the pass has been checked, punched and your wrist is cuffed with another security code), you can learn how to cook strudels and fruit dumplings at a stall manned by a patisserie chef from Vienna, you can place a bet at Ladbrokes, have your shoes polished, buy art or flowers.

Johnny Herbert's mother, who was worried about her hair in the photographs with her victorious son last year (having camped for three nights), might like to know that you can even have your hair done, courtesy of a mobile Vidal Sassoon salon. After the problem of obtaining hot and running water had been solved, the stylists reported a lot of re-style work, and there were long queues for consultations. Having left at five o'clock on Friday and Sunday mornings and still had time to 'read' a map of Great Britain several times in one traffic jam and catch up on a month's admin in another. I have no trouble in nominating my best adventure. It was Saturday, courtesy of Asprey, major sponsors to Ferrari, who naturally believe in doing things with style.

Apologies for gloating, but the day started with coffee in the library at Althorp House, home to the Spencer family (which, on the day after the Royal Divorce was agreed, added some poignancy to the memory) and a leisured stroll among the Rubens, Van Dycks, Reynolds and Gainsboroughs in the picture gallery. The helicopter landed on the lawn ('Where are your shades?' a fellow guest asked. 'You can't arrive in a helicopter without sunglasses') to whisk us across a solid M1.

We had Champagne, an anecdote-filled pit-stop lesson from the Ferrari press officer (Nigel Mansell used to sing over the radio when he started leading a race), a funny visit from Eddie Irvine ('Driving this car is not very pleasant. You're out there hanging on for your life … '), before a lunch of salmon carpaccio al pesto, paella, lamb brochette and apple tart with almond parfait and marinated sour cherries. From front-row grandstand seats, the cars looked pretty good, too.

2 SEPTEMBER 1996

RETURN OF STEWART TO THE GRID

Robert Philip

Paul Stewart was eight when he heard his father had been killed via a news flash on Swiss television. '6 October 1973, but I can see and hear the announcer yet, "Jackie Stewart and François Cevert met death today … " and feel the lightning bolt through my heart. I was staying with family friends outside Geneva because my parents were obviously away, and all I could say was, "It can't be my father, he's too good a driver. It can't be".' A subsequent bulletin confirmed Jackie Stewart was alive and well, but that his Tyrrell teammate and close friend Cevert had perished in a crash while practising for the following day's United States Grand Prix at Watkins Glen in upstate New York.

Twenty-three years on, Paul Stewart's eyes flick over to Cevert's portrait in the corner of the managing director's office on the top floor of Formula One's newest team factory at Milton Keynes. 'So although I was naturally very sad to learn François had died, the overwhelming emotion was one of unspeakable relief. Talking about it to you now after all this time seems really weird because the memory remains as sharp as if it had happened only yesterday.'

Though a grief-stricken Jackie Stewart, already assured of his third world drivers' championship, would withdraw from the race and announce his retirement – 'I lay in bed one night counting all the people I'd known who had died racing and after a while, maybe an hour, I'd reached 57' – not even the death of the much-loved Cevert could extinguish the fascination felt by both father and son for motorsport.

And so, when the first grand prix of 1997 is staged in Melbourne in a little over six months' time, two spanking new Stewart-Fords will be on F1's showroom floor alongside the familiar company cars of Williams, Benetton, Ferrari, McLaren and Jordan. Paul will serve as *chef d'équipe,* but Jackie, just as he has been for 31 years, will be standing off to one side, quietly advising, coaxing and assisting.

'It's eerie but my first recollections of motor racing revolve around tragedies,' muses Paul, who, as well as acquiring his father's passion for fast cars, inherited his dyslexia, business acumen, dark good looks, gentle west of Scotland accent, and old-fashioned courtesies. 'I knew from a very early age that my father was involved in racing. I also understood it was highly dangerous.

'I used to attend boarding school in Switzerland with the children of some of the other drivers, the sons of Jo Bonnier [killed at Le Mans in 1972] were at the same school, as was Natasha Rindt [daughter of Jochen, died Monza, 1970]. And I was actually trackside at Brands Hatch when Jo Siffert was killed in '71. I was only six but I can remember seeing this pall of black smoke rising up into the air, then all the mechanics rushing out of the pits across the circuit, then all the cars stopping.

'I can tell you exactly where I was, exactly what I was doing, exactly what I was wearing, when every driver was killed. When Jochen was killed, for example, I wasn't quite five but I recall being in the back of a car heading down a mountain. I must have known something was terribly wrong because I suddenly asked, "Where's Jochen?" and my parents sitting in the front looked at one another. They didn't say anything for a long time then my mother told me, "He's gone to heaven". And I thought, as you tend to do as a young kid, "That's a shame. I'm not going to see Jochen again". It was obviously far more difficult for my mother and father to accept than it was for me.'

The list of those he would never see again makes you want to weep: Peter Revson, Ronnie Peterson, Lorenzo Bandini, Bruce McLaren, Patrick Depailler, Piers Courage, Gilles Villeneuve ... but, blessedly, Paul Stewart's childhood also came generously sprinkled with magic dust. 'Like the afternoon in '73 when Graham Hill drove back to the Villa d'Este hotel to tell me my father had won his third world title at Monza and would be arriving at any moment by helicopter. A helicopter! Can you imagine the excitement? I'd stayed behind with my brother Mark, you see, to play with Damon Hill and his sisters, Bridget and Samantha, while our fathers had gone racing.' (Thanks to a £125 million deal with the Hong Kong and Shanghai bank set up by his father, Paul and Damon, so the latest rumour goes, could be play-mates again come Melbourne).

Sensitive to Jackie and Helen's steely determination to prevent their son from ever discovering for himself the unique thrills associated with the family business, the youthful Paul always professed to be far more interested in driving a fire engine than a Ferrari. 'Whenever lift doors opened, say, and people saw the two of us standing there they'd always speak to me rather than my father. I suppose they felt too shy to launch into a conversation with Jackie Stewart. They invariably asked the same question, too. "And are you going to be a racing driver when you grow up?" "No", I'd growl menacingly.'

Thus, while Schumacher, Coulthard, Häkkinen and Senna began their graduation into F1 through karting (which they had all taken up around the age of seven), Paul Stewart, like Damon Hill, rode off on a powerful motorbike with the stated purpose of seeking an alternative career, a world removed from the racetracks of Silverstone, Monaco and Spa. 'My parents made it clear they were not in favour of me going into motor racing. I think that's why my father bought me the bike at rather an early age. At the time, it seemed an odd thing for him to do. It wasn't Christmas, it wasn't my birthday – not that I'd have expected anything like that anyway. I think his motive was to try and give me something with a bit of speed in it to get it out of my system. If that was his theory, then it backfired somewhat.'

Having acquired a sense of adventure on two wheels, the lure of climbing into a tiny cockpit proved altogether too seductive. Thus, during his final year at Duke University in South Carolina, where he took a degree in political science, Paul Stewart – with his father's knowledge, if not his whole-hearted blessing – signed up for a course of lessons at Brands Hatch under the pseudonym Robin Congden. 'I knew if they discovered who I really was, then I'd be given special treatment. And I had to know whether Robin Congden, not the privileged son of Jackie Stewart, had what it took to succeed.' Stirling Moss, on the circuit that day testing a saloon car, remembers hearing excited pit-lane chatter of 'an American who's turned up from nowhere and who looks pretty damned quick'. Quickness was never to be a problem, but Stewart's belated entry into the sport as a mature 21-year-old and his lack of karting experience were seriously to hinder any chance of his emulating his father.

'I was fast, as fast as anyone in Formula Ford, Formula 3000 or whatever, but I wasn't a racer. People like David Coulthard and Mika Häkkinen had been racing for 13 years at that age. They knew how to overtake. I knew how to drive quickly. Big difference. Damon's learned to deal with the same handicap, but if you look at the guys who've been karting since they were seven or eight, they're able to do certain things I wasn't.'

As a driver, the younger Stewart was swift without being bellicose, fearless without being foolhardy, ambitious without being fanatical. After seven years, he had to make a stark choice: either to concentrate on the burgeoning team which bore his name, Paul Stewart Racing, or to accept one of three offers to drive an F1 car. 'If I'd genuinely been Robin Congden, son of a building society manager, then I might have carried on driving. But I'd arrived at a point where I'd enjoyed my racing and I knew if I continued I would become frustrated.

'I'd earned a respectable reputation, and I didn't want that to be tarnished. I was only 28, and I knew I was good enough to be a Formula One driver – not just to potter around as a tail-ender – but I also knew deep, deep inside I was not destined to be world champion. The ultimate aim in launching Paul Stewart Racing in 1988 was to compete in Formula One, and now, finally, I am only a few months away.'

With a £100 million contract with Ford to use their new V10 engines, the team has been able to employ the best, like Alan Jenkins, who has joined from McLaren as technical director-chief designer and whose half-scale prototype Stewart-Ford is currently undergoing wind-tunnel tests in San Clemente, California. The entire project is top secret. We were not allowed to photograph a single component or a scaled-down skeleton of the mono-coque being assembled behind blackened windows in a locked room in Milton Keynes.

Even the car's livery will not be revealed until the tarpaulin is removed at a ceremony in London in December, though the fact a Racing Stewart plaid has recently been lodged with the Scottish Tartan Society may provide a clue. Potential drivers, too, have been wined and dined in strict privacy. Though Paul would love to have Damon aboard, Denmark's Jan Magnus-sen and Brazilian Gil de Ferran (both of whom have made sensational entries into Indy Cars) look the likeliest pairing.

What, no Scots? 'We'd like to have David Coulthard, obviously. But he's under contract to McLaren next season. Still, in years to come you never know. I'd also give anything to see Damon behind the wheel of a Stewart, but he might come a little bit pricey these days.' And if no top name is avail-able? 'Then I guess you'll see me and father on the grid in Melbourne.'

And where exactly on the grid do the Stewarts expect to be when they go wheel-to-wheel against Williams, Benetton, Ferrari and the rest? 'If you give the "big five" the top ten qualifying places, then anywhere from 11th- to 16th-fastest in practice would be pretty satisfactory. But our ambition is to become the best.'

The best, after all, is what Paul Stewart has been surrounded by all his life. By his desk is a photograph of him as a 12-year-old nonchalantly leaning against the Alfa Romeo of a beaming Juan Manuel Fangio; on a ledge of the window rests the helmet of Jackie Stewart; and, in a secret room downstairs somewhere, the first Stewart-Ford is being assembled.

14 OCTOBER 1996

STYLISH HILL SIGNS OFF WITH A FLOURISH

Timothy Collings at Suzuka

He sat with Georgie, his wife, on the pit-wall and could not stop smiling. He answered the photographers' calls for a kiss and he kept on smiling. It was a perfect day for Damon Hill as he succeeded Michael Schumacher, his one-time arch-rival, on the long and glorious scroll of Formula One world drivers' champions. No one could argue that he deserved his hour, evening and night of triumph after dashing any doubts about his nerves, talent or composure. His eighth win of the season, and 21st of his career, in only 67 races, was delivered in the most commanding style. It was his second Suzuka success in three years at the Japanese Grand Prix and, if it was not his most spectacular, it was certainly one of the most controlled and assured races of his life. A perfect *adieu* to Williams.

Yet even after fulfilling his lifetime's ambition, after becoming the first son of a former champion to take the title, and after doing it when the struggle for glory had gone down to the final race, a joyous and Champagne-soaked Hill remained as self-effacing as ever. Asked if it was his greatest achievement, he replied: 'Oh, I don't know about that. But it has certainly been the most difficult thing I've ever done in my life … you should try it sometime.'

Victory released the confidence and humour which had been bottled away since his last taste of Champagne on the podium at Hockenheim back in July. Since then Jacques Villeneuve had trimmed his 21-point lead down to nine with a succession of strong performances, but if anyone thought Hill would be a bundle of nerves, they were wrong. He dominated this race as he did the first half of the season and stayed cool, relaxed and confident through the weekend.

In dedicating the race victory to his team and his championship to his wife, Hill showed the generosity and thoughtfulness which make him one of the sport's most popular champions. With all due credit to Villeneuve, whose challenge finally expired when his left rear wheel bounced, at massive velocity, like a wayward missile into a safety fence on the 37th circuit of the 52-lap contest, there never was much doubt about Hill's success.

Villeneuve's plight made life easy for Hill yesterday, but after his struggle to wrap up the title in Monza and Estoril, it was impossible not to share his joy. For neutrals, as well as those who have followed his career these past six years, it was a pleasure to see that nice guys do win, and that all Hill's hard work since his sorry departure from Suzuka a year ago had paid off.

14 OCTOBER 1996

LETTER TO THE SPORTS EDITOR

WORLD TITLE PROVES JUST REWARD

Sir,

I congratulate Damon Hill on clinching the Formula One world championship in Japan. I think he has done a very good job this year and deserves to be champion. The way he has worked with the team and developed the car for the past three seasons has proved that he has grown in stature as a driver. I know a lot of people are saying that Hill only won because Michael Schumacher was in the Ferrari. Well, I don't think the Ferrari is as bad as everyone makes out.

Some say anyone could have won in a Williams, but that's rubbish. As a driver for Mercedes in the International Touring Car Championship, I've watched some of Hill's qualifying laps, and he is so smooth and so in control it almost looks like he is on a Sunday drive. He won the championship in the right style in Japan, because many critics say he cannot handle the pressure. Well, look at the way he led from the start and took the chequered flag. But just a word of warning to him: he may be hoping that he will win Britain's next world championship as well, but I am marching forward in my career and I hope just as much that it will be me.

Dario Franchitti
Edinburgh

20 FEBRUARY 1997

THE LONG JOURNEY BEGINS IN ATTEMPT TO LAY SENNA TO REST

Paul Hayward in Imola

Everyone knows what they were doing when the news of Ayrton Senna's death came through. My own recollection is of turning on a silent television in an American hotel room and seeing a still picture above the words: 'Ayrton Senna, 1960–1994'. It was an unthinkable thought, too big to comprehend, Kennedyesque in its ability to stop the world turning.

Cut to Imola nearly three years later and a civic office above an Italian café where shrunken old men are playing cards and making a coffee last all afternoon. In the courtyard outside the trees are blackened and stripped of foliage. Time passes slowly at the other end of the speed-scale to Senna's death, which took place at almost 200mph just half a mile away across the Santerno River.

This is the makeshift courthouse where a local magistrate will hear a charge of manslaughter – *omocidio colposo* – or culpable homicide against Frank Williams, Patrick Head and Adrian Newey of the Williams Formula One team, plus three race officials from the Autodromo Enzo e Dino Ferrari, where Senna died on 1 May 1994 when his Williams car struck a concrete wall coming out of the Tamburello bend. Anyone expecting an Italian Old Bailey will be surprised to find a temporary provincial magistrates court in a tiny square dominated by a convent with peeling terracotta walls. Above the café and the high windows of the building are the words Casa Dopolavoro, which means 'the house after work'. But there will be plenty of work done here over the next few months. The upper floors are a kind of social or cultural centre used primarily for small exhibitions, and were requisitioned when the real magistrates court was judged to be too small to stage a trial of such magnitude.

At 9.30a.m. today the Salone del Circoli, as the café is called, will be a madhouse of journalists and camera crews, while small-town Italian jurisprudence labours to uphold its authority amid a scramble for soundbites that will steadily give way to a protracted, labyrinthine hearing which is unlikely to produced a lasting conclusion that will be accepted by all.

In this melée Senna will die all over again. Legally, he has yet to be laid to rest. The trial is the product of a 600-page report completed by an investigator in Bologna, 30 kilometres to the north west, over two painstaking years. At issue is whether Senna's steering column broke as a result of faulty engineering in the pits or when the car piled into the wall after Senna had failed to negotiate the normally straightforward Tamburello bend. Tamburello means tambourine, which is a curiously innocent title for a place where the world's greatest racing driver lost his life in a brutal crash.

The high windows of the Casa Dopolavoro suggest a desire to let in light, to see things clearly. But most Formula One people think the Italian judiciary are fumbling in the dark trying to apportion blame for Senna's death. Italy is good at trials. Much of the country's history over the past five years has been taken up with the prosecution of people in high places. Turn on the news here and somebody is coming down the steps of a courtroom. It has been said that nearly 50 per cent of all cases passing through the Italian courts collapse. The Senna trial – the *Processo Senna* – could limp on for years.

Some deaths just will not end. Another thing you notice in Italy is the proliferation of memorials to the dead. Death is big here, which may be why they are trying to solve the mystery of Senna's crash, to close the file on a couple of seconds which returned F1 to the bad old days of car wrecks and fireballs. It is said that the assassination of John F. Kennedy is the most persistent television image of the 20th century. Senna's death, broadcast live to hundreds of millions round the world, is unquestionably sport's most shocking and indelible televisual memory.

A visit to the Imola track, which stages the San Marino Grand Prix, confirms the seismic nature of the event. There his annihilation no longer seems something disembodied but a real happening. On the eve of the trial fresh-faced Italians were roaring round the circuit in touring cars, and the Ferrari flags were fluttering against a milky winter sky. The bend has been replaced by a chicane, but the sense of a ghostly presence remains. Senna was not the only driver to die at Imola that weekend. Roland Ratzenberger was killed in practice the day before.

Imola, the town, does not relish its status as the Dallas, Texas, of sport, which could be why the old men in the café study visitors suspiciously. The local paper speaks of a cross, or affliction, that the town has had to carry for three years. Workmen were splashing yellow paint on metal fences on the track – a reflective gloss to keep the accusations and memories at bay. Irony of ironies, Imola is known chiefly as a machinery manufacturing town. It was the most sophisticated machinery in the whole sprawling automobile industry which carried Senna to his end.

The significance of the trial may be largely bureaucratic, but it seems somehow encouraging that somebody is willing to ask questions of the F1 hierarchy. Williams, Head and Newey may turn out to be the victims of excessive legal diligence, yet the principle of an investigation into the death of a man in such bizarre circumstances is surely sound. It was valid to wonder why Senna's car went straight on when it should have taken a rela-tively gentle bend, and whether the severed steering column came to be snapped before or after the impact of a crash that rendered Senna's transfer to the Maggiore Hospital in Bologna a token act.

The charges which relate to 'negligence or fault', and are used as a catch-all in Italian jurisprudence, have been laid out in article 589 of the Italian penal code. If they are upheld, Williams, Newey and Head would be very unlikely to serve any of the maximum five-year prison sentence. But they would be landed with a criminal record, an outcome that would probably produce a Formula One boycott of Italy. The other defendants, if they can all fit into the Casa Dopolavoro, are two officials at the Imola track, Federico Bendinelli and Giorgio Poggi, and the race director, Roland Bruynseraede.

As with all great unsolvable mysteries, conspiracy theories abound. The prosecutors here say they will not be swayed by new evidence which suggests Senna may have been affected by a piece of debris from an earlier collision resting in his path. The more one studies the evidence, the more one feels that nobody will ever be able to prove beyond reasonable doubt why Senna drove into a wall when he should have turned a corner. The absence of a black box, and the difficulty in determining when exactly the steering column broke, increase the likelihood that the trial will run aground on its own technical complexities.

The Williams team are not obliged to attend today's hearing, which will deal with procedural issues. The start of the most exciting F1 season for years is 18 days away, and Williams have important work to do in Australia.

Senna's life was complex, unfathomable, and his final death rattle will be, too. The old men in the café downstairs will still be playing cards, and the convent walls still peeling, when Ayrton Senna is finally allowed to rest.

4 JUNE 1997

THIRTY CANDLES ON COSWORTH'S BIRTHDAY CAKE
Sarah Edworthy

Today is the 30th anniversary of the remarkable debut victory in the 1967 Dutch Grand Prix of the Ford-Cosworth DFV engine. Not a date on which most of us would bring out the cake and candles, it has to be said. However, even at a time when Formula One is complicated by a stock-market flotation, by a proposed ban on cigarette sponsorship and by the introduction of new regulations, its significance is hard to overlook.

When the DFV-powered Lotus driven by Graham Hill claimed pole, and team-mate Jim Clark took the chequered flag, 30 years ago at Zandvoort, it was clear that this engine had revolutionised F1 from its first competitive revs. How? At boffin level, it introduced a concept that remains fundamental to F1 today: the idea of the engine forming a structural part of the car. It was based on Lotus boss Colin Chapman's concept of a compact, simple engine with a wide torque range. On a historical level, Walter Hayes, who, as head of public affairs at Ford of Britain, commissioned the engine for a mere £100,000, is best qualified to explain.

'It won first time out when Jimmy Clark hadn't even seen the car until practice, because he was in tax exile in Paris. It took pole for the next nine races and went on to win more grands prix than any engine of all time. But what it mostly did was to cement Britain as the hub of motorsport. If a team hasn't got a British manager, engineer or chassis today, it isn't actually going to be successful in grand prix. We have a secondary motor industry in this country, employing thousands of people, turning over huge sums of money. It will be very sad if the tobacco ban happens and all the races go to the Far East, because there could be a huge technology transfer to the Japanese or Koreans.'

We are familiar with the dominance of the McLaren-Honda in the late 1980s and of the recent run of Williams superiority, but the Ford-Cosworth's impact was embarrassing in its era. Hayes had to tell Graham Hill to slow down because, from a marketing point of view, he wanted it seen on television that he was in front of the second-placed car. Hill was so far in front no one could see he was leading. It was like that from the outset. 'We had such superiority that Jim Clark and Graham Hill were chasing each other around in practice,' recalls Hayes. 'I said to Colin Chapman, "You tell those drivers to report to me because we are not having this. We're going to toss a coin to decide who wins". The answer is Graham won the toss but Jimmy won the race. Towards the end, I thought I heard a splutter in Graham's engine and beckoned Clark on. When the race was over, the first thing Clark did was to rush back to Hill and say, "They told me to, they told me to, I kept the agreement". We had such outstanding supremacy, I said to Chapman, "If we keep the engine exclusive to Lotus, we'll kill the sport. We're going to have to make it available to anyone that wants it." And Chapman agreed.'

Different times, indeed. A time when Frank Williams was scrounging vans, when Ken Tyrrell claimed you could go and buy a couple of chassis and a couple of Cosworth engines and anyone with a bit of sense could be world champion (which he did with Jackie Stewart), when Bernie Ecclestone ran the Lotus Formula Two team for Chapman. Most of all, it was a period of wonderful racing and a sudden flowering of genius in British motorsport. 'They just came out of everywhere, and we've gone on and gained from it,' says Hayes. 'The huge technical competence of Williams, for example, and the Walkinshaw set-up must benefit from the early technological advantage they had.'

Hayes is not one to hark back to a golden past. 'It was different, not necessarily better,' he maintains of the pre-sponsorship days. 'It was Indianapolis that showed them the potential of commercial sponsorship. When Jimmy won in 1965, it was $150 for each lap you led on. He led for 190 of 200 laps. Jimmy never talked about money but he was so enchanted by this idea. He said: "It was so funny. I was like a cash register. I kept going around thinking, click – $150, click – $150", but even that was so little money compared to today.'

Clark died just as Lotus signed the first sponsorship deal in 1968 with tobacco giant Gold Leaf. It was Yardley, though, who set the precedent. 'Just imagine. In 1968 men who used scent were dagos or something. Yardley wanted to sell men's perfume, and quite soon every man you met was smelling like a ladies … ' says Hayes, lost for words. 'It set the example to other companies. If by going motor racing you could turn men into walking pomade parlours, it had to be good for your business.'

The Ford-Cosworth and its derivatives won 155 grands prix, the last coming in 1983 before the turbo era kicked in. Sadly, Clark never benefited fully from the DFV engines. Today, as Hayes officially inducts him into Ford's Hall of Fame at a ceremony at Donington Park, the reputation of the shy brooding Scot gains yet more respect. Besides giving Ford a more youthful, exciting image, the purpose of commissioning the magic engine was to win the world championship again for Clark. Unlike Hill or Stewart, his amazing talent was forged in the record books without it.

14 JULY 1997

HIGH ON EMOTION AT GRAND OCCASION
Chris de Burgh

What a day and what a night … not only did I enjoy myself at the British Grand Prix, but I stayed on last evening to take part in my pal Eddie Jordan's now traditional post-race party. He had asked me to sing, and after sharing in Damon Hill's success, being soaked in Jacques Villeneuve's victory Champagne and sharing in Eddie Irvine's disappointment, I was in just the mood for a great night out. It was an exciting race, and I'm sure it made excellent television. But it is possibly a good thing that last night's party was not broadcast as well.

I saw the start with Jordan and I stayed there for about 15 laps before the first refuelling stops, then I made my way along the pits. To be around when the teams are changing tyres and filling the car up with fuel was very exciting and tense. I get a tremendous buzz out of the British Grand Prix. I love motor racing, and this is my fourth grand prix this year. There are a lot of parallels between my business and this business, except this is on a far bigger scale. The organisation that goes into a Formula One race still amazes me. They may not have to cater for 210,000 people over a weekend, but to see all the motorhomes and the work that goes into looking after a team is amazing.

My first personal contact with the sport was when I met up with Nigel Mansell, and I remember being with him at Spa-Francorchamps in 1992, the year he won the championship. He took me in a Renault Espace around the circuit on the Friday night, and it was a real white-knuckle ride. He was just lounging in the front seat, one hand on the wheel, and he was telling me about how fast he would be going through each corner, with the tyres screaming and the smell of burnt rubber. I was sitting there with my knuckles completely white and he just said, 'How do you like that?' What amazes me is that these men can drive around at these speeds, because I think it is absolutely amazing that they are getting close to 200mph at Silverstone. When you get here and see and hear what Formula One is all about, there is a great thrill.

I'm a good friend of the Jordan team, so I would have loved to see them getting on the podium here, but I'm also very fond of Irvine. He lives just down the road from me, and I slept at his house last weekend, drinking some wine and teaching him how to play the guitar – which was kind of interesting. Irvine is one of those wonderful characters in Formula One. He is a blunt Ulsterman, and he is a damn good racer, too. To be second to Michael Schumacher makes him almost one of the big drivers in the world.

I was not too upset to see Villeneuve win, though, because I like seeing him do so well after so much fuss was made of his hair. He is a damn good driver, irrespective of anything else, and I think the same of Damon Hill. He is obviously in a car that is not responding to his particular talents, and it shows brutally how important it is for a driver to have a good car. I think he would have won a few more races if he was still with Williams, so I'm thrilled he scored a point yesterday. It is probably equivalent to winning a race. When he came in sixth my wife and I were in the TWR hospitality box, and there were scenes of great happiness.

But the memory of the British Grand Prix that will stick in my mind came immediately after the race. The new press officer at Williams, Ffiona Welford, said to me: 'Thank God you're here. The last time you came to a race it was Barcelona and we won.' I was standing with her when Villeneuve was spraying the Champagne, and he sprayed it all over us. Afterwards he apologised for getting me soaked, but I said he could spray me anytime because I just adored being there watching the race.

After that, it was party time and my chance to get up on stage. I had been in the studio recording my new album until late on Friday, but this time it was just for fun. And Irvine – even after my guitar lessons – was not expected to stay long. He told me he was off home to Rome.

16 OCTOBER 1997

ERROR-PRONE VILLENEUVE DOES NOT DESERVE TITLE

Eddie Irvine

Whatever the final race produces in Jerez, the Japanese Grand Prix at Suzuka on Sunday will surely prove to be the most memorable of the season. Jacques Villeneuve started the weekend as a near certainty to claim the world championship, but after that run-in with the stewards and an unimpressive race, he ended it with the odds stacked against him. For someone who has consistently had the fastest car, he doesn't deserve to win the title. He makes too many mistakes.

For myself, while it makes a change to be declared a hero – even in the Italian press, who have sacked and replaced me with a different driver each month – my podium finish was disappointing. I was quickest in Friday's practice, third in Saturday qualifying and I don't see how I wouldn't have won the race had I not been called upon to play the team-mate role and help Michael Schumacher to the ten points he needed to upset Villeneuve.

Normally it is on with the next race, but this week I have been bombarded with questions about the 'master strategy' we at Ferrari devised to outwit Villeneuve. So for the record I can report that there is nothing as complex as people imagine. The only plan we sat down to discuss was to pinpoint corners where I would let Michael overtake me if I was in front. Otherwise my role was obvious: to get between Michael and Villeneuve and let Michael get on with it. My race strategy was to do two quick sprints and then put a load of fuel on board to hold up Villeneuve at the end.

Of course it didn't happen that way. Villeneuve led off the start with Michael, Mika Häkkinen and myself close behind. We didn't need a mole in the Williams camp to know that the only thing Villeneuve could do – as he was racing under appeal, knowing that he would lose whatever points he scored – was to try to help other people beat Michael by bunching up the cars so that Michael could be overtaken during pit-stops. However, Villeneuve should have gone along the pit-lane and told the other teams what he wanted them to do, because none of the other guys looked like even thinking of overtaking. They were plodding around on a Sunday drive.

My car felt fantastic. Having found half a second with an improvement to the front wing in testing after the Nürburgring race, and knowing Suzuka as well, I was flying and jumped ahead of Michael in a very satisfying manoeuvre. I said to Michael beforehand that I thought it was possible to overtake on the outside at turn six, and he didn't reckon it was, so he was only half-surprised to see me take them both. I have to say it was a great feeling sweeping past them.

Once I got past Villeneuve, I did what any racing driver aims to do and cruised into as much of a lead as I could. I knew the team would call me over the radio when they needed me to hold up Villeneuve. Sure enough, after 20 laps or so of glory, the call came. They just said: 'Back off, Michael's second now', and then 'Slow down more', and then 'Keep going slow'. It was amusing being part of such teamwork, but at the end of the day I was on the losing end of it. I had to give up a 12-second lead in a grand prix to finish third. And the extra responsibility in racing for someone else's world championship prospects kills some of the immediate enjoyment.

Annoyingly, I had a bad second pit-stop while Heinz-Harald Frentzen in the second Williams had a good one. Having disposed of the Villeneuve threat we then had Frentzen chasing Michael. But he could handle it. Two questions I have been asked. Why could I overtake Villeneuve but not Frentzen? That doesn't look good on the CV, I know, but it was because I had so much fuel on board. Why can't I drive like that all the time? When the car is good you can do the job, and our car hasn't been competitive in some races.

Jerez will be Ferrari's biggest race for 18 years. It's the nearest the team have been to a title since Jody Scheckter. It's not easy racing with the extra onus of responsibility but I will do everything I can to help Michael claim the title within the rules. I won't be aiming to take Villeneuve out, but I will certainly put my car in his way whenever possible.

27 OCTOBER 1997

VILLENEUVE FLAVOURS SUCCESS WITH TOUCH OF POETIC JUSTICE

Timothy Collings in Jerez

The drivers' world championship, which appeared to have been removed from Jacques Villeneuve's grasp so many times this year, by various means, was yesterday delivered, wrapped up with poetic justice, in the most sensational, satisfying and extraordinary circumstances at the European Grand Prix in Jerez. By passing Michael Schumacher's Ferrari and then surviving the German's ill-judged lunge at his Williams, he turned potential calamity into a triumph of such proportion that it prompted a roar of approval among even the most neutral of professional observers, avenged Adelaide '94 for his team and inspired his crew of mechanics to dance in their white 'Billy Idol' wigs on the pit wall.

While their driver was hoisted on to the shoulders of the victorious Mika Häkkinen and David Coulthard on the podium, it was the sight of these temporarily demented Williams men that provided the defining image of the day and the season. This was Jacques' hour, and it was the year he put a broad grin back on the face of grand prix racing. All the conspiracy theories, suggesting that the Italians had the title in the pocket beforehand, were scattered in the winds that kept the temperature down after two days of searing heat. It was a sublime moment for Formula One, providing those who recalled the acrimony of the 1994 Australian Grand Prix, when Schumacher's collision with Damon Hill brought him his first world title, with a chance to celebrate in the joy of a sporting victor.

As it turned out Villeneuve, his car damaged in the controversial collision on the 48th lap, slowed down on the 69th and final lap of a pulsating contest to allow the two McLarens of Häkkinen and Coulthard to pass him. It was Häkkinen's first Formula One win and came in his 96th race, courtesy of gentleman Jacques. Villeneuve, son of the renowned Ferrari driver Gilles

Villeneuve, who was killed in qualifying for the 1982 Belgian Grand Prix, thus became the first man to win the IndyCar World Series – which he dominated in 1995 – cross the Atlantic and then conquer Formula One. In the final reckoning, as Schumacher and Villeneuve were called to see the stewards – they concluded, incredibly, that it was a racing accident and no further action was necessary – there was no doubt that the Canadian's honesty, his doggedness and his huge-hearted approach deserved to be rewarded. In short, he had stuck it out.

Schumacher, a controversial victor in Suzuka two weeks earlier – when Ferrari's tactics paid off fully, following the disqualification muddle surrounding Villeneuve – finished the season with five wins and 78 points to the Canadian's total of seven wins and 81 points. Schumacher was not just beaten this time, he was humiliated. It may have been a narrow, last-gasp win for Villeneuve, but by surviving the double champion's smash-and-grab attack for a third title, he did the sport's image, as well as his own standing in it, an honourable service as the sun set on Andalusia and a roller-coaster year. Villeneuve said: 'This championship feels great. It's been such an up-and-down season. We've been the most competitive team since the beginning of the year, but there have been many races where we didn't get the job done, races where I made a few mistakes. The team also made some, and somehow things didn't go right when they should have gone right. But, after the disqualification at Suzuka, it feels great to have won the title here, and I'm really delighted. My deepest thoughts are private now, of course, and I'm keeping them to myself, but I'm very happy.

'I wasn't really surprised when Michael decided to turn in on me. It was a little bit expected from my point of view. And I knew I was the one taking the risk because I braked too late. But when he touched me, we banged wheels and my car really jumped off the ground and into the air. I really felt that the crash had broken something. Luckily, he went off the road, but my car felt very strange, especially in the right-hand corners, and the rear end wasn't stable at all after that. I could only push hard for a few laps because the tyres were heating up in a very strange way and it was tough to keep on pushing. But I knew right away that Michael was out of the race, because of the way he hit me. He hit me really, really hard. I'm surprised that I was able to actually finish the race. When he came over on me, I couldn't move over any further because I was already on the grass. Either Michael had his eyes closed or, somehow, his hands slipped off the steering wheel or something.' He added: 'I half-expected him to try it and I was ready. He just turned in on me, but he just didn't do it well enough – and he went out and I didn't.'

Villeneuve's refreshing candour, his willingness to go where others fear to tread, and his ability to smile when all around him appear to be on the point of a nervous breakdown, has earned him friends and foes this year. But despite the disappointment of Monaco – where the heavens opened for Schumacher and Ferrari, and Williams forgot to look at the skies – and his skirmish with the ruling body before embarrassment in Canada, he came through unscathed.

Damon Hill, who was expected to play a major role, ended up among the spectators when, after starting fourth on the grid, he retired on the same lap as Schumacher's shunt-helped exit with a gearbox problem. Hill said of Schumacher, his old nemesis: 'He showed his true colours today and he got what he deserved. I said before the race that I didn't think he would do anything like that again, because it would spoil his image, but I was wrong.'

The race, overshadowed by the crash, appeared to be going Schumacher's way from the start when, with the help of his electronic differential, he made a tearaway start to build up a lead of 5.2 seconds at the first pit-stop after 22 laps. Villeneuve, on used tyres for the first section, had Frentzen to thank for letting him rise from third to second, but it was only when he was on new tyres before and after his second pit-stop that he could attack with real venom. He closed the gap, drove with passion and caught the Ferrari, taking advantage when Schumacher, in a rare lapse of concentration, presented a gap on the inside at the Dry Sack curve. Schumacher drove his right front wheel into the middle of the Williams sidepod and, as the car recovered, bounced off into the gravel. Schumacher said: 'Jacques had nothing to lose and he went for it. To be honest, I would have done the same. I braked as late as possible, he braked even later. ... He took a chance and it paid off.'

28 OCTOBER 1997

FERRARI TEAM DETERMINED TO GO ONE BETTER

Eddie Irvine

I hear Michael Schumacher has been summoned before the World Motor Sport Council following his incident with Jacques Villeneuve in Sunday's

European Grand Prix, but it isn't my place to comment on this challenge to his reputation. I thought it was a great race, and I have to say, a great move by Villeneuve to steal the championship from my Ferrari team-mate. There was nothing wrong with Michael's car when Villeneuve slipped up the inside of the Dry Sack curve and caught him on the hop. Michael slowed down a bit to look after his tyres, and Jacques caught him off guard. Michael was very depressed after all the build-up, but as a team we can't complain. In fact, right after the race we were having a good laugh because Willi Weber, Michael's manager, had ordered 100,000 Michael Schumacher World Champion 1997 commemorative caps and 250,000 T-shirts.

We were always going to have an end-of-season party, win or lose. Strange as it sounds, ours was the most cheerful, according to those who did the rounds of all the teams' celebrations. Ever since the Japanese Grand Prix, where our teamwork put Michael into a potential winning position, the pressure has been intense. To be so close to a title after 18 years, in Ferrari's 50th year, had the whole of Italy stirred up.

In a sense I wasn't part of that because I didn't have the responsibility to shoulder. After my role at Suzuka, life was easier: everyone in Milan was suddenly my best friend, which hasn't always been the case. But at Jerez it even affected me. I don't normally notice that kind of atmosphere, but it was overwhelming. I made a mistake in qualifying, which left me disappointed with seventh on the grid. We had a car set up so that it was capable of pole, but I forgot to change the brake balance going into one of the corners on my best lap. It probably annoyed Michael because we had our plans about my potential role in supporting his championship prospects, but after qualifying on the fourth row there was very little I could do. I'd been working on tyre and fuel evaluations for his benefit and that meant I couldn't focus on my own qualifying as much as I'd have liked.

People will talk and talk about the way Michael reacted to Villeneuve's move but you have to conclude that the best car won. Our Ferrari was nowhere near as good as the Williams, and yet we were fighting for both the constructors' and drivers' titles in the last two races of the season. Williams gave us that opportunity because they made mistakes, both the team and the drivers. We weren't expecting championship glory this season but by the end of the year it was tantalisingly close. It was going to be a big deal whether we won or lost. Now we've seen a taste of what we can do and we're coming back even stronger next year. The close finish on Sunday showed how competitive the sport has become. Even I, the total buffoon, could have finished two seconds behind the leader if Giancarlo Fisichella hadn't been messing around holding everyone up in the final laps. Next year we could be awesome.

3 NOVEMBER 1997
LETTERS TO THE SPORTS EDITOR
FORMULA ONE'S RULING BODY MUST ACT NOW

Sir,

Your headline ran 'Villeneuve flavours success with touch of poetic justice', and we all celebrated his escape from the clutches of a blatant cheating attempt. What would have been the headline if Villeneuve had been forced to retire immediately, or if his car had suffered damage leading to a fatal accident some laps later? The fact that he has won gives the sport's governing body their greatest ever chance of penalising cheating with the deduction of world championship points. They must act now to avoid future denigration of the sport.

Simon Hester
Pulborough, Sussex

Sir,

The unconcealed elation of sportswriters at the defeat and humiliation of Michael Schumacher is predictable, but does not make appetising reading. Schumacher appears to have been already tried and condemned with no credit being given to his own account that the incident in Jerez was a misjudgment, an account accepted by the stewards in Jerez at the time. The fact that Schumacher has never been forgiven in this country for allegedly depriving Damon Hill of 'his' championship title in 1994, a view made all too apparent by the mean-spirited reaction to Schumacher's accident by Hill himself.

Now, in the midst of rejoicing over Schumacher's perceived comeuppance, can we please remember that this man is not only the outstanding driver of his generation, but that throughout his nightmare first season with Ferrari in 1996, and the cruelly dashed hopes of 1997, he has never uttered a word of criticism or reproach towards his car, his team or his fellow drivers.

Yvette Moyse
London SW19

SCHUMACHER 'LET-OFF' SPARKS ANGRY REACTION IN PADDOCK

Timothy Collings

Formula One insiders and observers reacted with anger and dismay last night after Michael Schumacher escaped serious punishment for his 'road rage' ramming of Jacques Villeneuve in the European Grand Prix at Jerez last month. Damon Hill, Jackie Stewart and Ken Tyrrell led the amazed reactions on a day when motor racing's high court appeared to bow to commercial pressure and duck out of an opportunity to make an example of the German double world champion.

Instead of punishing Schumacher and Ferrari and sending a warning to all in the sport that reckless driving and unsporting behaviour would not be tolerated, the verdict from the extraordinary meeting of the World Motor Sport Council of the ruling body, the Federation Internationale de l'Automobile (FIA), confirmed that Schumacher was beyond reach. He was expected to be handed a points penalty for next season and perhaps fined, but was instead stripped of his runner-up spot in the 1997 season and asked to perform seven days of work promoting road safety.

Experienced reporters who crowded into the white frilly-trimmed marquee inside the RAC Motor Sports' Association's headquarters at Colnbrook, near Slough, declared the sentence a whitewash and a scandal, and the FIA's president, Max Mosley, was subjected to a series of hostile questions. None of the answers, however, proved satisfactory for the journalists present, or the many Formula One insiders who followed the hearing and its aftermath through the media or by other means.

Hill said: 'It is not the kind of heavy sanction that we were expecting, or that we were promised by Max Mosley at the drivers' briefing in Jerez.' Hill, whose chance of winning the 1994 world drivers' championship perished when Schumacher collided with him in Adelaide, added: 'He has said his move on Jacques was instinctive – but it is also instinctive to try to avoid an accident and far more natural. I think it is a long way short of what constitutes a serious sanction and it is hard to take it seriously.'

Stewart, three times a world champion and now chairman of the Stewart-Ford team, was stunned by the decision not to hit Schumacher with the kind of draconian punishment promised for any miscreant drivers in Jerez. His views made it clear that he believed the World Motor Sport Council had failed in their duty. He said: 'My chief concern is that this was a very good opportunity to drive home to every single racing driver, from Formula One to Formula Ford, that if you behave in a manner that is unbecoming to the sport, you won't get away with it. I don't think they have taken this opportunity, and it is disappointing.'

Tyrrell, the most experienced team owner in the pit-lane, said: 'Schumacher has not been punished at all. Losing second place in the drivers' championship will have no effect on him. In my opinion, he should have been allowed to start the season, but been given a points penalty.' Former grand prix driver Derek Warwick, who tangled with Schumacher and nearly punched him during a fracas at a sports car event at the Nürburgring in 1991, said: 'The one thing the FIA have to be is consistent. So, you have to ask, if it had been [Shinji] Nakano, or [Tarso] Marques, would it have been the same?'

However, triple world champion Niki Lauda, who prior to the hearing had said that Schumacher's actions were deliberate, described the sentence as 'brutal' last night. 'I'm surprised by the harshness of it, because Schumacher, until Jerez, had had a good season in difficult conditions.' The Austrian, who has been advocating football-style red and yellow cards to punish drivers, said the decision had serious implications for the sport. 'I fear that if this type of decision becomes commonplace then people will lose interest in motorsport because spectacular manoeuvres will effectively be outlawed.' Gerhard Berger, who drove for Schumacher's former team, Benetton, last season, said: 'In the end it's not a bad solution. It's acceptable for Schumacher, and everything is set for next year's championship.'

David Richards, chief executive of Benetton, called it 'a creative compromise and not one that I had envisaged', while television commentator Murray Walker said: 'I like to think that what happened at Jerez was an involuntary reaction to someone coming down the inside of him. That being the case, I don't take as grave a view as some. I'm mindful that Alain Prost and Ayrton Senna, two of the all-time greats, each did something similar and got away with it.'

Schumacher, who arrived wearing a heavy black leather overcoat in a red Alfa Romeo, accompanied by his manager, Willi Weber, and Ferrari sporting director, Jean Todt, said he was looking forward to a holiday and a chance to recharge in readiness for 1998, but few of those who witnessed the shunt in Jerez, or yesterday's proceedings, could feel much warmth at either prospect.

FORMULA ONE TEAM ACQUITTED OF MANSLAUGHTER CHARGES

Timothy Collings

Frank Williams and his team had every reason to sigh with relief and lift a celebratory glass last night when Judge Antonio Costanza acquitted technical director Patrick Head and former chief designer Adrian Newey, now with McLaren, of all manslaughter charges relating to the death of Ayrton Senna during the 1994 San Marino Grand Prix at Imola. For Williams, his team and Formula One, it was the end of a dark chapter in a glorious history. Williams, Head and Newey were charged, along with race director Roland Bruynseraede and two track officials, Federico Bendinelli and Giorgio Poggi, in a verdict which was widely greeted as a victory for common sense.

Delight, as expected, quickly spread throughout the Formula One fraternity. After a period of embattled efforts to polish up an image tarnished by the Jerez grand prix, collusion allegations, £1 million donations and tobacco rows, it was the most welcome news of the year. 'I never doubted the team or their integrity in any way, and this is the right outcome,' said Damon Hill, who was Senna's team-mate on the afternoon he died at the Tamburello curve in a 192mph collision with a concrete wall. 'I have always known that Williams's cars were both safe and competitive. If I didn't believe that, I wouldn't have driven for them. I know that this trial has been hanging over the whole team, and I'm very happy that the court has reached the correct verdict at last.'

Veteran former team owner Ken Tyrrell, who has been active in grand prix motor racing longer than any other principal, said he was very pleased with the decision, read aloud in the court in Imola by the judge. It took Costanza less than 60 seconds to bring three years, seven months and 15 days of official investigations and legal suspense to an end. 'Like other teams, I'm delighted,' said Tyrrell. 'They brought in the right verdict. This idea that Williams, the most successful team in racing history, could be put in this position, or have made any mistake, was quite extraordinary in the first place. The fact that Frank and the rest of his team have coped with this major problem during a championship year says something about the Williams team. In motorsport we have our own governing body – the Federation Internationale de l'Automobile – and they should have dealt with it, not a court of law. I know it's Italian law, but if there's going to continue to be racing in Italy that has to happen in future. Any other verdict could have put motorsport in Italy in jeopardy.'

As the rejoicing and the recriminations about the trial began to swirl, the Williams team stayed calm. Even in the hour of their vindication, the Grove-based outfit adopted a sober and dignified stance in keeping with their position throughout the protracted inquiries which resulted in 31 court sessions. 'Our legal advisors inform us that the prosecution has an automatic right of appeal,' the team pointed out in a statement. 'Clearly, we would hope that this matter will not be pursued further. We firmly believe that this was the only appropriate outcome of the trial, and we now look forward to the 1998 season with confidence and enthusiasm.'

The ruling body, the FIA, were equally prudent in their initial reaction. 'The FIA has noted today's decision … but will not comment until it has examined the full text of the decision and studied its implications,' said a statement from Paris. Like everyone else connected with Formula One, the FIA's president Max Mosley will now hope this is the end of the whole Senna tragedy.

The Williams team solicitor, Peter Goodman – whose life has been consumed by constructing the team's successful defence against allegations that faulty welding in the modification of Senna's car's steering column led to a steering failure which caused the crash – said: 'It's the right verdict. The trial was correctly done. And Williams will be pleased that it's all over and that it has gone successfully for him.'

The prosecuting magistrate, Maurizio Passarini, had advised the judge last month that there was no case for Williams, Bruynseraede or the two circuit officials to answer, but called for convictions for Head and Newey, together with one-year suspended sentences. He said they were responsible for 'microscopic' errors in the modification of the steering column of Senna's car, a claim dismissed by yesterday's brief, dramatic and, hopefully, final scene.

The family of the Brazilian, who won the world drivers' championship three times and who was revered in his native land, were never involved in the proceedings, but followed them through their lawyer, Giovanni Carcaterra. He said: 'The family did not seek a conviction, but wanted only an explanation of the circumstances.' In the event, they will probably agree with Frank Williams's assessment after giving evidence in October when he said: 'We'll probably never know what happened for certain.'

WINNING ONE CHAMPIONSHIP HAS DONE NOTHING TO QUENCH MY THIRST FOR VICTORY

Jacques Villeneuve, F1 World Champion

My first world championship title now seems the stuff of memories, and there are many. I think it was in Canada that I first realised what the title really meant. I was in Montreal to see my fans just one week after the last grand prix, and I was overwhelmed by the warmth of the reception. But after the euphoria of victory in the United States it was time to come back down to earth and think about training again.

If 1997 was an exceptional year, it ended on a sour note. I was skiing in France with some friends, including a former Swiss national ski coach. Together we took the slopes at a lively speed when I made a mistake that sent me hurtling into the trees. I got back to my feet and continued my descent. When I got to the bottom, my friends commented that I didn't look too well and I did feel slightly faint. I told them not to worry, but they insisted on taking me to hospital where I was diagnosed with a mild concussion, which made me calm down for a few days.

But it takes more than that to keep me off the slopes. As soon as possible I had my skis back on. This winter, I started slalom training again as I had done while at school in Switzerland. It is a new challenge and a useful form of physical training. I was also able to get in two days' skiing off-piste on the slopes of the French Alps. Days on the slopes were interspersed with promotional activities and, from December, with the testing programme.

My car, the FW20, was to get its new livery at the beginning of the year, and my team, Winfield Williams, launched it at the end of January at Silverstone. After a press conference and a photo opportunity, I was in my seat to try out the new car. First impressions were very positive; a different sensation compared to last year, but it has potential. The many test sessions in February allowed us to put in some hard work on the tuning. As always, these tests were carried out in an atmosphere of friendly co-operation. Thanks to good working relationships between the members of the team, improving and putting the final touches to the new car became all the more interesting.

The regulations coming into force will certainly cause a few surprises during the first races. But it is difficult to make any exact predictions before tomorrow's race in Melbourne. The teams test by themselves without really giving anything away. Journalists are always asking me what I think of this team who completed the fastest lap on a circuit this year, or that team who have some problem. In the sport of Formula One predictions and suspicions provoke endless discussions and fill up the pages of the motor-racing press. For myself, I simply want to be in my FW20 on the Melbourne circuit. Only then will we see who has the best car.

I am impatient to get started. Winning one championship has done nothing to quench my thirst for victory; a second world championship is my goal for 1998. The newcomers who have marked the beginning of the season only serve to heighten my determination to prove myself against the other drivers. My team-mate, Heinz-Harald Frentzen, and I have already covered many kilometres in our FW20s in training, carried out calmly and without pressure. I am more composed and relaxed than I was last year and will be cool and calm here in Australia.

I wonder what is likely to stir up the media: a new tyre war, a team of outstanding superiority, or maybe a driver with a new hair colour? That's the fashion with sportsmen. Those who dyed their hair red for the Winter Olympics included a gold medallist snowboarder and the winner in the men's slalom. One thing is for sure: the pressure mounts, the engines roar. Let the games begin.

21 MARCH 1998

HILL DESPERATE TO TURN UP HEAT AND RUIN FORMULA ONE SOUFFLÉ

Giles Smith

'The truth of the matter is that the last three races have been fixed,' said Damon Hill. We were sitting on the upper deck of the Jordan Grand Prix motorhome, parked behind the garages of the Catalunya racetrack near Barcelona, the site of this week's Jordan car testing. Hill was wearing a leather jacket, white jeans and a polo-neck jumper which, along with a new, grey-flecked beard, lent him something of the look of a French student, circa 1968. 'The last three races have been affected by agreements either between teams or between drivers in the same team,' Hill went on.

So let's just recap. A fortnight ago there was Melbourne, where David Coulthard and Mika Häkkinen did their 'After you/No, after you' routine, to widespread dismay. Before that, at the end of last season, there was Jerez, when Jacques Villeneuve, with the world championship safely his, let the McLarens slip through to enjoy some sponsor-appeasing podium action. And before that, there was Japan.

'Do you remember Jacques went really slowly?' asked Hill. 'What was supposed to happen there was, McLaren were supposed to win the race to prevent Michael Schumacher scoring maximum points, but it backfired rather badly.' Indeed. Eddie Irvine in a Ferrari nipped past, like someone who couldn't quite believe his luck. And, in a way, he was right not to. 'With Coulthard and Häkkinen, that's contrived,' Hill said. 'It's good PR for Mercedes and McLaren to appear to have everything under control. But the public didn't want that. The public want to see cars racing. And David doesn't want to graciously hand over his hard-earned race to Mika. And Mika doesn't want to hand it over to David. But they're caught in this bloody sponsorship and PR bloody soufflé, and it's ruining everything.'

Thus, Damon Hill on the state of Formula One in 1998. And apparently a few more personal spats wouldn't go amiss, either. 'You've got the seeds of something going on with Jacques and Michael,' Hill said. 'But really they should be fuming. They should be at each other's throats. Jacques should be saying what he really thinks. I know Jacques, and I know what he really thinks about Michael. But no, it's all played down. The team don't want it, and the sponsors don't want bad feeling. But actually it would make the sport alive again.'

I asked Hill if the McLaren pre-race pact wasn't justifiable in terms of team tactics. 'Who's interested in the team result of Formula One?' he replied. 'Mercedes are interested in it, and McLaren. But the fans aren't. People who turn on motor racing do not watch it to see which team wins the constructors' championship. There's an obligation, I believe, to provide the public with an unadulterated event.'

Two days after our interview, Formula One's governors proposed unspecified punishments for all future arrangements, which are embedded deep in drivers' contracts and in private motorhome dealings. In the end, it's probably only the teams and sponsors who can make any difference. 'The only time pressure will come to bear,' Hill said, 'is when people start watching something else. Then they'll pay attention.'

Currently, Hill drives under no team orders—except a pleading command that he win something. At 37, he has signed for two years with victory-less Jordan, with the option of a third year. Hill could finish his career there, but this will not be some casual, twilight phase. The fixing of races angers him but it does not appear to have softened his enthusiasm for racing. 'I'm looking to get back up the front,' he says firmly. It is an outcome many of us would enjoy. Hill's cruelly public dismissal from the Williams team in 1996 – after six years of service and three races from the end of the season, when Hill was ten points away from winning the world championship – was a bad thing to happen to a nice bloke. 'I very much took the view that I was stuffed,' Hill said. 'I make no bones about it. I was very hurt by what happened, by not being kept on. I had to go through a year at the back of the grid as world champion, which was not something I particularly enjoyed. I can't shake that off. I could have knocked it on the head, but I felt I drove better at the end of 1996 than I'd ever driven, and I thought I got better again last year, so I have the feeling I can bring something to the equation that's of use.'

Hill could have spent last season with Jordan, but he was lured to Arrows by Tom Walkinshaw, who got up a high wind of optimism about the team's prospects. 'I didn't go for Jordan because I had more belief that if things worked well with Tom then the potential was greater, because Tom's resources are greater, to be frank,' Hill said. 'He's an extremely well-backed businessman. But it was always going to be touch and go.'

As it turned out, last season for Arrows was mostly touch and stop. 'The engine kept blowing up, so we hardly got any testing done between races,' Hill said. It threatened to take Hill from British sporting hero to an Eddie the Eagle figure in a matter of months. Except that Hill bore with dignity twists which would have humiliated a weaker person. He was to be seen assisting the marshals in the removal of his stricken car, and he was probably as heroic in that moment as at any point in his career. We can probably rely on Hill not to dwell on last year. He does not seem to go in much for looking back, not even at videos of his races. 'They have a sort of soporific effect on me when I see them afterwards,' he said, and laughed noisily. 'Even races I've been winning.'

After our interview, Hill had supper with the team in the garage and talked at length with his engineers. It was dark by the time we got back to the hotel. The car park was full, but these are the moments when it helps to be alongside a Formula One driver. Hill distinguished himself by getting the car across a pavement and on to a small triangle reserved for motorbikes.

The next morning, Hill arrived at the track shortly after 8.30a.m., consumed a large bowl of fruit, a larger bowl of cereal and a mug of coffee and then went and changed into his flame-retardant overalls. After the political electricity of Williams, and the shortage of most kinds of power at Arrows, it's possible that Jordan – widely agreed to be the carefree, rock'n'roll team in Formula One – offer Hill a place to breathe more easily. I asked Gary Anderson, Jordan's technical director, why they chose Barcelona for testing. He replied: 'Because the wine's good and the food's good.'

That said, the garage was the scene for the kind of quiet and serious application which might accompany heart surgery. Chiefly, testing is long periods of inactivity broken by sudden phases in which absolutely nothing happens whatsoever. Then abruptly, the engine will fire up, the car will go out, magnificently rupture the tranquillity of a warm Spanish afternoon for a couple of laps and then return beneath the mute gaze of the mechanics.

People declare Hill an uncommonly professional and attentive tester. One Jordan team member said he had been surprised by how much talking Hill does on the intercom, both in testing and racing. 'He wants to know everything,' he said. Ralf Schumacher, Hill's team-mate, can blow hot and cold in testing, according to his mood. Hill stays even. But then, as Hill said: 'What most drivers crave is to have a clear track, new tyres, low fuel and give it the max.' Most of us can only begin to imagine what that might feel like: some life-depleting cocktail, no doubt, of wired nerves and adrenal mayhem accompanied by bowel-slackening horror. But, as Hill explained it, it sounded more like yoga. 'If you're going a second quicker, you are aware of it. Even half a second. That's the addiction,' he said. 'That's the thing people get hooked on. It's like a meditation; you're completely in touch with that split second. Which in a way is a kind of relaxation as well. Your head's so muddled most of the time with all the things you've got to think about. But there's nothing else at that particular moment that matters. So it's quite a tranquil experience as well.'

And out of this meditation may come the transcendent moments which only the best drivers know. 'Sometimes you get it right, where the car goes through a corner at a speed you want it to do which you didn't believe the car was capable of doing. And you get a real buzz from that. Or you clip the apex at the right place, you just go right to the edge of the kerb on the exit and you're on the power really early, and it's all flowed beautifully ... '

Did he think many such moments lay ahead for him this season? 'I don't think there's any reason why Jordan can't elevate themselves into the position of a front-running team. It's not quantum physics, it's simple physics. We're confronted with a simple problem: how to make a racing car go round a circuit two per cent quicker.' He sounds emphatic and determined like this a lot of the time. 'Believe me I want to win,' he said at one point. 'I do not want to be tugging around in ninth place, or whatever I was last weekend.'

'Eighth, actually,' I said, in an attempt to be optimistic.

'Big difference,' Hill said.

2 NOVEMBER 1998

HÄKKINEN COMES OF AGE ON 'SPECIAL DAY' FOR McLAREN

Timothy Collings at Suzuka

He smiled, danced and waved to the massed flag-waving Finns who had made the long but rewarding journey east. He even sang aloud and whistled in his car as McLaren team chief Ron Dennis, on the pits-to-cockpit radio told him the news. 'Michael Schumacher is out of the race and you are the world champion'. Mika 'the Iceman' Häkkinen melted yesterday, at last. He made no effort to conceal his delight at becoming only the second man from his homeland to win the world drivers' championship on his way to victory in an extraordinary Japanese Grand Prix.

One thousand days after his life-threatening accident in Adelaide in 1995, a year on from his maiden victory in the European Grand Prix at Jerez, the man from Helsinki came of age. It was his eighth win of the season, his ninth in all, and with it came a championship built out of hard work, teamwork and determination, even if yesterday his rival was eliminated by a combination of misfortunes.

To his credit, Schumacher was the first to congratulate the victor in the *parc fermé*. Changed back into his civvies of jeans and Ferrari-red sweater, the German showed commendable sportsmanship and regained the sympathy of many former admirers who had been upset by his move on Jacques Villeneuve in last year's title-decider in Spain. He recognised that this season belonged to Häkkinen and his Mercedes-powered McLaren team, and that Bridgestone had won the tyre war against Goodyear. It was only a shame, for the public, that the long-awaited showdown never really happened because the Ferrari driver's race was over before it had begun.

Not one but two starts were aborted, the second because Schumacher had stalled his Ferrari in pole position. That he then drove from the back of the field to reach third position in 22 laps in quite coruscating fashion counted not a jot. It may have been all over when his right rear tyre exploded, and he was blown out of the title race after only 32 of the 51 laps contested, but the blunders on the grid killed this one for Ferrari. 'My heart sank because it meant we could not fight from the start,' said Ferrari president Luca di Montezemolo afterwards. It was a spectacle made to savour, with Schumacher and Häkkinen sharing the front row, but one that was wrecked by an overheated clutch in front of 148,000 spectators.

With Schumacher's car removed to join the also-rans, Häkkinen started the race with no one to obscure his view. He took control, drove flawlessly and claimed a victory that was a credit to his temperament and talent. He came home, after two pit-stops, 6.5 seconds clear of Eddie Irvine in the second Ferrari, with David Coulthard third in the second McLaren. It was a comprehensive triumph, McLaren's first in the drivers' title race since 1991, when Ayrton Senna also carried them to their seventh constructors' crown.

'This is a very special day for me,' said Häkkinen later. 'It has taken me a while to win the championship but now it has happened I feel very happy. The team achieved a lot this season, and this is the perfect result for us all, not just me. The two false starts meant I had to stay focused despite the disruptions, and I have to say that the team did a fantastic job to keep the car at its optimum.'

Häkkinen's remarks about his car's condition were important. For, while McLaren's mechanics swarmed out to keep his car cool with packs of dry ice, Ferrari's were content to give Schumacher only the minimum of attention. 'They did great work and cooled my car down,' said Häkkinen. 'But that didn't happen to Michael, so I guess he had a problem with engines or clutch or temperatures, or something like that. ... I did not know what was happening. So I just tried to focus, and then they said they were moving him to the back of the grid, and I thought, "That's nice", and it made me feel it was done.'

So, while Schumacher was consigned to double trouble, Häkkinen was left with only his own nervous system as an enemy. 'It was easier than some races his year, but the pressure was on me,' he said. 'It disturbed me a little, but the team played a big part in keeping me supplied with information. But the problem when you are leading like that is that your mind starts thinking about things other than driving. But Ron [Dennis] came on the radio and he reminded me to stay cool. It worked.'

12 JULY 1999

SCHUMACHER THE SURVIVOR

Paul Hayward

A popular complaint about modern Formula One is that there is no over-taking, no edge, no danger. There is a short piece of cockpit video footage from yesterday's British Grand Prix which scotches that theory. It shows Michael Schumacher encased in an 800-horsepower carbon-fibre chassis hurtling towards a wall as dramatically as Ayrton Senna's wheeled coffin at Imola. Then the Ferrari strikes, and the picture disintegrates into electronic waves and snow.

In that moment of visual breakdown, Schumacher's life might also have lost its force. Last night he was nursing a broken right leg in Northampton General Hospital after being airlifted from the Silverstone medical centre by helicopter. Before the chopper rose, the world's most gifted driver was able to phone his wife and family in Switzerland to tell them he was alive. In the Williams garage, Schumacher's brother, Ralf, was given the same news. Pale, pained around the eyes, the younger of the Schumacher boys climbed back into his own million-pound land-rocket and chased home David Coulthard and Eddie Irvine to finish third, two places ahead of Damon Hill, who may decide today whether to race on to the end of the season.

Schumacher broke both the tibia and fibula in his right leg and was oper-ated on last night as his crumpled Ferrari was flown back to Maranello for tests. The team's engineers are saying officially that the cause may have been defective rear brakes. The blood-curdling nanoseconds in which Schu-macher fizzed off the track on the opening lap at the end of the ultra-fast Hangar straight were a reminder that racing drivers and prize fighters risk a personal apocalypse every time they dress for work. The crash also provided a fresh perspective on Hill's unending dilemma. As the race was restarted, with Schumacher being driven away in an ambulance, the eye fell on the yellow Jordan of Hill, who might have been tempted right there to turn off the ignition on a distinguished career.

Hill raced on, and so, too, did the brother of a man who has confessed to whipping every ounce of effort out of the Prancing Horse in his pursuit of Ferrari's first drivers' championship for 20 years. 'It's not easy getting back in the car when your brother's just had an accident,' said Ralf, who was kept informed of his brother's condition over the car radio. For three years Michael Schumacher has had his foot to the floor chasing a Ferrari world title. As smoke billowed from his tyres, and his car flew perilously on when it should have been turning Stowe corner, it was reasonable to wonder whether he had just tipped himself over 'the edge' which Ferrari have been occupying in their attempt to pull back the superior McLarens of Coulthard and Mika Häkkinen, who retired after 35 laps. In sixth gear, and at speeds of up to 182mph down Hangar straight, disfigurement and even death are only a tiny miscalculation by toes or fingers away.

'Brake late here,' wrote Coulthard in his programme notes. But did Schumacher push that policy too far? The dread chill that settled over Silverstone spoke of a trauma far deeper than the one he finally endured. For the tearful Ferrari fans who watched the gathering swell of medical personnel at Stowe Corner, haunting memories of the 1999 British Grand Prix will endure. The raising of a white sheet as Schumacher was removed from his buckled car was hideous. As they loaded him into the ambulance, there was a white sheet at the back and a green one at the side. The front of his car had disappeared. Safety stewards pulled out bits of metallic debris from the triple bank of tyres. It was like watching the aftermath of an air crash.

By then, a Ferrari official was on his way to the grid to speak to Ralf. Schumacher rose from his sunken chamber and rushed into the Ferrari garage to hear the latest news. Soon, his brother's car came back on a lorry marked Trowbridge Vehicle Contracts. It seemed too prosaic for such a potentially momentous event. The Ferrari engineers threw a red cape above the car and lowered it into the pits. From above, they looked like red insects reclaiming the shattered shell of their king.

Schumacher's chance of winning the 1999 title has surely gone. It is a measure of his stature that people were willing to bet last night on him being back in his hot seat before the end of the summer. A more compelling question is whether there will be any lasting psychological damage when he resumes the task of trying to win races in the sport's second most proficient car. Even a driver as implacably certain of his own abilities as Schumacher is entitled to feel a gush of trepidation next time he tries to eke out an extra split second on a difficult corner. This F1 campaign is now severely diminished. Without a Schumacher–Schumacher rivalry, an already quiet season is in danger of turning into an extended victory lap for the McLarens. Bernie Ecclestone, the game's ringmaster, will be rifling through his manual of impresario's tricks to get the punters rolling in for the second half of the season.

The 200 sensors that fill an Fı car are no help when a wall of tyres is rising before you at 100mph-plus. Nor is a reputation as the world's most capable and ruthless car-jockey. In those seconds, the machine has conquered the man. Senna was destroyed in one when it struck a concrete wall that came to be seen as the hard outer limit of one sportsman's genius. The technology that Schumacher has spent his life trying to control was suddenly and perhaps fatally in charge of him. But somewhere in Switzerland, his voice was heard at the end of a telephone line conveying the news that he was safe. Motor racing's reputation as a test of mortality is equally secure.

19 JULY 1999

THE MAN WHO REPAIRS THE LOOSE SLATES

Michael Parkinson

When Michael Schumacher crashed at Silverstone, the thought occurred, not for the first time, that those who drive racing cars have a slate loose. The theory is substantiated by the man who is in the best position to judge. Apart from being one of the world's leading neurosurgeons, Sid Watkins has not missed a grand prix since 1978. Officially, he is chairman of the FIA medical commission; unofficially, he is the family doctor of the whole shebang.

He says: 'As a neurosurgeon, I should hardly be required at a motor race, because the drivers do not have any brains, otherwise they wouldn't race.' There's an alternative, more vivid opinion that racing drivers have small brains but large balls. He is joking, of course. On the other hand, whatever brains racing drivers possess have been made safer by Sid Watkins.

When I met Watkins the other day, he told me that had the Silverstone safety measures been applied at Imola in 1994, then it was more than likely Ayrton Senna would have survived. When he went to his first British Grand Prix, at Brands Hatch 20 years ago, he found the medical centre underneath the stand without access to the circuit. The rooms were inadequate both in terms of equipment and personnel. On his first tour he found two ambulance men drinking beer. He asked to be shown the oxygen supply. They couldn't find the spanner key required to turn it on.

Imola 1994 was the watershed. Before the race Watkins expressed the view that the gung-ho, dashing, devil-may-care world of Fı was out of tune, that sociological changes were so marked that the old panache of Fı was no longer acceptable. The death of Senna at that meeting gave terrible weight to his prophecy. He was particularly close to Senna, and when I asked him what made a racing driver he told me a story about a visit they made to the Jimmy Clark Museum in Duns, Scotland. They were lost and looking for directions when Senna said: 'There's a sign.' He pointed ahead. Watkins couldn't even see the signpost. It was 100 yards away, yet Senna said: 'It says Jimmy Clark Museum.' It did. 'Extraordinary visual acuity,' is how Watkins describes it. Further proof they are not like you and me, says I.

In the crusade to make F1 a safer sport, Watkins gives particular praise to two people. Jackie Stewart was the man who originated the crusade and Bernie Ecclestone the one who embraced it. Ecclestone's unchallenged power within the sport provided the cutting edge for swift change. At one grand prix, Watkins was having a problem persuading the locals to see things his way; they were reluctant to implement a safety precaution he felt was necessary. The drivers were on the grid and waiting for the off when Ecclestone intervened. After Watkins had explained the problem, Ecclestone said to the objectors: 'I am going to walk down on to the starting grid. When I get there, I will look back to where you are now sitting. If Professor Watkins gives me the thumbs-up, we go. If he gives me the thumbs-down, then we all go home.' The race went ahead.

Ecclestone's domination of the sport is not uncontroversial. But what is indisputable is that he has created a well-run, beautifully presented sport with the largest worldwide audience of any, including football. Moreover, in the important area of learning from its mistakes, particularly in the crucial area of safety, it has created an enviable reputation. As Peter Hamlyn, another neurosurgeon, wrote in these columns last week, the evaluation of what happened at Silverstone will be used to make the sport even safer. You begin to understand what Watkins meant when he told me: 'The Michael Schumacher crash was a very important one.'

Hamlyn is to boxing what Watkins is to F1, but without the co-operation and the wherewithal. Instead of the support of one man, Hamlyn is confronted by the intransigence of a multiplicity of governing bodies. Instead of consensus, there is anarchy. In spite of the gruesome evidence of what happened to fighters like Michael Watson, change is resisted by apologists for no better reason than they fear the truth.

For God's sake, there are still those in the fight game who will tell you that Muhammad Ali's present pitiful state has nothing to do with the noble art. The sooner Bernie Ecclestone takes over boxing, the better. After that, he can bring cricket into the 21st century before stepping in to prevent football going down the gurgler. What those sports have in common is that it's not only the participants who have a slate loose. Which is how they significantly differ from F1.

HÄKKINEN CUTS THROUGH ACRIMONY TO RETAIN CROWN

Timothy Collings at Suzuka

It was sad, but somehow inevitable, that Mika Häkkinen's masterful victory in the Japanese Grand Prix yesterday, which enabled him to retain his drivers' world title, should be overshadowed by a bitter row between his McLaren team-mate David Coulthard and Ferrari's Michael Schumacher. Coulthard last night threatened to take legal action against Schumacher in one of the most extraordinary post-race rows in Formula One history.

Less than an hour after Häkkinen had retained his title Coulthard replied to earlier comments about his driving, made by Schumacher, as the thinly veiled war of words between Ferrari and McLaren was reignited in the most spectacular fashion. Schumacher, who was held up by Coulthard when the Scot rejoined a lap down after spinning off, said: 'If you have been lapped, you should give space. David had passed many blue flags and he had some kind of problem but he was really zigzagging. Actually, I am not sure now whether I should believe that what happened at Spa last year [when they collided in heavy rain] wasn't done purposely, the way he behaved today. I didn't expect such a thing from him when it was clear he was out of contention for the race and had been lapped. That situation cost me, I think, about ten seconds. So, I am very disappointed about that.'

Coulthard hit back strongly, and said: 'He only lost two seconds, not ten. He thinks there is one set of rules for Michael and there is one set for everyone else. I am very disappointed he is questioning my integrity over Spa. What he has said is slander and libel, and if he doesn't apologise and retract his remarks, there could be legal repercussions. If he wants to discuss something, he should discuss it with me, not the whole world. It is just ludicrous and shows that, despite what we discussed at the time, he holds grudges and is not able to get over things. He has a real problem admitting his mistakes. I am not denying I held him up, but it was not a deliberate attempt to ruin his race. I am sorry, but I am not going to be held responsible for the fact he finished second. Anyway, I would say that deep down he is quite happy with the result, because he didn't want Eddie [Irvine] to win the championship, despite the very public image of being out there to do all he could after Malaysia. He will be happy because he wants to be the Ferrari champion.'

All weekend, indeed every day since the post-race capers at Sepang, where both Ferrari cars were disqualified, relations between the two teams, whose garages and offices were separated only by packing boxes, had been strained to breaking point. Yet Schumacher deserved better. Rising to the challenge of delivering only his second victory in ten races since the Canadian Grand Prix in Montreal in June, facing unrelenting pressure in a torrid atmosphere soured by the aftermath of Ferrari's successful appeal in Paris last weekend, rightfully concerned at his and his machinery's vulnerability, but determined to succeed, he delivered one of the greatest races of his life.

Driving from the front, Häkkinen scorched away from Schumacher's lurching, wheel-spinning Ferrari at the start and never really looked back. Schumacher led only briefly, following Häkkinen's first pit-stop, and never threatened again, regardless of his claims about Coulthard's interference. It was Häkkinen's fifth win in the season, and the 15th of his career, and it was entirely well-deserved, as Irvine so manfully accepted after he had come home third, behind Schumacher, to seal Ferrari's first constructors' title since 1983. 'I have to say Mika deserved the title,' conceded the Ulsterman. 'He did a fantastic job and won it in style.'

Few argued with that, not even Schumacher, upon whom Irvine was depending for a victory to keep his own championship aspirations alive. As it happened, however, it was the twice world champion who was unable to deliver his part of Ferrari's pre-race plan for double title glory. To cap all that, however, Häkkinen's triumph made him only the seventh man since the championship began in 1950 to defend his title successfully. His name now follows those of Alberto Ascari, Juan Manuel Fangio, Jack Brabham, Alain Prost, Ayrton Senna and Schumacher in the record books.

CHAPTER SIX
THE 2000s

EVEN THE BEST GET IN A SPIN

Andrew Baker

It was a small but delicious consolation for the fans: the same swampy grass that ruined so many weekends for those unable to get into flooded car parks also did for the victory hopes of Michael Schumacher. Accelerating away from the grid at the start of the British Grand Prix, the world championship leader tried to pull a fast move on his rivals by sticking a couple of wheels on the verge. As anyone who had tried to get a vehicle into Silverstone over the weekend could have told him, this was a bad move.

The Ferrari's wheels started to spin, Schumacher lost momentum and in a split-second his chance of a win disappeared. Jenson Button swept past him on the inside, then Jacques Villeneuve slipped by and – this is the bit he really disliked – his little brother Ralf nicked a position as well. Heaven for the majority of fans at Silverstone, who felt that four victories in a row for Schumacher would have been at least one too many. They would happily have settled instead for a win by any other driver, so to find the top step of the podium occupied by a Briton at the end of the 60 laps was almost perfect. If the reception accorded to the winner was marginally less than ecstatic, David Coulthard need not mope. It was amazing that anyone turned up at all, and those who had struggled into the grandstands after upwards of five hours in traffic jams must have been hard pressed to keep their eyes open as the race unfolded into a high-speed procession.

Coulthard did his best to wake everyone with a magnificent passing manoeuvre to take the lead from Ferrari's Rubens Barrichello on lap 31. Shortly afterwards Barrichello contributed further to the afternoon's entertainment by spinning in front of the grandstands at the complex before the pits, spinning again trying to recover and then splashing across two enormous puddles en route to the pits. There his car was retired with what was described as 'hydraulic problems', which is the technical term for 'it's full of water'.

The result that the Silverstone crowd really craved – a win for Jenson Button – was never really on the cards, but once again the 20-year-old drove with impressive maturity, holding off his team-mate Ralf Schumacher and, later, the world champion before his two-pit-stop strategy reduced him to a fifth-place finish. It has been suggested by senior members of the Williams team that Button is being over-hyped and that in the run-up to this race he was spending rather too much time plugging his own brand of T-shirts and baseball caps and not enough time swotting up on braking points, or whatever it is grand prix drivers do for homework.

But, on the evidence of yesterday afternoon, Button has taken to celebrity just as comfortably as he has taken to the wheel of a Formula One car. Assuming that he retains his seat at Williams for next season – and it is an assumption that becomes easier to make with every assured performance – 'Button-mania', which was largely a figment of the tabloid imagination last year, will be a noisy reality by the time the grand prix circus returns to Northamptonshire next year. Whether that return occurs in April or July is, of course, in the lap of the gods or, to be more precise, in the lap of the little god who spends his grand prix weekends in a grey bus at the head of the paddock. Maybe Bernie Ecclestone should have tried getting his bus into one of the car parks.

9 OCTOBER 2000

SWEET MOMENT FOR SCHUMACHER

James Allen, member of ITV's F1 commentary team

So he has done it. The man who has carried Ferrari's hopes for the past five seasons, the most successful and controversial driver in their history, has finally given them the world title which had been missing for 21 years. It has been a long wait for Ferrari, but also for Michael Schumacher, whose last world title came five years ago. Their joint success brings to an end the sport's longest-running soap opera, but it also poses a new question: where do Schumacher and Ferrari go from here?

In many ways this has been a strange season for Formula One's top driver. He won five of the first eight races, before a series of retirements sapped morale and allowed Mika Häkkinen back into the chase. The pressure was relentless, and it looked at times as though it was getting to him. The man whom Damon Hill once criticised for being 'robotic' learned this year to show his human side. He burst into tears after winning the Italian Grand Prix, his emotions stirred partly by memories of Ayrton Senna, whose record of grand prix wins he had equalled, and partly by the warmth of the reception he received on the podium from the Italian fans.

The accident at Silverstone last season, when he broke a leg, was a major turning point. After seven years of unbroken pressure as the sport's star performer, the enforced three-month absence brought an opportunity for him to rest and to see the wider picture. The Schumacher who returned was stronger and more determined, but at the same time more mature, able to admit his mistakes and even to laugh at himself. Schumacher may be Formula One's current hero, but he has often been its villain, too. He won his first world title in 1994 by driving Damon Hill off the road in Adelaide, and three years later unsuccessfully attempted the same trick on Jacques Villeneuve. The incidents showed his malevolence and put a stain on his character as a sportsman. He remains the only driver to have been disqualified from the championship results table for unsportsmanlike conduct. 'Jerez is the black spot on my image,' he said then. 'I will have to carry it around and live with it, but hopefully there will be some brighter moments in the future.'

He is now enjoying the brightest of those moments. But once the celebrations have subsided, there will be some awkward questions to be answered. How much longer will Schumacher continue to race? Those close to him speak of his likely retirement at the end of the 2002 season. If Schumacher leaves, then the elite team of engineers, drawn from Britain and elsewhere, who have laboured for five years to secure this title, will surely disband, and Ferrari will be forced to restructure. All that lies ahead. For the moment the controversial genius is free to enjoy a period of quiet celebration. Until the next F1 title quest begins, and the pressure kicks in again.

26 JANUARY 2001

BOY RACER BUTTON COMES OF AGE
Sue Mott

Jenson Button is a young man in a hurry. We know this because he was once caught doing 142mph down a motorway in France, which resulted in his removal to the local police station and a heavy fine. We also know this because he was doing 200mph round Silverstone this week in what sounded like the world's largest and most demented bluebottle. So far this has only resulted in his being pitchforked into world fame, dating a girl band member, earning (approximately) $4.5 million (£3.2 million) this year, moving to Monte Carlo and holding his 21st birthday party (last Friday week) in a flash London disco with beds in it. Still, he's only young. Things could get better.

I think we can safely say, given man's undying love for Castrol GTX and related hardware, that Button is living nearly every boy's fantasy. He gets to wear overalls with his name on them and is poised on the brink of his second Formula One season, having more or less confounded his critics during his debut year for Williams. Progress report: 17 races, 12 points, eighth place in the drivers' championship, which placed him above Heinz-Harald Frentzen and Eddie Irvine, among others. Also, one sticky story in *The Mirror*, one split with school sweetheart, one house with swimming pool bought in Weybridge, one Jackie Stewart forced to eat words that a move from 'kindergarten to university' would be asking too much of a boy of 20.

Button emerged from his baptism of firing engines with maturity and credit. Frank Williams has let him go to Benetton for the next two seasons, but with an option to renew. There are no hard feelings, or at least they have been swept under the hard carapace of commercial reality. His replacement at Williams is Juan Pablo Montoya, who is good, Colombian and hugely popular in North/South America (where BMW would not mind selling a few cars).

Button is wisely not taking this personally. His future has the same rosy hue as a rather large pile of £50 notes. His manager, David Robertson, has total faith. 'Jenson will win three or four world championships. He will be a megastar in F1. He will be The Man. I think he's going to be better than Michael Schumacher.' Button's father, John, the 1976 runner-up in the British Rallycross Championship, is similarly sanguine. 'He's Beckham with brains,' he said succinctly.

You might, after this introduction, expect an ego-crazed prodigy to lurch into view, entirely drunk on the exhaust fumes of his premature hype. Instead: 'Hello,' he said matily, shaking hands and looking rather like Jamie Oliver, the Naked Chef. He is not young enough to have pimples still, nor old enough to make a complete go of facial hair. We talked about bicycles. Needless to say, the last time he was on one he went at 45mph downhill.

'You'll meet him and become a fan,' Robertson had warned, and – despite one's best intention to thoroughly dislike an individual so blessed with talent, youth, riches and garden statuary – the bandwagon was definitely rolling in that direction. He is so amiable, he bears no malice to Frank Williams at all. 'We still talk on the phone. He's a great bloke.' And he's still paying his ex-racer a retainer. (Best guestimate: $1 million a year). 'Yeah, exactly,' Button said. 'But it was really important to stay friends with him. He gave me such a chance in F1. You've got to respect that. It doesn't feel like demotion. He had already geared up for Montoya coming back. He's very truthful. Very good with handshakes.

'I'm good friends with Montoya, too. He's said some good things about me. I've said some good things about him. Lots of people have been trying to put us against each other. Hasn't worked so far.' And anyway Button has to knock Giancarlo Fisichella, his Benetton partner, off the track first. 'Nooo, he's my team-mate,' Button said with just the right pantomime outrage. 'Don't say that. We get on really well. Hopefully I'll learn some things from him.' He stopped and added confidentially: 'I think he's down there actually.' He peered down the steps of the Benetton motorhome, in which the Queen could throw a medium-sized knighting ceremony. No response. 'Mmmm, he could be asleep.'

He accepts graciously his elevated position in life. 'I suppose if you asked any 20-year-old if they want to be an F1 driver, 90 per cent would definitely say yes. But they don't realise what goes into it. It's not just driving round in circles. Even when you're not testing you're doing stuff. Sponsors and other things.' But the downside is not immediately apparent, not when he has a yellow Ferrari for fun, a few others ('I can't remember how many') and soon, a Renault V6 Clio. I wonder if this puts us on similar footing because I happen to have a Renault Clio, too. Blue one. He just laughed. 'Mine's a boy racer car,' he said, as kindly as he could.

He does not mind being called Jenson, despite attracting the nicknames Jennifer and Genitals in his youth. His father named him after a Scandinavian racer, not the car, which improves matters, and one day that singular name might be as resonant as Elvis or Madonna in its field. Button is certainly not ambivalent about fame. 'I love it,' he said. 'I'm sure some people are waiting for me to fail, but hopefully that won't happen.' Instead, he shares the vision of his management – entirely backed up by his short, sharp past into which he condensed being a karting phenomenon, living in Italy and Belgium from the age of 14, winning seven Formula Ford races in 1998 (including the unofficial world championship at Brands Hatch) and propelling himself into a Formula Three Renault-backed team in 1999 before he had remotely finished with his teens.

Michael Schumacher is in his sights. 'Oh, I want to be world champion, and I think he's the person to beat. He's a great driver, the best driver in the world *at the moment*. [My italics]. And the most experienced. And I think he's going to be at the top *for the next couple of years.* [My italics again]. I'm not here to finish second. I want to be Michael Schumacher. It's not going to happen this year. Maybe next year it will. But it's *definitely* [his italics] going to happen in the future.'

Button has been compared to Ayrton Senna. 'Crazy people,' his dad calls those who insist on this view. It is wildly premature. To hold young Button up against the gigantic shadow left by Senna is rather like mistaking a boy scout doing a good deed for John the Baptist. But absolutely no one would deny the youngest Briton to drive in Formula One (beating Stirling Moss by a year) is jam-packed with the skill, reflexes, confidence and maturity required in this high-octane crucible.

Button reckons Stewart has been answered. 'It was difficult to know whether he'd really said it, or not at first. But then he repeated it. I think I know myself more than he did. He didn't know enough about me at all. About my driving or personality. I had to go for it and I definitely feel I've vindicated myself. The best moment was Spa. Qualifying was quite amazing.' He started third on the grid. 'Also the first three laps of the race were pretty special, before I collided with Jarno Trulli. Because I was the second quickest on the circuit, pulling away from Michael. To be pulling away from the red car that had Michael in it – pretty special feeling.'

Many of his feelings just now must be pretty special. He once lived with his father along *Men Behaving Badly* lines, but now divides his time between London and a two-bedroom apartment in Monte Carlo. Quaintly, he chose the latter not for its renowned tax haven qualities but because he likes to be beside the sea. 'I've always wanted to live by the seaside,' he said. And Cromer just wouldn't hack it. His dad accompanies him to every race. 'A lot of dads can get in the way. So I've heard. But he doesn't at all. He sort of works for me,' Button said. They have not yet decided on the correct title. Odd-job was originally favoured by John, but he has now come around to 'Director of Something or Other'.

Likewise, Button's girlfriend, Louise, is a frequent companion. 'We have a very, very good relationship. We've been going out for five months. She's in the singing business.' I involuntarily gasp at the similarity to the Beckhams. 'Sssssh,' he hissed. 'Don't say that. There's a group of four but I can't say what their name is.' I infer that she utterly rejects the slightly shabby notion of riding to fame on the back of her boyfriend's celebrity. Another mature decision. The girl thing is naturally an issue in Formula One – it being a well-known fact that one of the greatest mechanical aids to arousal in women is the Benetton Renault Sport B201 and its pit-lane ilk. 'Um, difficult one. To begin with it was slightly strange. I suppose there are a lot of girlie fans, but – I don't want to sound big-headed or anything – now that I'm in Fɪ there's a lot of younger girls involved. If you look at my website, their average age is about 14 to 18. But no, I don't feel in danger ever.' Not on the track either. Rocketing around the track at warp speed holds no fears for him. 'It's the same as being in an aeroplane,' he said, but frankly there are crucial differences. He hasn't got a little pair of towelling slippers or an air stewardess in the Benetton cockpit. It is slightly more labour intensive. It remains, whatever precautions taken on its behalf, a death-defying sport.

Button is not concerned about this. He has a bluebottle to test and off he goes, back to the machines and machinations. He has enormous potential but there are no guarantees. It is not even certain he will go back to Williams when his Renault contract ends in two years. 'Maybe,' his father said. 'But money talks.' Clearly young Button has learned to steer round more than hairpin bends.

3 FEBRUARY 2001

ECCLESTONE: BOY RACER TO SELF-MADE MAN

Sue Mott

We had a terrible pile-up on the starting grid, Bernie Ecclestone and I.

'Crap! Absolute crap!' he shouted, pounding on his desk and leaping to his feet, within approximately two minutes and fifty seconds of my audience with the most powerful man in British sport. I swiftly inferred from this that I was being shown the exit, not even stopping in the pit-lane for repairs, and adopted the brace position. There was only one manoeuvre left. Cringing. 'Oh, please. Oh, please,' I begged. 'I'll be in terrible trouble.' 'You are in terrible trouble,' he said, with menace forged in Dante's *Inferno*. 'With me.' Call it the survival instinct or just arrant cowardice, but we left aside at that point the sometimes suspected possibility that Formula One racing, over which Ecclestone has exercised a deity's control for three decades, can just be a little, teeny-weeny bit manipulated, tweaked, you might say, to maximise its sex appeal to the masses.

My next question, after the restart, was: 'Can you describe the love and joy you have got from car racing?' Oh, faint-heart. I had about as much chance as Minardi of reaching the chequered flag in this interview. In retrospect, I believe he might have been capable of feigning that rage. To lay down the road markings for the encounter, to stress his pole position, to demonstrate most vividly who was boss. As if I was in any doubt.

When a singular man takes home £29.7 milllion, as he did in 1994 in his role as chairman of the Formula One Constructors' Association; when he is reputed to be worth a billion pounds and one of the richest men in Britain; when in July last year he signed a 100-year deal to exploit Formula One's commercial rights; and when the motorhome he parks at every grand prix is universally known as 'The Kremlin', you have a pretty good idea of his pre-eminence, professionally, financially, socially.

But that certain knowledge is belied by the first illusion. Entering his offices overlooking Hyde Park in London, all you can see is a small man behind an oceanic desk of smoky glass feeding paper into the shredder that sits beside him like a pet. The impression is all benign. White, spiky fringe, neat, framed specs, soft-toned voice, muted grey tie. Unforewarned, you could mistake him for Miss Marple's younger brother.

Then the Napoleonic mogul explosively appeared. That is the story of his life. From potato-picking in Suffolk to owning the Brabham Formula One team by 1971. From a double newspaper round as a schoolboy to holding global sway in one of the most unyieldingly glamorous and cut-throat industries devised by man. So great, in fact, is his power perceived to be that the European Commission last week insisted he step down as vice president of the sport's governing body, the FIA. They think it's all over? Is it heck.

Ecclestone is 70. He has the money to retire on and a statuesquely beautiful former model Croatian wife, 30 years younger than himself, to retire to. Why keep going? 'Because the thought of doing nothing would put me in a graveyard,' he replied. 'I'll do it for as long as I think I can. I'm not afraid of death. I've done a lot in my life. Everything's a bonus for me. I mean, the Bible says you should live for three score years and ten and I've achieved that. So I'm on borrowed time. But I'm fit and well. I don't feel any different now from how I did 30 years ago.'

He had a triple heart by-pass operation in 1999. 'Forget it,' he dismissed the subject. 'I feel great. I recommend everybody has one.' They said he was back at work within two weeks. He looked scandalised. 'Before!' He did admit that he avoided the telephone for the first day after the operation. 'But the day after that I was back on it.'

One would hazard a guess that he enjoys his mystique, which has mushroomed around him, fed by gossip, guesswork, mischief and shredded facts.

'The rubbish about the Great Train Robbery. I sued in Canada, I sued in France but, you know, I haven't got time to spend in court. The story started because Graham Hill, who drove for me at Brabham, knew the guy who drove the getaway car. When he came out of prison Graham sent him to me to see if he would make a racing driver. I said, "Well, you haven't had much practice for a few years. I think you're wasting your time." But as he was a gold and silversmith I got him to make a trophy for us. Still use it today. Then all of a sudden I'm the guy who organised the Great Train Robbery. Complete joke. There wasn't enough money on that train for me.' Cue laughter. But is he joking? He is the only sports administrator I've ever met with a sculpture of a pile of hundred-dollar bills in his outer office. Money matters to Ecclestone, not as spending spree material but as a benchmark.

'I measure whether I've done well the only way I can. By how much money's in the bank. Basically, at heart, I'm still a racer. To be honest with you I'd probably rather be running McLaren or Ferrari than doing what I'm doing. They get more satisfaction than I can get, because after each race they know how they've done. They've got a result. My result is whether we're commercially successful. It's satisfying but perhaps not so satisfying.'

He was a devil-may-care racer of motorbikes and cars. 'I'd either win or crash.' Then he translated the policy to business. He went for the gaps. Only instead of the pencil-thin bar of daylight between smoking wheels at high speed it was the gaps in the market he spotted. He did the deals that packaged Formula One as a television product worldwide. It went from a sport in greasy overalls to an industry in sponsored spacesuits. Even allowing for the two world championships he won with Brabham, the highlight of his career must be success as an entrepreneur. 'Highlights? I don't think of it like that. Emotionally, I don't have highlights. I expect to do well, so I can't be happy about it.'

Well, lowlights then. There must be some sense of rise and fall of human emotions in his life. He admits to this. He was there, trackside, when his friend, the Austrian driver Jochen Rindt, was killed during a practice session at Monza. Before that, he had been planning a team around a young driver called Stuart Lewis-Evans when the ambition perished with the man at the 1958 Moroccan Grand Prix. 'When young Stuart got killed, I more or less took a back seat for a year or so.' (Even his imagery is centred on the car.) 'But I was drawn back again eventually. I'm a racer.' But surely he has felt moments of wild elation. 'All the time,' he said in an ironic monotone.

'Except now!' he added with a smile that flexed muscle but flagrantly avoided his eyes. I was clearly still vole to his sparrowhawk.

This should not imply that he isn't charming. He is. And he has the virtue of unflinching directness. This is different from ruthlessness. 'I'm not ruthless,' he said, putting forward an not entirely independently sourced opinion. 'I make sure people I do deals with are happy. I don't think anyone can genuinely say that isn't true. Of course, I have enemies. More than I know. There's an awful lot of people jealous. I don't know why. I'm not jealous of anyone. Why bother? I could say I wish I looked like Robert Redford (not as he is now; as he was then) but that ain't going to happen. So I can look in the mirror,' he paused, '... when I'm shaving.' Maybe a man with a billion or so doesn't need to be pretty.

Ecclestone's needs are different. Vision, commitment, energy. Does morality fit in anywhere? 'There's different types. The "what can I do without getting locked up" morality or the "I really want to do good for the world" morality. My view is beware the self-righteous. I wonder how many people are really like that. Mother Theresa, maybe. Not too many.'

He does, however, want to do good in the world. 'I feel sorry for people.' His money is contributing to charity work in Brazil, his wife looks after a children's hospital in Croatia. He is taking a corporate table at next week's lavish grand prix dinner to raise funds for the Brain and Spine Foundation. But, as for the spillage of human emotion on a day-to-day working basis, he regards it as akin to an oil slick. He was present at the birth of his two daughters but refuses to romanticise the fact. 'I can't claim it as an achievement. Babies are born every minute of the day. It's just a moment that's personal to you.'

He does not know the genesis of his prowess as an empire builder. 'Not from my parents, that's for sure. I think I was born with it, exactly the same as an artist. I was born a dealer. I didn't have a tough upbringing. In those days living in the country was very relaxed. No shootings. Nobody got mugged or raped, not that anybody would want to rape me. It was all very carefree. But I had realised very early it was better to be independent. I did two paper rounds every morning. I absolutely did it for money. You think I'd get up at bloody 5a.m. for anything else? I worked Saturdays in shops. In holidays I used to go and pick potatoes and tomatoes. I did it all for money.'

So began the work ethic which led to this place: full-throttle domination of a world sport and its fortune. He has no holding bay for regrets. They are expunged. He doesn't even regret the million-pound donation to the Labour Party that they shakily denied and then returned in 1997. It had an unfortunate proximity to a Government decision to allow Formula One to retain tobacco sponsorship. You don't have to know Latin to suspect a *quid pro quo*. 'You should be able to do what you like with your money, if you haven't stolen it and paid your taxes. We just shouldn't have politicians running the country.'

Ecclestone would never have considered such a flawed arena of combat. 'There's nothing worse than being an "ex". If you're someone like John Major, you're chucked out of your house, out of everywhere and then you have to go and get a job.' You make money, I pointed out. 'You're still ex,' he said conclusively. Ecclestone will never be ex. Body and mind willing, he will stay there, suspected and respected in equal measure and as ferocious in his job as the German Shepherd that once bit a chunk off his nose in Los Angeles. It is the only time he has resorted to plastic surgery. 'Had to. Had blood pouring everywhere and the dog still chewing a bit of my nose.'

That turned out to be my last hairpin bend. 'You've been completely dishonest with me,' he said, but not unkindly. He meant I had promised to be only ten minutes and devote all my questions to Formula One. Instead, I was an hour and had deviated into death, wealth, tomatoes and dogs. We finished with the abstract. Did he trust anyone? 'I trust everyone until I find out they can't be trusted.' What happens then? 'They're like MPs.' 'Ex?' I hazarded. He nodded.

5 MARCH 2001
STEWART LEADS CALL TO TIGHTEN SAFETY NET
Andrew Baker in Melbourne

The moment of triumph was tinged with tragedy. The Champagne was left unopened as the drivers trooped off the podium, and that was when the crowd began to fear the worst. Everyone had seen, on the giant television screens, the ambulance drive slowly from the scene of Jacques Villeneuve's terrifying crash. But then the Australian Grand Prix had resumed, and fears had been suspended in the elation of competition.

When the engines fell silent, though, the bad news spread quickly. Michael Schumacher set the tone in a sombre press conference, and it was all too easy to recall his tearful reaction to a similar fatality at last year's Italian Grand Prix. Track marshals are held in very high regard by racing drivers, and the shock when one is killed is almost as intense for them as the loss of a racing rival. The marshals are there to help keep the drivers safe; but by the most unpleasant of ironies they seem to be more vulnerable than the sportsmen they have volunteered to look after. Motor racing is dangerous, and those whose work takes them closer to the track than spectators would be allowed know the risks that they are running. But that does not mean those risks cannot be reduced.

To have one marshal killed by flying debris looks like an unfortunate accident. But when the circumstances of that accident are repeated five races later a dangerous trend can begin to become apparent. Rule-makers, designers and drivers all need to contribute to the debate on how to avoid a repetition of yesterday's carnage at Albert Park's turn three. The family of the dead marshal will not see it this way, but the incident could so easily have been worse. As the German driver Nick Heidfeld put it, 'thousands of pieces seemed to be falling from the sky': pieces of Villeneuve's car, which could have fallen into spectator areas. As it was, half a dozen members of the public received minor injuries.

Jackie Stewart, who has campaigned for greater safety at racetracks since his own days as a driver in the 1960s and 1970s, led the calls for more work on car and circuit safety last night. 'We need to do some housekeeping,' Stewart said. He identified three areas that he felt could be improved. 'We need to look at wheel attachment,' he said, 'at debris-fencing and at where the marshals stand and how they are protected.' All could contribute to what Stewart called the 'containability' of an accident. 'This is something that needs to be addressed,' Stewart continued, 'because of the amount of debris in the air following an accident like this. At 200 or 300kph, these things become missiles.'

Any changes that are made can only be a matter of degree. A Formula One car's wheels are already attached to the chassis with cables that are supposed to prevent them from flying off in an impact. Recent regulation changes have strengthened the cables, and no doubt they could be made stronger still. But ultimately they can only be as strong as the chassis to which they are attached. Debris fences can undoubtedly be made higher – those at Albert Park are no more than ten feet or so tall – but fragments of Villeneuve's car and Ralf Schumacher's Williams could be seen flying as high as the trees next to the track. How high will be high enough? Marshals can undoubtedly be better protected, but will still need to be close enough to the track to be able to do their jobs effectively and swiftly. There would be little point in making the marshals' jobs safer if by so doing the risk to drivers was increased.

Part of the problem is that modern Formula One cars are designed to fall apart, to some extent, on impact. So-called 'deformable' structures absorb energy when they are destroyed, so lessening the forces to be transferred to the driver's body. Regulations could be changed to make the cars themselves — and in particular their fragile aerodynamic wings — stronger. It is even conceivable that the wheels could be enclosed within some form of protective shield, so that the launching-pad effect which catapulted Villeneuve's car into the air could be avoided. But the drivers are not likely to be in favour of any change that makes the cars heavier, slower or more awkward to manoeuvre. As David Coulthard pointed out after yesterday's race, these are Formula One cars, not saloon cars. They represent the peak of speed and technology, which is what the fans pay to see. Such drastic changes will no doubt be avoided. But some change is undoubtedly necessary. Recent innovations seem, happily, to have made the cars safer for their drivers. It is time for technology to turn to the service of those who watch them being driven.

17 MARCH 2001

MALAYSIA IMMUNE TO F1'S COSTLY APPEAL

Martin Johnson in Kuala Lumpur

Most of the perimeter placards around the Sepang motor racing circuit are the usual invitations to fill your engine with a particular type of oil, or your lungs with a certain brand of cigarette, but one of them reads more like the kind of thing you would hear from your doctor at morning surgery. 'You have F1 fever!' is the message, although the temperature reading on the Malaysian public's thermometer ahead of their own grand prix tomorrow barely suggests a runny nose, never mind a fever.

There are, however, one or two more possibilities, not least the fact that you can pull up a seat at any road junction in Kuala Lumpur and witness — entirely free of charge — driving that is a hundred times hairier than anything Michael Schumacher is liable to produce tomorrow. The world champion might be relatively fearless inside his Ferrari cockpit, but put him in the back seat of a KL taxi on the Jalan Kuching highway at rush hour and technical FI language like 'rear-end instability' would refer to the need for fresh underwear rather than fresh rubber. Schumacher's suggestion the other day that more people would turn up to watch a grand prix here if a Malaysian driver were involved was probably spot on, if only for the fact that the local boy's upbringing would make it mandatory for him to go round the wrong way and propel anything within shunting distance straight into the gravel trap.

Another reason for the Malaysians' reluctance to stump up for tickets may well have been contained in a front-page newspaper headline on Wednesday which read: 'Rumour Mongers Held!' Arresting people for gossiping is a hard concept to grasp, but here it was – complete with a quisling phone number inviting people to shop suspected tittle-tattlers. Oddly, though, there was no actual indication as to whether Plod had moved in to nab anti-government agitators, or two women in a laundrette whispering: 'Hey up, have you heard about that Mrs Chang at No. 12?'

Which leads to the obvious conclusion, given the Malaysian government's natural anxiety to promote a successful race, that they were rounding up rumour-mongers for putting it about – and thus having an adverse effect on sales – that Formula One is actually quite boring. This would certainly have warranted action under Malaysia's Internal Security Act, which is thought to invest the police with almost as much power as Bernie Ecclestone.

The Formula One supremo presides over a sport that commands massive worldwide television audiences and yet is so technology-driven that working out which car is likely to win is hardly the stuff of a Mensa test. Malaysian motorists overtake in any lane (though the hard shoulder is generally the preferred option), and shelling out hard cash when a driver rarely gets passed unless he has pulled in to the FI equivalent of Newport Pagnell Services rates as even less of a thrill here than it does elsewhere.

Formula One changes its regulations more often than its drivers change socks, usually embracing the permissible width of a wheel nut, or something equally exciting. If they have to have pit-stops, maybe they should consider forcing drivers to fill up like the rest of us. Imagine the consternation in the Ferrari garage if Schumacher's credit card would not swipe properly, or he had to join a queue of people lining up to buy anything from petrol to a bar of Kit Kat. Despite its obvious merits, this seems an unlikely scenario, in which case the next change – due for the fifth race of the season, in Spain – is the introduction of traction control. This, in effect, means that wheel spin will be eliminated, and brings us a little closer to a scenario in which the cockpit's resemblance to the flight deck of a commercial airliner will also include an auto-pilot button.

Tony Hancock fans will recall that this city first came to prominence for technological advances when – perched in his East Cheam attic in *The Radio Ham* – the highlight of his evening was an SOS call to send a tray of bread pudding to Kuala Lumpur. Nowadays, of course, communication is a good deal more sophisticated, nowhere more so than in Formula One. Driver feedback is still important, but not half as much as what the computer is telling them back in the garage.

Formula One rarely has a season without a buzz phrase, and this year it is 'tyre war'. Michelin's arrival to compete with Bridgestone has apparently brought about such improvements in grip that it has more than negated F1's attempts to slow down the cars with their close-season rule changes. Faster cornering, though, still does not mean more overtaking, as in the days when Nuvolari and Fangio drove around on the kind of inner tubes that had the pit crews getting ready with the Halfords puncture repair kit.

However, if technology has helped to make F1 less of a spectacle, it has also brought about many benefits, not least in survival rates. The last driver deaths were in 1994, when Ayrton Senna and Roland Ratzenberger were both killed at Imola, and Jacques Villeneuve provided further evidence in Australia that the most serious medication likely to be required after a high-speed collision these days is a couple of aspirin. The track marshals have not been so fortunate, with two deaths in the past five races, and it was a flying tyre which caused a fatality in Melbourne two weeks ago. The clerk of the course here at Sepang, a Mr S. Subramaniam, this week responded by warning his marshals to 'keep an eye on oncoming traffic', which is not quite up there with some of F1's more impressive safety measures.

Tomorrow, as usual in grand prix racing, there will be oncoming traffic, and traffic apparently going the other way. The Formula One pit-lane is a bit like *Upstairs, Downstairs,* with the aristocracy at one end, in the shape of Ferrari and McLaren, and Prost and Minardi at the other, with a relative working area that would have a Kwik Fit fitter checking the Shops and Factories Act. Imagine what it's like being a Minardi driver. You go out there and race to the teeth-jarring limit, just like Schumacher, but with an engine note that sounds more like the bloke next door mowing his lawn, and a budget that pales by comparison with the quarter of a billion dollars spent by Ferrari. You half expect it to come out of the garage with one of those metal coat-hangers by way of a radio aerial, and it is rare not to find the words 'Minardi' and 'plucky' in the same sentence.

When journalists descend on the Minardi pit, it is not so much to chase after an exclusive driver interview as Minardi's reputation – as befitting an Italian team – for brewing the best coffee on the circuit. Sadly, however, the car itself is not very espresso, and there was serious talk about the bailiffs being called in during the close season. The team had no engines, and their owner had packed it in with a stomach ulcer. However, they have since been rescued by an Australian who owns European Airlines, which now means that the team are officially called European Minardi. More appropriate, perhaps, would be Eurovision Minardi, given last season's familiar haul of 'nul points'.

Australians, however, do not sit comfortably with the tag of gallant underdogs, and their new benefactor, Paul Stoddart, is cheerily upbeat, and pursuing what he describes as a 'business deal – not a hobby'. His countrymen also have a reputation for gambling, which would appear to be borne out with this transaction, but Stoddart himself prefers to cite Australia's other reputation for 'achieving what we set out to do'. At the moment they are setting out to do no more than win one point more than they did last season – namely, one point. 'That would be enough to put us in the top ten teams,' said Stoddart, 'and we were encouraged enough by the way we performed in Melbourne to reckon we can do it. Let's face it, if the guys at the top end of the grid do their jobs, there aren't all that many points to go around for the rest of us, but I wouldn't have stepped in if I didn't think there was a long-term future for this team.'

Long term it will certainly have to be, judging by yesterday's lap times in free practice – with the two Minardis kept off the bottom only by Juan Pablo Montoya's Williams, which went round so slowly (34 seconds behind the leading car clearly indicated a major problem) that he was in danger of being wheel-clamped. Minardi are this year giving a drive to the Spaniard Fernando Alonso, 19, who would probably not win a single race were he in a Ferrari, but neither would Schumacher in a Minardi. The top drivers graduate to the top teams, but they are not so good that they can make an inferior car competitive, which is what makes Formula One too predictable to be thrilling for everyone.

British fans will make sure the alarm clock is set for tomorrow's start time (7a.m. GMT), while detractors may decide to tape it for viewing late at night, just to make sure they can drop off to sleep watching it. But that's the nature of Formula One. For some, it's vroom vroom; for others, it's drone drone.

2 1 AUGUST 200 1
THE ULTIMATE PLAYBOY RACER
Sue Mott

Eddie Irvine is without doubt the most shameless, chauvinistic, sexist, hedonistic, superficial, self-satisfied, skirt-chasing egotist you could wish to meet. An appraisal which will delight him no end. Women would be mad to go near him, but, owing to the quirk of fate that allowed him to emerge from his dad's scrapyard in Northern Ireland and hatch into the Formula One-driving, *Falcon*-flying, yacht-owning multi-millionaire with a leprechaun's lilt and the cheek of the devil, his girlfriends make a habit of peeling his grapes.

Not just peeling them. Biting them open and taking the pips out before they feed him like a gummy, helpless newborn babe in overalls. 'Women like looking after men,' he said with utter confidence. I goggled at him. No, they like looking after multi-millionaire racing drivers with a Polynesian-style beach house being built in Miami and Jaguar paying him £7 million a year to drive a car. He waved away this petty objection. All women like mothering Irvine, he has discovered. If it's not grapes, it's slivers of drooled-upon mango. I think it sounds disgustingly unhygienic.

'Men are dogs,' he continued. 'Men are animals. We have a primal need to have sex.' It is truly amazing how the half-heard snippets of fourth-form biology seem to stay with men all their simplistic lives and furnish the excuse for the morals of an alleycat. Unfortunately, the maintenance of a hard heart against this ridiculous force of nature is impossible. Spend a couple of hours with him in a good mood and you find yourself wondering how bad grape peel can be.

Formula One is extremely fortunate to have him. With Michael Schumacher sewing up the world championship for the second year in succession. and exuding all the charisma of a wheel nut (plus, I'm told, a hideous dress sense), the sport needs every character it can find in the supporting cast. Irvine is it. He is living every man's fantasy. Cars, sex and money no object. 'Put it this way. If I wasn't me I'd want to be me,' he said. But the good mood is crucial. A curious feature about this day which he was devoting to one of his sponsors was the number of organisers remarking on his good mood. True, it involved two gorgeous models poured into green lycra, but even in such enlivening circumstances he has been known to be fiendishly grumpy. 'Thank God, Eddie's in a good mood,' they all kept remarking to each other, relief and joy awash in their expressions. Apparently, when he is not in a good mood he is rude, unco-operative and/or hits people.

He once had a fight with Bernie Ecclestone's own security guards at a racetrack. He had suffered a crash, was out of the race, came steaming back towards the pits and was not allowed through a security gate. The guard pushed him, Irvine punched him as hard as he could, the guard fell over a rail, now with the fighting Irishman clutching him to prevent the victim falling 15 feet on to concrete. But he hadn't catered for the guard's mate coming to the rescue and effectively (and painfully) ending the scrap. Ecclestone bought him a T-shirt from Notre Dame University (motto, 'the Fighting Irish') commemorating the event.

There doesn't seem to be any correlation between this bleach-blond lotus-eating brawler and the quick-thinking, cool-headed professional behind the steering wheel of a 200mph machine. But you know there must be. Jordan, Ferrari and Jaguar cannot all be wrong. True, McLaren turned him down in 1999, and Ecclestone has hinted that the playboy lifestyle has inevitably hurt his career, but he cannot see it, does not believe it. 'I enjoy that side of life, so why not? It doesn't affect my job. But it would be very unwise to dispute anything with Bernie Ecclestone. I understand where he's coming from. If it stopped me going to McLaren after Ferrari, then maybe it has affected my career.'

He nearly won the drivers' championship in 1999. Perhaps one less vodka, one less 'lashing' aboard his yacht, the *Anaconda*, one less *Falcon* flight to Greenland or Egypt or Alaska, would have made the difference. 'I look at mistakes I made on the track in 1999 and wish I hadn't made them, so in that way I failed. But you've got to say, "Right!" And learn from it. The first championship you go for, there's so much pressure, attention and distractions, it's easy to take your eye off the job. If it comes around again, a second chance — I think it will be a lot easier.'

But the trouble is: he has only scored four points this season with Jaguar, he is 35 ('going on 17') and Schumacher exists. 'It is a bit depressing with him there. It's not like he's more intelligent. It's not like he's a better dresser —

that's for sure. It's pure speed. And that's a very difficult thing to beat. But there's hope. Formula One is not like the 100 metres. You don't have to have the most talent to win. If you're more intelligent than the other guy you can beat him. You can set your car better, work more cleverly, get yourself into better situations.'

This all seems to imply Irvine rates his own intelligence very highly. 'Um … I used to be conceited but now I'm perfect – that line, so to speak. No. Er. Yeah. I do. I guess.' He had the good grace to laugh. Actually, this is perfectly valid. He is highly aphrodisiacally intelligent. Any man who has set himself up with a limitless supply of fast cars, women, global notoriety and the speed boat that used to belong to Nicolae Ceausescu, Romania's executed dictator – and done so with such blatant honesty that no scandal can touch him – has got to be possessed of a wily mind. He has held down a pretty good job for 15 years or so too, albeit in the shadow of Schumacher. They don't like each other much, you can deduce. 'No, I don't particularly like his personality, but that's because we're opposite. We worked well together at Ferrari, but personally I wouldn't go out socialising with him. His sense of humour isn't my sense of humour. What he likes I don't like. We've nothing in common.

'But he's won the championship and he deserves it. Ferrari have the team, the people, the continuity and the best driver in the world. Ever. It's a tough call, comparing different eras and all that, but I think Michael gets the edge. But he doesn't drive in a gentlemanly way. Eventually I think we've got the FIA to understand that what he does at the start of a race – the zigzagging – is not in the rules. It's not allowed, even though it has been allowed. I think now you will see an enforcement of the rules as they are written.'

This is quaint. Hellraiser turned authoritarian. Irvine seems to be a seeker of justice. Perhaps only where it affects him, but possibly on a wider scale. He believed it was wrong in 1994 that Schumacher's title win was made so difficult. Schumacher was running away with the drivers' championship following the death of Ayrton Senna until disqualified in two grands prix and banned in two more. 'I don't think it was rigged. But it was slightly massaged,' Irvine said. 'Michael was banned for two races. I think it went too far. A lot of unjust things were done.' A number of cynics think Formula One is rigged year in, year out. 'Bernie's ruthless, without doubt, but at the end of the day he loves motor racing.'

So, as with a number of elements in his life, Irvine lies back for the massage option. Maybe nothing else could be expected. His mentor, for heaven's sake, when he was a tender 21, was James Hunt. One memorable tutorial, Irvine reminisced fondly, consisted of catching a train from Paris to Marseille complete with two bottles of blue vodka, two acquired young ladies, a man with a small stove (don't ask) and several dozen matelots returning to their boat. The mind boggles. Irvine adored Hunt. Thought him a massive, charismatic, enviable character and promptly made him a role model. 'Not like the bubblegum sports stars of today,' said this sports star of today dismissively. He thinks, for instance, that David Beckham is overrated. Not many people in Britain would dare say such a thing.

As a matter of fact, he makes a number of utterances beyond the daring of most men. The one I particularly liked was his theory of dating. 'If you're out with a beautiful woman who's dumb, you have to go out with your mates so you can have a laugh and leave her to the end.' Or, 'You have to speak to a beautiful woman, but if she's average you can nail her without bothering.' Thank you for that.

Later, he disputed this last gem. 'I didn't say "nail her", did I?'

'You did.'

'No, I didn't.'

'You did. You said, "nail her". I had witnesses.'

'Oh, all right,' he surrendered gallantly.

He has a daughter, Zoe, aged five, by his former girlfriend, Maria. She gave up on him after one story of flings too many, but they remain close friends. Many people, including his mum and dad, who seriously thought about calling their son Edmund 'Stirling Moss' Irvine when he was born, would like him to settle down with Maria. He did ask her to marry him once but claims he cannot remember it now. He is still resisting.

'It probably would be a very sensible, logical thing to do, but I like the freedom. I like to go where I want to go when I want to go and not annoy anyone by doing it.'

However, he can lay claim to a long-term relationship with his current girlfriend, the mango depositor, now running into its tenth month. Is he faithful? 'Very,' he said. 'When I'm single, I'm very single and when I'm not single, I'm very not. I do what I want to do. If I'm single and go out and meet three girls who want to have a good time, I have a good time. I would never say, "Oh I can't do that, it's immoral". If I think I'll have fun, I'll try it. It's all a game, isn't it? Work's a game. Making money's a game. Chasing a girl's a game. If you're winning, feeling good, carry on.'

But it is a dangerous game, you would have thought, Formula One. Does dying cross his mind. 'No, you close that off,' he said immediately. 'I want to live to spend all this money. It would be a shame to turn your socks over at 35.' So he will live to be an old man. What sort of old man you can only surmise. 'Oh, a miserable bastard,' he said with conviction. I can't see it. Where there's an Eddie, there's a gorgeous girl spitting grape pips into the nearest available ashtray.

I OCTOBER 2001

FOND FAREWELL TO COMMENTATING'S KING OF THE COCK-UP

Giles Smith
Sport on TV

The world is a quieter place this morning. With a lump in his throat the size of a Bridgestone tyre, Murray Walker has bidden us all farewell. Or rather, as he would prefer to put it: 'Fare! Well!' All the rest is silence – or at least tinnitus. It was a shame, in some ways, that the scene of the great man's final commentary turned out, by a quirk of the motor racing calendar, to be Indianapolis. As is the case with Cliff Richard, America is the one market that Murray has never quite managed to crack. Indeed, it's one of the few places in the world where you can abruptly, and loudly, say: 'Unless I'm very much mistaken … I am very much mistaken!' and not get back immediately a warm look of recognition and comradeship. Try it next time you're there.

Ideally, we would have liked him closer to home for those final, breathless laps of the circuit. Purists may even feel that the proper send-off happened in July at Silverstone, when pilgrims gathered with banners and quilts in Murray's honour. In which case, this weekend's celebrations were merely pageantry for tourists, a bit like the Queen's official birthday. At the same time, Indianapolis could not be said to be without its historical resonances and was no bad place to cap a broadcasting career of noble longevity (52 years, to be exact; Walker has been commentating on motorsport since pretty much the age of the horse). And really the whole point about Walker was that wherever he shouted his hat off, that was home.

Walker's survival to the age of 77 at the pinnacle of his business is a testament to many things – not least to his own professionalism (a swimmer and a worker-out even now), but also to the increased safety standards in

Formula One commentary boxes, where his explosions and burstings into flames don't necessarily have the ruinous consequences they would have had in the sport's infancy.

He left yesterday clutching an authentic Indianapolis Motor Speedway brick – one of the ones from which the circuit was originally built nearly a hundred years ago. It was presented to him on Saturday as a mark of respect from the track's owners – which provides a rare instance of a brick being offered to a performer in appreciation. (Can you take a brick on an aeroplane these days? Let's hope so, for Murray's sake. Otherwise he could be in an airport interrogation room at this very moment, saying: 'This! Is! Merely! A! Paperweight!')

At the brick ceremony, Formula One drivers took it in turns to read aloud their favourite Walker moments. Without fail, these were cock-ups. Eddie Irvine's was: 'I'm just going to stop my start-watch.' Michael Schumacher remembered a lengthy and misguided sentence of Walker's which had concluded with the phrase 'the boot is on the other Schumacher'. Jenson Button, for his part, recalled the time Walker had referred to him as a teenager of 20. And so forth.

In truth, though, straightforward Colemanballs were not Walker's big thing. Rather, he pioneered and perfected a unique and more comically rich kind of cock-up all his own: the hapless prediction. When Walker noted that someone was doing well, it was a reliable indication of imminent disaster. It endeared him to people as a kind of Harry Worth figure, forever dusting himself down following still further evidence of the world's conspiracy against him.

Forged in the grit and mud of rallying – where one line of smooth commendation from Walker was enough to put a car on to its roof in a bush – it was a skill he carried over into Formula One. Walker was widely blamed for preventing Nigel Mansell from being still more successful and for keeping Damon Hill back from winning the world championship until the latter end of his career – all by the force of his enthusiasm and fondness for those drivers and his desire to see them do well.

We would be failing in our duty if we didn't note that Walker's last few seasons had seen a slight increase in the number of unforced errors; and that, every now and again, one has had occasion to be grateful for the presence of Walker's deft co-commentator, Martin Brundle – someone unafraid of moving in swiftly with a water-soaked towel to point out that, actually, that wasn't Michael Schumacher, it was Rubens

Barrichello, and so on. But again, enthusiasm seemed to be at the root of it.

These lapses weren't necessarily a matter of Walker having gone off the boil; it was usually a matter of his boiling too hard. It might also be worth taking a moment, amid the jokey farewells, to reflect that Walker did more than just cock things up. He commentated live on a sport which could, at any minute, leave him staring at death. And much though one cherishes the memory of Walker shrieking like a man who has just had a shovel-load of hot coals tipped into his pants, one shouldn't forget entirely the quieter tone he could slip into when the moment arose. He had a lower gear. It's just a happy feature of Formula One that recently he seldom had cause to use it.

Peter O'Sullevan, David Coleman, Brian Moore, Murray Walker: one by one the big voices go. They leave a big hole.

13 MAY 2002

FORMULA ONE IS THE LOSER
Andrew Baker in Spielberg

Formula One demands a great deal of its visiting dignitaries. Pelé was entrusted with the chequered flag at the Brazilian Grand Prix and waved it at the wrong man. Yesterday Dr Wolfgang Schüssel, the Chancellor of Austria, stepped up to the podium at the A-1 Ring with the seemingly simpler task of presenting the trophy to the winning driver, only to find that the winning driver did not want it.

According to the official results, Michael Schumacher won yesterday's Austrian Grand Prix, but in every respect other than the accumulation of maximum points, the German, his Ferrari team and the sport of Formula One were losers. Schumacher's determination to hand the trophy over to his team-mate, Rubens Barrichello, displayed his discomfort at being handed victory as a result of orders from his team. His demeanour after the race, when he was obliged to field a barrage of hostile questions, was a combination of defiance and gloom. He had helped to score a huge own goal, and he knew it. So did the crowd, thousands of whom greeted the victor with their thumbs down, like spectators at the Coliseum dooming a gladiator. So will millions of Ferrari fans all over the world, who saw the reputation of their beloved team tarnished by an ill-advised exercise in corporate greed.

We have been here before, in every sense. Last year, at this very race, Barrichello was ordered to move over and donate second place to Schumacher, a scenario that left the Brazilian devastated. Enzo Ferrari, the founding father of the team, started the tradition, for he would often impose team orders on his drivers, though they were not always obeyed.

Schumacher trotted out the usual excuses, which are based on the idea that he might win the world title by one point at the end of the season, when yesterday's decision will look clever. He also alluded several times to the amount of money Ferrari spend in pursuit of the title, and insisted several times that he, himself, was unhappy with yesterday's endgame. But overtaking the car in front of you is a voluntary decision, even if it slows down to let you pass. Schumacher could, quite simply, have refused to win this race, and that he considered the option and then took the action he did cannot but reflect badly on his character.

All the indications – from Schumacher and others – are that the order for Barrichello to slow down came from the very top, which can only mean Luca di Montezemolo, the ultimate boss of Ferrari. But Schumacher is the most powerful man in the sport, and plenty big enough to refuse such an order without getting the sack. A sportsman who is – almost – bigger than his sport has special responsibilities. As Schumacher considers his healthy championship lead today, he should also ponder the health of Formula One. How many people tuned into yesterday's race on television will have turned off their sets at the end in disgust? And how many will want to watch next time?

13 MAY 2002

LETTER TO THE SPORTS EDITOR

MOCKERY OF RACING SPIRIT

Sir,

I understand that Michael Schumacher was only 'following [team] orders' in the Austrian Grand Prix on Sunday when he swapped position with team-mate Rubens Barrichello and went from second to first place, but surely he, with the support of a bank balance of millions, should have recognised what he should have done by disregarding those orders.

Grand Prix racing has become a test of who can whizz round the fastest in practice and then change tyres, replace wings and fill up quickest. Racing has gone out of the window. If Schumacher really wanted to gain any respect, he would have ignored the team orders and let the race take its natural course. Giving the trophy on the podium to Barrichello was a meaningless, hypocritical gesture. There is no doubt that Schumacher is a very good driver, but he must prove this on the track, and if another driver can beat him on the day, then so be it.

Schumacher appeared, on the podium and in the press conference afterwards, to have disagreed with the team decision. He should, as a true sportsman, have made this clear on the track. No doubt money talks, everywhere, although it is interesting to note that on this occasion the Ferrari team officials have been ordered to appear before the International Automobile Federation.

Martin Billingham
London SE6

8 JULY 2002

SCHUMACHER USES BRAIN AND BRAWN TO TIGHTEN GRIP ON TITLE

Timothy Collings

The last time Michael Schumacher led Rubens Barrichello home in a Ferrari one-two, in Austria on 12 May, the result was followed by a furore over race-fixing and pandemonium on the podium. Yesterday, after a rousing British Grand Prix run in mixed weather conditions at Silverstone, there were no such controversies as the scarlet scuderia recorded their fifth such triumph of the year and left the opposition in forlorn pursuit.

In finishing first, just 14.5 seconds ahead of his Brazilian team-mate, Schumacher secured only his second British victory in 11 attempts, and its significance to him was clear in the way he jumped into Ferrari technical director Ross Brawn's arms and then skipped in delight on the podium. It was, perhaps more importantly, the 60th win of his record-breaking career and came in his 171st race, a statistic that is stunning when it is realised that Alain Prost, the previous record-holder, collected his 51 wins in 199 grands prix.

Schumacher can now win the drivers' world title at the French Grand Prix on 21 July, a prospect that could see him crowned champion earlier in the year than anyone in the 52-year history of the world championship. It would also bring him a record-equalling fifth crown, putting him alongside the legendary Argentine, Juan Manuel Fangio, in the record books. Fangio, who died on 17 July 1995, after winning his five championships with 24 victories from 51 grands prix, completed his last race, the French Grand Prix, in fourth place, at Rheims, on 6 July 1958, 44 years to the weekend before yesterday's rain-hit adventures. For Schumacher, therefore, this win added symmetry as well as history to his record-breaking achievements.

The 33-year-old German, however, was less interested in such details than the reality of his commanding performance in difficult conditions yesterday as he made the most of his rivals' mishaps and the excellence of Brawn's tactical calls, on tyres and pit-stops, to sweep to a majestic triumph. Once he had passed Juan Pablo Montoya's Williams down at Club on lap 16, there was little doubt about the outcome. 'This is a very special win for me,' said Schumacher. 'I have not finished first so often here, and it is my 60th win. It is also ideal for the championship. The whole package worked well, and the real problem was when to use what tyre in those conditions. I have to thank Ross for making the decisions for me – and for making all the right ones.'

Barrichello, having been squeezed out of pole position by a late flying lap from Montoya on Saturday afternoon, endured a bitter-sweet day. Fastest in the morning warm-up, he went to the grid confident he could repeat his victory at the Nürburgring two weeks ago, when Ferrari ordered Schumacher not to attempt to pass him, but instead of zipping away at the start, he stalled on the formation lap and had to begin the race at the back of the field. Remarkably, with a performance that demonstrated the supremacy of Ferrari, he climbed from 21st to second in the opening 19 laps. Only a spin during the middle section of the race – when teams were switching tyres with gay abandon as the rain fell, stopped, and fell again before the circuit dried out – prevented his mounting a serious challenge to his team leader. However, that, in its own way, only emphasised that in unpredictable conditions it is Schumacher who has the flawless class of a champion. Schumacher now has a 54-point lead in the championship, with 86 points to Barrichello's total of 32. Only if the Brazilian produces a miracle can Schumacher be stopped from lifting his fifth title.

27 AUGUST 2002
STILL HUNGRY FOR PODIUM FINISH
Jenson Button

It was fun to be back in the car for the Hungarian Grand Prix after the three-week summer break. I spent half the time in Mallorca on my boat, and half in Monaco. Drivers are lucky in that we normally have three or four days off between races, but for the mechanics the summer break is a great opportunity to relax away from the relentless routine of the Formula One calendar.

After a break that long, though, I couldn't wait to get back in the car. The result was not satisfying – though, overall, the Renault team's fourth position in the constructors' championship was reinforced – but the occasion was great for a number of reasons. I particularly enjoyed the first lap of the race, where Juan Pablo Montoya and I hit each other twice fighting for position, and it was cool to see my old rival Anthony Davidson making his Formula One debut. He and I used to race each other in go-karts from the age of eight.

I gather television viewers saw Anthony apologise fulsomely to me via Louise Goodman's pit-lane report because he thought he had caused my spin into retirement on lap 31. He went a bit wide ahead of me, when he was being lapped, and brought dirt on to the circuit, but the fact I spun off wasn't his fault at all. I was finding the car really difficult to drive at that point. We had started the race on tyres that had already done 15 laps because we were concerned new tyres would blister or overheat (the Hungaroring is renowned as the circuit where the highest temperatures of the season are reached, and the slow, twisty layout increases the wear on tyres and the challenge of cooling the car). Twenty-five laps into the race – when the tyres were 40 laps old – we completely lost grip front and rear, and I was an 'off' waiting to happen.

It was interesting to hear Anthony's comments on his first F1 race. It is easy to forget how difficult it is to adjust to F1. He said being lapped was 'unbelievably hard', and it is. The Minardi is one of the slowest cars on the grid, and to see the Ferraris of Michael Schumacher and Rubens Barrichello suddenly loom large in your mirrors, would certainly increase your heart-rate. You have to get out of the way, without slowing down too much, and it is difficult to gauge that kind of thing on your first outing. Drivers tend to make debuts for teams lower down the grid, but they have most likely come from leading a junior championship and are not used to racing in the scrum.

I feel sorry for Justin Wilson, who lost the opportunity to make his grand prix debut because he is too tall at 6ft 3in to conform to safety regulations. When I was talking to other teams recently, before signing for BAR Honda for next season, a few of them said: 'You're very tall. It could be a problem.' I'm 5ft 11in. I think cars should be built to accommodate drivers of heights up to 6ft 3in or 6ft 4in, because at the moment shorter drivers enjoy an unfair advantage. Shorter drivers are normally lighter, and because of the minimum weight – whereby cars carry weight that can be moved about to change the centre of gravity – the smaller drivers have more weight to move about to find the optimum balance.

People have asked what it's like driving for Renault, knowing that in five races' time – at Melbourne 2003 – I'll be behind the wheel of a different car. I have to say it makes no difference. I still want to drive as well as I can to help Renault in the constructors' table and to ensure I finish the season where I stand now at seventh in the drivers' championship. The top three teams' drivers are ahead of me, so to finish the next best would be a fantastic achievement for me.

30 SEPTEMBER 2002

FERRARI SEW IT UP

Will Gray in Indianapolis

World champion Michael Schumacher controversially handed his team-mate Rubens Barrichello his fourth victory of the season at the Indianapolis Motor Speedway yesterday, as Ferrari once again demonstrated their dominance by appearing to orchestrate the result of the United States Grand Prix. Schumacher had led the race, with Barrichello never more than three seconds behind, but the German slowed in the final corner to hand Formula One's closest-ever victory to the Brazilian. Schumacher claimed that he was trying to finish alongside Barrichello in Formula One's first dead-heat, and instead lost out by one hundredth of a second. But he admitted that the result offered some personal compensation for Ferrari's decision to force Barrichello to sacrifice victory for him in Austria in May.

He said: 'It was just that I felt Rubens deserved to win this race. I did ask before whether I could let him by and the team said, "No". There was no plan. The team did not want this but, in the end, I did not feel particularly happy with what happened in Austria. I now feel to some degree I equalised this. We said we wouldn't do this, but it just happened.'

Schumacher declared before the race that he and Barrichello were free to fight for victory and insisted afterwards that they had been racing throughout. But their formation finish, which secured them a championship one-two, ignited controversy, and Barrichello tried to dampen the fire. 'It was not planned,' he insisted. 'We had a lot of fun in the race, and at the end ... what can I say? Just thank Michael very much. We have got everything now: first, second, constructors ... '

It was the Italian team's fourth consecutive one-two finish and their 14th win in 16 races. It leaves them one victory away from equalling the record number of wins in a season. David Coulthard claimed the only spare spot on the podium after a one-stop strategy, and a collision between Williams pair Ralf Schumacher and Juan Pablo Montoya allowed him a quiet and careful race.

28 OCTOBER 2002

FORMULA ONE RUNNING ON EMPTY

Damon Hill

I could save Formula One. All I need is a fire hose and access to the Terminal Four Heathrow Hilton conference room today where the whole power-crazy bunch will be working out how to stuff each other, yet still come out looking like responsible custodians of one of the world's biggest sports. Make no mistake. The problem with Formula One is not simply regulations, it is to do with power. Not horsepower, but political power. You, the Formula One fan, have not been invited to see this spectacle, which is a shame, because there will be no team orders in there, believe me.

Every material thing in my life has been paid for by Formula One, from my education to the house in which I now live, so I have to thank the sport for an awful lot, and in that respect I share something in common with every key player in that room. Sure, some have turned it around and made it what it is today. But what exactly is it? Is it a show, or a sport? In 2002 it was too often neither, and no amount of ballast-adding or grid-shuffling will change the fundamental problem with Formula One, which is that no one is acting as its guardian, by which I mean protecting that 'thing' that cannot be owned by anyone – the spirit of sport.

Formula One still has all the ingredients for a fantastic show. I have just spent the past season commentating for Formula One Sky Digital, Bernie Ecclestone's new baby. I have enjoyed the best coverage possible. I have interviewed all the protagonists and seen every car from every angle. Nothing was missed. As far as coverage goes, it blows away every other sport. Except it was £12.50 per race, and there wasn't one. There was racing, for sixth place, but not at the front and, call me old-fashioned, but I want to see who will come first. I had trouble keeping awake sometimes – and I was being paid.

The sad truth is that Formula One has relinquished its autonomy to outside forces, and the billion-dollar golden-egg-laying goose that is television has been sent to the *foie gras* farm. The controlling shares in the television rights are held by German bankers. Ecclestone has kicked the ball out of the ground, and no one is big enough to go to get it back.

The car manufacturers have been lured in by promises of control in the sport and access to the huge global audience and revenue. If they don't get it, they are threatening a rival series. But if what we have seen with Ferrari this year is a precursor to a manufacturer-run championship, then God help us! For too long Ferrari have been given *carte blanche* to do whatever is necessary to win, in the mistaken belief that the world is so hungry for Ferrari success that this will, in turn, catapult Formula One viewing figures into unimaginable territory. Well that backfired! Why? Because Ferrari showed they no longer care about the millions who watch, by dangling a race under their noses – as they did in the Austrian and US grands prix this season – and then taking it away on the last lap. But what is more worrying and telling and shocking is that they can't see what they did wrong. Nor can half the people in Formula One.

Those two events tipped me over the edge this season. There we saw what Ferrari care about and how much they understand about the reasons for the sport's appeal. They care about share prices and historical success. We will all be long gone before Ferrari produce their last car. They are no longer here for today's race; they just want to build on the brand, as do all the manufacturers. Well, I'm not buying. I spend my life being bombarded by commercials. What I want is a little bit of the old 'escapism' that Formula One used to offer. It would take us to Brazil on a dull March Sunday, to see playboys risk their lives for whatever their particular motive happened to be – girls, money or adrenalin. It had characters, people who spoke their minds, as distinct from the blurb from a Mercedes E-Class brochure. 'The track is shit,' Niki Lauda was fond of saying after having just won. Drivers would race each other and disregard team orders.

We can improve this sport if we simply provide a formula in which the drivers are given the freedom to do what they are genetically programmed, or psychologically compelled, to do, which is perform. The first thing would be to listen to what they have to say. They are the best drivers in the world, after all. According to last week's *Autosport* they would, nearly to a man, reduce down-force. But I'm not going to be distracted and embroiled in the technicalities, despite having a burning desire to see my personal set of regulations put to the test.

The problem this season has simply been that Michael Schumacher is the best driver in the best car, with team orders for him to win. If I could have negotiated that deal, I would have. However, by doing so, Ferrari betrayed themselves, and the sport, by conducting business in sporting hours. Industry interests are interfering with the actual racing, and I feel as though we are supposed to just sit there and be fascinated, or feel humble or privileged to watch. Well, we don't. We boo!

The Ferrari red dream became one big raspberry-red nightmare in 2002. So who is ultimately to blame? Well, who is supposed to be in control? Who is minding the sport? Max Mosley and Bernie Ecclestone? Aren't they the bosses? Or is it Ferrari? Who is making the rules here? Sorry, I'm lost!

The only way to make Formula One enjoyable again is for the untouchables to remember that 90 per cent of viewers only want to look forward to a Sunday in front of the television watching highly paid egomaniacs fighting over a tin cup. I personally doubt if any of them care if Ferrari or BMW win. I think they are more likely to remember the driver. Also, a large section of viewers are now children and teenagers. If it was difficult to explain the US GP result to a ten-year-old, then imagine what it was like for an American to understand it. I know you want to know what I would do. Here it is: put Michael Schumacher and Juan Pablo Montoya or Jacques Villeneuve in the same team, or better still, all three together. Arrows have vacancies.

SPEED KING WHO RULED GOLDEN AGE

Robert Philip

According to legend, when John Surtees decided he had enjoyed his fill of the Machiavellian manoeuvrings and intrigues of Ferrari and decamped to Cooper-Maserati immediately after his victory in the 1966 Belgian Grand Prix at Spa, his farewell conversation with Enzo Ferrari, the Godfather of motor racing, went something like this: 'Do you know what, Enzo? They should make you Pope and have done with it.' 'And why is that, John?' 'Because then we would only have to kiss your ring ... !'

Ah, but once a member of the Family Ferrari, always a member, which is why Surtees, now 69, will be avidly following the fortunes of Michael Schumacher and the famous black, prancing-horse motif when the Formula One season begins. Surtees won the world drivers' championship for Ferrari in 1964 and was forever considered a favoured son, even after taking his talents elsewhere. 'I had a good relationship with the old man [who died at the age of 90 in 1988],' says Surtees with tangible fondness. 'But what has happened at Ferrari in recent years could never have happened in his lifetime. Enzo could never have presided over such a united team; he was of the old school who believed you had to introduce elements of controversy, doubt and conflict to motivate your drivers. It was all a game, and we were puppets on a string. He loved stirring things up, but what you can never take away from him was that he created a legendary name; Ferrari represents everything that is Italy – style and passion. I suspect the old man will be up there looking down on Schumacher on the grid in Australia smiling away ...'

Surtees was already a national hero in Italy, having ridden an MV Augusta to seven motorcycling world championships, plus six Isle of Man TT victories, so when he opted to switch to Formula One in 1960 it was inevitable that he would be summoned before Enzo Ferrari to discuss his career prospects. 'The first time he offered me the drive I turned him down because I didn't feel ready. His secretary took me aside and whispered, "You don't say no to *Il Commendatore*, Ferrari doesn't ask anyone a second time ..."'

After he finished fourth in the 1962 world championship behind the wheel of a Lola-Climax, a second invitation was forthcoming, however, and this time Surtees agreed. 'I reckon I was missing the pasta and vino of Italy ...' Two years later Surtees justified Enzo Ferrari's faith by becoming the first man in the history of motorsport to win the world championship on two and four wheels, in Mexico City, where he, Jim Clark and Graham Hill all went into that climactic grand prix vying for the title. Needing to finish first or second to be guaranteed the title, Hill's hopes vanished just before the halfway stage when he was in a collision with Italian Lorenzo Bandini in the second Ferrari ... on the last lap, and with the championship seemingly his for a second successive year, Clark slowed to a halt with an oil-pipe leak, handing American Dan Gurney victory ... at which point the Ferrari pits signalled Bandini to allow Surtees through (and you thought team orders were a recent phenomenon) into second place and triumph by a single point from the unfortunate Hill.

'Luckily, fate smiled on me as it hadn't done earlier in the year, but I should have won the title long, long before the Mexican Grand Prix. In Austria, for instance, the suspension fell apart when I was leading, and over the course of a season, luck tends to even itself out. We might have won the world title three years in a row and I was actually leading the championship in 1966 when I finally walked out after one argument too many with the aptly named team-chief, Eugenio Dragoni. But I loved my years in Italy – I was even named Italian Sportsman of the Year – because they have this flair of creating beauty, whether it's a pair of shoes, a dress, a painting or a motor-bike or car. They never regard the main objective as being practical or usable; whatever they make has to be beautiful and this shines through to the people.'

Having brazenly favoured Italians Bandini and Ludovico Scarfiotti, Dragoni would come to realise how much he owed to Surtees's driving skills and technical knowledge when Ferrari waited 11 long years before Niki Lauda won the team another title in 1975. 'Shortly before his death, Enzo Ferrari said to me, "John, we must always remember the good times and not dwell on our mistakes". I didn't mind leaving it like that.'

Curiously, although Formula One drivers are faster, richer and more powerful than ever before, as personalities – Schumacher apart – they seem diminished in comparison to the golden age of the 1950s and 1960s when Surtees, Mike Hawthorn, Stirling Moss, Jim Clark and Graham Hill provided a dash of Hollywood-style glamour. 'The public need heroes,' Surtees believes. 'They've latched on to David Beckham because, frankly, there isn't that much else out there. What Formula One needs is an exciting young person to contest the world championship. Look at Schumacher; you see that sparkle and bounce as he climbs on to the podium, there's a vibration.

Now, whether one loves him or loathes him, he inspires emotion. Have you seen any of our drivers create that emotion? The answer, sadly, is no. With all respect to your fellow-countryman [David Coulthard, I presume] he's like a dead duck. For motor racing to compete with the antics and frolics of the Beckhams, we need personalities who sparkle and generate human interest. Juan Pablo Montoya has it – I think he's got to grow up, but at least he creates comment and emotion.'

Surtees is equally concerned that, by tinkering with the rules in an attempt to drag Schumacher back into the pack, Formula One is in danger of losing credibility. 'I don't like what I'm seeing at the moment. It's almost like Lennox Lewis flooring someone in the first round and being forced to fight with one arm tied behind his back in his next bout. That situation has arisen simply because Ferrari have become the most complete team in history – driver-wise, mechanic-wise, engineering-wise, management-wise, you name it. The others, who haven't done the same best of jobs – whether it's McLaren-Mercedes, Williams or whatever – were shown up, but that's no reason to change the rules. It's like dumbing down school exams to make everyone equal, the other teams should be encouraged to improve their own programmes.

'You have to achieve a balance; the purist will say engineers must produce the best cars they can within the rules, whereas thrill-seekers reckon that even if you have to introduce an artificial element, we want more smoking tyres, more spectacle, more entertainment. Throughout the years, some teams have always had an advantage; 30 years ago, for instance, Lotus were way ahead of the opposition. It would be a privilege to be able to drive a car built to today's standards. In my day, we sat in a petrol tanker which, if you happened to spin off, could go bang! In the 1960s, teams were run on a shoe-string in comparison to 2003; F1 cars used bits and pieces of Triumph Heralds, they were back-yard specials. Were they fun to drive? Aye, if the wheels didn't come off. Certain cars you drove at your peril.'

Now a highly successful industrial property developer living on the edge of the Ashdown Forest (where he also restores antiques and timber-framed buildings), Surtees remains heavily involved in motorsport as chief mechanic, team manager and sponsor to his 12-year-old son, Henry, who is carving out a precocious reputation in karting. Four decades on from his world championship-winning year with Ferrari, it is not the memory of that triumph which sustains him, nor even his reign as the King of Bikes. 'The highlight of my career was the moment that sparked it all … at 17, winning a relatively unimportant road race in Wales riding a Vincent which I largely built myself. It was the first time I felt man and machine came together. ... I'll never forget the vibe I felt knowing I was part of the bike ... it flowed ... I was flying ... that was the day the future was born.'

4 APRIL 2003

WILLIAMS KEEPS EYE ON FUTURE

Sarah Edworthy

Frank Williams is adamant that he is not in the nostalgia business. 'What matters is today or tomorrow,' says the man and founding principal behind the Williams Grand Prix team. 'The dictum that one is only as good as one's last race is uniquely true in Formula One. It's been a number of years since we won the championship – I know the number but it's too painful to mention – and every year that goes by the gap inexorably widens.'

Be that as it may, the Williams team celebrate their silver jubilee this season – and have reason to revel in the memories of their seven drivers' championships (won by Alan Jones, Keke Rosberg, Nelson Piquet, Nigel Mansell, Alain Prost, Damon Hill and Jacques Villeneuve), 108 grand prix victories and nine constructors' championships.

Williams flew off to Brazil earlier this week 'looking forward to the fight', and to seeing his charismatic charges, Juan Pablo Montoya and Ralf Schumacher, strive to build on the promise shown so far by the new car in the sort of exciting race habitually conjured by the Interlagos circuit and its long 'man-size' straight. After two eventful rounds, the team are fourth in the constructors' championship on 14 points, behind McLaren on 26 and Renault and Ferrari in joint second on 16. 'We've made quite a lot of improvements, we believe, to our cars since the last race: a little bit here, a little bit there – it all adds up to a useful amount. I can't predict how much, but we will be more competitive than in the first two races,' Williams said.

If Montoya's fate in Malaysia was frustrating, given his loss of the rear wing in the chaotic opening lap, you would think Schumacher Jr's admission that he is struggling with the new format of single-lap qualifying must furrow the Williams brow. 'I'm not sure that is the case or not. Ralf's got this nonsense in one of the German scandal papers about being gay and his wife going off with other blokes. I don't think there's any truth in it at all, but it's on his mind. He says it's not, but he'd say that anyway. If I said, "Is there something on your mind?", he was not about to break down in tears, wait for me to put my arm around his shoulder and say, "Come come, talk to Frankie boy". It's a man's world.'

It certainly is. In the book published to coincide with the team's milestone, *Twenty-five Years of Williams F1: The Authorised Photographic Biography*, a caption reveals that Williams's partner, Patrick Head, once admitted that the experience of working with Alan Jones, the tough and ambitious Australian driver who signed for the team at the start of the 1978 season, effectively shaped his attitude towards Formula One in the future. 'Alan was a man's man and I can understand why he appealed to Patrick, as he did to me – he was very straightforward, determined, and he had a ruthless streak in him when it came to his competitors,' Williams said. 'He had the necessary skills to make him a world champion. I'm not saying he was the very best driver that we ever had, but his character was very complete as a racing driver. He had no important weakness in the complexion you need to be a racing driver.' A 'Williams driver' has now become part of paddock vernacular, referring not necessarily to a driver under contract to the team but one who has the aforementioned characteristics – which Frank is happy to elaborate on. 'They are characters who are strong internally and externally, get in, get on with the programme and deliver. And don't make a fuss while doing it.'

The commemorative book tells the 25-year story with fulsome captions brimming with fascinating detail: a picture of Williams running with Jones comes with the fact that, before the accident in 1986 that put him in a wheelchair, Frank would run great distances at six-minutes-a-mile pace. There is Ken Tyrrell, in a Goodyear cap, who had left his own team's pit at Silverstone to join in the wild salute to Williams's first race victory delivered by Clay Regazzoni. And Rosberg in fluorescent yellow branded overalls 'regarded at the time as terribly extrovert and offensive to the sensibilities of F1 traditionalists'.

The collage offers little glimpses of another era – Williams sitting on the pit-lane wall in a picnic chair; Rosberg chain-smoking all the way on to the grid. To read this team history is to realise how very British the Williams team are, and how for many fans the recent history of Formula One is generally interpreted through the events surrounding the Williams team. Mansell's reputation was probably exaggerated thanks to his acrimonious partnership with Piquet ('They had no time for each other whatsoever. In fact there was pretty intense dislike on either side, I think. ... it was not anticipated and maybe I wasn't tough enough about it at the time, but they couldn't help themselves.')

Ditto Michael Schumacher's ambition after that controversial championship-winning incident with Hill in Adelaide. There were the dramatically won laurels for Hill and Jacques Villeneuve – both imbued in the romance of racing through their fathers' achievements. The horrendous tragedy that befell Ayrton Senna in only his third race in his long dreamt-of Williams drive. The chirpy debut season of Jenson Button, followed by the arrival of Montoya, the so-called 'Colombian firecracker' at whose very mention the team principal thrills. 'He's a great character, a great character,' Williams repeats with admiration.

'We've had our trials and tribulations with one or two of these individuals along the way, but a man who wins a world championship ... let's take Alain Prost – you might say not explicitly a Williams driver, but he was a wonderfully skilled driver, highly intelligent with his racing and self-preparation. He won that championship [1993] masterfully. He won it at the lowest possible speed he could get away with and at the least possible risk to himself. It was frustrating once or twice at races, but the bottom line is he just handsomely won the title, which is why we asked him to get in the car in the first place.'

You never stop learning, from putting assets in your experience bank. That is the only way Williams cares to look to the past. Surely he feels some sort of collective pride in what he and his dedicated workforce have achieved. 'Not really, because I think that would be self-indulgent,' he answers bluntly. Was there a moment when he suddenly realised the team he and Head had created had become one of the leading players in the sport? 'You sort of realise it, but you equally realise how precarious the whole thing is. It is, like any international sport, very competitive and everyone else in it is trying to pull you down. And, once they have you, they try to trample you into the ground. That's the nature of competition.'

LET'S CELEBRATE MEMORY OF GREAT MAN THEN MOVE SWIFTLY BACK TO BUSINESS

Juan Pablo Montoya

There has been a lot written and spoken about Ayrton Senna leading up to the San Marino Grand Prix. I think the media are missing the point here. I agree with Ayrton's family this should be a celebration of his life rather than his death. And I would also like everyone to remember that Roland Ratzenberger died that weekend. I think the media were hoping that a driver would come out and say he would be thinking of Senna as he went through the Tamburello curve, or something. That would be a great story, big headlines: 'Drivers scared', and so on. But that is wrong and was never going to happen. My focus this weekend is on the race. Nothing else. That is how it has to be.

The Senna thing was ten years ago. Sure, I looked up to Senna as a kid. He was my big hero. I recognised that he had a fantastic talent, but I never met him. I remember where I was when I heard the news. I was going to watch the race but had to leave early because I was racing myself in Colombia that day. When I got to the track they told me he had died. I could not believe it. It was like saying Superman had died. But at the same time it is racing, and it happens. A year later I moved to Europe, and my own career was under way.

It is sad to say that they needed someone like him to die to make an improvement in safety. Last year at Silverstone I went straight into a tyre wall at Becketts at 175mph. That is plenty of speed, top gear just wide open. I was thinking, 'This is going to hurt'. I was a little sore, but you just get out and get on with it. Formula One has never been safer, and we have Senna to thank for that.

In fact I'm a little surprised to hear the current rumblings about speeds being cut back. I don't see the need for that. People are talking about a fifth groove on the tyres. What are they trying to do? There are no high-speed corners as it is. That's why we all love the old tracks. The lap times are coming down because the tyres are getting better. I think they have overcompensated a little bit. What are they going to do next? Put an eject button on the cars? Safety needed to improve but it's getting ridiculous. Have you seen the size of the run-off areas? No one ever goes off any more. I maybe go wide about twice in a weekend. I'm happy with the safety of the car but you also need the speed, too.

You never think about the risks anyway. If you did you would never get behind the wheel in the first place. You would say, 'I'll take the train, thank you very much'. There is always a risk. It is part of what we do. I love driving, pushing myself to the limit, going quicker than anybody else. Going slower is not what the sport is about. I think that's crazy. Hopefully we can be quicker soon. I'm giving it 100 per cent. There is not one thing we need to do to go quicker, it is a little bit of everything to improve the package generally.

Last year we spotted one thing that needed putting right. When we did that we saw a huge improvement. No one has found anything particularly wrong this time. The car was quick out of the box but the developments have not perhaps come along as we would have liked, and Ferrari are just that little bit better at the moment.

Ralf [Schumacher] has had an engine retirement this season, and in Bahrain I had a gearbox problem. You don't even hear a misfire in a Ferrari. At least in Bahrain I had ten laps to calm down after getting stuck in fourth. I knew the car was going to stop early so I radioed the garage and asked if they would mind if I crossed the finish line then pulled over. I did not want to walk back to the pits.

5 JUNE 2003

SCHUMACHER CAN PUT HIS FOOT DOWN BUT, AWAY FROM THE TRACK, HE PUTS HIS FEET UP

Sarah Edworthy

At the end of the final race of 2002 – with the world championship sewn up in record time four months beforehand – the Ferrari mechanics were hanging around in the Suzuka paddock itching to party. Michael Schumacher had ordered 12 bottles of Bacardi (mixing Cuba Libres, cigar dangling from lips, is his end-of-season speciality), but celebrations were delayed. And delayed further. The champion remained absorbed in discussion in a briefing room, buzzing with ideas for next year's car. Hadn't he asked for an additional function on one of the 19 buttons on his steering wheel? This would give a small advantage if it were fitted now before the winter break.

Schumacher's success stems from his groundedness, his focus, the fact that his motivation remains the same: he simply loves the challenge of taking a car to its limits. Ask about his dreams, his secret wishes, and the man now deemed the equal of Juan Manuel Fangio responds swiftly and always with the same word: anonymity.

After 11 full seasons in Formula One, five of which have seen him crowned world champion, the trained mechanic from Kerpen who concedes he would be equally happy fixing go-karts for a living, is uncomfortable with global-hero status. 'I don't want it, I have a problem with it. I'm just like everyone else, I just happen to be able to drive fast,' he says. The longest stretch of invisibility he has achieved was the winter break in 2001, when he, his wife Corinna and family retreated to Norway. 'Or maybe the time after the accident I had in Silverstone 1999, when I stayed at home in Switzerland with a broken leg for around three months,' he ponders.

Schumacher, conducting the interview a month after his mother's death, also admits that the environment which has put his image in petrol stations and on advertising billboards the world over is not one to which he wants to introduce his young children. He never brings Gina and Mick into the F1 paddock lest they mistake this 'artificial world', as he dubs it, for normality. If little Mick grows up to announce a passion for racing, will the legendary father be happy to guide his son? 'If I could, I would prefer to steer him away from a racing track on to some golf course because I have seen with Jacques Villeneuve or Damon Hill, or even with my brother Ralf, what a burden a name can be, and I would not want him to be constantly compared with me or to not be able to establish his own name,' he says. 'But then, if he has a passion – you know, like our parents who always supported Ralf and myself in anything we really wanted – I would support my son as well.'

Schumacher was talking on the publication of a book he has collaborated on with journalist Sabine Kehm. Gloriously unguarded – the German recalls how nothing in life has outraged him as much as the incident at Spa in 1998 which caused him to accuse David Coulthard of wanting to kill him; Corinna talks about her fears, her raceday rituals, even how they bath together – it teems with insightful anecdotes and gives a genuine sense of how Schumacher, the icon of his sport, functions as a human being.

As a competitor, Kehm likens Schumacher's philosophy to that of Sepp Herberger, coach of the 1954 World Cup-winning German football team: 'After the game, the game is only beginning.' He has never been a dreamer. He doesn't even do hope. His starting point is a fundamental pessimism. In the car he is immaculately precise, the embodiment of control, but, surprisingly, race weekends are often marred with sleeplessness. He travelled to

Japan in 2000 – where he ultimately brought Ferrari their emotional first championship crown for 21 years – with this attitude: 'It could have been on the cards that I would leave Japan two points behind the winner. That's the way I have to approach such matters. It's simply the way I am: I always start by being pessimistic.'

Schumacher's F1 debut at Spa in 1991 came after a blistering test at Silverstone in a Jordan to see whether he was good enough to stand in for absent driver Bertrand Gachot. Only now does Schumacher reveal how he squirmed as his manager, Willi Weber, told a 'little white lie', confirming the difficult Belgian circuit was part of Schumacher's repertoire when in fact the 22-year-old had no experience of the track at all. However, Schumacher's tendency to worry has never extended to his ability inside a cockpit. 'Of course I was concerned! I mean, as I had this test in Silverstone before I was OK, I knew I could handle the car, but still I had the vague feeling of F1 as a "superior" racing class and wondered if I could be a part of it – testing is different from racing. On the other hand I was calm, as I knew worrying about it would not change anything in the way I drove.'

Just as fulfilling as a qualifying lap that puts him on pole can be the perfect testing lap. As Ferrari principal Jean Todt puts it: 'The track is his drug.' Can the driver himself foresee a time when he loses his addiction to the challenge? 'To be honest, I don't know. At the moment, very clearly, I could not imagine this passion to stop. It has always been part of my life, and I never had a feeling it is weakening. To me, a life without motorsport is unthinkable – having four wheels around me is perfect. You know, in the end I am crazy enough to participate in karting races against boys who have half my age after a long season. No, I cannot foresee such a time when this is gone.'

A black spot on this boyish enthusiasm remains Jerez 1997, the championship-deciding race in which Schumacher turned his car into Jacques Villeneuve's – described in the book as an 'act of desperation' for which he was punished by the FIA. Were his children to ask about it in years ahead, how would he describe it? A moment of impetuosity, or madness? A mistake? Something he is ashamed of? A lesson learnt? 'Maybe all of this? I could not describe it better than you did here now. It was clearly a mistake, and if I could re-do something in my racing life, that would be it,' he agrees.

If this act betrayed the hot-headed human behind the cool tactician, his show of tears at Monza 2000 prompted a reassessment of Schumacher, the otherwise robotic performer. That was the race in which he equalled

Senna's 41 wins but also saw a marshal fatally injured. The German newspaper *Bild* ran the headline 'Schumi we have seen your heart'. Was it a relief, after all, to be seen as someone who harbours admirable emotions? 'Yes and no. Sure I felt better because of this, but on the other hand I had anyway never really understood that perception of me being cold, so at the same time I did not feel the need to "prove" I am just a bloke like others. Actually I had difficulties with this attitude: OK, he cried, so he is human, so he must have emotions. Strange, isn't it? I mean just because I don't show them in public it does not mean I don't have them.'

Corinna Schumacher tells how her husband, the glue of the Ferrari team, has the same role at home. 'With Michael, everything is so harmonious,' she says. 'It feels as if there is a link between us, at all times. We are always touching each other, we do it automatically. We simply have to. Our children now do it, too. When we are eating, for example, we all sit very close together. Sometimes, I have to laugh, because we are pressed up so closely together that we can hardly eat. And it's not as if we don't have a large table.'

At the end of 2002, the relentless success of Schumacher and Ferrari bored spectators. Putting himself in the place of an average paying spectator, would he have decried the lack of excitement too? 'I think this opinion was also partly down to the fact that many people concentrated very much on the top of the drivers' field. But motorsport is not only about the top, there were a lot of fascinating battles in the area behind, which too few people were concerned with. I think I would have watched the race from out of the eyes of a motorsport enthusiast and enjoyed the level of battling for positions.'

Schumacher left Benetton after two world championships saying he needed fresh motivation. Where does he get that now he has collected three more world titles at Ferrari? 'There is always a new race to come, so there is always new motivation. You know, I love what I do, so I do wonder why people wonder why I am motivated in doing this. Plus, why should I be less motivated because I have had success? It's the other way around, especially – and this is the nice thing about sport – as it is always only the next race that counts. The last one is over. You do not win something because you won in the past.'

'IN THE PRESENT CONDITIONS, WE SHOULD LOSE THE DORITO BAG IF YOU DROP YOUR SPEED TO 22MPH'

Giles Smith

When Juan Pablo Montoya swept across the finish line to win the Monaco Grand Prix earlier this season, he accidentally left on the intercom in his car, with the result that his private and none too cool cries of elation were broadcast for all and sundry to hear.

'Embarrassing,' Montoya said afterwards. But he's not the only driver this year to have been exposed by a radio link with the pits, as the following exclusively obtained transcripts reveal.

Kimi Räikkönen (McLaren)
Intercepted at the Canadian Grand Prix, Montreal, 15 June.

Pit: Kimi?
Räikkönen: Yep.
Pit: Yeah, you've picked up something, looks like a crisp packet or something. It's sticking just below the air induction, behind you. On the left-hand side.
Räikkönen: So?
Pit: Could you try and lose it?
Räikkönen: But I'm in the frigging lead here.
Pit: I know, I know. It's just that it's covering the Hugo Boss logo and we've got sponsors going completely ape. The guy from Boss is jumping all over us in here. He's saying they don't pay us five million a year so we can go around advertising hot barbecue flavour Doritos.
Räikkönen: Well, tell the guy from Boss he can [expletive] my [expletive].
Pit: He's right here, as it happens, Kimi. And he says you can [expletive] your own [expletive]. Hang on. [Pause] And he says you can [expletive] his, too, for all he cares.
Räikkönen: Damn it all. Doritos, you say? Well, let me see if I can reach it. ... I'm just waiting for a straight. ... OK!

[Noise of safety harness unbuckling followed by scrambling sounds.]

Räikkönen: No, it's no good. I can't get to it.
Pit: [Expletive] Hold tight, Kimi. We'll come back with something.

[Extended pause]

Pit: Kimi? Could you try weaving?
Räikkönen: Weaving?
Pit: Yeah, from side to side. We're thinking if we can change the wind pressure on the side of the car, we might be able to get some air under the Dorito bag and flip it off.
Räikkönen: Give me a second, I've just got to get past this Minardi. [Pause] OK, here I go.

[Noise of squealing tyres]

Räikkönen: Is it gone?
Pit: One second … no, it's still there. Give us another moment, Kimi.

[Even more extended pause]

Pit: OK, we've been back to the airflow log, on the computer simulation, and, according to the best available data, and in the present wind conditions, we should be able to lose the Dorito bag if you drop the speed to 22mph. Understood?
Räikkönen: Understood, but you realise I'm going to lose race position. I've got Alonso right up my pipe here.
Pit: Priorities, Kimi.
Räikkönen: OK.

[Brief burst of screaming brakes. Muffled crunch.]

Pit: Kimi? You OK?
Räikkönen: I'm fine. But where did Alonso go?
Pit: Not sure. There's a lot of dust.
Räikkönen: Is the bag gone?
Pit: Hang on. … Well, it's further back than it was, so that's something. Ah, hell: would you frigging believe it? Now there's a Chewits wrapper on the TAG Heuer patch. Kimi, you're going to have to pit.

David Coulthard (McLaren)
Intercepted at the Australian Grand Prix, Melbourne, 9 March.

Coulthard: Anybody there?
Pit: *[After long pause]* Hello, David.
Coulthard: Who's that?
Pit: Robin.
Coulthard: Robin the wheel-bolt guy?
Pit: Yes.
Coulthard: How are you, Robin?
Pit: Well, I'm pretty busy right now, what with ...
Coulthard: Robin? Can I talk to you for a while?
Pit: Well, perhaps it would be better if ...
Coulthard: Do you ever think about the universe, Robin? I mean, really think about it? Like, the concept of an infinitely expanding space?
Pit: I just do the wheel-bolts.
Coulthard: Only, sometimes when I'm out here, behind the wheel, and there's nothing ahead of me but road, I get to wondering about the vastness of everything. Because if the earth is but a grain of sand within the universe, what does that make all of us, Robin? What do we all amount to?
Pit: I have to go now.
Coulthard: But if all we are is specks of dust, then explain why ...

[Radio contact lost]

Antonio Pizzonia (Jaguar)
Intercepted at the French Grand Prix, Magny-Cours, 6 July.

Pizzonia: Hey! I don't believe it!
Pit: What now?
Pizzonia: I just went by a huge banner with my name on!
Pit: Yeah, right.
Pizzonia: No, I did! A big one with Pizzonia painted on it! You know what this means?
Pit: I'm sure you'll tell us.
Pizzonia: That somebody loves me! That I may have been a miserable disappointment all season, thoroughly outdriven by my team-mate; that I may have managed to crash the team road car

during a corporate presentation day; that rumours of my imminent sacking may have come almost every hour, on the hour.
Yet, I, Antonio Pizzonia, still have a fan.

Pit: Takes all sorts.

Pizzonia: Hang on, I'm about to go past it again ... here it comes ...
the sign of love ... ah.

Pit: Problem?

Pizzonia: Actually it said pizzeria.

David Coulthard (McLaren)

Intercepted at the French Grand Prix, Magny-Cours, 6 July.

Coulthard: Is Robin there? Robin the wheel-bolt guy?

Pit: *[After extremely long pause]* This is Robin.

Coulthard: Do you think there's such a thing as objective reality, Robin?
Or is the world just the way we each of us perceive it in our
own heads? So it's like we're all going around the place, thinking we see the world as it is. But in fact we're only seeing the
world in the way that we see it. And maybe the way that you
see the world and the way that I see the world have nothing
at all in common. That's a terrifying thought, isn't it, Robin?

Pit: *[Pause]* I just do the wheel-bolts.

Michael Schumacher (Ferrari)

Intercepted at the European Grand Prix, Nürburgring, 29 June.

Schumacher: Into sixth gear. Oil pressure holding. Temperature normal.
OK, going for the overtake. Down to fourth, move out
wide. Adios, sucker!

Pit: Sounding good, Mike.

Schumacher: Accelerate: fifth, sixth. Congestion ahead! Drop to third,
duck inside. Yaargh! Eat my dust, headless pond life!

Pit: Super!

Schumacher: Fourth! Fifth! Sixth! Double de-clutch, brake, second gear.
Approach barrier. Show ID. First gear. Drive through. Find
empty bay. Select neutral. Handbrake. Engine shut down,
ignition off.

Pit: Beautiful, Mike. OK, when you've finished parking up, come on over
to the garage so we can start getting ready for the race.

19 JULY 2003

PIERS COURAGE LIVED LIFE TO THE FULL AND WAS TIPPED FOR GP GREATNESS

Sarah Edworthy

The crowded roof of the pits at Zandvoort on 21 June 1970. Sally Courage, elegantly settled in a folding camping chair with her pad of blank Ferodo-supplied lap charts and pencil to hand, reads a Nevil Shute paperback to calm her pre-race nerves. As the cars leave the pit area one by one, Bette Hill, Nina Rindt and Helen Stewart sit at their respective pits, poised to perform similar time-keeping duties for their husbands.

Later, just 23 laps into the Dutch Grand Prix, a thick plume of smoke rising behind the sand dunes, and the non-appearance of her husband's car in pursuit of the No. 26 of Clay Regazzoni, were the first indications of the unthinkable for Mrs Courage. It was an agonising wait, but soon the whispers were confirmed. Less than a month after his 28th birthday, and 18 months into a promising Formula One collaboration with close friend Frank Williams, Sally Courage's husband of four years and father of her two young sons, Jason and Amos, had been killed instantly when his De Tomaso crashed, rolled and exploded into a fireball.

Telegrams of condolence came from the Queen, from Enzo Ferrari, from the grieving parents of Bruce McLaren in New Zealand, from all over the world of motor racing. 'He was a great man, highly popular, and I remember clearly that when he died a nation grieved, as did all of us in Formula One at that time,' writes Sir Frank Williams in a foreword to a stirring new book which celebrates Piers Courage as the last of the gentleman racers. Thirty-three years after his death, Courage, known to his friends as 'Porridge', is treasured as one of the most life-enhancing Englishmen to go motor racing. He had contested just 28 grands prix and finished second in two of them, at Monaco and Watkins Glen.

However, his story is not just a moving tribute to lost potential (Williams maintains he would have become one of Britain's premier sportsmen), it is also a celebration of that special brand of friendship that comes of shared enthusiasm. For Courage and his car-mad gang, racing was informal, hazardous, full of japes, incredible fun – and he, in particular, had a gift for inspiring camaraderie. As Monny Curzon, a cousin of Sally's with no motor racing connections, comments in the book: 'Piers did have a magical quality, be it part charm, part the nature of his spirit, that made his loss deeply and lastingly felt. It acted as a magnet to people so that they remember the period when he was around as being, in different ways, centred on him. Perhaps it was the quality of loving life, and showing friends how to live accordingly.'

Courage caught the racing bug at Eton, but it was not until the summer after he left that he was able to experiment as a participant. On Sunday mornings he disappeared with the family Morris Minor Traveller. Once out of sight he would decorate it with peel-off go-faster stripes ready to go racing around the perimeter of the former RAF base at Chalgrove, where a gap in the hedge and lax security encouraged a field of like-minded petrol-heads to charge around. His racing career began more officially when his father bought him a Lotus Seven, in kit form. Richard Courage later helped to buy his son's next car, a Merlyn (only after his wife walked out until he agreed to do so), but thereafter Piers was on his own as far as finance was concerned. It was a dramatic step to choose not to follow six generations of Courages into the family brewing business.

A hand-to-mouth existence ensued to pursue his racing ambition with endless amusing tales of life with Jonathan Williams, Charles Lucas, Frank Williams, Charlie Crichton-Stuart and Anthony 'Bubbles' Horsley. The stories that emerge from a flat in Harrow – Flat 6, 283 Pinner Road – suggest a blue plaque is in order to commemorate the partying, the ducking and diving, the people sleeping on floors, the visitors such as Jochen Rindt and Innes Ireland. In the lock-up garages in the backyard the racing cars were prepared lovingly for their next outing. No one had money, and here emerges Frank Williams's first entrepreneurial ways in raising money – charging local policemen to come in and watch blue movies.

For all the fun – and the most entertaining stories involve incidents like Piers ramming his car backwards to reshape a damaged chassis, or crashing his road car into a skip in Montpelier Square, Knightsbridge, such was the legendary awfulness of his road driving – and for all his easy manner, the *Who's Who*-ish facts suggest serious racing ambition. He could have had a different lifestyle, but gave up a lot to go racing. After towing his own Formula Three car around Europe, he became a regular winner and was acknowledged as Britain's most promising driver when he received the 1965 Grovewood Award from Jim Clark. A premature move into Formula One, and a series of crashes in a Formula Two McLaren, meant he rather poignantly set off to salvage his reputation, racing as a privateer in the 1968 Tasman series. The following year he joined forces with Frank Williams to run first a private Brabham, then the ill-fated De Tomaso in F1.

His skill in the fast corners of the fast circuits earmarked him as a fearless talent. He was always part of the slipstreaming group. Sir Jackie Stewart recalls him 'driving like a tiger' at Monza, very quick and clean round the big high-speed test of the Curva Grande. 'Piers had made a lot of progress. He had the style and the education. Frank had incredible steel, determination and confidence, so they complemented each other perfectly. I have no doubt Piers would have been a major player in grand prix racing,' said Stewart in a short film shown at a moving tribute to Courage at the Goodwood Festival of Speed last weekend. 'He was a very good racing driver, a very good friend, a typical aristocratic Englishman with great style, great manners, great humour. He was a very nice person to have around in those turbulent and exciting years.'

Indeed, the only bad experience in reading Adam Cooper's enthralling book is that, having had this particular period of motor racing brought so dramatically to life (with the Beatles playing and Courage himself pioneering Carnaby Street fashion sense), you know the awfulness of the Zandvoort incident looms. The pages before and after his death are peppered with reports of other fatalities. It was that dreadful era, 'one disaster after the other', as Bernie Ecclestone recalled when Rindt's luck ran out only 11 weeks later.

However, his story is a testament to living life to the full. 'Thirty-three years later his friendship is still there, he had a huge effect on my life,' says Horsley in the Goodwood film. 'What more can you say other than that he was the dearest friend you ever had and you miss him every day,' says Charles Lucas. 'He was the greatest fun, utterly charming. They don't make them like that any more,' says Sir Frank Williams.

2 APRIL 2004

OASIS AWAITS ITS DESERT STORM

Andrew Baker

It is not unusual for a motor racing circuit to be in the middle of nowhere. A track takes up a great deal of land, and the cars are noisy. But it is unusual for a motor racing circuit to be in the middle of nowhere, in the middle of a desert. As Bahrain's Sakhir circuit rises above the horizon, shimmering in the heat haze, the first impression is that it surely must be a mirage. It is anything but. It is a solid, substantial facility, and the truly remarkable thing about it is not its location, about 20 miles from Bahrain's capital, Manama, but the fact that it was completed in only 16 months, and no less than six months ahead of schedule.

The Bahrain Grand Prix, the first Formula One event to be held in the Middle East, was scheduled for September. But then the sport's calendar underwent one of its periodic shake-ups, and the Bahrainis were suddenly staring at a pleasingly uniform but frighteningly imminent date: 04/04/04.

As recently as three weeks ago, the race looked in some doubt. The organiser, Philippe Gurdjian, called Formula One commercial rights holder Bernie Ecclestone to tell him that the race would have to be cancelled. Ecclestone, whose future strategy for the sport is based on expansion into the Middle and Far East, refused to allow this to happen. The Bahrainis hired more workers, and got on with the job. The chairman of Cebarco Bahrain, the construction company who built the track, is finally able to rest peacefully in his bed. 'I'm a bit relieved now that it is all over,' Khalid Abdul Rahim said. 'For the last six months, I couldn't sleep without taking a pill, but in the last few days I have had a sound sleep. The project was a big challenge, and moving the race date made our job even harder.'

None of it has been easy. The track's German designer, Hermann Tilke, selected the location from a choice of six sites he was offered by the Bahrainis. The attraction for him was the slight change in elevation – no more than 18 per cent – across the site, which offered a rare chance of variety in such a flat land. But the chosen spot was not problem-free: it was covered in boulders, which had to be blown up and carted away. 'It was all rocks here,' Tilke recalled. 'Blasting them was quite boring in the beginning. But with close co-operation between all departments concerned we were able to complete the project on time and as planned.'

Connoisseurs of such things will recognise the track as a typical Tilke design, wide and characterised by long straights leading to sharp turns. The first corner is particularly reminiscent of the first corner at Sepang in Malaysia, another Tilke track. Viewers on Sunday may feel they are watching a flashback to a fortnight ago. But there is one key difference between Sakhir and every other track on the calendar: sand. This is pretty enough as a background, but has a nasty habit of blowing around, and the drivers are concerned that if sand blows on to the track during the race it may get into engines, and will undoubtedly reduce the grip of tyres. The circuit constructors have responded to this threat by laying kerbs that are 33 per cent wider than usual, and then bonding the area of sand closest to the track with cement and water. This allays some worries, but sand blowing from outside the circuit perimeter may still cause problems. Fortunately, only light winds are expected this weekend.

Haste of construction has caused one other area of concern: the track surface. It is usual when constructing a track to allow the asphalt time to settle, and then to run test events with increasingly demanding vehicles. But this will be the first race at Sakhir, and sticky-tyred, powerful Formula One cars en masse may, some fear, start to tear up the track's top layer. There are precedents: the 1985 Belgian Grand Prix at Spa was postponed when a newly laid surface disintegrated. But let us hope that these problems, and the much-touted security concerns, fail to materialise. Formula One thrives on novelty, and that has been rare on the track this season. If we cannot have a new winner, at least we can have a new track, and a new country on the grand prix calendar.

Luminaries of the sport arriving in Bahrain over the past couple of days have all expressed themselves optimistic for the weekend, and the mood in the desert is upbeat. Sir Jackie Stewart put it best. 'What they use in the engines of the racing cars comes from this part of the world,' he said. 'So it only makes sense to have a race here.' Formula One breaks new boundaries: petrol's coming home.

22 MAY 2004

A DRIVE FOR LIFE

Sue Mott

There was a phase, if I remember rightly, when the Great British constabulary used to pull errantly speeding motorists to the side of the road, not with the erstwhile, 'Who d'you think you are, Stirling Moss?', nor with the subsequent, 'Who d'you think you are, Nigel Mansell?', but with the far more thrillingly exotic, 'Who d'you think you are, Emerson Fittipaldi?'

You can just imagine how gratified and preening the wayward driver would feel in his Austin 7, clocked at 73mph on the A4, even as he was hauled down the nick with his driving licence. Fittipaldi was a gloriously romantic figure, a Brazilian blessed with the touch of an angel and the tactics of a chess grandmaster. He was the youngest man to win the drivers' world championship in 1972 at the age of 25. He had the longest sideburns in grand prix history, even longer and bushier than those of his dear friend and rival, Sir Jackie Stewart. 'He was a man of average height with long sideburns. At the time it was necessary,' said Sir Jackie from Monaco yesterday.

They remain close, survivors of an era when the risks of Formula One were far more horrific than those faced in Monte Carlo tomorrow by the modern breed of racers. 'In the 1970s I lost a lot of friends in grand prix racing,' Fittipaldi said. 'Jochen Rindt, Jo Siffert, Jo Bonnier, you name it. The odds were 7:1 to survive. At the beginning of the season there were always 20–22 drivers, and by the end of the year always three would go away. Now the odds are 1000:1. The last one to go was Ayrton Senna and that was ten years ago. There are still a lot of crashes, but people don't get hurt. Thank God.'

He is a religious man, and he would need to be to enjoy a speedster career that spanned four decades and involved his travelling at up to 230mph as a 50-year-old in the IndyCar series in America. Most of us at that age would only hit such a speed on a shuttle flight to Manchester. There was little he did not accomplish in those years of flair, panache and a few accidents, but funnily enough, Monte Carlo was one that got away. Even now it rankles. 'I missed so much not winning at Monaco. I have much sadness about it. Always I had mechanical problems. The ghost I had all the time was mechanical failure. In a fraction of a second you can go from a driver to a passenger.'

But not always. Sometimes the ghost was replaced by a much more substantial being, like Stewart's rear axle. 'I had a great dice with Jackie in 1973. He was leading all the way, but for the last ten laps I was in his gearbox. But on that course, unless the guy in front makes a mistake, you cannot overtake.' Stewart did not make a mistake, unless you count during the victory lap. 'I finished only a second behind Jackie, and I came next to him on the cooling-down lap to congratulate him. But he was busy saluting the public and he drove over my car. He didn't see me. I [was] up in the air on two wheels and nearly turned upside down. I said to him, "Never again will I come alongside you after a race". During the race, no problem. But after the race was too dangerous.' Sir Jackie confirms the story but tweaks it a little. He was not saluting the crowd. He was taking his gloves off and simply failed to look in his rear-view mirror. Either way, he was hideously apologetic. Almost to the point of meaning it. 'I'd just won a race, so I wasn't overwhelmingly upset,' he said.

Monaco had special resonance for Fittipaldi. He loved street circuits, so familiar to him from his junior kart-racing career in Brazil. 'Always I have good feeling for street racing. Very twisting, so you have to be very precise. At the same time you have to be very aggressive. This is the advantage Michael Schumacher has today. He is fast, aggressive, but at the same time very smooth. Always you have to be on that edge. There are not many drivers who can master this. But I have great admiration for Schumacher and the way Ferrari set up their cars.

'Unfortunately, yes, Formula One is also boring. I love and adore the sport but even myself, watching the Spanish Grand Prix, I thought after the pit-stop it was just a question of Schumacher administrating the race. Like a business administration. Like another business day in his office. All you think is: how far [behind] is going to finish the second guy. Historically, the young talents could, even in their first season of F1, show their potential. Whether they were world championship material, immediately you could see. Now that doesn't happen. Now, if you take a great potential young talent and put him in a Minardi, you don't know how good the guy is. We are losing the main goal: the race for the world championship of drivers.' Now we just have the world championship of Michael Schumacher: not much anticipation there? Fittipaldi nods his head in acknowledgement.

It is uncanny how much he resembles Alice Cooper these days – two 1970s icons who refuse to get their hair cut. They cannot, however, be one and the same. No man as charming and urbane as Fittipaldi would dream of biting the head off a chicken, while Cooper would not have enjoyed a post-rock'n'roll career belting around an IndyCar oval at more than four times the speed limit in America. The former singer famously prefers the more sedate pace of golf carts. Karts of a different kind inaugurated Fittipaldi's career. His father, Wilson, was a prominent racing correspondent and friend of Argentina's hero, Juan Manuel Fangio – five times the world champion, a superman of the sport renowned for his fierce competitiveness, allied with tender care of his car. 'When I was about five years old my father took me to Interlagos racetrack, and it was so beautiful, I loved it. I saw the race cars go by and said, "This is what I want to do for the rest of my life". Fangio was my big idol. I saw him race for the first time when I was seven.'

As if these antecedents were not spur enough, Fittipaldi's mother was also a racer. 'She was unusual,' he says in wild understatement. 'At the beginning of the 1950s, she raced Citroen and Mercedes. Saloon cars. Amateur races. I remember going to Interlagos with my elder brother and watching her race in a black, four-door Mercedes. It was a 24-hour race. Beforehand, she came to the paddock and drew a big circle on the asphalt with chalk. She said, "You have to stay in here while I'm racing".' As any mother of seven and ten-year-old boys will tell you, the chances of them staying faithful to such an instruction are about the same as Victoria Beckham learning Spanish. It is a measure then of the little Fittipaldis' passion that they stayed glued to their spot, watching the same corner hour after hour.

Before he could lay his hands on a car at 18, the younger Fittipaldi raced anything, everything. 'Boats, hydroplanes, motorcycles, karts. I won a few. I never had an accident. Then in my very first car race I had a crash. It was a Renault in a race in Rio. At the end of the straight I suddenly had no brakes. Finished, the brakes. The only way to stop the car was to turn the steering wheel. The car started flipping over and over and went over the fence, into the crowd. Thank God, it never hit anybody. So I had just turned 18, it was a brand new car and it had been lent to me by a friend.'

Freakishly, the only other bad accident Fittipaldi suffered was at the very end of his career, two bookends of mangling action that bring a neat symmetry to his life. It was 1996, the first corner of the first lap of the US 500 in Michigan. 'The Michigan Speedway,' he says with due reverence, 'is the fastest oval track in the world. Two miles long with banking. I had qualified fourth on the grid and I wanted to get to the front from the start. There was this particular young guy from Canada, who actually got killed two years after. I passed him on the outside and he just touched my rear wheel. I spun, went backwards through a wall, broke my neck, collapsed my lung and suffered internal bleeding. I was critical. Thank God, I am still here.' God and a chassis conforming to better safety regulations. 'It was a tremendous impact when I hit the wall. I survived. But in the 1970s the car would have disintegrated completely.'

The nostalgic tug of a name like Fittipaldi is tremendous. He and his fellow racers were risking limb and mortality in a very candid way, yet they were fed by a blind-to-all-else passion. Not competing was not an option. But the range of options was pretty limited. Glory or death. When you talk about the 'fragile lotus', most people would take that to mean the flower. In his case it was the car. In his grand prix debut at Monza in

1970 his Lotus 72 crashed heavily during practice at the Parabolica. It was at precisely this place that the team leader, Jochen Rindt, smashed into a barrier and died on his way to hospital. Fittipaldi's F1 career began in a state of mourning.

Yet such are the advances in safety that he is already supporting his seven-year-old grandson Pietro in a fledgling kart-racing career. Once petrol is in the blood, it seems no distillation process will remove it. The family hardly needs the money. Since retiring, Fittipaldi, a member of the Laureus World Sports Academy, has become an entrepreneur with his own racing team and a huge orange plantation in Brazil.

Where Fittipaldi stands in the pantheon of great drivers is not a preoccupation for him. He won a relatively modest 14 grands prix, but this was predominantly due to his loyal transference to the non-competitive team run by his family and sponsored by the Brazilian sugar company, Copusucar.

'If you get a time machine and gather up all the great champions going back in history for one race, all in their prime, all in a Ferrari, can you imagine how fantastic that would be. Who would win? Ah, it is very difficult to see. It could be Jim Clark, it could be Fangio or Jackie Stewart or Michael Schumacher. I know who would be the most aggressive: Nigel Mansell. Senna told me: the way Nigel drives is always acrobatic. Always like an emergency.'

Senna confided a great deal in Fittipaldi, fellow countrymen, fellow racers, fellow admirers, but only one survivor. It affects the elder man greatly still. 'I remember the moment I heard. I was testing at Michigan, going at 230mph, when my team manager shouted, "Emerson. In, in, in." It took a long time for me to slow down and roll into the pit. Someone said, "Your family's calling". I took the phone and my wife just said: "Ayrton's just got killed". I remember the shock to this day. For me he was immortal. Not just because he was a friend and a boy I had introduced to grand prix racing as a new world champion, but because of his position in F1. It was such a tragedy.

'There is no other sport that has this instant line of life and death. It is safer now, but still the risk is there. Especially at Monaco. When you think of the speeds they go and the very narrow track, there is not much protection for the public. It would be easy any time for an F1 car to jump and go over the fence. The risk is always there.'

'F1 IS NOW A PERFECT MERITOCRACY. YOU HAVE TO PAY TO PLAY'

Paul Hayward

Bernie Ecclestone turned the British Grand Prix into roadkill yesterday, squashing it without sentiment in his haste to do mega-deals with governments in the oil-rich Arab nations and Far East. If the Tower of London was still trading, he would be in it, yet the decision to drop Silverstone is entirely consistent with the ruthlessness of Formula One. Like a James Bond villain, Ecclestone must have given his cat an extra stroke last night when blame was heaped on the Government, who have invested £8 million of public money in roads around Silverstone but refuse to subsidise the multi-millionaires of the F1 paddock. Quite right, too.

Does anyone other than Sir Jackie Stewart and the British Racing Drivers' Club seriously think the state should make up the £3 million shortfall between what Silverstone are offering and Ecclestone has in mind? Bahrain, who spent £127 million building their new circuit, and Shanghai, who lavished £300 million on the inaugural Chinese Grand Prix last weekend, have their own motives for wanting to be on Ecclestone's map of rampaging egos.

If F1 wants to shred loyalty and tradition in search of untapped markets, the British taxpayer can hardly be expected to respond to such emotional blackmail. F1's overlord and impresario is taking care of business. Plainly Ecclestone can't bring himself to sacrifice a valuable date in the calendar to a hard-up track just to please 100,000 British petrol-heads and to keep cars whizzing round Luffield, Stowe corner and Copse. It may yet be, of course, that he is playing brinkmanship with the Government and the BRDC, who have until 13 October before the sport's governing body ratify his cold-heartedness. But there is a pattern of attacks on Silverstone, which looks more dated each time Ecclestone opens a new frontier. For years now he has been chipping away at its credibility.

F1's product – the race itself – has lost its old competitiveness and its dare-devil allure. So it may be no coincidence that the top man has driven the industry into new markets at a time when Michael Schumacher and Ferrari have turned it into a one-horse race. In this context the word sport hardly applies. F1 is a money-circus – deals on wheels – and so it matters not that there are 40 grand prix firms in the UK or that Northamptonshire has been a host since F1's inception in 1950. Ecclestone saw that governments outside Europe would be willing to pay silly money for the kudos that building an F1 track brings.

For China, the investment was linked to the automobile industry. Belgium had already been dispatched when the British Grand Prix was left bleeding on the tarmac yesterday. In Ecclestone's world view, F1 is now a perfect meritocracy. You have to pay to play. The British motorsport industry is entitled to feel traumatised. It's as if the tennis authorities had reached down and taken the oldest grand slam event away from Wimbledon.

Motor racing is deeply embedded in the British psyche. After a lull, Nigel Mansell and Damon Hill showed us how feverishly the hordes would flock to Silverstone to see a British driver extend the legacy of Hawthorn, Hill, Surtees, Clark and Hunt. A telling statistic is that Britain has fielded almost twice as many drivers in grands prix as Italy, its nearest pursuer.

The heart shrivels to imagine no Silverstone next year. But if Sir Jackie and the big hitters of British F1 mind so much, they should organise a whipround and then turn the BRDC into a proper consortium of patriots and investors. Our £3 million would be better spent on school sport.

30 OCTOBER 2004

SCHUMACHER DRIVES ON TO IRREFUTABLE GLORY

Kevin Garside

The 2004 Formula One season was about one man. Michael Schumacher. He would be a threat in a Citroen 2CV; in the best grand prix car Ferrari have produced in the 54-year history of the world championship, Schumacher was in a class of his own.

Arriving on the last weekend of August in Spa-Francorchamps, the Belgian circuit where he made his debut in 1991 and took his maiden win a year later, Schumacher had won every race but one, 12 out of 13. Had Juan Pablo Montoya not clipped his rear while running behind the safety car in the Monaco tunnel, Schumacher would probably have won in Monte Carlo, too. At Spa he required only two more points than his team-mate, Rubens Barrichello, to win the world championship for a record seventh time. Ironically he managed it while suffering his first genuine defeat of the year: coming second to Kimi Räikkönen was enough to get the job done.

Schumacher made the odd contribution to the record books along the way. Most wins in a season (13), and most consecutive victories (7). The only landmarks he does not hold are the number of poles and grands prix contested. The former is sure to fall to him next year (Schumacher is just two behind Ayrton Senna's 65 poles, a figure once thought unassailable); for the latter to be his (Ricardo Patrese is 44 ahead on 256), Schumacher must race beyond 2006. Don't bet against it.

The shame is that much of Schumacher's work attracts opprobrium rather than praise. The succession of uncontested victories from the start rapidly drained the drama from the season. Elite sport, by definition, is about competition, about testing oneself against adversaries more or less able, about meeting the hardest of challenges in the fiercest environs. Ferrari's supremacy meant that Formula One failed to meet the basic criteria, and therefore robbed the season of the oxygen of intensity. Not Schumacher's fault, of course. But until McLaren, Williams and Renault give Räikkönen, Montoya, Button, Webber and Alonso the means to compete, Schumacher will be denied the chance to put flesh on the statistical bones, to demonstrate his genius. Muhammad Ali was demonstrably a brilliant fighter. However, he became a greater fighter when forced by another to dig deeper during molten exchanges with Joe Frazier, Ken Norton and George Foreman. Räikkönen, Montoya, Button, Webber and Alonso may yet do for Schumacher what Frazier and Foreman did for Ali. Spa apart, they never came close in 2004. As a result the season's enduring memory was not one of Schumacher leaping into the stratosphere after yet another grand prix win, but of the champion elect sliding out of the Monaco tunnel sideways on three wheels, his unblemished start to the year kiboshed by a comic collision.

20 JUNE 2005

DAY OF SHAME FOR F1

Kevin Garside at Indianapolis

The future of Formula One in the United States hung in the balance last night after what must rank among the greatest PR disasters in the history of this or any other sport. The failure of the teams to agree a solution to a tyre problem that first emerged 48 hours earlier shamed all involved in grand prix racing. More than 120,000 people paid to watch the fastest, most technologically advanced cars negotiate the most celebrated track in American motorsport. What they got was the equivalent of Chelsea versus Rushden & Diamonds. The record books will show that Michael Schumacher won his 84th grand prix at the Indianapolis Motor Speedway, fighting off the challenge of Ferrari team-mate Rubens Barrichello plus the combined might of Jordan and Minardi.

What it will not record is the anger and frustration felt by an outraged American public utterly baffled by the decision of 14 cars to return to the pits after the parade lap. Vernon King, a citizen of Indianapolis and one of the many to walk out immediately, called for Formula One to be banned in the United States. Others, more realistically, just wanted a refund. The American market is one that the sport's power-brokers are desperate to crack. All that was required to put on a show was unanimous agreement to build a temporary chicane at turn 13, the fastest part of the track. With 14 cars affected by Michelin's error in producing a tyre too unstable to run at 200mph-plus on this track, the weight of the argument lay with them.

Sadly, Ferrari and the sport's governing body, the FIA, did not see it that way, refusing to acquiesce. With Michelin unable to guarantee the safety of the cars for anything more than ten laps, the teams they supply were left with no option but to stand down. The rules do not allow a change of tyres, once a choice has been made. Neither of the two specifications brought by Michelin were fit for purpose. A mistake was made. The question was how best to deal with it. A chicane was the only plausible solution. When agreement could not be reached after talks lasting 48 hours since the problem emerged on Friday, embarrassment was guaranteed.

Bernie Ecclestone, Formula One's commercial rights holder, said: 'I'm furious at the stupidity of it all. There should have been a compromise but we could not get one. I tried a million things and thought that if we could get them on the grid we were halfway there. But it did not happen. We were just starting to build a great image in America on TV and with the fans. All of that has gone out of the window.'

David Coulthard, one of 14 emasculated by Michelin's advice not to race, spoke for all. 'I'm shocked. I find it hard to put into words how damaging this is for F1. It throws into doubt the future of the race in US,' Coulthard said. 'The bottom line is Michelin made a mistake. But after that the FIA had it in their hands to find a solution and ensure we all raced out there. The most important people, the fans, have been forgotten in all of this. It is them I feel sorry for. We did not know what speed the tyres would burst at. Not just the speed but the loading.' Jenson Button added: 'I feel sorry for the fans, but if Michelin tell us it is too dangerous you can't race.'

Most, including those draped in the red of Ferrari, did not hang around to watch the farce unfold. There was no joy to be had watching Ferrari pound the Jordans and Minardis into the asphalt. 'This is going to leave a long-lasting bitter taste in people's mouths,' Coulthard added. 'Quite frankly, as a driver, I'm embarrassed to be involved in this situation. The fact is that mature adults were not able to put on a show for everybody. It's a very sad day for racing.'

Disbelief silenced the crowd when only six cars took their places on the grid. When people realised what was happening, that silence turned to anger. Fingers were raised and boos rang out. One fan showed his displeasure by throwing a can on to the track. Before the cars had completed a lap the first of those to leave had left their seats and begun walking through the tunnel and out into the car parks.

With 22 laps to go Schumacher exited the pit-lane to a near-miss with his team-mate. The Ferraris survived unscathed after Barrichello ran across the grass, but the prospect of both being forced to retire after a coming together was there for one tantalising moment. But by the time Schumacher brought his car home first there was barely any interest to record. The German raised his hand in victory, but it seemed an empty gesture after what had gone before. The podium ceremony, which featured Tiago Monteiro of Jordan alongside the two Ferrari drivers, was also a surreal affair.

As fans arrived at the start of the day, tickets for the 2006 United States Grand Prix were being advertised on the huge, electronic screens that tower over the pit straight. After this, they will not be able to give them away. Schumacher certainly took no delight in his win. 'It was not the right way to win my first grand prix this year,' he said. 'I would have wished to fight under normal circumstances.'

20 JUNE 2005

THIS LOOKS LIKE THE END OF GRAND PRIX RACING IN AMERICA

Jackie Stewart at Indianapolis

There are no winners in this. Any sympathy towards Formula One in this country will have gone after this. There will be a lot of ramifications. I can see what has happened here today having a domino affect on F1 in America and perhaps in other countries, too. The contract in the United States is up next year. Whether the people here will want to renew it now is another thing. There are not many promoters in this country who will want to take on the responsibility of hosting an F1 GP, given the difficult financial situation surrounding the sport at this time.

The US government do not get involved in supporting racing in this country in the way so many others do. The state of Indiana does not help financially, either. Tony George, the chief executive officer at the Indianapolis Motor Speedway, has been put in a difficult situation. This is bound to have a significant impact, and I'm very disappointed that a solution was not reached.

Any form of crisis management requires a compromise. I believe the United States Grand Prix should have taken place in the proper way. For that to have happened you would have needed a chicane to be put in place. It was a technical issue that was certainly unforeseen and that affected all but six cars. The chicane should have been accommodated – there was plenty of time to do that. The governing body has to be open to some kind of compromise when faced with unique or unusual situations of this kind. Especially so in this part of the world.

A crisis emerged at a time when F1 does not need this kind of negative element being introduced. I was in a suite with some very important business figures, and they could not understand why something could not have been arranged to allow the race to go ahead in some sort of normality. You would not allow the drivers to go out with a set-up that potentially could lead to a dangerous situation on the track. There will be another time when something like this arises. Hopefully when it does, a better solution will be found. What is clear is that F1 cannot afford too many days like this. Especially days like this that can be avoided.

6 SEPTEMBER 2005

LAP OF HONOUR FOR A CANNY SCOT

Sue Mott

'It's great to remind yourself where it all began,' shouted Sir Jackie Stewart over the racket of whirling rotary blades as the rooftops of Milan swept by beneath him and the rising stands of the racetrack at Monza swirled into view. It was a pilgrimage in a sense, revisiting the scene of his first triumph in a Formula One grand prix exactly 40 years ago. The son of a Dumbarton garage owner entered the pantheon of fame in that moment. 'My life has been like a magic carpet ride ever since.'

It was like walking into a wall of noise, excitement and petrol fumes as the running of the 76th Italian Grand Prix was gearing up on Sunday. But even young *aficionados* in their bright red Ferrari T-shirts stopped to stare at the small 66-year-old Scotsman in tartan trousers marching purposefully towards the paddock. Then they encircled him, begging for autographs, photographs, a word. Time goes by, but motor racing does not forget its greatest champions. Stewart was three times world drivers' champion, runner-up twice, won 27 of his 99 grands prix. He was a hero of the track and a campaigner off it, fighting against often fierce and sneering opposition to make the sport a safer environment. He buried too many friends to let it rest, and he was too attached to the sport to let it go.

Heading for the Williams motorhome, where the Champagne was waiting on ice and the walls were decked in photographs of his triumphant career, he was greeted warmly by old friends and new fans. Even Bernie Ecclestone, with whom he has enjoyed a long-running feud over the future of Silverstone, stopped by to shake hands and hug Helen Stewart, Jackie's wife of 43 years. Typically, his favourite venue was the Williams truck, where he opened drawer after drawer filled with highly polished nuts, bolts and nails. 'Look at that,' he said rapturously. 'Fantastic. The attention to detail is vital. When we ran Stewart Racing, I used to jack up the trucks and turn the tyres round so that the name Bridgestone was exactly positioned on the top.' The meticulousness of F1 vastly appeals to him. His target is perfection. Even his personal assistants are Sandhurst-trained. The new one, Niall, comes fresh from employment as a UN Conflict Zone reconstruction officer in the illegimate, *de facto* non-state of Abkhazia in the former Soviet Republic of Georgia. Good training, I'd say.

Stewart took a tour of the Williams garage and stopped to admire the shell of a driver's seat. 'You have four fittings for a Savile Row suit,' he said. 'But for these a driver has six fittings.' The three Williams cars were lined up in the pits ready for the race, the focus of activity for a staff of 85. 'When I drove for Ken Tyrrell, there were 14 of us in total. We didn't do tyre changes in those days unless you got a puncture, and the catering corps consisted of Ken's wife Norah making the sandwiches.' We looked around Red Bull

Racing's hospitality and dining suite, which was constructed on three floors in the paddock, and every pencil-thin model in a microskirt in Italy had been drafted to lounge tantalisingly on the steps.

Stewart spotted Jacques Laffite, the former French driver. 'He's 61 and he's just signed up to race in the new Masters' series they've created. Nigel Mansell's doing it. So's Alain Prost.' Stewart went over to give the Frenchman a friendly hug. 'Silly old bugger,' he muttered as he went. There is absolutely no danger of Stewart racing again. He announced his retirement in 1973, aged 34, at the US Grand Prix, Watkins Glen. 'It was probably the best decision of my life,' he said. He went out at the top, the reigning world champion, but it was not a time of unbridled celebration. It rarely was in those days. One of his dearest friends, François Cevert, was killed in practice for that grand prix. Stewart was one of the first to reach his car. It was clear that Cevert was dead, but it remains a regret with Stewart to this day that he did not, could not, stay there with his friend by the mangled remnants of the car for a few minutes longer. 'I couldn't do it. I was so sickened and disgusted. I walked away. But I really wish I had stayed.'

There are smiling pictures of Cevert in polished frames in Stewart's study at his immaculate home, which is the former gatekeeper's lodge at Chequers. The Frenchman is not the only one. Graham Hill, Jim Clark, George Harrison, King Hussein of Jordan, all friends, all gone, all remembered in portraits or just happy holiday photographs around the Stewart home. The house is unpretentious but stunningly appointed. Obviously, an alarm bell is primed to ring if a crumb drops to the floor. At one point Stewart disappears behind a door frame. What was he doing, I inquired. 'I thought I saw a leaf on the floor,' he said unapologetically.

'It can be a bit exhausting, but you get used to it,' confided his wife on the private jet back from Milan which, according to the visitors' book, had been recently hired by Prince Charles, Madonna and Wilbur Smith. This was a glimpse of the Stewarts' globetrotting life, typical of a multi-millionaire businessman and sporting icon. But it certainly was not the life they might have imagined for themselves when Jackie was an apprentice mechanic working in the grease bay of his father's garage, and Helen was the friend of the blind date that he went to meet at Dino's Radio Café in Helensborough. 'The friend didn't fancy me,' Stewart explained. You have to bet she's sorry now.

'I was born on 11 June 1939, to the son of a gamekeeper and the daughter of a farmer. His name was John Young, and it was on his farm that Rudolph

Hess crashed during the war.' That might have been enough excitement in the life of some families, but the young Stewart brothers, Jimmy and Jackie, both had other ideas. Jimmy was the first of the brothers to become a racing driver, while Jackie, even as he learned the trade of a mechanic, became a clay-pigeon shooting champion. He missed by one point qualifying for the two-man British Olympic team to Rome in 1960. He would not miss the pinnacle in his second sporting career.

There was another spur to his eventual global success, his dyslexia. 'My schooling at the Dumbarton Academy was a total disaster,' he said. 'I was stupid, dumb, thick. The torment, the humiliation, the frustration – you cannot believe the frustration. Just to be so abused by your teachers, your peers, even your family, who didn't understand that it was not just a matter of being lazy or not paying attention. I was eventually diagnosed at the age of 42 because my sons were dyslexic. We discovered this when one of them was asked to leave his school in Switzerland, the second most expensive school in the world, Aiglon, because he couldn't keep up academically. He didn't leave. There are no problems, only solutions. I had him tested in London, and I was saying to the consultant that I was never any good at school either. He said, "Come this way". I did the test, and that's how I found out. I tell you, it was like someone had saved me from drowning.

'Honest to God. I thought of all those years when I had thought I was the stupidest boy in the class. Of all those times when I had tried to read aloud, all the tittering and laughing because I was unable to do it. You can't imagine the damage it does from the beginning.' The diagnosis was a life-line, but the problem still exists. 'I'm still unable to do certain things. A balance sheet, for instance, is a jungle to me, and I'm on the board of a number of companies. I have to get people to explain things to me. I have to consume it and understand it painstakingly. But once I have,' he tapped his forehead, 'I've got it in here forever.'

This would explain his amazing recall of dates, numbers, names, speeches, even the lines he learned in 1967 for the first TV commercial he made. 'It was for British Railways, and I was standing in Waverley Station in Edinburgh in a sports jacket saying, "The most powerful engine that I've ever driven produced 750 horse power. This beauty produces 7,500 horse power. And it's fast. Very fast. It can take you from Edinburgh to London in under five hours. And even I can't do that".' He stopped, looking highly pleased with himself. 'Jackie, that was 40 years ago,' I said, amazed by the filing cabinet capacity in his head. 'Thirty-eight years ago,' he corrected me, typically.

You absolutely see what Helen means.

They married in 1962, the year that Jackie began racing in a Marcos for a benefactor, Barry Filer, he had met through his work as a mechanic. Helen could only just afford half a yard of Stewart ribbon, which she glued to his helmet and then painted over with clear nail varnish. 'It never did quite meet at the back because I couldn't afford the full yard,' she said. The newly-weds lived in joyful frugality to the point of penury. 'I remember being so depressed during the Cuban missile crisis that I went out and did something madly extravagant. I bought myself a lipstick.' She laughed – an elegant, handsome grandmother (of seven boys and one girl) with access to every luxury money can buy, looking back on simpler times.

Stewart continued to work as a mechanic throughout his rise through the racing ranks. By 1963 he was racing for the Scottish team, Ecurie Ecosse, for £500 a year plus expenses. In 1964 he contested 53 races in 26 different racing cars in a variety of classes including F3, F2 and Le Mans, and won 23 of them. In 1965 there was Monza. 'That's when the rocket really took off.' The pictures look positively quaint, like the Dinky toys we all had as children. His round-topped BRM, No. 32, immortalised in static black and white. The driver, gimlet dark eyes looking steadily in front of him, topped by a helmet hardly more protective than the ones mods used to wear on their Vespas. Stewart drove for BRM until the end of 1967, then he went to work with Ken Tyrrell. Twenty-five of his 27 wins were for Tyrrell, and all three world championships. By 1969, when he won the first championship, Monza was crazy about him. The crowds went so wild after the race, he and Helen locked themselves in a loo to escape and eventually crawled to safety out of the back window.

By 1971 his fame had reached the point that his friend Roman Polanski came to Monaco to film *Weekend of a Champion*, the inside story of Stewart at the Monte Carlo Grand Prix. Helen remembers Polanski discovering she had got up and washed her hair in preparation for filming on the Saturday morning. 'He threw me back into bed and messed me up so it looked as though I had just woken up.' A mere two years later, it was over. 'I was burnt out,' Stewart said. 'Burnt out to the point I was getting more aggravation than satisfaction from one of the most stimulating things that life will ever give you.' He walked away to his new life, business, which he claims has given him as much exhilaration, and certainly as much security, as motor racing did. He has enjoyed long-time relationships with Rolex (since 1968), Moët et Chandon (since 1962), Ford (he resigned from the board after

40 years in 2004), ABC television in America, where he was a colour commentator for 15 years. Now he is an ambassador for the Royal Bank of Scotland, on whose behalf he was making a speech in Copenhagen last night to a throng of conservative suits.

You wonder what he must talk about. There is surely not much a banker has in common with a racing driver, except vast wealth. Wrong. 'You can talk about the art of the calculated risk,' he said, smiling. The calibrations of his calculations are very precise. Just as he would relay information to his mechanics on every facet of every corner of every race, so he has been a very careful, very successful businessman. 'Before telemetry was invented, if I could tell my team what was happening to the car better than anybody else, I'd have a better racing car. I needed an invitation not a challenge. If I'm trying to keep up with a bitch of a car, I can't create optimum speed.' Same in business. When Stewart gave up the Stewart Racing team after three years of F1 competition, winning their first grand prix after 31 months, he had no overdraft to pay back. 'I never believed in hire purchase. Still don't,' he said. He and his elder son Paul, with whom he ran the team, reportedly sold the going concern for well over £100 million.

This must be slightly sickening to some team owners, who seem to throw their money into a vast, black, oily pit for very little return except political angst, financial strain and burst eardrums. But Frank Williams holds no grudge. Despite years of mock English versus Scots warfare between the two, Williams unequivocally put Stewart in his top five all-time racers along with Fangio, Clark, Senna and Schumacher. 'What he had as a driver is a quality he shares with many of his compatriots,' Williams said. 'He was canny.'

'François Cevert, Jochen Rindt, Piers Courage, Jim Clark, Mike Spence, Bruce McLaren, Ludo Scarfiotti, Jo Schlesser ... ' Stewart was reciting the names of the dead, friends and fellow racers who died from their sport. 'We were going to funerals and memorial services all the time. You saw the families grieving. Helen would go and clear bedrooms, pack suitcases, for the widows and girlfriends. It was terrible.' Reminded of those dark times, Helen can remember letting herself into the hotel of Cevert after he was killed and the shock of seeing the indent of his head on the pillow. It is 31 years later but tears still swim into her eyes. 'Jackie says why do I still cry all these years later, but he does, too, you know,' she said.

The old days. 'I never make the mistake of thinking they were better than now,' Stewart said. 'More exciting perhaps, but not better. The circuits were dangerous. The cars were dangerous. Fire was a far greater hazard. And yet the resistance that *aficionados* and the media put up against change was incredible. They saw us as gladiators. They said they paid us to do it. But I never thought I was being paid danger money. I thought I was being paid for my skill. You know, in all those years of racing I never spilled one drop of my blood.'

Williams was right. He was canny. It was part his Scottish inheritance and part his experience as a shooter that always kept his feet on the ground. 'I won the first event I competed in. I went on and did very well. There was a short period of time when I genuinely thought I was God's gift. Big mistake. Suddenly you lose it. You lose your timing, your perspective. I had gone through all of that by the time I got to racing. I wasn't going to make the mistake of thinking I was God's gift to racing.' It was a good lesson. 'I remember coming out of the gates to walk to the front row of the grid at Monza, and suddenly 150,000 people stood up for me. The whole stand erupted. I was the reigning world champion by then. It was a very intoxicating experience. But on the start line the drive shaft broke. So I'm grounded. Everybody passes me. I get out of the car and the entire crowd started whistling and booing at me. The same people. So why get intoxicated? Why get suicidal? That's how you keep your feet on the ground.' He is not afraid of his own mortality, either. He, Helen and his son Paul have been through cancer scares of various intensities, but his attitude remains unaltered. 'I have absolutely no fear of dying. I think racing drivers of my generation have a different view of dying anyway. I don't think of death as other people do. So many friends died, and I still see them. I see them every day of the week. They'll never be out of my life. They were very important people in my life, and I feel their spirit is still there, lingering on, long after their physical death. Don't get me wrong. I don't want to check out unnecessarily early. But whenever I go, I've had the most fantastic life.'

I NOVEMBER 2005

NO ONE LOOKS LESS DIFFERENT, MORE HUNGRY, THAN OUR OWN FORMER WORLD F1 CHAMPION

Sue Mott

Eight men in silver suits are smiling into space on the edge of a field in Northamptonshire. They are one of two things: either on a bus trip from their home for the bewildered, convinced that the aliens are coming for them at last; or else members of the superannuated driving force who will comprise the Grand Prix Masters series, soon to be unleashed on the sports world.

A slightly nasal laugh drifts across the tarmac. Excitement and petrol fumes fill the air. This is Silverstone. There can be no doubt about it any more. Nigel Mansell is back. He is not only back, he is thrilled. 'I think this is more exciting than Formula One,' he has been saying over toast and strawberry jam in the breakfast marquee. And this is just a practice session; the first time the drivers have climbed into the cars, the 650 brake horsepower beasts with Cosworth-Nicholson engines (very fast, to you and me), that will soon carry them down the straight at nearing 200mph in a fearful reprise of the old days. Fearful to us. Wonderful to them.

What was it like? 'Very nice,' said the German Christian Danner. 'Good. So far,' said Emerson Fittipaldi. Patrick Tambay just beamed. He has widened a little, like the M25, since we last saw him. He is deputy mayor of a suburb of Cannes. Life was good, but it can always be better. The lure of fast cars to middle-aged men proved irresistible. Here they are. But no one looks less different, more hungry, more delighted than our own 52-year-old former world F1 champion and special police constable, Mansell. 'There's a senior golf tour and a senior tennis tour. Really it's just a natural progression to have the same thing in grand prix racing. Listen to the noise of the engines. The cars look like F1. It's just tremendous.' He looks like a boy. 'A big boy,' he amended before charging off to sit in the cockpit of his new noisy toy.

Autosport, the magazine, has christened this series the 'Gramps' Prix Masters in honour of seniority of the drivers. But the combination of famous names, ferocious speeds and Murray Walker, who has been lured out of retirement to commentate, could make this package more than a little attractive. The first race is at the Kyalami circuit in South Africa in November. Christina Aguilera supplies the music, Delta Motorsports the cars, and the old boys the passion that has never really gone away. 'The neatest drug in the world that is legal is adrenalin,' said Mansell, returning from a practice session, grinning. He was fastest, by the way. 'You go out there and scare yourself, and it helps all your aches and pains. Then the aches and pains come back and you have to go out again. We live longer that way.'

Ten years ago he left Formula One. It could have been yesterday to look at him. He has not gone grey, he has not fattened out, his engineer's enthusiasm for driving has not dimmed one iota. He is mad about the car. 'It has surpassed all my expectations as a race car. It's better than some of the F1 cars I drove. It worked straight out of the box. There's no question this is a thoroughbred of a car. That has surprised me a little bit. I thought it might have been a little more docile. But this is a stallion of a car to drive. You've got to hang on to it. There's no traction control. There's no power steering. There's no automatic gear shift. It's all driver inputted. It's fantastic.' He burst into laughter, a pure outbreak of glee. 'It wakes you up.'

This is the reason for the drivers' expectations. Unlike F1, the series represents a level playing field similar to the A1 Grand Prix series. The cars are all the same. No dominant Ferrari or Renault with a computerised astronaut at the helm. Information will be transparent and engines equally powerful. Fernando Alonso, the new world champion, would find this an alien planet. 'I'm sure Alonso would find it a shock to the system. This is stepping back in time. We've put the driving of the car back into the hands of the driver, which is how it should be. All the F1 drivers would find this a bigger handful. Wouldn't it be nice to have a guest appearance by a regular F1 driver. See what he does. I think they'd have a bit of a shock.' He thinks he would beat them, doesn't he? 'I'm not saying anything,' he said, grinning.

They would love it, the grandpas. But it would be crazy for a current F1 driver to accept the challenge, a hiding-to-nothing on wheels. It would be a little bit like a modern footballer in his Porsche being overtaken by an old lady en route to the library. Not quite, actually. The cars so beloved by Mansell are, in fact, genuine F1 lookalikes, so light on their wheels and yet so powered-up, that they are hailed as the second fastest circuit vehicles on earth. Not one of the silver-suited racers returned to base with anything less than a look of bemused rapture on their faces.

The same may not apply to the families of those involved. 'Totally supportive,' said Mánsell of his wife Rosanne and three children, Chloe, Leo and Greg. But there is more to this story. 'We've had a terrible last 18 months because my wife's been so poorly. She's had four operations. We almost lost her last year. We're now much more fatalistic as a family than before. I've been devastated. Through that my sons have had a change of heart about their direction in life. They're racing now, and I've gravitated back to it. What you do is realise that life is precious. Which is almost a contradiction in terms when here we are driving at 200mph. But what you've got to do is make the most of your life. With the GP Masters, everything has come alive again.'

Lord, how can this be the same man who earned a reputation among some of moaning, for perceiving slights in every comment, for bearing chips on his silver shoulders? He is the happiest middle-aged man I have met. 'I got labelled as a moaner, and it was totally untrue,' he said. 'I'm a qualified engineer. I wouldn't settle for second best. I was just trying to get the job done. I wasn't playing at it. But it was just a few people who did me down. I'm very phlegmatic about it. I'm very honest. A lot of people in the press said I had no talent. So ridiculous, it's untrue. Ultimately I'm a very strong person and took no notice.' He must have taken notice to have noticed, as it were. He is one of those people, like John McEnroe, with an infinite capacity to be irritated. You could put them in the back of the smoothest-running Rolls-Royce and they would still hear a rattle in the engine.

Perfectionists. But then Mansell would have to be in order to turn his eight karting championships (1968–75) into the world F1 drivers' championship 1992. He was heroic, aggressive, unflinching and Brummie in the process, a style that caused Ferrari's devotees to christen him *Il Leone*. 'Fantastic,' he said, of the nickname. 'Even now, when I go to an Italian restaurant, they won't let me pay for the meal. So I go to as many Italian restaurants as I can.' He has another good laugh with himself.

Not all former heroes (who must be over 45 and have spent at least two years in F1) are ready and willing to compete again. 'You have to look at yourself in the mirror and say, basically, "Are you ready to put yourself on the line today?" If you are, you can be a race car driver and a good one. It's frightened a few of them. A few of them should be here that are not here. But I won't mention any names. It's the opposite in my case. What attracts me is the level playing field. It's absolutely fantastic and tremendous.'

Now it is true that Nigel Ernest James Mansell, twice Sports Personality of the Year (so, for all those who disliked him, there were more who adored him) is being paid as an ambassador for the GP Masters, but his enthusiasm is patently honest. 'The thing is I haven't always loved the rules and politics of racing, but when it's in your blood, that's it. It's just wonderful to be reunited with so many drivers.' Reasonable people might wonder whether they are all taking a hellish risk. Elderly people tend to wander from their lane or meander the wrong way up motorways. They cannot hear oncoming vehicles, let alone see them. These drivers might drop their glasses in the cockpit. As it is, before Fittipaldi can climb into the car for a photoshoot, someone triggers off his fire extinguisher by accident threatening him with white froth. There are just no end of hazards.

This is disgustingly ageist and utterly dismissed by Mansell, who has not aged one millisecond in the last ten years. 'There is too much suggestion in sport these days that when you are over 30, you're past it. Total nonsense. I'm doing this for the over-forties and the over-fifties to demonstrate life goes on.' He had a hospital check-up, as required. 'Being English, of course, you couldn't cheat the system. I know a few people who have just gone to the motoring authorities and said, "Give me a licence," and they were given a licence. I was on a treadmill doing a stress test for 20 minutes because they couldn't get my heart up high enough. I thought, "I'm going to die in a minute". We had a good laugh.' How is his eyesight? He feigned missing his head with his hat. 'Oh, not too bad actually,' he joked. So his eyesight is fine and his sense of humour is terrible.

These are early days for the GP Masters but, given the combination of men, car and ball-bearings, inextricably mixed with nostalgia, the formula may be a winning one. Mansell, who will talk to anyone about revs per minute (10,800 on this car, if you really want to know), cannot wait to begin. Nor for Michael Schumacher to turn 45. 'Or let's get him in now,' he said excitedly. 'Bring 'em on. I think it's wonderful for motorsport to embrace something as special as this,' he said over the deafening of eight engines. 'I think history is being made.' He is wrong there. The history has already been made, this is grown men reliving it.

5 MAY 2006

PUTTING THE BRAKE ON PRESSURE

Mark Webber

Jenson Button thinks he has problems. He should try being an Australian and not winning races. The same questions that are put to Jenson about his failure to cross the line first are also fired at me. And the Aussies don't hold back. It's frustrating, not least because Formula One is one of the hardest sports for people to understand. It's like me watching yacht racing. I respect the guys who do it but I don't really know what I'm looking at. You can't tell that the guys in the boat are rubbish; you just don't know. In other sports, such as football and cricket, it is easy for people to demonstrate their ability and to show what level they are at. In F1 it is not easy to convey such qualities if your car is not as quick as the front-runners.

In the 1980s when I was growing up watching F1 as a fan, there was a lot more attrition; the cars were more spread out. There were some brilliant races, too: Prost, Senna, Mansell, Piquet, that sort of stuff, but you got more surprising results. Look at Michael Schumacher last year. Apart from Indy, which he won by default, he didn't win a race. That didn't suddenly make him a bad driver. The car wasn't there. At the moment there are only two or three cars capable of winning. Last year, it was Fernando Alonso and Kimi Räikkönen.

I'm going to work this weekend knowing that I'm unlikely to win. The key, of course, is not to let that frustrate you. You have to bring the bar back down so that expectation matches reality; you have to set yourself achievable goals. In the San Marino Grand Prix I came home in sixth position. I thought that was all right, behind Michael Schumacher, Alonso, Juan Pablo Montoya and Räikkönen. That's where we are.

I've been in sports cars with Mercedes. We turned up and won. That was it. Bang. Every week. That didn't make me the world's best driver. However, I believe I'm pretty good at what I do. Jenson the same. He is getting single-lap performance out of the Honda, as I used to do at Jaguar. Jenson doesn't hold himself back in the race. He is up against a team in Renault who have all the boxes ticked, a very crafty outfit with a sound racing car and a brilliant driver in Alonso. As a package they are tough to beat, but it won't always be that way. Ask Jenson. When he was at Renault four years ago they were running at the back with Minardi. They have turned it round brilliantly under Flavio Briatore and look in great shape again this year.

But there are a lot of good blokes in this paddock trying to bring them down. Eventually someone will succeed in doing so. I'd like to tell you that I would benefit from that cycle. I'm sure Jenson would, too. The reality is that it is impossible to say. The key is not to put pressure on yourself, and I'm not sure that Honda have managed their early disappointment as well as they might have.

29 MAY 2006

SCHUMACHER A SLIPPERY CUSTOMER ON SKID ROW

Sarah Edworthy in Monte Carlo

What a race. Consigned ignominiously to the back, he started from the pit-lane, scorched through the field, finished fifth, and set the fastest lap. That is Michael Schumacher all over. Determined. Unemotional. Undeterred by a force-field of opinion that declares his reputation is in tatters. At the close of the race, he even took Rascasse with one hand as he waved to the crowds – sweetly rounding the very right-hander at which he ineptly faked an accident during qualifying by apparently not being able to steer around it.

'Does he think we are all fools and idiots?' Keke Rosberg, the 1982 champion, had raged after the parking incident. 'It was the cheapest, dirtiest thing I have ever seen in Formula One. He should leave F1 and go home.' 'A ******g disgrace,' fumed Flavio Briatore, the man who shared two successful world championship campaigns with Schumacher at Benetton in 1994 and 1995. 'How can a seven-times world champion make a simple mistake like that? Of course it wasn't a mistake!' 'It was too blatant ... a very agile mental management job. ... I am sure he knew Alonso was on a fast lap. It reflects on him and Ferrari,' was the verdict of three-times champion Sir Jackie Stewart. 'If that was a mistake he should not even have a Formula One superlicence,' raged 1997 world champion Jacques Villeneuve.

The resounding reaction to Schumacher's 'dodgy pole' – later deleted by race stewards – was overwhelming. The paddock was electric with indignation. Not one voice stood out to suggest he had done anything other than deliberately stop his car in the dying seconds of qualifying to prevent anyone beating his time. No one gave him the benefit of the doubt. That was chilling.

So why did Schumacher risk his reputation with such a clumsy tactic? History shows this instinct is woven into his psyche. Clinically competitive, he has an 'at all costs' flick-switch deep inside his mind. When his superiority is challenged, the margin closes and the offender is a competitor of threatening stature, that switch flicks on. Mika Häkkinen suffered from it in Macau in 1990, Damon Hill in Adelaide in 1994, Villeneuve in Jerez in 1997. In police parlance, Schumacher has 'previous' when it comes to doing unsporting things at important moments.

Gaining pole at Monaco in 2006 was an important moment. Alonso seems indomitable, yet Schumacher wants to retire at the end of the season with a record eighth title, to go out in a blaze of glory. But in paying the ultimate compliment to Alonso, in betraying his desperation to come out best, Schumacher has undermined his career achievements. Schumacher's credibility as a worthy champion is in tatters. In the nine years since Jerez he had become his sport's elder statesman, but now it is back to square one, this time with no path left to redemption. It is unprecedented for a driver of his calibre to (a) face blunt claims of cheating, and (b) be sent to the back of the grid.

The question now is: how will he handle it? Yesterday the team issued a statement in which principal Jean Todt said: 'Ferrari notes with great displeasure the decision of the race stewards... We totally disagree with it. Such a decision creates a very serious precedent, ruling out the possibility of driver error.' Surely, reiterated the opposing consensus, a stewards' study of data traces, video evidence and testimonials lasting eight hours examined every possibility? Briatore – who, as Renault sporting director, lodged the protest – had feared that, because this was Ferrari in Monaco, justice could not prevail. But the evidence was overwhelming. The FIA-appointed officials concluded: '[We] are left with no alternative but to conclude that the driver deliberately stopped his car.'

'Never apologise, never explain' is a line taught at business school. Schumacher drove around Rascasse 78 times in race mode yesterday, and he probably didn't give the corner any more resonance than being turn 18. Pressed on the issue, he rued mucking up Alonso's qualifying lap but denied he is a cheat. 'If you know Michael, he's not an emotional man,' said Willi Weber, his manager.

15 JULY 2006

MODEST ALONSO ON COURSE TO REPEAT HISTORY

Andrew Baker at Magny-Cours

One hundred years ago the first motor racing grand prix was held in France, on a circuit in the Sarthe, to the east of Le Mans. The winner drove a French car, a Renault, which ran on French Michelin tyres. Annoyingly for the organisers, though, the driver was not French: he was a Hungarian, Ferenc Szisz.

Plus ça change, plus c'est la même chose. A century later, the favourite for this weekend's French Grand Prix will drive a Renault on Michelin tyres, and he is not French. But then national pride is not top of Fernando Alonso's list of priorities.

The Spanish world champion was born in Oviedo but lives very happily in Oxford. He says that he has three 'home' grands prix: the Spanish, the British and, in honour of his team, the French. He won at Magny-Cours last year and remembers the feeling well. 'That was one of my best races,' he said. 'Everything was right, and the crowd were fantastic. The grandstands were blue with Renault fans, and I could feel the support, feel the emotion.'

At that time Alonso was on his way to becoming the sport's youngest world champion, at the age of 24. This year, he is on his way to becoming the youngest double world champion. He has a healthy lead over his closest rival, Michael Schumacher, and is starting to think about adopting the same conservative approach to the latter half of the season that served him so well in 2005. 'I wouldn't say I'm feeling comfortable – I'm never comfortable – but I certainly prefer being first to being second. It is similar to last year, the way we opened a gap in the championship and tried to keep the advantage.'

Last year, it was Kimi Räikkönen and McLaren in pursuit. Now it is Schumacher and Ferrari. 'The difference is that Ferrari are not having mechanical problems,' Alonso said. 'Last year McLaren were quicker than us, but they weren't finishing their races.' McLaren are still not finishing their races, and they are no longer quicker than Renault. Which must give Alonso pause for thought as, after six years under contract to the French team, he has signed to join the British team next year. It is, on the surface, a perplexing decision. McLaren have a great winning history but have struggled for consistency in recent years. Renault, with tighter budgets, have constructed a lean and efficient winning machine around the talents of Alonso. But now, the driver feels, it is time for something different.

'I need a new motivation,' he explained. 'I just feel that this step of my career is finished, and I wanted to change.' But … having seen the way that McLaren have performed this year? 'I have no regrets. I would make the same decision today. I don't know if the car will be better, but if it is not I will work hard to make it better.'

He will be missed at Renault, where his easy-going ways fit in well with the team's intimate, friendly ambience. They think he is that rare combination of nice guy and winner, and he will miss them, too. 'This is the team who brought me into Formula One,' he said. 'Even when I started, with Minardi, I had a Renault contract. This is the team who developed me in F1. All my experience is here. All my memories, and the first world title that I will never forget. This team will be in my heart always.'

They look after him well. Throughout our conversation, in a motorhome in the paddock at Magny-Cours, attendants in Renault's blue livery flitted to and fro, ensuring that Fernando was happy, that Fernando was on schedule, that the TV was tuned to the channel that Fernando preferred. Not that he is an egomaniac. When he first arrived in Formula One the young Fernando was shy to the point of invisibility. Now, invested with the confidence that being world champion can bring, he remains self-effacing.

Like most successful drivers, he is short, and powerfully built around the neck and forearms. He has grown into his looks, but there is no preening: the only concessions to fashion are a flashy watch and rakish sideburns. This all fits: Alonso does not court attention. Like most of the other F1 drivers, he no longer lives in his homeland. Unlike most of his rivals, though, Alonso has not dived into tax exile in Switzerland or Monte Carlo. He lives instead not far from Renault's British base at Enstone. Assorted family and friends live close by. Unable to pursue a normal existence in Spain, where his fame approaches that of the royal family, he has exported all that means most to him to the Cotswolds.

Convenience is not the only factor. Last year, Alonso took a three-week holiday — get this — touring England and Wales. To most British people, long used to spending their down-time on the Costas, the idea that a rich and famous Spaniard would relish life and relaxation in our native drizzle seems extraordinary. But to Alonso it is no more than common sense. 'I wanted a holiday somewhere close to Europe where I would not get recognised,' he shrugged. 'England was a good choice.' The same logic drives his choice of home. But isn't it sad that he cannot live in Spain? 'It's just not possible,' he said. 'But all the people that I love, my family and closest friends, have come to Oxford.'

The television in the motorhome was tuned to the Tour de France, an event that Alonso, a keen cyclist, would normally follow closely. 'This year, I think, a little bit of interest has gone,' he said. 'People don't watch too much any more.' The reason, of course, is the doping controversies that have removed many of the leading contenders.

'Doping is important, for sure,' Alonso said. 'But it is frustrating as well. You don't know much about the real situation, and you don't want to believe everything that you read.'

It is not a scenario that is likely to occur in Alonso's own sport, because the last thing a Formula One driver needs is chemical intervention. 'We are dominated by the car,' he said. 'What we need above all is concentration. If you are doing 300kph and something interferes with your concentration, you are in big trouble.'

Cycling is not the limit of Alonso's extra-curricular interests. He loves football, in particular Real Madrid, and his favourite player is Zinedine Zidane. 'Of course I am disappointed by what happened to him in Germany,' he said. 'There are things that you cannot do on the field. But in the same situation, I am sure I would have done the same.' Alonso also enjoys tennis – he used to play regularly with Toyota driver Jarno Trulli – and he has been following the progress of his young compatriot Rafael Nadal, whom he views as a kindred spirit. 'Rafa is stronger than me, more powerful,' he said. 'But he is a fighter, just like me. He chases every ball.' And does Alonso play tennis like Nadal? 'Sure. I hit the ball with the same power as him, but my ball always flies out of the court.'

Back to Formula One. Michael Schumacher has been telling anyone who will listen that this year's title battle is still on, that Alonso can be caught. His reaction? 'Of course Michael is saying that. He will fight to the end. That is his job. But this time last year, Kimi was saying the same thing ...' Expect No. 1 on Alonso's McLaren next year.

7 AUGUST 2006

BUTTON SAVOURS THE 'WOW FACTOR' OF FIRST WIN

Simon Arron in Budapest

Tousled and bearing the scars of Champagne warfare following his maiden Formula One victory in yesterday's Hungarian Grand Prix, Jenson Button grinned sheepishly and offered a brief apology. 'I'm sorry if my voice sounds funny,' he said. 'It's because I've been screaming so much.' Touted as the next Ayrton Senna when he was still a schoolboy armed with no more than a kart, and lauded as Britain's next surefire F1 winner when he made a blazing entrance with Williams in 2000, Button had to wait 113 races to record his maiden success. But the manner of delivery could not have been sweeter. In treacherous conditions that caused rivals to commit a litany of errors, Button never put a foot wrong.

'Wow, what a day,' he said. 'Winning feels normal already. It's amazing. The weather made the race very difficult for everyone, so to come through from 14th and win ... I couldn't have done it in a better way. We didn't just go out with the best car and win. We thought hard about this and won through a mixture of speed and strategy.' Button's weekend began with a spectacular engine failure on Friday, but he insisted the possibility of a repeat never occurred to him. 'During the last ten laps I didn't want the race to end,' he said. 'When you're in the lead I suppose it normally feels as though things go on forever, but I loved it. We turned down the revs a lot, so I knew we'd get to the end. It was the best feeling, knowing you're on the way to winning your first grand prix.'

Down below, in the sea of faces beneath the podium, Button's father John – a former rally-cross driver and devoted supporter of his son's career – admitted he hadn't been feeling quite so sanguine. 'I went through the roof when the chequered flag came out,' he said. 'Before that it was strange. When Jenson got the lead he started putting in these blistering lap times, and suddenly there were ten laps to go. I started wondering what might happen or what might go wrong. When he crossed the line it was unbelievable. There were a few tears – I was emotionally dead by that stage.'

There was little time for Button to savour the moment. PR commitments in Shanghai dictated that he had to be whisked away for an early-evening flight. 'I think my dad will look after celebrations,' he said. 'I could see his face when I was standing on the podium – and from his expression I'd guess that he plans to stay here tonight.' That prediction, like his judgment in adversity and his team's strategic nous, proved to be spot on.

11 SEPTEMBER 2006
SCHUMACHER EXITS AT PEAK OF HIS POWERS
Kevin Garside at Monza

The only dry eyes in the house belonged to Michael Schumacher. As Monza wept at the news of his retirement the Teutonic bottom lip held firm. In the circumstances it was as towering an achievement as the Italian Grand Prix victory he had recorded moments before. Emotion is rarely in short supply in this part of the world. How it erupted when the most decorated champion Formula One has known confirmed his going at the season's end. The face of Ferrari general manager Jean Todt, who had learned of Schumacher's decision in Indianapolis three months before, was awash with tears as he embraced him like a son at the end of the race.

Sabine Kehm, a loyal press aide for the past seven years, wept uncontrollably. The Ferrari rank and file, kept in ignorance for three months, learned the truth as Schumacher crossed the line, the message being delivered on the radio. The length of the start-finish straight was a sea of red mourning, the heartbroken *tifosi* reduced to awed silence as Schumacher's valedictory speech aired eerily through the public address system. 'This has been a very special day for me,' Schumacher began. 'To finish it in this style, looking at the championship and what is going to happen in future, it was overwhelming. There has been a lot of discussion about my future. Sorry it took longer than people wanted. You have to find the right moment. This is my last Monza. It has been a really exceptional time, 30 years in motorsport. I have loved every single moment, the good and the bad. I thank my family, my dad, my late mum, my wife and kids. Without their support it would have been impossible to survive in this business. The day has to come. I felt this was the moment.'

So a career that started in a kart knocked together by his father, Rolf, in the nondescript Rhineland outpost of Kerpen, edged inexorably towards what could yet be a glorious end. This is how the great should go, on top, still rattling the bones of their fiercest rivals. One recalls the tearful exit of Andre Agassi at Flushing Meadows a week ago, of Jack Nicklaus taking his leave of St Andrews in 2005, sporting giants both, but neither winners any longer. At 37 Schumacher is as good if not better than the earlier vintage that dominated for five successive years from 2000. The height he reached on the podium with a trophy in his hands would shame many a centre-forward at the far post. His concern was with the future, with the corrosive potential of time on the iron in his soul. 'I wanted to go out at the top. Not with my best days behind me,' Schumacher said.

He gave himself every opportunity, making the most of the greatest stage available to Ferrari to ram home the advantage inherent in his car. It did not need championship rival Fernando Alonso to perish with four laps remaining to make his day, but this being Schumacher, providence collaborated to deliver maximum reward. Inevitably there was controversy, too. Alonso blamed his blown engine on the strain of having to battle from tenth place on the grid instead of the fifth spot he lost when deemed to have hindered Ferrari's Felipe Massa in qualifying. As Schumacher was closing to within two points of the leader with his 90th career win, Alonso was hoofing down the paddock towards the Renault motorhome, thunder rumbling beneath his visor. 'Many people will be happy today. I hope they sleep well,' Alonso said, the use of irony the only weapon left with which to strike a blow.

Kimi Räikkönen, who fittingly followed Schumacher home, will assume the German's mantle at Ferrari next year. The right choice according to Schumacher. Robert Kubica, in only his third race, became the first Pole to stand on the podium. Even in his home town of Krakow, Kubica's momentous performance was a footnote on a day as portentous as this.

Luca de Montezemolo, Ferrari's president, led the tributes to Schumacher. 'We have lived through some unforgettable times together, achieving results that will be hard to equal. He has earned the affection of all of us and of our fans.' Todt added: 'Michael has been the author of a unique chapter in the history of Formula One, and of Ferrari in particular. What he has achieved extends over and above the results obtained.'

Others outside Ferrari are less enamoured. The cynical removal of Damon Hill in Adelaide in 1994, which resulted in his first championship; the failed attempt to bury Jacques Villeneuve in similar circumstances three years later in Jerez; the malicious parking of his Ferrari at Rascasse during qualifying for the Monaco Grand Prix, are examples of a Schumacher character flaw that does not permit universal worship. But those who lingered in grandstands dappled by Monza's early-evening sunshine, hoping for a glimpse of their champion, cared little for that. To them and millions of red-clad worshippers for whom Ferrari forms an important part of their Italian identity, Schumacher sits with the gods.

23 OCTOBER 2006
GENTLEMAN FANGIO WAS THE BEST EVER
Stirling Moss

Looking at today's Formula One cars, I would not have liked to have driven with all the electronic aids the drivers have today. I feel it would have taken away much of the skill that was required to balance the car. To be able to control wheelspin and traction, balance oversteer and understeer, and make the car slide when I wanted it to, were all happy and gratifying experiences.

When I said this to Michael Schumacher, whom I would place equal fourth in the top five of drivers, he did not agree. Michael explained that having all the modern gizmos allowed him to concentrate more on the driving itself. I can't understand that, but he certainly has the credentials to prove his point. But that is one good reason why it is difficult to compare drivers of different eras. Another is the importance of the world championship. When I started racing, the thing that mattered to me was to try to win that day's race. Then the world championship was introduced, and that became the big prize; even bigger than winning races. This is great in one way, but it is not always good for pure racing. I remember well the championship of 1956, when driving a Vanwall at the last race in Casablanca I had to win, record the fastest lap, and Mike Hawthorn not be second. I did win and took the fastest lap. Mike was third with one lap to go, then Phil Hill, correctly, let him take his second place. The title superseded the race, which I suppose is correct.

Safety is another aspect. At 18, to me one of the most important ingredients was the danger. The bravado of youth, I guess. Fortunately F1 cars and circuits are much safer now, but this has brought with it a change in ethics. Fangio, Clark or myself would never have pushed each other off, as this was too dangerous, or cheating, that was for others, but now it seems to be accepted, or tolerated. Michael has a few black marks on his record, but that is today's integrity. For some reason I can accept dirty driving more easily than cheating, provided it is not dangerous. Sometimes it may happen in the heat of the moment. But Michael's decision to stop on the track at Monaco this year, so hindering Fernando Alonso, was not only premeditated, having ascertained that he was still on pole, but stupid as well. Surely he should have bent the nose a bit, got out and thrown his helmet on the ground. We would all have felt sorry for him! He demeaned his status as a world champion.

In my view Juan Manuel Fangio was the best there has ever been, but then I am biased. I drove with him and against him. I knew how fast he was, always, whatever car, whatever the conditions. I could beat him in sports cars, but F1 was, and is, the pinnacle. I beat him once in F1, at Aintree in 1955, but I'm not sure that he didn't allow that as a gesture. He was humble, a great champion, and a gentleman.

In second I go for Ayrton Senna. A great natural talent, also with some black marks, who was killed before he had time to show how truly great he might have been. Then Jimmy Clark, who was a very polished driver. With Colin Chapman at Lotus to help him, he became unbeatable. I would put Michael Schumacher in fourth. He has shown how fast, consistent and talented he is. He makes mistakes, but is magic in the wet. Equal with him was Tazio Nuvolari, a man with terrific charisma who would drive the wheels off all his cars – to win.

SUPERSTAR ACT HARD TO FOLLOW

Kevin Garside

What next for Michael Schumacher? What next for Formula One? As the cleaners and ground staff swept through Interlagos yesterday clearing up in the wake of Schumacher's epic leaving do, F1's principal players were still coming to terms with the events of the previous day and their consequences. It seemed absurd to most observers that Schumacher could be leaving the sport after a performance like his. One respected F1 pundit had Schumacher at eighth in his list of all-time greats before Sunday's heroics. He took a dim view of Schumacher's cynical approach to racing and the number of uncontested victories he had engineered with Ferrari.

Schumacher shredded that analysis as he had the field with a demonstration of the art of racing as pure as any he had given before. Could Fangio, Senna, Clark or Gilles Villeneuve, the darlings of the nostalgic tendency, have bettered Schumacher's Interlagos valedictory? Unlikely. In one astonishing afternoon Schumacher not only underlined his driving credentials, he signalled in red the scale of the difficulty Formula One faces without him. Namely, how to replace its superstar?

Fernando Alonso, the champion of the past two seasons, now has a fantastic opportunity to stamp his own authority on the next decade. Alonso proved himself a match for Schumacher on and off the track, matching him inch for inch in combat (remember his overtaking manoeuvre around the outside of Schumacher at Suzuka's feared 130R corner in 2005), and in managing expectation at race weekends. As he continued his championship celebrations down the Interlagos paddock, Alonso raised a finger to Ron Dennis, the team principal at McLaren, where he drives in 2007. 'Number one next year, too,' he said, sending an emphatic message to the Woking team to raise their game to match his own.

This is Alonso's next great challenge. To truly emulate Schumacher he must do as the German did after leaving Benetton as a double world champion: resurrect a sleeping giant by building the McLaren team around him. Sir Stirling Moss claimed in these pages yesterday that Schumacher's unique legacy was indeed that: his skilful moulding of a fallen Ferrari into a team of world-beaters the like of which none had seen. Make no mistake, Schumacher had the heat turned up to full this year in the hope Alonso might melt in the championship furnace. There were times, particularly at Monza, where he was docked five places for blocking Felipe Massa in qualifying, when it appeared Alonso had reached breaking point. His response was Schumacheresque in character, rousing the team, controversially in China with his 'I feel alone' speech, to a new and ultimately successful peak.

The same preternatural ability to manage and motivate will be required to knock McLaren into shape. Should he take them to the drivers' and constructors' titles as he did Renault, then Alonso will walk on sacred ground in Formula One. As you might expect, he fancies his chances. 'I feel that for the next three years at McLaren I will have the opportunity to have a good car,' Alonso said. 'Hopefully I will find new motivation with McLaren, a new challenge, new people and a new way to work. Hopefully I can fight for the championship. But it's difficult to repeat what Michael did, being in the dominant position for so many years.'

19 MARCH 2007

SHEER BRILLIANCE OF HAMILTON DEBUT HAS MOSS PURRING

Kevin Garside in Melbourne

Kimi Räikkönen won the Australian Grand Prix on his first outing for Ferrari, only the third scarlet rapier to win on debut, claiming pole and setting the fastest lap. Yet, despite the purity of his drive, even he had to surrender the plaudits to a 22-year-old from Hertfordshire, who finished on the podium in his maiden race in Formula One. Today is the first day of the rest of Lewis Hamilton's life. The little-known figure who entered Australia was left behind at Albert Park, buried along with a racial stereotype. When F1's first black driver crossed the line behind Räikkönen and McLaren team-mate Fernando Alonso, Hamilton's world went bananas as the great and the good of F1 queued up to acclaim his display.

Sir Stirling Moss, that incomparable post-war cavalier, held court from his shooting stick in the middle of the Melbourne paddock. Moss said he had witnessed the performance of a future world champion, hailing Hamilton as a 'revelation, the best thing to happen to F1 in my time. Lewis is a very, very humble man with enormous talent. It is just a question of time, whether it be this year or next. He could have been second easily. To do that in your first race is indicative of how good he is. I was like him, a racer. You watch – if there is a gap he is in there. That is a quality you cannot ask someone to find. They either have it or they don't.'

Niki Lauda, three times a world champion, echoed the sentiment. He also understood the wider significance of Hamilton's emergence for a constituency that for too long has been unrepresented in F1. 'He's the best because he's black. Very simple. The best young guy in his first race I've ever seen. Now we have to watch it. He has the same speed as the world champion. Alonso will have a fight on his hands,' Lauda said.

An assault on the *Marlboro Grand Prix Guide*, F1's *Wisden*, revealed that only three drivers in the history of the world championship had bettered Hamilton's debut. The first was an obscure Italian, Giancarlo Baghetti, who won at Rheims driving a Ferrari in 1961. The second, a little-known Englishman, Mike Parkes, who contested only six races, was runner-up in 1966, also at Rheims in a Ferrari. Finally, Jacques Villeneuve drove to second for Williams in Australia 11 years ago.

Of course, Hamilton benefited by having at his disposal a McLaren, the most potent marque after Ferrari on yesterday's grid. Without the machinery no driver can hope to compete. Conversely, it takes a special talent to ram home an advantage on debut. And Hamilton proved to be extraordinarily special, even leading the race for five laps around the pit-stops. Had he not been hindered by back-markers as he came in for his second stop with 15 laps to go, Hamilton would have led home Alonso, F1's youngest world champion. He made his mark by the first corner, where, having been overtaken and pushed wide by Robert Kubica off the line, he braked hard, swung left and flew around the outside, retaking Kubica and passing Alonso into third. In that split-second of intuitive brilliance Hamilton set a career ablaze.

The excitement around Hamilton's debut was not limited to Britain. On race morning Australian readers of *The Age* newspaper woke to a broadsheet banner dedicated to Hamilton, his image filling two thirds of the front page. Räikkönen and Alonso had to settle for head-shots in the margin. And as he crossed the line, fists pumping with abandon, a Brazilian journalist who had faithfully recorded the career of Ayrton Senna, sought the ear of your correspondent to argue that Hamilton was the better man at the same age. Blimey!

The only one not getting carried away was the tyro himself, absurdly self-assured in the aftermath of his incandescent drive. 'To lead in my first grand prix was fantastic. It was extremely tough when you have a two-time world champion behind you for most of the race. I was unfortunate in the second stop. But all in all, a new experience for me. I thoroughly enjoyed it. To be on the podium after my first race, I could not be happier.' Asked if he was thrilled to better Alonso as early as the first corner, Hamilton replied coolly: 'Not really. It was only the first corner. You can't get too excited about it. I lost a place to Robert and needed to get it back. That's what I did.'

For every contented son there is an ecstatic father. Locked in the throng beneath the podium, Anthony Hamilton led the homage to his progeny, clapping proudly as the Champagne corks popped. It had been a long road, often involving three jobs to cobble the cash to allow the infant Lewis to dream. 'The emotions are just absolutely incredible. I knew we were going to be in trouble the moment we arrived here this week because Lewis was just so happy. Whenever he is happy I know there is something special to come. Nothing surprises me with Lewis. The move at the start was classic Lewis. All those years in karting paid off in that one corner. This whole roller-coaster ride, there are not enough superlatives to explain it. This is a fantastic milestone. Sixth would have been great. Third ... bloody hell.'

I I JUNE 2007

CHEQUERED FLAG PUTS HAMILTON OCEANS APART

Kevin Garside in Montreal

They say after a first win the floodgates open. Lewis Hamilton's rivals had better man the lifeboats. In a grand prix of unremitting drama, when more experienced men were losing heads on a circuit that permits few errors, Hamilton drove the world's best drivers into oblivion. His grand prix career is only six races old, yet, incredibly, he leads the championship outright for a second time. The holy trinity of pole position, fastest lap and chequered flag fell to him in Montreal in another demonstration of talent seemingly without limits.

During a madcap afternoon of missed turns, spectacular smashes and black flags, Hamilton rode serenely through the chaos. Three times he saw a carefully constructed lead wiped out by the safety car. No matter. He simply rebooted that preternatural racing brain of his and caned the field anew. Set against the travails of his McLaren team-mate, double world champion Fernando Alonso – who went off four times at turn one, suffered a time penalty for sinning under the safety car, and was overtaken by Takuma Sato – and title rival Felipe Massa, black-flagged for leaving the pit-lane under a red light, Hamilton's deeds acquired even greater weight.

The madness began at the first turn. The principal threat to Hamilton was on his shoulder to the right, bang on the inside line into turn one. The way Hamilton bolted out of the slot for the formation lap told Alonso, positioned on the front row, what to expect when the lights went out. He did not disappoint. Hamilton drifted first to the right to cover Alonso then left to assume the correct line. Alonso, braking beyond the limit, missed the turn completely, allowing Nick Heidfeld through for second place as the cars burned around turn two. This was grand prix driving at its most exhilarating, the novice making a mug out of the double world champion. The error was a disaster for Alonso, subsequently marooned behind Heidfeld while carrying the lighter fuel load. It would get worse.

With wide open space in front of him Hamilton turned the timing screens purple with a succession of faultless laps. Montreal had delivered a blue-sky afternoon, temperatures nudging 30°C. The capacity crowd was held spellbound by the meteor in the yellow helmet. By lap 14 there was not a car to be seen in front or behind. Hamilton was, literally, in a class of his own.

Behind him matters were going from bad to worse for his team-mate. At the start of lap 20 Alonso again missed the apex at turn one under pressure from Massa. The Ferrari was through in a flash. The gap to Hamilton was 19 seconds. McLaren responded by bringing Hamilton in almost immediately for his first stop. Then drama. Adrian Sutil smashed into a wall on lap 22, bringing out the safety car. Though Hamilton had completed his stop, so too had Alonso. Or had he? The new rules state cars cannot pit on the first lap of the safety car. He was judged to have done so and was handed a ten-second stop-go penalty. The safety car had barely retreated when it was called out again after Robert Kubica ploughed horrifically into a wall at high speed as he approached the hairpin at turn ten. Kubica left immediately for hospital – he will be released today – taking Hamilton's 19-second lead with him. He was left to build again. This time, of the front-runners he had only Heidfeld for company. And not for long. In the space of a sequence of spell-binding laps, the lead was again 19 seconds.

However, enter Christijan Albers, whose disintegrating rear wing initiated yet another collision with concrete. Out came the safety car again, and back to square one went Hamilton. Again he readjusted without fuss. This is how heroes proceed. This race was another demonstration of Hamilton's wizardry, the kind of performance the marketing men at Adidas had in mind when they coined the slogan 'Impossible is nothing'; the kind of display that had the Canadian media in raptures. The Canadian daily *The National Post* devoted a whole broadsheet page to Hamilton on Saturday morning. The competition were reduced to a single column on the opposite page under the headline 'Other drivers to watch'. The editor understood his market.

As the drivers made their way to the grid, Hamilton was pursued by a legion of photographers. An hour later as Hamilton parked the McLaren on pole for the first time, there was none of the uncertainty leading up to his debut in Australia. He assumed his familiar post beneath the umbrella held by his father before answering nature's call. Two hours later, he was drowning in Champagne. His rivals were just drowning.

7 JULY 2007

A WINNING FORMULA

Rory Ross

With two grand prix wins in his first seven races as a Formula One driver, and podium finishes in the rest, Lewis Hamilton has made the most sensational debut in the history of motorsport. In five months, the 22-year-old from Stevenage has shot from near obscurity to global celebrity, but remains the normal boy next door. The story of how Hamilton, a boy racer of 60cc go-karts funded by his devoted three-jobs father, was spotted by a fairy-godfather in shining Kevlar – Ron Dennis, the head of the McLaren F1 team – who funded him, groomed him and eventually gave him a seat in a McLaren F1 car, is a modern-day fairytale, except that it is true.

Hamilton's performances this year mark him out as a future world champion, a man who can drive on water. He is already outdriving and outwitting Fernando Alonso, his Spanish team-mate, the double world champion who toppled Michael Schumacher, who is probably thanking his lucky stars he quit when he did. At the equivalent stage in his career, Alonso was coaxing a slow, unreliable Minardi around the track, before Renault appointed him test driver. Hamilton has leapfrogged this stage of his career altogether and now flies on a far steeper, faster trajectory.

Rewind the clock back to the Monaco Grand Prix in May. Besides the yacht parties, there is only one place to be: backstage with the McLaren Mercedes F1 team. I am introduced to McLaren's communications centre, a mobile, two-storey, tinted-glass-and-steel office cum hospitality gazebo, the team's HQ at European grands prix. It is one part of McLaren's travelling circus which tours Europe in six articulated lorries, attended by around 120 mechanics, engineers, technicians, caterers, PRs and senior management. While I am being shown around the offices, kitchens, press room, conference suites, IT rooms and soundproofed drivers' quarters, the cars are on the circuit practising. Averaging just over 90mph on the tortuous street circuit, they make a high-pitched howl like a swarm of demented bees, interspersed with agricultural spluttering as they skirt Rascasse, one of the slowest corners, at a pedestrian 40mph.

After the session has ended and the howl is replaced by the rat-tat-tat of power spanners as the mechanics get to work on the cars, Hamilton approaches in his overalls, preceded by a posse of photographers running backwards. He is soon working his charisma in the communications centre. He beams at everyone and pumps every hand, including mine. You couldn't find a brighter ray of sunshine. He then disappears into his driver's suite, where he can be seen chatting with his father Anthony, his half-brother Nicholas, who has cerebral palsy, and his stepmother Linda.

McLaren have forbidden me to talk to Hamilton in Monaco, but have granted an eyeball-to-eyeball interview at a later date at their factory in Woking – for a stopwatched 20 minutes. I had little idea what currency a 20-minute one-on-one with Hamilton is worth in the F1 paddock until I bump into a friendly motor-racing scribe.

'Hi, what are you doing here?'

'Feature on Lewis Hamilton.'

'Oh … really?'

'Yeah, but nothing special. I've only been given a 20-minute interview.'

'The full 20 minutes!'

'Er, yes …'

'That's outrageous. I've been trying to get five minutes with Hamilton for the last six months. I'm going to complain.'

After that, I pretend I'm sightseeing.

'Lewis is just a very kind boy,' says Lyndy Redding, McLaren's chief caterer, who has been feeding Hamilton since he joined McLaren on their junior driver scheme in 1998. 'He still seems younger than he is,' she adds.

'He always comes into the kitchen to say hello.' According to Redding, Hamilton's favourite food is toasted chicken sandwiches and fillet steak. 'Lewis has grown up with us. He is the nicest person. He has fun. Yesterday, I saw Lewis and Fernando playing a computer game together. What other team would have two drivers doing that? They get along. They are both nice people. No egos.'

The British public have been quick to embrace Hamilton. His third place at the Melbourne Grand Prix in March boosted ticket sales for this weekend's British Grand Prix by 200 per cent compared with the equivalent time last year. British television audiences have soared by 30 per cent on last year. In May, Hamilton topped a BBC poll to determine front-runners for Sports Personality of the Year. He polled 44 per cent; Andy Murray came second, on 23 per cent; Joe Calzaghe third with 14 per cent. Hamilton's popularity has spread like morning sunlight. In Brazil, he has eclipsed Felipe Massa, the Brazilian Ferrari driver, especially in the favelas, where they see in Hamilton one of their own doing well. In Spain, he is more popular than Fernando Alonso, much to the irritation of the Spanish champion.

Hamilton's father, Anthony, is the son of immigrants from Grenada; his mother, Carmen Larbalestier, is white; his parents split up when he was two, and Lewis lived with his mother until he was about ten. Inevitably, as the first mixed-race driver in Formula One's 57-year history, Hamilton has inspired Tiger-Woods-on-wheels comparisons. I ask Bernie Ecclestone, the chief executive of Formula One, if Hamilton's colour is significant. 'I think people want to write about him being black, but that doesn't make him any quicker or slower,' Ecclestone says. 'He is a young guy who has done some things that a lot of people who are older than him have not done.'

'His blackness isn't important,' Ron Dennis has said. 'I have constantly said to him, the moment that you exploit your blackness, you are going to have a problem with me. You've got to develop your career on your ability to drive a racing car.' The Tiger Woods comparison doesn't impress Hamilton either. 'My colour is an advantage in that it's something people talk about,' he once said. 'But the bottom line is that it is clearly not why I'm in this position. I'm happy if other black kids see what I'm doing and realise it can be done, but that's not what motivates me. I'm doing it for me, because I want to win in F1 and because I believe I'm good enough to do that.'

Actually, Tiger Woods had better watch out: Hamilton has taken up golf. A Hamilton industry is hastily swinging into action. Already, there is talk of the 'Hamilton brand', the 'Hamilton effect' and, perhaps a little prematurely, the 'Hamilton era'. Some have predicted that his potential earnings could soon reach £100 million a year, and £1 billion in his career.

David Wheldon, the global director of brand and customer experience at Vodafone, who sponsor McLaren to the tune of £35 million a year (I nearly fell off my chair), is thrilled with Hamilton's ascent. 'Were you to write a film script, no one would ever believe it,' he says. 'It is an astonishing story of a kid chasing his dream, living it and fulfilling it, made more so by his being an extraordinarily nice, modest and focused young man who stops for pictures and autographs, and has time for everyone. Lewis is a regular guy from Stevenage who loves his brother. We are getting 33 per cent more from McLaren than we got when we sponsored Ferrari.'

According to Wheldon, Hamilton will soon eclipse David Beckham. 'We sponsored David when we launched Vodafone Live. He overexposed himself. He took on too many other sponsors. Hamilton is in a bigger circus. Premier League football is nothing compared to the best of Formula One. Beckham's marketing persona was superstar fashion icon. Lewis's is a regular guy who is a potential world champion. I've met a few superstars, but this guy is very special. To remain modest and real in Formula One is fantastic.'

A few days after Monaco, my clearance to interview Hamilton at Woking arrives, courtesy of one of the team's sponsors, but hedged with caveats, provisos and qualifications. I had already spent two days walking on plovers' eggs trying to get around the McLaren protocol in Monaco; now some of those eggs were beginning to crack. A row was brewing about the fact that, at Monaco, our photographer had had the temerity to Go Off And Take Pictures Without Authorisation. The ensuing exchanges bordered on the surreal.

'So what? That's what photographers do.'

'Yes, but she didn't have the authorisation.'

'Well, you invited her. Why invite a photographer if you don't give her authorisation?'

'She was just meant to be soaking up the atmosphere. Anyway, a lot of people are annoyed. As for you, you are not allowed to quote any of the people you interviewed at Monaco.'

'Why not?'

'Because you spoke to them without authorisation.'

'So? The people I interviewed were more than happy to speak to me on the record.'

'Yes, but you didn't have authorisation.'

'Then why did they agree to be interviewed?'

'Well ... OK, you can write what they said, but just don't put it in quotes. And you are not allowed to mention the team orders issue at Monaco [when Hamilton let slip that the team had prevented him from trying to overtake Alonso during the race].'

I arrive at McLaren's HQ in Woking on the Monday before the Canadian Grand Prix. Approaching it along an innocuous wooded country lane, the visitor is confronted by a gate that opens on to a landscaped field, into which is half-sunk a glass-faced, curved building fronted by a koi-carp-filled lake. Welcome to the nerve centre of Formula One's most successful racing team, a £200 million, Foster-designed masterpiece of contemporary architecture, completed in 2004.

A staff member waltzes me around a mind-bending, high-tech labyrinth of spotless, hushed vistas of glass and light. The retired F1 cars of world champions Emerson Fittipaldi, James Hunt, Niki Lauda, Ayrton Senna, Alain Prost and Mika Hakkinen stand silent and still, time's relentless march already making them look boxy and crude compared with the more menacing silhouette of Hamilton's MP4-22 car. I visit the wind tunnel, where, for 19 hours each a day, the team tests 60 per cent scale models of Hamilton's car, and the machining workshop that produces 6,000 components each week for the cars. The staff – mechanics, designers, technicians, machinists and widget-tweakers – all wear black clothing by Hugo Boss, and look like cloned inmates of a French jail. Boss has dressed McLaren for 26 years. Each year, they supply some 22,000 individual items of clothing, T-shirts, trousers, socks, sweatshirts, jackets, shirts, travel uniforms, suits and formal wear. 'Whenever an employee represents the team, they wear Boss, including Mr Dennis,' Till Pohlmann, the head of sport sponsorship at Hugo Boss, says. 'Even on a Tuesday morning in the factory, Mr Dennis will wear Boss.'

You can't miss the trophy cabinets. Crammed with thousands of cups, vases, plates, goblets, chalices, whorled sconces and hideous things set in Perspex, harvested from 41 years of racing, the cabinets are located next to the canteen, winking at passing staff to remind them that the sole purpose of McLaren is winning. It is as though the staff have been brainwashed into believing one thing. I feel a religious experience coming over me. I suspect the factory doubles as Ron Dennis's tomb. Somewhere here, he will be laid to rest in a sealed room surrounded by his trophies and winning F1 cars, whereupon he will be sped to the afterlife aboard one of his carbon-fibre chariots.

I look up and notice that the clones are converging on the canteen from all directions.

'Are the clones all going to meet their controller?' I ask my tour guide.

'Ha-ha! No. It's the three o'clock tea break.'

'Tea break? I'd have thought that in this temple to technology, those would be a thing of the past.'

I end up in the Emerson Fittipaldi Room, where Lewis Hamilton eventually arrives, casually dressed in a fleecy brown top with rolled-up sleeves. His angelic features are shrink-wrapped in a radiant, flawless complexion that seems almost back-lit. His hair is closely cropped, like iron filings. His grip feels like something mechanical crushing my hand. He looks tougher in the flesh than on television. He is 5ft 10in, 10st 10lb, and has a 16.5in neck, broad shoulders and a superbly developed upper body. His forearms are streaked with pulsating veins like brown thunderbolts.

For six months before the start of the season Hamilton was groomed for his F1 debut. Every day, including weekends, he submitted himself to two three-hour training sessions: he swam two kilometres, cycled 50 miles and spent two hours in the gym. 'It's all about endurance,' he says. 'There is nothing worse than getting to mid-race and starting to fatigue, because your mind needs to work doubly hard to give energy to the rest of your body, and then you lose focus and you can crash. It is about your mind being at ease that you are fit enough.'

While I was being given the tour, Hamilton had been running through computer simulations to get a feel for the unfamiliar Canadian and Indianapolis circuits. They clearly did the trick because Hamilton won both races. 'I'm a fast learner,' he says. 'That has always had to be a strength of mine. Some drivers don't have it. I needed it because in GP2 [the feeder series to F1] we had very short test sessions: ten laps on tracks I didn't know. So I could go to Canada and Indianapolis without doing simulations, but this job is not just about driving. We need to make sure the car is set up right. There is so much detail that goes into setting up a car, mechanically, on the tech side, the software. To have that all set up with traction control, the hydraulic diff . . .'

'Hydraulic diff?'

'You have it on your road car, but it is a lot more sophisticated on a Formula One car. We can control how much the brake is clamped around each corner. If you go round a right-hand bend, the outside wheel has more distance to cover than the inside wheel, so the differential compensates for that, and you control whether it stays locked or how much it eases up so it allows the outside wheel to move.'

'It sounds like you need a degree in engineering.'

'You do. I am the driver, but I need to have a very, very good feel for the car and communications, because development of the car is the key to the team moving forward. To get your car on the front row, it is not a case of going out and driving it. You need to have the set-up, and to get the set-up right, you have to give the right information to your engineer. That is why, before my first race this season, I was here every day, spending three to four hours engineering.'

Cramming the technology and mechanics of his car is part of an F1 driver's job the public never sees; I suspect some F1 drivers don't often see it either. 'I don't know what other drivers do,' Hamilton says, 'but I study the data. My whole apartment is covered in sheets of paper that I have gathered from six months before my first race: details of the strategy, the starts, the launch sequence, the pit-stops, any problems we might have.

'No one really understands this job,' he adds. 'It is so demanding. We need to be fit to do all the travelling, and then be really sharp. Because as soon as you get in the car, you don't focus on all that stuff. You have to make sure you feel what the car is doing. You don't just go out, then come back in and go out again. You go out and you have to store all the information, all the small vibrations you get, any problems you may have had, any problems with the engine, or if you lock up and flat-spot a tyre, or if you miss a gear shift. You have to remember everything. When you get back to the garage, you wait a couple of minutes, then say, "Turns 2, 4, 11, I've got this problem. Fix it".'

Hamilton's car is his exclusive bespoke office. The cockpit is built around a mould of his spine, ribcage and shoulders. His steering wheel, pedals, gloves, boots and overalls are all made to fit. Whenever Hamilton folds himself into his car, it becomes part of his central nervous system; and he in turn becomes an integral component of the car, so that when he races he literally feels his way around the circuit.

The car has a nervous system, too. One hundred and twenty sensors embedded in the chassis measure engine performance, aerodynamic efficiency, oil pressure, tyre grip, brake wear, hydraulics and the driver's performance, such as the angle he takes into a corner and the moment he lifts off the throttle. As the car goes round the circuit, the sensors beam this data – known as telemetry – to the garage in the pit-lane, to the communications centre and to the McLaren factory.

At Woking, they do all sorts of clever things with the telemetry. It can be fed into a replica of Hamilton's car, which is then subjected to the forces of a full grand prix distance to test each component. If any widget needs altering, the team can redesign an improved version – with a pico-millimetre added on or shaved off – then machine it and fly it out in time for the race. For the Monaco Grand Prix, McLaren reserved seats on flights from London to Nice on the Thursday, Friday and Saturday nights before the race, in case a component needed to be rushed out.

They also feed the telemetry to the strategy room. This room contains an exact replica of the pit-wall gantry where Ron Dennis watches each race. The data is fed into a computer that uses it to run through different scenarios of what might happen during the race, in order to project possible outcomes. All sorts of 'what ifs' are introduced, such as what if it rains, what if the safety car comes out, or what if a satellite spins out of control and hits Alonso on the head on lap 37, and so on. The computer produces the best race strategy, which is then communicated to the track. Having the strategy room in the sequestered quietude of Woking ensures that no racing decision is ever made on an *ad hoc* basis in the heat of the moment at the track side.

Hamilton is wise enough to know that his relationship with his engineers must be every bit as close as between him and his car. In order to extract the most from his car, he must consider himself part of a team, and not just a driver who pitches up every now and then. Pre-season, Hamilton and some 30 team members went on a training camp to Finland to get fit and bond together. 'They are a great bunch of lads,' he says. 'There is nothing worse than those guys working, and then all I do is turn up, get in the car, get out and bugger off. I think they have had that with other drivers in the past. They feel free to speak to me when they want. I know they will give 110 per cent, even if they have had a whole week with no sleep. There is nothing better than having that belief in a team.'

Lewis Hamilton's uncanny hand-eye co-ordination was evident early on when, aged six, he appeared on *Blue Peter* to show his skill with remote-control cars. When he was about eight, his father took him to a kart track on a whim. When Lewis crashed, Anthony Hamilton thought that would be that. Instead, Lewis leapt back in, and began to race in earnest in 1993 in a series for novice kartists called the 'black plate' category. Drivers are required to complete six races before progressing. Hamilton won all six. To fund Lewis's racing, Anthony Hamilton, who then worked for British Rail, took a second job, and at one point was also being paid £15 a go to put up For Sale signs in Hertfordshire.

'As a kid,' Hamilton says, 'you look up to your dad. We have come from nothing. We lived in a one-bedroom flat in Hatfield, and in a council house in Stevenage. I went to a normal school. We didn't really have any money. My family have sacrificed a lot. They gave me an opportunity and I grabbed it with both hands. I didn't waste it.'

The story of how Hamilton caught Ron Dennis's eye at an awards dinner in London in 1995 has already gone down in the annals of motor racing history. Dressed in a dinner jacket and clip-on bow tie, Hamilton, then ten, the youngest winner of the British Cadet Karting Championship, went up to Dennis and asked for his autograph. 'It was 12 years ago,' Dennis said, speaking pre-season. 'He just walked up to me, not that I'd noticed at the time because he was probably only three or four feet tall, so he didn't come into my sight line, and there was this young chap with his hand out.'

When Hamilton asked if one day he could drive for McLaren, Dennis gave him his number and told him to ring back in nine years' time. Three years later it was Dennis who rang, having watched Hamilton's astonishing karting career. 'There are some traits there that you see in the greats,' Dennis said. 'By and large, all the great grand prix drivers are from karting. It is the right place to start.'

Anthony Hamilton broke the news about Dennis's phone call when Lewis got home from school that day. 'That changed, to a degree, our whole lives. All of a sudden, Lewis has got an opportunity – he never expected to make a career in motorsport. Even at that time, we never thought he'd become an F1 driver. There is this nice guy, Ron Dennis, who said, "I'll look after Lewis and help him through school and everything else".' The McLaren team supported Hamilton's career from 1998, on condition that Hamilton did not neglect his education. 'For years, I'd realised that so many drivers, in their determination to get into motorsport, do so to the detriment of their education,' Dennis said, 'which then gives them a weakness if and when they get into Fɪ.'

Lewis was supplied with a top-of-the-line kart, plus technical support and transportation around Europe, amounting to £100,000 a year. He then progressed to Formula Renault, backed by McLaren, and won the British championship in 2003, followed by two years in F3, winning the crown in 2005. All in all, McLaren are reckoned to have plunged some £5 million into Hamilton's pre-Fɪ career. As Dennis put it: 'He climbed; we paid.'

In 2006 Hamilton moved up into GP2. Few who witnessed him race last year at Nürburgring, Monaco and Silverstone will need convincing of his mystical gifts and animal instincts behind the wheel. Driving fast is one thing, but a winning driver must think even faster. Hamilton has an Ayrton Senna-like instinct for making the right snap decisions. 'He has developed into a very complete motor racing package,' Martin Whitmarsh, the chief operating officer of McLaren Group, says. 'He has also been able to carry that in-born capability through the successive formulae, and has been able to focus on the capability to grow with the technical understanding, physical preparedness, mental toughness and ability to single-mindedly focus and commit. He is quick, committed, brave, a phenomenal overtaker and he just does not give up.'

The question of an Fɪ drive was discussed. 'His domination of GP2 in 2006 was outstanding,' Dennis says. 'Because we were a team in transit looking to change one or both drivers, ultimately all of us decided to give him a chance. He has a uniqueness and determination that is rarely seen in drivers, and he is prepared to make personal and emotional sacrifices you have to be mentally able to accept to become the best.'

At the Monza Grand Prix last year, where Hamilton was racing in GP2, he was watching the Formula One cars as they lined up on the grid. He walked to the front, looked down the track towards the first corner and imagined what it would be like to sit in the leading McLaren car, then occupied by Kimi Räikkönen. Dennis took Hamilton to one side and said: 'I'm going to give you a chance. You are going to have to work hard for it, but I'm going to give you a chance.' Unsure what Dennis meant – a race drive or a test or what? – Hamilton put on his professional smile, but felt ecstatic underneath.

On 23 September, Dennis invited Hamilton and his father to his house in Woking to tell them that Lewis would get a Formula One drive in 2007 for a salary rumoured to be 500,000 euros a year. This pales beside Alonso's

16 million euros, which in turn pales besides Räikkönen's 35 million. (But Hamilton is said to have been offered a bonus scheme that could easily double his salary, depending on how many races he wins. Such a generous bonus scheme is unusual, but then nobody expected Hamilton to do as well as he has.)

For Dennis, this was all a calculated risk. McLaren had never employed a rookie driver, and they were on one of their longest losing streaks. The team failed to record a single victory in 2006. Between 2001 and 2004, McLaren won only eight races. You have to reach back to 1999 for their last drivers' title (Mika Häkkinen), and 1998 for their last constructors' title. Fernando Alonso was hired at the Brazilian Grand Prix in 2005, after he had won the first of his two back-to-back titles. As the youngest world champion at 24, he was signed specifically to turn around McLaren's fortunes. Hamilton's appointment was much more of a gamble.

'The decision was not mine alone,' Dennis has said. 'I deliberately took a slightly back seat in the process, to make sure it was something supported by everybody. I didn't want to find myself in a position where if he had struggled, people would be saying it was my decision.' Hamilton had become the monster to Dennis's Frankenstein, and there remains the lingering suspicion that he was not born in Stevenage but in fact created in a genetics laboratory in an obscure wing of the McLaren factory. 'I think I am a fairly normal guy,' Hamilton says, shrugging. 'I love very much being a family man, not just my immediate family but aunties and uncles and cousins. Every year we meet up to have a big weekend together. I spend a lot of time with my brother, who is my best friend. I gain a lot of energy from my family and friends. I find it hard to trust people, and so I really feel trust needs to be earned. I can count my friends on one hand and I keep those closest to me. The others, they're friends, but it is so easy to see the people that are just trying to cling on or have just popped out of the woodwork all of a sudden. The qualities I admire in people are politeness, respect for others, loyalty, honesty. I like people who are just themselves and don't try to be anyone else.

'I love making people laugh,' he adds, 'and enjoying myself. I'm very, very determined, very focused on achieving my goals and will always put family first, racing second. But nothing will ever come between me and my dreams and my goals. That has really helped me. You need that push. You cannot have everyone kicking you up the arse all the time. You need to be able to do that to yourself. Even when you make mistakes when you are racing, you need to be able to bounce back. I have a really strong team behind me in my family who have really helped guide me in the right way and made me say the right things. But, as I said, I like having fun. It is all about enjoying what you are doing. I love my job; I believe it is the best in the world.'

Given his natural ability as a driver and his grasp of mechanics, I wondered what specific challenges Hamilton has had to overcome. 'The biggest challenge is defeating your opponents mentally,' he says. Well, he has already out-psyched Alonso, whose outbursts to the Spanish media about favouritism after the Canadian Grand Prix show a driver who has cracked. 'You have to be able to control your mind, even when you have bad days,' Hamilton says. 'If you have a really good day, you feel fantastic, and it is a big boost of confidence. If you have a really bad day and you crash when everyone has worked so hard for you, the biggest challenge is to bounce back, come out looking fresh and happy. Give your team a good feeling, and get in the car and do a better job. It is about mental energy and being able to balance yourself. You cannot be too aggressive. You cannot party too much. You can work yourself into a hole. I think that is why I have a very good team at home where I spend time relaxing with my family. If I get out of the car and I've had an incident, I go back to my brother, and he recharges my batteries and I go back out. Over the years you learn to cope with it.'

Expecting media overkill on the Hamilton sensation, I was prepared to be disappointed. But I found him even more impressive in the flesh than in the media. In sport, Britain rarely does 'complete packages'. Sebastian Coe and Steve Redgrave spring to mind, but we haven't done it in football, cricket, golf or rugby. Does Hamilton have a weakness? 'The biggest danger is yourself – letting yourself get into trouble, go off the rails, enjoy life too much, getting involved with the wrong people. I have won every championship I've competed in. I'm one of the youngest drivers. I don't know anyone who has my CV. I've won a lot of races, and I'm still going.'

4 OCTOBER 2007

LEWIS HAS LIFTED OUR SPIRITS
Murray Walker

I have been involved closely with three British world champions: James Hunt, with whom I shared 13 years in the commentary box, Nigel Mansell, who is very close to my heart, and Damon Hill. But Lewis Hamilton is a phenomenon the like of which I have never seen before and, I think it is fair to say, one that has never existed in the history of motorsport. Not Formula One, nor grand prix racing, which preceded F1.

Never has anybody come in and been as successful at the top level as consistently and quickly as he has. And with such dignity, cheerfulness and commonsense. He has rekindled worldwide interest in F1 at a time when the domination of Michael Schumacher had left the sport in a despondent state. His youth, and I suppose his colour to an extent, has revived it in a way I have never seen before. If I were still behind the microphone, I would have been through the roof with great consistency.

I always say even the most processional race in F1 has something interesting to talk about, if you know where to look. You would not have to look too far with Hamilton. You would just have to look at the front. Kimi Räikkönen, who is regarded as a great hot shot, Fernando Alonso, double world champion, and Felipe Massa have been all been blown away, and with such maturity. I have people coming up to me all the time in my local village of Ringwood, in Hampshire, saying: 'Murray, is this Lewis Hamilton as good as people say he is?' and I say: 'No. He is better.'

James was an extremely good driver. You don't get to be world champion unless you are, especially when you are racing against someone as calculating, experienced, successful and good as Niki Lauda. James had a natural talent. I don't know how hard he worked at being a racing driver. I suspect not much. For Lewis it is a lifetime vocation. I often wonder how James would have been in these days of telemetry, etc. The sport was a lot less professional and serious in his day, and a lot more fun.

I have always had a soft spot for Nigel. Few have sacrificed as much, financially and bodily, as Nigel. The stories are legion. He remortgaged his home, he broke his back testing for Colin Chapman. But Nigel was a fighter. He needed adversity in order to motivate himself. For me, as a commentator, Nigel was manna from heaven, possibly more so than Lewis, because wherever he was on the circuit, something dramatic was happening. He was passing Gerhard Berger at the Peraltada in Mexico, which was physically impossible; he was grabbing Ayrton Senna by the throat in Belgium; or his wheel was falling off in Portugal; or he was marching to the stewards to complain about something; or he was saying he would not be driving for Williams any more in the most dramatic circumstances, at Monza. He then went and conquered America.

I'm a motorcycling chap really, so Damon, being a motorcycling champion, makes him a very special hero to me. Damon was not an obvious F1 superstar. He did well in Formula Ford without winning any championships. He won races in Formula Three without winning any championships. The same in F3000. He got the Williams test-driving job by the sweat on his brow. He became No. 1 when the team were in crisis, after the death of Senna, and had an inspired season.

People used to accuse me of thinking of smart-arse things and writing them on the commentary box wall and waiting for the appropriate moment to produce them. But one of the things I'm apparently remembered for was the line in Japan when Hill won the title in 1996: 'I've got to stop now because I have a lump in my throat.' It was genuinely spontaneous. I'd seen Damon come up through the hard times and adversity and, like his dad, through a combination of natural talent and grit achieve superstardom. In those circumstances, when you have the adrenalin pouring out of you, and subconsciously you know you are addressing millions across the world for whom what you say matters, it can all well up and boil over. You are supposed to be neutral, but in the end you are British. Nigel was one of us, and my mate. So, too, Damon and James. I make no apology for getting behind them.

And now we have Lewis, *Boy's Own* hero come to life. I was a commentator for 53 years. We all have to stop sometime. I don't regret it, and I do. I wanted to stop with dignity when I was ahead. But I would have liked to have gone on and believe I could still do it. The young man has lifted all our spirits. We have only had 15 races of Lewis, but there is no doubt that if he carries on as he is he will be one of the greatest drivers of all time. More than that you cannot say.

22 OCTOBER 2007

HAMILTON'S CHASE NEVER GETS INTO GEAR

Kevin Garside in São Paulo

It is not enough to be good. Sometimes you need luck to endure. As another English dream lay skewered on a sporting battlefield, Lewis Hamilton will look back at the random intervention of a dodgy gearbox eight laps into the Brazilian Grand Prix and an unscripted trip to a Chinese gravel trap in the penultimate race as the moments that wrenched glory so painfully from his grasp. A mighty slap on the back goes to race winner and new world champion Kimi Räikkönen, who has known his own disappointments. Six victories, two more than Hamilton or McLaren team-mate Fernando Alonso, were just reward for a season's toil. But were it not for the ghosts that entered Hamilton's machine yesterday, and the bizarre decision to leave him on bald tyres in Shanghai, the Finn would be celebrating little this morning.

The race did not start brilliantly for Hamilton. Räikkönen jumped him at the start off the clean side of the track. Stuck behind the Ferrari through the Senna Esses, Hamilton was then taken by Alonso, who carried the greater momentum through the inside of turn three. It was still some move. Hamilton should have sat back but, being the racer he is, tried to go around the outside at the end of the back straight. Big mistake. Off he slid on to the grass and down to eighth. Pulses were through the roof. Hamilton took Jarno Trulli into turn one to claim seventh, then hauled in Nick Heidfeld's BMW for sixth.

The in-car radio must have been melting. It had experienced nothing yet. On lap eight, as Hamilton stoked the fires for an attack on Robert Kubica, speed suddenly drained. The world championship dream was fading like ice in the desert. As cars streamed past, Hamilton could be seen in the cockpit physically trying to urge his car along. It looked for all the world a forlorn hope, but then, as suddenly as power had disappeared, it returned. The problem, it transpired, was with the gearbox. Hope surged and Hamilton gratefully resumed the throttle. He was now down to 18th.

A year ago a puncture dropped Michael Schumacher to the back of the field. The Ferrari, he said, had insane pace, enough to finish fifth. Hamilton did not get close. By the time he came in for his first stop at the end of lap 22 he was up to 14th. McLaren equipped him with the quicker, super-soft compound and fuelled him for a short stint. Sadly, there was too much to do. He made up five places in all before coming in for a second stop at the end of lap 37. He returned ninth but 30 seconds adrift of David Coulthard. The championship was gone. Hamilton drove like a dervish to the flag to claim seventh, enough to finish the championship second on a count-back, with Alonso third.

6 JULY 2008

STEWART VOICES CONCERNS OVER VIABILITY OF DONINGTON TO HOST BRITISH GRAND PRIX

Kevin Garside

Sir Jackie Stewart has cast doubt on the viability of the British Grand Prix at Donington and believes Silverstone is still the best place to host the race. Bernie Ecclestone, Formula One commercial rights holder, and F1's governing body, the FIA, confirmed a ten-year deal for the British Grand Prix at Donington beginning in 2010. Work has already begun on revamping the Leicestershire circuit, but the money behind the deal is shrouded in mystery. The person bankrolling the £100 million investment is said to be a shareholder on the board of the company that leases the circuit, Donington Ventures Leisure Ltd, from owner Tom Wheatcroft.

Stewart has grave concerns about Donington. 'They have to knock down the pit and paddock complex and build a new one. That will cost a lot of money. If you consider the added cost of enlarging the circuit and making it safe … there is not enough run-off area at almost any corner to hold a grand prix – so a complete redesign is required,' he said. 'Money can buy it. The problem with that is people with a lot of money like to make a lot of money. I do not see how the British Grand Prix with the economics as they are determined by Formula One Management and CVC [F1's joint commercial rights holders] permit a race to be economically sound. There is no profit to reinvest in the circuit. That is wrong.' When Silverstone were still at the negotiating table, the asking price to host a race in 2010 had been set at £11 million by Ecclestone, who denies he is an investor in the new scheme.

3 OCTOBER 2008

LETTERS TO THE SPORTS EDITOR

THE FARCE THAT IS CALLED FORMULA ONE

Sir,

It's so exciting! Now that we know that Lewis Hamilton will be doing his very best to finish safely in second place for the remaining three world championship heats (please, no more calling them 'grand' prix; 'petit' prix is more apt), the paying spectators will no doubt be ecstatic at getting their money's worth on the overpriced tickets, knowing that the leading contender will now not be fighting for a win with his main rival, but instead aiming to finish just behind him.

With each passing year F1 becomes more fatuous and farcical. The idea of a fuel-empty car not able to enter the pits to fill up is as mind-bending an example of its ridiculous rules as one can get.

William Pender
Stratford-sub-Castle, Salisbury

3 NOVEMBER 2008

HAMILTON KEEPS COOL TO BECOME YOUNGEST WORLD CHAMPION IN RAINY BRAZIL

Kevin Garside at Interlagos

Nothing comes easy with this boy. Hamilton was seconds from heartbreak on the circuit where a year ago he lost the world championship by a point in his rookie year.

The random intervention of rain looked to have wrecked his dream again when Felipe Massa crossed the line first in the Brazilian Grand Prix believing he was Formula One's 30th world champion. The celebrating mechanics in the Ferrari garage shared that view. But that did not take account of Hamilton's incredible late surge to reclaim the fifth place he needed with just two corners of the final lap to go. 'My heart was in my mouth. I was almost exploding. I don't know how I kept my cool. It was the toughest race of my life. I don't know how I did it.'

Nobody did, which elevates this achievement among the most incredible in British sport. In 1959 Sir Jack Brabham pushed his car up the hill at Sebring to win his first world championship. Hamilton comfortably trumped that, and arguably any other sporting finale. Hamilton's victory also saw elite sport's most stubborn stereotype bite the dust. Formula One has a black champion at last, a detail of enormous import which carries greater weight than the other historic component blitzed, the lowering of the age barrier.

With six laps to go Hamilton was cruising home in fourth. Then down came the rain. With two laps remaining after a chaotic dash for wet tyres Hamilton slipped out of the championship equation after losing fifth to

Sebastian Vettel. That he was put at risk was down to the gamble by Toyota to keep Timo Glock out on dry tyres. Glock, nowhere hitherto, was suddenly cast in a pivotal role in the unfolding drama. Hamilton's heart must have been breaking. A sense of disbelief hung over Interlagos. The Brazilian crowd could hardly believe the hand fate had dealt them. Massa was supreme all afternoon, victory was never in doubt. But his performance did not look like yielding the main prize. Then Vettel squeezed past Hamilton as the McLaren struggled for grip, and an amazing result for the Brazilian was suddenly in his grasp. He took the chequered flag to huge cheers. His father went berserk in the Ferrari garage. They hoped for this but never really believed it was possible.

The McLaren garage was stunned. Bottom lips were shaking. How could it have come to this? How cruel sport can be. Then, without warning, the championship started to swing back his way. Performance was draining from the Toyota. It lost a total of 18 seconds on that final lap as the gamble to stay on dry tyres unravelled at the death. Massa's hopes died with it. To his credit Massa was fulsome in his praise for Hamilton. 'He deserved it. It was tough to lose the championship in that way, but I can have no complaint. Hamilton did a great job all year. He is a worthy champion.'

7 NOVEMBER 2008
LETTERS TO THE SPORTS EDITOR
SIGN OF A SPORTSMAN

Sir ,

Hats off to Felipe Massa for the way he conducted himself in the aftermath of the Brazilian Grand Prix. Having just driven a flawless race to take the chequered flag in front of thousands of his adoring fans, the Ferrari driver must have been devastated to find he had lost the title to Lewis Hamilton by a single point. Yet he took it on the chin, with exceptional grace and dignity. Lewis has had two terrific seasons and is undoubtedly a worthy winner. But Massa actually won more races this year and would have made an excellent champion too.

Hugh Terry
Reading, Berkshire

24 MAY 2009

HAMILTON LAPPED AGAIN

Tom Cary in Monaco

Having entered the race weekend with high hopes of defending the crown he picked up in the Principality last year, Lewis Hamilton had to be satisfied with 12th position after a crash in Saturday qualifying for the Monaco Grand Prix had left him starting from the back of the grid. The McLaren driver, who has seemed far more relaxed in recent days after his traumatic start to the season, was unable to make much progress on a track where overtaking is almost impossible. 'It was an extremely tough race. I feel quite satisfied though, because I wanted to finish. I was thinking of one of the *Rocky* films when he says, "I just want to see the end of the fight", and I got to the flag having pushed as hard as I could throughout the race.'

The 24-year-old world champion, who survived an early scare when he made contact with the BMW of Nick Heidfeld, managed a nice manoeuvre on Jarno Trulli towards the end. However, it was more a matter of pride than in any hope of securing points. Hamilton's day was summed up when he was lapped by Jenson Button for the second race running.

7 JUNE 2009

BUTTON WINS IN ISTANBUL

Tom Cary in Istanbul

Forty seconds. That was all the time it took for Jenson Button to quash fanciful notions that this year's title race might still be alive. Sebastian Vettel's dazzling drive to pole on Saturday had raised the possibility, however remote, that Red Bull might have still something to say in the matter. Then the youthful German ran wide at turn ten, and that was that. Game over.

One and a half hours later, as Jenson Button show-boated down a deserted home straight in Turkey for a sixth win in seven grands prix, the true, devastating superiority of his Brawn machine had been made painfully clear to all concerned. 'Thanks guys, you have built me an absolute monster,' he screamed down his team radio, just in case anyone hadn't noticed.

Those who did make the trip over the Asian border to the Istanbul Park circuit witnessed another step in what is becoming an inexorable march to world title glory. Hypothetically, Button could still be caught. But with team-mate Rubens Barrichello returning nul points after a disastrous race that saw him stall on the start line, the Briton's lead has been stretched to a fearsome 26 points. Third-placed Vettel is 32 points behind Button and requires at least four races of extremely unlikely antics to usurp the Briton.

So the season is turning into an assault on the record books. Button already has more wins — six — than Lewis Hamilton managed in the whole of last season when he claimed the world title in the most dramatic fashion imaginable at the final round in Brazil. Button is now in the exalted company of Alberto Ascari, Juan Manuel Fangio, Jim Clark and Michael Schumacher in winning six of the season's first seven grands prix. All of them went on to win the world title. And the bad news for everyone else is that the Brawn is only getting better. 'The car was immense,' Button said simply. 'This was the first race where it has been absolutely perfect. I could have carried on driving for a few laps at the end I was enjoying it so much.'

The race was itself won on the first lap. Vettel and Button both got away cleanly but the German's hopes of keeping the Brawn driver at bay for any length of time were dashed when he lost control at the exit of turn nine and ran wide into turn ten. Button did not need a second invitation and quickly established a lead of almost 12 seconds.

Behind the leading pack, Lewis Hamilton drove a typically determined race on a one-stop strategy to finish 13th. 'I actually thoroughly enjoyed the race, considering I started back in 16th. I just pushed and pushed,' he said. 'I didn't have anything left, and that's why I'm kind of smiling now.'

15 JUNE 2009

BRAWN HAS FORMULA ONE RIVALS IN A SPIN

Kevin Garside

We all know the story; the death sentence imposed by Honda's withdrawal, an eleventh-hour reprieve, a car quick out of the box, supremacy. Jenson Button arrives at his home grand prix with six wins from seven and a 36-point lead in the world championship. While the return to predictability might appear achingly dull to some, to the 400-odd people who survived the cull after Honda's exit from Formula One last November, the monotony is beautiful.

The man largely responsible for boring the nation rigid on Sunday afternoons is Ross Brawn, a candidate for manager of the year. Guru status has settled on Brawn. Championships won at Benetton were repeated at Ferrari and are now projected at the team that bears his name. Astonishing. Unprecedented. There is a quality in the demeanour of Brawn that inspires trust. Plenty might question the suitability of that term given the proximity of controversy during his years with Benetton and Ferrari. High achievers in the ridiculously complex warren that is Formula One are vulnerable to a coating at the hands of sport's standards and morals committee.

Nevertheless, if Brawn is batting for you then you walk to the crease with The Don or I.V.A. Richards, with the best there is. That said, not everyone at Brackley believed. 'If you are a guy on the shop floor, and someone with a name turns up, you are expecting him to transform your fortunes,' Brawn said. 'Twelve months after I arrived we were bottom of the championship with a pretty lousy car. I was saying, "Be patient, we are going to do it". But for a guy who doesn't know you very well, who doesn't see the detail, it requires a lot of faith. One or two pointed out that I had not made much difference. I respected that. I saw it from their perspective. When Honda pulled out there was potentially a whole load of people who might have left thinking I had made no difference. That was a huge frustration at the time.'

For much of last winter it was more than that. Brawn was attempting to consolidate the F1 operation by focusing effort in the UK. The plan was to cherry-pick the best engineers from Japan and relocate them to Brackley. When Brawn met with Honda executives in November he assumed it was to rubber-stamp the scheme. 'Instead it was *arrivederci*. I went with my briefcase full of new plans. I didn't get to open it. It was a shock.'

How different the scene today. Laurel wreaths, F1's emblematic victory salute, decorate the hoarding at the entrance to Brawn GP. An enterprising local knocked up a fly poster celebrating the Australian Grand Prix win, a branding exercise perhaps on behalf of the local council: welcome to Brackley, grand prix central. The staff took the idea on. 'They said they would come to work after a race and there was no sense that we had won. At Ferrari we had flags. That was nice but I didn't want to copy that. Someone in graphics came up with the idea of the laurels on the wall.'

Brawn is more than 30 years in this business, yet this is a departure. He is the largest shareholder. His mobile rings off the hook. A queue builds at his door. The answers to questions are in effect focused reflection. And he is happy to talk about his past; about the key relationships that shaped him. 'Ferrari was a fantastic experience. Never regretted a minute. Wonderful people. It will never leave me. I still have a lot of friends there; still have a house in Italy. When I moved to Ferrari I was ready to experience a different culture, ready to face a different challenge. It was wonderful for me in that period. I stopped voluntarily, and that was me saying it is time to do something else. I don't think they took it in for a while. Michael [Schumacher] was always aware of it. I have never asked him whether it made a difference or not to his decision to go. But we were close. I know that if I had a crisis in my life there are a few people I could turn to. Jean Todt is one, Michael would be another, friends in the truest sense who you could go to for unconditional support.'

This precious period of Button dominance begs the comparison with the driver who constructed a skyscraper where the FI records office used to stand. Brawn, as you might expect, has joined the Jenson appreciation society. 'I had no idea what he was like to work with but from a distance there were impressive performances. In 2004 the only team giving Ferrari and Michael a bit of a hard time was BAR and Jenson. He out-qualified us at Imola. He didn't make mistakes and withstood pressure. What I found when I came was a guy who is frank and open; a genuine, straightforward person. For me Michael was the same: very straightforward. We had a great relationship. We could tell each other what we thought. If he made a mistake he would admit it. Jenson is the same. You hate it when a driver says he doesn't understand what happened – that something must have gone wrong. You waste hours that way. Last year was the second in a pretty mediocre car – it knocks the stuffing out of you. This year everything is flowing naturally and it is very impressive. The qualifying performances give you a tingle. He does it with such a lack of fuss. You don't see it coming. You wouldn't quite know he was on a flying lap. It just happens. Amazing.'

26 JULY 2009

FORMULA ONE 'MUST REMAIN VIGILANT' ON SAFETY

Tom Cary in Budapest

The 'freak' nature of the accidents involving Felipe Massa in Hungary on Saturday, and, fatally, 18-year-old Henry Surtees in a Formula Two race at

Brands Hatch a week earlier, should not deter world motorsport from striving for improvements to car safety. That was the overriding verdict from within the Formula One paddock on another anxious day for the sport, after Massa was hit on the helmet by a metal spring that had fallen off Rubens Barrichello's Brawn GP car during qualifying for the Hungarian Grand Prix. Massa was airlifted to hospital, and underwent emergency surgery and remained in an induced coma for 48 hours following a 'reassuring' CT scan.

It was quickly confirmed that a full investigation would be launched, conducted by world motorsport's governing body, the FIA, and the Brawn team, whose car suffered a failure in its rear suspension. It will attempt to discover the causes of the incident and whether any changes are required to improve safety with regard to [drivers'] exposed heads.

'We need to keep a perspective on it,' Ross Brawn said. 'From what's been seen, we need to have a proper study to see if we need to do anything. We must take a balanced approach. You can have covers or canopies, but you have to be able to get at the driver and extract him if there is an accident. And you don't want anything that collapses down on a driver. If there's a need to react, I'm sure F1 will do so promptly. But we must make sure we don't do something that makes the situation worse.'

Brawn's view was backed up by fellow team principal Martin Whitmarsh, of McLaren. 'I think that was very much a freak accident, but that doesn't matter,' Whitmarsh said. 'We have to be vigilant. I think we can do more work developing safety on cars, and we can do more work on helmets, visors and systems. If you have got a coiled spring coming at you at 160mph, or whatever it was, then it's very, very difficult. You could put thick glass there, but it would come whistling straight through that and you would have an even bigger problem. Having a windscreen isn't necessarily the solution. It's very difficult, given the speeds at which Formula One cars travel. Yes, it was a freak accident, but, like everything, let's take it as an opportunity to study it and see what else we can responsibly do to enhance the safety. Since 1994 the teams and the FIA have worked well together, and we can do a lot more.'

Bernie Ecclestone, the chief executive of the Formula One Group, said that he had instructed Professor Sid Watkins, formerly the FIA's Formula One safety and medical delegate, to look into the issue. 'We can learn from any accident, and I want to get Sid Watkins to look at how Felipe was injured and see what can be done. We need to look at helmet technology, what can be improved in what the drivers wear, study the visors. We might be able to learn from other sports. Look at ice hockey, where the goalies have to be able to see clearly but still have a visor that is strong enough to withstand the impact from a puck going like a bullet. We all hope Felipe will be back as soon as he is fully fit. I went to the hospital to hear from the doctors myself how he is doing, and I will be keeping in touch until he is ready to drive again.'

I I AUGUST 2009

SCHUMACHER CALLS OFF RETURN FOR FERRARI

Simon Arron

It would have been one of the most engaging tales in a Formula One season full of intrigue, but Michael Schumacher's Peter Pan moment – a return to the Ferrari cockpit after a 45-race absence stretching back to Brazil 2006 – has been called off because of fitness concerns. Ferrari spokesman Luca Colajanni said there was now 'no possibility' of the German standing in for the injured Felipe Massa during any of the season's remaining seven races.

As much a perfectionist in retirement as he was during his competitive heyday, the 40-year-old has been forced to accept a painful truth: his neck simply could not cope with the demands of a grand prix – the consequence of an accident he suffered in February, while testing a racing motorbike in Cartagena, Spain. Massa is recovering from head injuries sustained in an accident during qualifying for the recent Hungarian GP and Schumacher was due to take his place in the Grand Prix of Europe in Valencia. The team's regular test and development driver, Luca Badoer, will now fill the breach.

Although teams are barred from testing current chassis during the season as part of a programme of cost-saving measures, Schumacher had been preparing for his return by driving a two-year-old Ferrari at Mugello, Italy. In a statement released on his website, he said: 'I tried everything to make a temporary comeback, but much to my regret it didn't work out. We did not manage to get a grip on a neck pain that occurred after my F1 day in Mugello, even though we tried everything medically and therapeutically possible. The consequences of injuries caused by my bike accident in February, fractures in the area of my head and neck, turned out to be too severe. I am disappointed to the core and awfully sorry for the guys at Ferrari and the fans who crossed their fingers for me. I can only repeat that I tried everything within my power.'

Schumacher chalked up 91 world championship wins and collected seven F1 titles, the last five of them back to back between 2000 and 2004. A former Ferrari press officer provides an interesting insight into the German's methodology during that period of dominance. 'On one occasion Michael had been in action all day at our test track, Fiorano. In the evening I noticed a TV was still switched on in one of the briefing rooms. I wandered in and saw a human shadow – Michael was sitting there, watching a movie, but he had his crash helmet on and 40kg of weights attached. He saw it as an opportunity to do a few extra neck exercises . . . It made me realise why the others didn't stand a chance.'

Schumacher's acute attention to detail remains intact, but an unquenchable sense of adventure means the same no longer holds true for his once peerless physique.